ANTHONY DOWSLEY has been a police repo[rter]
since 2004, specialising in crime and corrupti[on].

Since 2014, Dowsley has been the driving force in exposing the 'Lawyer X' scandal, which has wide-ranging implications for the justice system. Dowsley and colleague Patrick Carlyon have written extensively on the topic, including on the royal commission triggered by their investigation. They collected three Walkley Awards, including the Gold Walkley, for their work in 2019.

Dowsley has also investigated the conviction of Jason Roberts, who is serving a life sentence over the murders of two police officers. Dowsley's work forced an anti-corruption inquiry and was central to having the case returned to court.

Dowsley lives with his partner Siobhan. In his spare time, he dreams of another Western Bulldogs premiership.

PATRICK CARLYON has been a senior features writer at the *Herald Sun* for a decade. He has won two Walkley Awards for feature writing, one for his coverage Victoria's Black Saturday bushfires, the other for his account of a war medic in Afghanistan.

In 2019, he shared three Walkley awards with Anthony Dowsley for their coverage of Nicola Gobbo's role as a police informer, including the Gold Walkley.

His book *The Gallipoli Story* was a Children's Book Council of Australia Honour Book in 2004.

Carlyon lives with his partner Susie, his kids Charlie and Chloe, Susie's kids Tom, Maddie and Jack, and two young dogs he plans to train any day now. In his spare time he drinks red wine and forgets to put out the bins.

LAWYER X

ANTHONY DOWSLEY   PATRICK CARLYON

HarperCollins*Publishers*

HarperCollins*Publishers*

Australia • Brazil • Canada • France • Germany • Holland • Hungary
India • Italy • Japan • Mexico • New Zealand • Poland • Spain • Sweden
Switzerland • United Kingdom • United States of America

First published in Australia in 2020
by HarperCollins*Publishers* Australia Pty Limited
Level 13, 201 Elizabeth Street, Sydney NSW 2000
ABN 36 009 913 517
harpercollins.com.au

A catalogue record for this book is available from the National Library of Australia.

ISBN 978 1 4607 5806 9 (paperback)
ISBN 978 1 4607 1183 5 (ebook)
ISBN 978 1 4607 8113 5 (audiobook)

Cover design by HarperCollins Design Studio
Cover image by Damien Horan/Newspix
Typeset in Adobe Caslon Pro by Kirby Jones
Printed and bound by CPI Group (UK) Ltd, Croydon, CR0 4YY

To Les Carlyon,
who was the kindest of teachers,
and the wisest of thinkers,
but most of all just a great dad.

Contents

Dramatis Personae

THE PLAYERS

Mick Gatto: A former heavyweight boxer who becomes a member of the Carlton Crew. Gatto's links to the underworld begin in the fruit and vegetable markets and illegal gambling venues in and around Lygon Street. He is now a mediator who resolves business disputes. He becomes a household name after the shooting of Gangland hitman Andrew 'Benji' Veniamin in an Italian restaurant in 2004, and is later acquitted of murder on the grounds of self-defence.

Horty Mokbel: The second-eldest Mokbel brother, mistrustful of Gobbo.

Kabalan Mokbel: The Mokbel brother least involved in crime. Regardless, he goes to jail for drug trafficking.

Milad Mokbel: A one-time butcher and the youngest of five Mokbel children, Milad follows older brothers Tony and Horty into a life of crime. Gobbo gets one of his underlings to sting him.

Tony Mokbel: Born in Kuwait to Lebanese parents, the oddly charismatic Tony is the third of five children. After owning a milk bar and a pizza shop, he becomes a Melbourne drug lord. His prolific drug-supplying is emboldened by the demise of other 'Mr Bigs'. Tony Mokbel is one of Gobbo's key clients and she, in turn, becomes part of his criminal network.

Faruk Orman: As a working-class kid growing up near Andrew 'Benji' Veniamin, Orman eventually comes under the wing of Mick Gatto. He is targeted by the Purana Task Force and faces two murder raps. In 2009, a jury finds him guilty of murdering underworld heavy Victor Peirce, seven years after the killing. Ten years later, Orman's conviction is overturned because his lawyer, Gobbo, was a prolific informer against him.

Andrew 'Benji' Veniamin: A hitman who dies violently in 2004 before he can be convicted of up to six Gangland murders. A gun for hire, he keeps switching allegiances and everyone fears his drug-fuelled unpredictability.

Carl Williams: A drug trafficker shot in a suburban park by half-brothers Mark and Jason Moran in 1999. It sets off the Gangland War, with Williams-ordered bullets killing Mark, Jason and eventually their father, Lewis. Williams's life expectancy is shortened the moment he cooperates with police regarding the murder of police informers Terry and Christine Hodson.

George Williams: Carl's father makes millions of dollars from drugs with his son and then loses the lot. To his dying day, he fights police over the death of his son in prison and the tax office over a tax bill imposed on his ill-gotten gains.

Roberta Williams: A street kid attracted to abusive criminals. As the wife of Carl, Roberta becomes infamous. She sticks by him, even after Carl shoots at her one Christmas Day.

THE DRUG BARONS

Pasquale 'Muscles' Barbaro: The son of a Calabrian mafia boss, Barbaro is convicted as the head of a drug-trafficking syndicate that imports 15 million ecstasy pills into Melbourne. Gobbo, who is responsible for stinging the syndicate, joins his defence team to get him bail. He is sentenced to thirty years' jail.

John Higgs: A veteran drug trafficker credited with being the founder of the Black Uhlans bikie gang. Higgs meets Gobbo through his lawyer, her boss 'Levi Diamond'. Higgs is convicted over his role in the drug importation headed by Pasquale 'Muscles' Barbaro and is sentenced to eighteen years.

Rob Karam: A docks expert who imports tonnes of drugs for the likes of Tony Mokbel and the Calabrian mafia. He meets Gobbo through Mokbel and they strike up a close friendship. His audacious drug trafficking unravels when he gives Gobbo a shipping document, which she copies and delivers to Victoria Police. As a result, the world's biggest ecstasy importation is seized weeks later, hidden inside more than 3000 tomato tins.

Dramatis Personae

THE LAWYERS

Joe 'Pino' Acquaro: A lawyer who primarily serves Italian clients, some involved with the Calabrian mafia. The suave Italian uses Gobbo as a barrister for some of his key clients. His life concludes at the wrong end of a gun in 2016, outside his Italian restaurant.

'Levi Diamond': A colourful solicitor who hires Gobbo as the young star of his criminal practice. Their working relationship lasts little more than a year before she leaves to become a barrister. He suspects Gobbo is too close to cops and criminals, but treats her like a daughter. She becomes a police informer for the second time and tries (unsuccessfully) to convict him as a money launderer, a charge he has always denied.

Zarah Garde-Wilson: Garde-Wilson arrives in Melbourne as a young solicitor just when the Gangland War explodes. She becomes the de facto partner of crime figure Lewis Caine, but loses him in the war. She doesn't trust Gobbo from the start.

Nicola Gobbo: A University of Melbourne Law graduate and a 'spectacularly good liar' who craves attention from both crooks and cops. Gobbo is first registered as an informer in 1995 while still a student. She is registered twice more, in 1999 and again in 2005 when she assumed her Informer 3838 designation. Her willingness to inform on her colleagues, criminal associates and clients makes her an intelligence gold mine, which ends the Gangland War, puts away drug barons and murderers, and leads to a royal commission into the scandalous use of a defence barrister as a police informer.

Fin McRae: Victoria Police's chief legal officer from 2007 and an award-winning lawyer, he is lumbered with the Gobbo secret when it's too late.

Robert Richter: An eminent barrister who defends the hardest cases, including Mick Gatto's and Faruk Orman's murder trials. Gobbo sometimes acts as his junior, and, like many, he is blindsided by her duplicity.

THE DETECTIVES

Stuart Bateson: A member of the Purana Task Force who primarily targets Carl Williams. Gobbo tells Bateson about her colleagues and her clients. She helps Purana and Bateson to secure convictions against Gangland hitmen, who score reduced sentences by implicating, or 'rolling on', Williams and others.

Paul Dale: A cop who quits the force when he is investigated over allegations of corruption and murder. Dale has been charged with burglary and with the murder of Terry Hodson, but he was never convicted. Along the way, his one-time police partner David Miechel has been jailed and Carl Williams was brutally killed in prison after agreeing to testify against him. Dale has always maintained his innocence. He shares secrets with Gobbo, his sometime legal advisor and ultimate betrayer.

Peter De Santo: An unflinching investigator who jails corrupt detectives. He builds a relationship with Gobbo to gain information from drug criminals on dirty cops.

Dale Flynn: A Purana Task Force detective at the centre of a police sting using Gobbo to bring down the Mokbels.

The Handlers: Members of the highly secretive Source Development Unit, known only by pseudonyms such as Mr Black, Mr Green, Mr Fox and Mr Anderson. They are all burned out by handling prolific informer Nicola Gobbo, whom they refer to as 3838.

Jim O'Brien: In charge of the Drug Squad, he is shocked when one of his own, David Miechel, is caught burgling a drug safe house that is the target of an operation. O'Brien runs Purana Task Force for several years and has direct dealings with Gobbo.

Jeff Pope: An Asset Recovery Squad officer who registers Gobbo as an informer in 1999 in an effort to nail her boss for money laundering. Years later, when Pope has risen to the rank of assistant commissioner, Gobbo tells police she had a sexual affair with him, a claim he denies at the royal commission. He helps shut down the covert department that handles Gobbo, the Source Development Unit.

Paul Rowe: A drug detective who meets with Gobbo after Tony Mokbel asks her to betray a client in 2005, which leads to her becoming a registered informer for the third time: Informer 3838.

Gavan Ryan: Sometime head of the Purana Task Force, Ryan brings down Carl Williams and his cronies. He supports Gobbo when she is taken through secret coercive hearings about the murders of Terry and Christine Hodson.

Wayne Strawhorn: As a hard-nosed detective in charge of the Drug Squad, he is drawn to Gobbo, a young criminal barrister, in the 1990s. He gleans information from her in an 'unofficial' police–informer relationship. A lauded officer, Strawhorn ends up in jail on drug corruption charges.

'Sandy White': The head of the Source Development Unit, who recruits Gobbo as Informer 3838 in 2005 to crack Tony Mokbel's drug empire. It is meant to be a one-off sting, but the force gets hooked on Gobbo.

VICTORIA POLICE TOP BRASS

Noel Ashby: An assistant commissioner who is the target of a sting along with police union boss Paul Mullett. They are investigated for leaking information about a clandestine police task force probing the killing of the 'vampire gigolo' Shane Chartres-Abbott. No charges are upheld, but their careers are ruined.

Graham Ashton: Australian Federal Police trained, Ashton's career follows that of his former AFP boss, Simon Overland. His interest in Gobbo begins with the Hodson murders in 2004 and he later learns she is a police informer. In 2018, as chief commissioner, he loses the fight to hide Gobbo's secret informer role.

Neil Comrie: A former chief commissioner (1993–2001), Comrie authors a secret 2012 report that raises serious problems with the police's use of Gobbo as an informer. The force tries to bury the report.

Luke Cornelius: Australian Federal Police trained, Cornelius is known as the third of the 'three amigos', alongside Ashton and Overland. The trio make the tactical decision to use Gobbo in two major murder investigations.

Sir Ken Jones: Deputy commissioner from 2009 to 2011, he questions Overland's tactics and reports Gobbo's use as an informer before he is ousted.

Christine Nixon: The first woman to lead a police force in Australia, her stint as Victorian chief commissioner from 2001 to 2009 is marked by the Gangland War and her pursuit of dirty cops. She claims that her subordinates did not tell her about Gobbo's informing; Overland says he didn't but later changes his mind and says he did.

Simon Overland: A former Federal Police officer and trained lawyer, Overland joins Victoria Police to end the Gangland War and stamp out police corruption. His time in the force from 2003 to 2011 is plagued by controversy as he rises to chief commissioner. Gobbo becomes his key weapon in landing major Gangland convictions.

THE SNITCHES

'The Assassin': A merciless hitman who kills men in front of their children. He is arrested with Shifty hours after a broad-daylight murder in October 2003. He becomes Supergrass Number Two.

'The European': As the last member of Williams's key 'hit team' to be arrested, the European is encouraged by police to turn on Gangland bosses and hitmen. He becomes Supergrass Number Three.

'Jack Price': A triple Gangland killer who confesses to killing 'vampire gigolo' Shane Chartres-Abbott in 2003 and triggers an ill-fated $30 million police investigation.

'Shifty': A hitman whose Nazi-sympathising parents beat him as a child before he graduates to violence, drugs and killing. He joins Carl Williams's murderous 'hit' crew until his arrest in October 2003. Gobbo helps turn him into Supergrass Number One.

THE JOURNALISTS

Patrick Carlyon: A *Herald Sun* feature writer who joins the Lawyer X investigation in 2017 and becomes part of the fight to expose the truth behind Victoria Police's use of Gobbo as an informer.

Dramatis Personae

Anthony Dowsley: A *Herald Sun* crime reporter who breaks the Lawyer X story in 2014, leading to internal police reviews, anti-corruption body inquiries, Supreme and High Court battles and, ultimately, a royal commission.

Damon Johnston: The *Herald Sun* editor who publishes the 2014 Lawyer X story and fights numerous court battles to get the story told.

Chris Tinkler: The *Herald Sun* deputy editor who, in response to the constant legal wranglings of telling the Lawyer X story, adjusts stories and re-shapes the paper, again and again, night after night.

Timeline

7 October 1991: Nicola Gobbo, then a Melbourne University law student, is at the Tunnel nightclub on the night Collingwood footballer Darren Millane dies while driving home drunk. She later tells the coroner he was usually 'the life of any party'.

September 1993: Gobbo, still studying law, is arrested in a raid on her Carlton house, which uncovered 1.4 kilograms of methamphetamine with a street value of $82,000, and cannabis worth $3000. She pleads guilty to drug possession and escapes without conviction.

1995: Not yet practising, she is registered as a police informer for the first time.

1996: She wades into a federal election scandal by publicly claiming a Liberal staffer forged letters purported to be from Jeff Kennett.

7 April 1997: Gobbo is admitted to the Victorian Bar to become a defence solicitor.

19 November 1998: Gobbo becomes a barrister.

13 October 1999: The Gangland War erupts when Carl Williams is shot in the belly by the Moran brothers in a tiny park in the north-west of Melbourne.

1999: Among Gobbo's contacts are Drug Squad detectives and emerging drug criminals. Gobbo is registered as a police informer for the second time.

2001–2002: Gobbo approaches Gangland kingpin and her former boss's client Tony Mokbel in jail. She becomes Mokbel's defence barrister in a major drug case, and a close confidante. She also meets his co-accused, Rob Karam.

2003: AFP agent Simon Overland joins Victoria Police as Assistant Commissioner (Crime). He establishes the Purana Task Force to investigate organised crime and end the Gangland War.

2003: Gobbo establishes a close bond with her client Carl Williams. She is MC at his daughter's christening at Crown Casino.

21 June 2003: Jason Moran and Pasquale Barbaro are killed in a van in front of children at a junior football clinic, increasing community and political pressure on police to contain the escalating Gangland War.

15 May 2004: Gobbo's client Terry Hodson and his wife Christine Hodson are murdered in their Kew home, after a file revealing Terry Hodson's informer status is circulated in the underworld.

September 2005: Gobbo is officially registered for the third time as a confidential 'human source' and given a number: 3838.

March 2006: Gobbo is a junior barrister in an infamous cocaine-trafficking trial from which Mokbel absconds (escaping to Bonnie Doon and then Greece).

April 2006: Milad Mokbel and other drug associates are arrested and subsequently convicted after Gobbo, their lawyer, informs against them.

5 June 2007: Tony Mokbel is captured in Athens.

April 2008: Gobbo's BMW is torched in front of diners in South Melbourne. Thousands of dollars in cash is burned in the car.

8 August 2008: Mafia syndicate members, including Gobbo's client Rob Karam, are arrested over the importation of tomato tins filled with 15 million ecstasy pills. Gobbo led police to the illegal consignment before it arrived in Australia. She represents and gives legal advice to numerous members of the syndicate.

7 December 2008: Gobbo covertly records detective Paul Dale as part of an investigation into whether he organised the murder of Terry and Christine Hodson.

1 January 2009: Gobbo agrees to give police a statement against Paul Dale and become a key witness for the Crown case, along with Gangland boss Carl Williams.

March 2009: Gobbo exits Crockett Chambers where she had leased an office on a floor with Victoria's top criminal barristers. Victoria Police pay her $1000 a week until December 2009.

Timeline

28 March 2009: Gobbo gives another statement to detectives investigating the murder of 'vampire gigolo' Shane Chartres-Abbott. The statement is not signed amid concerns it would expose her as an informer.

April 2010: Carl Williams is bludgeoned to death in Barwon Prison. The Hodson murder case against Dale collapses.

25 September 2010: Victoria Police pays Gobbo $2.88 million in a confidential settlement.

January 2012: Former police chief commissioner Neil Comrie raises legal and ethical questions after he completes a review into Gobbo's use as a police informer.

2013: Paul Dale is found not guilty of lying to the Australian Crime Commission. During the committal proceedings, Gobbo is withdrawn as a witness because of threats made against her life.

31 March 2014: The *Herald Sun* reveals that a barrister, whom the paper dubs 'Lawyer X', was used by police to inform on her clients.

3 April 2014: The newly formed Independent Broad-based Anti-corruption Commission launches a probe into the Lawyer X informer scandal.

July 2016: Convicted drug trafficker Rob Karam is the first to fight for a release from prison on the 'Lawyer X' principle.

November 2016: Victoria Police launches an unprecedented secret fight in the courts to stop the Director of Public Prosecutions from sending out letters to Gobbo's clients, alerting them that their cases might have been tainted.

December 2017: Tony Mokbel begins appeal proceedings using the 'Lawyer X' principle.

September 2018: Gobbo, now a mother of two, receives a Premier's Award at Government House for her volunteer work in saving a Brighton childcare centre.

November–December 2018: Director of Public Prosecutions is green-lighted by the High Court to send letters to Gobbo's clients revealing cases could have been tainted, allowing the *Herald Sun* to reveal the extent of the scandal for the first time. The Andrews Government launches the Royal Commission into the Management of Police Informants.

6 February 2019: The Victorian Government expands the scope of the royal commission, revealing other lawyers were registered as informers and Gobbo's informing dated back to 1995, not 2005 as previously acknowledged by police.

1 March 2019: Lawyer X is revealed as Nicola Gobbo after a five-year fight by the *Herald Sun*.

26 July 2019: Faruk Orman has his murder conviction overturned after twelve years in jail because his lawyer Nicola Gobbo, who informed against him, was found to have subverted the case.

February 2020: Nicola Gobbo gives evidence at the royal commission.

19 May 2020: Steve Cvetanovski is granted bail after eleven years in prison after he cites concerns about Nicola Gobbo's use in his conviction. Many more such claims, including from those convicted for the Tomato Tins drug importation, are expected to follow.

30 November 2020: The royal commission hands down its final report.

Prologue

A Tip-Off in a Pub

2013

Herald Sun crime reporter Anthony Dowsley doesn't like beer. But he drinks it anyway. He has to. Contacts in his blokey realm would query his credibility if he didn't.

He is shouting rounds of beer at a South Melbourne pub when he gets a tip-off about the greatest legal scandal in Australian history.

The Palmerston Hotel is a friendly place where the 'Parmie at the Palmie' is an institution. The pub draws Victorian police officers from both elite squads and nearby stations. The afternoon sun streaks across the TAB TV screens as dozens of detectives gather in the Christmas haze of 2013 to swap war stories about blood and bastards.

Dowsley's chameleon charms are marked by sartorial indifference. He sports a buzz cut and wears crinkled clothes. He could be just another cop who finds criminals easier to negotiate than ironing boards. He's in his forties, and masks anxiety about his volatile waist measurement with self-deprecating lightness. People tend to open up in response to his easy curiosity, which explains both his familiarity with newspaper-office gossip and his knack for landing scoops.

Dowsley and his *Herald Sun* colleague, feature writer Patrick Carlyon, have written many stories together. They are united by a 1990s suburban newspaper editor who long ago declared that neither of them would amount to much. Let's call her Shirley.

Back then, Carlyon sported an earring, and Dowsley hair to his waist: memories neither cherishes. Both suffered as whipping boys under Shirley's tutelage, and both figured at the time that Shirley was probably right.

At the *Herald Sun*, theirs is a hunter–gatherer union, which they hope transcends the office chatter about how Dowsley needs an editor and Carlyon should remove his head from his behind.

Dowsley recently got a tip-off that the DNA of serial rapist and killer Adrian Bayley was not stored on a national database. It should have been. Bayley committed numerous rapes in the 1990s and early 2000s.

Bayley's DNA sample was not in the system on the day in 2012 when he killed Irish ABC worker Jill Meagher in a Melbourne laneway. Police had botched its inclusion in the database, in an administrative oversight that could have cost Meagher her life.

Dowsley dragged Carlyon to meet sex workers raped by Bayley. Carlyon gave out cigarettes to ease the victims back to the moment they thought they would die in the back of a van. The pair wrote a series of stories detailing the Bayley monster, and the justice system that freed him to return to the hunt.

The Meagher tragedy has been Dowsley's biggest story until now. Won him an award. Yet after nine years at the *Herald Sun*, Dowsley feels like he's surrounded by reporters with higher profiles, like he's a Toyota who wants to be a Porsche. His newspaper investigations have located a paedophile hidden by the State government near a school and triggered a cold-case murder charge. But he's still waiting for the career-changing breakthrough.

He doesn't know it, as he identifies friends and foes amid the hubbub of the Palmerston, but tonight he'll finally get that opportunity. The next six years of his professional life are about to be framed.

An ex elite-squad officer approaches Dowsley. They know each other well. The reporter suddenly finds he is answering rather than asking questions.

'Can you get birth certificates?' the officer asks.

'No,' Dowsley replies. 'Why?'

The ex-detective passes on a rumour about criminal barrister Nicola Gobbo, well known for her peroxide hair and plunging necklines. She's recently given birth to a daughter. The gossip says the girl's father is a former assistant police commissioner called Jeff Pope.

Prove it, the officer challenges. Get the piece of paper.

This detective is not the only one spreading stories. The evening drinks spill over into another bar, where Dowsley hears how Pope dropped out of Victoria Police six months ago, without the fanfare normally reserved for someone of his rank.

Pope has become well known in police circles since his recent review of the force's covert operations — including the acutely sensitive Source Development Unit (SDU), responsible for high-risk police informers. When he recommended the shutdown of the SDU in February, he hadn't spoken to the unit's head before dispatching him and his men into irrelevance.

The gathering buzzes with speculations about Gobbo, Pope and naughty sex. The rumour galvanises those who view Pope as an enemy. Pope *must* have fathered the child of the Gangland lawyer, the thinking goes, because Pope's detractors want to believe it.

Yet the claim doesn't sound convincing to Dowsley. The tip-off leading to the biggest story of Dowsley's career will prove, in fact, to be wrong.

He doesn't know Pope, but he wonders if the sex rumour has been muddled up with the anger at Pope's decision to close the SDU. Dowsley is wary of sex scandals. When he last wrote a story on the topic, a sports manager threatened to hurt him.

But the inclusion of Gobbo's name? This intrigues him greatly.

Gobbo represented many of the biggest figures in the drug turf wars — popularly known as Gangland — that gripped Melbourne between 1999 and 2010.

Dowsley already knows Gobbo can be fearsome. He once called Mick Gatto, then leader of the so-called Carlton Crew, about a Gangland story he was writing. Instead of Gatto, Dowsley got Gobbo.

Do not associate Mr Gatto with Gangland, Gobbo declared, spitting out her flat vowels with a venom that prompted her client, sitting next to her, to calm her down.

Gobbo doesn't slot into the usual conventions of lawyers, cops and criminals. Everyone seems to know *a* Gobbo story, and almost every one seems to lack nine-tenths of the full drama.

Dowsley has heard that Gobbo walked into police headquarters a couple of years ago and announced that she had once had a relationship with Pope. Tonight's love-child element is a fresh take on a long-standing story.

He leaves the Christmas drinks serenaded by police entreaties: Go on, do your job, find out who the father is. But his journalistic antenna tells him the story is *behind* the story.

He comes into work late the next morning, too dusty for the gym. He chats with a friend, defence solicitor Rob Stary, about the love-child business. Stary knows every criminal lawyer in Melbourne, and Gobbo has been on his mind. For some time he has been wondering about certain courtroom events.

In 2008, Gobbo wore a hidden police wire to record a conversation with former police detective Paul Dale. Her evidence was later critical to cases brought against Dale for lying to the Australian Crime Commission — and for murder.

It was odd, almost unprecedented, for a defence lawyer to wear a wire to snag a suspect. Stranger still was how Gobbo was dropped from the witness list for Dale's lying case after she received a death threat. Justice is blind, Stary argues. Police don't usually withdraw a witness just because they are threatened.

Stary doesn't know Gobbo well, and was never inclined to brief her as a barrister. But two of his former clients were close to her and they wound up dead. He's intrigued by the possible link Dowsley has now uncovered between Gobbo and the closing of the SDU. The SDU handled the highest-risk informers, whose identities had to be protected. Dowsley wonders at the links between Pope and Gobbo, and the extraordinary efforts of police to protect a criminal barrister.

'Something's going on here,' Stary tells him. 'It doesn't feel right.'

Dowsley has the first inkling of an unthinkable idea. It undercuts every ethical tenet that lawyers are bound to uphold. But it couldn't be right, surely? Was Gobbo a defence lawyer *and* a police informer?

Dowsley has been handed a jigsaw piece. The first of thousands. If he knew how many more were to be coaxed, begged and wheedled out of countless sources in coming years, he may have resigned then and there, and returned to his first job in a plastic-bag factory.

Dowsley visits dozens of contacts in the following weeks — police and otherwise. He gets a thumbs-up here. A denial there. No one wants to talk openly about Gobbo. Dowsley's theory bobbles and yaws, like a little boat confronting a big iceberg. He thinks of what happened to the *Titanic*.

He perseveres.

One Sunday in March 2014, he calls his boss, *Herald Sun* editor Damon Johnston. Enjoying a rare day off, Johnston is at the park with his daughter, watching her ride on the swings.

'I've got a yarn,' Dowsley says, with typical understatement.

As he painstakingly explains how Gangland history needs to be rewritten to include its biggest secret, Phoebe Johnston wonders why her father is no longer pushing her back and forth.

'They won't like it,' Johnston says. Victoria Police's media arm is well drilled in shutting down unfavourable news. But neither Johnston nor Dowsley has anticipated the police's response to the revelation that the police have cheated the courts and the cornerstones of justice.

Six years and tens of millions of dollars later, authorities still resist what Dowsley has uncovered. He has enlisted Carlyon and Johnston and countless others. He wants to finish his quest, then go on a holiday far from Carlyon.

A royal commission hears extraordinary suggestions. That Victoria Police broke the law. That some of Melbourne's worst ever criminals are victims. That the State's law enforcers care so little about the public's right to know that they are still seeking to suppress their scandalous use of Nicola Gobbo.

We know all this for only one reason: because a chronically underdressed journalist braced himself for another round at the pub and was told a secret he was not meant to hear.

Dowsley's investigation has led him to police stations, law offices, courtrooms and yes, more beer-drinking sessions. And to this book, too, which Victoria Police would prefer you do not read.

Authors' Note

On 1 March 2019, Nicola Gobbo was named as Victoria Police Informer 3838.

It was almost five years since co-author Anthony Dowsley had uncovered her double role as a defence lawyer and police agent. He wrote a 2014 newspaper story that did not identify Gobbo, but instead dubbed her 'Lawyer X'.

The telling of the scandal then stalled amid secret court processes. Dowsley fretted that the biggest scoop of his career would never be properly told.

The story of Gobbo's use as a police informer is no simple tale. The lines between good and bad are tangled in mixed motivations and hidden agendas. For the first time, we tackle them in their unwieldy wholeness. In Part 1 of the book, we tell Gobbo's story as it really happened. In Part 2, we reveal Dowsley's frustrating fight for the truth, shared by co-author Patrick Carlyon and the *Herald Sun*'s editor Damon Johnston. It also covers the legal restraints (and threats) that cost the trio so much sleep.

We've tried to tell Gobbo's tale — and ours — in chronological order. But often it's been necessary to jump into the future (particularly to the 2019 to 2020 Royal Commission into the Management of Police Informants) to expose the secrets of the past.

The journey to publishing this story has been a kind of years-long drip feed of insights. Major media investigations often are. How do you declare the existence of a scandal when you cannot say how you know the scandal to be true? That's the age-old conundrum of a journalistic scoop based entirely on anonymous sources, as this one is.

Those sources revealed themselves one by one to Dowsley in the early months of 2014. The information came from individual, off-the-record conversations, mostly in pubs or cafés.

There were no underground car park meetings, as depicted in the Watergate investigation by the *Washington Post*'s Bob Woodward and Carl Bernstein. Instead, a succession of brave people provided Dowsley with titbits of highly classified police material. No one whistleblower blew the lid on the Lawyer X scandal, but instead a series of surprising and mostly unrelated 'deep throats'. Some of them risked their careers and more to share these insights.

Their secret snippets were the starting points for Dowsley in 2014. He was on a quest. He could not recognise the bigger puzzle until the clues were gathered and arranged in such a way as to uncloak the bigger conspiracy.

Many of the sources knew the dangers of exposing a police culture built on slavish loyalty to the boss and an institutional aversion to transparency. The legacy of Victoria's highest-ranking officers, including three police chief commissioners, was blotted in doubt when Dowsley published his first story in 2014.

We would love to explain who told us what throughout the following pages. To parade them as exemplars of truth and integrity. But their conversations cannot be reproduced. We are ethically bound to shield our sources. They are free to reveal themselves, if circumstances permit, and we hope that one day some of them will do so. Until then, they are unsung heroes.

We later gained access to precious written records, in particular Gobbo's recorded police information reports, which we've been able to use and quote from. There are tens of thousands of pages of such documents.

Much of this information was not made public until long and tedious battles had been fought in the courts — secret hearings in which the sanctity of Gobbo's life was subsumed by the competing public interest to uphold justice.

We filled in many of the remaining blanks when witnesses from different periods in Gobbo's past gave evidence at the 2019 to 2020 royal commission, prompted by Dowsley's investigation. Knowledge gaps became facts that tilted understandings this way and that. The explicit references to Dowsley by name in historical police documents, and the threat of exposure he posed, underscores his place in this story.

In recent years, Dowsley and Carlyon have been asked to explain many aspects of the Gobbo story. Often, they feel that there is no easy way to do so. The events in this book follow such unexpected plotlines. They are driven by quirks of nature that define the bigger characters.

Carlyon holds to his initial response when Dowsley first told him about Gobbo in 2016. Her story is a Hollywood movie on steroids.

To this end, we have tried to keep the following chapters as simple as possible. It is why we chose to write this story by casting ourselves in the third person as characters. This style offers a detached clarity to events but it did not come naturally. A heightened sense of self is at odds with the humbling and often demoralising journalistic search for truth. The authors have lost count of the times their Gobbo-related inquiries were met with versions of 'fuck off'.

Bit by bit, Gobbo's story became our story. Yet it would still be untold without the unyielding resistance of the *Herald Sun* to the legal hopscotch played by Victoria Police. They fought the *Herald Sun* in twenty-eight separate contested hearings. They didn't want anyone to know that they had changed the rules of the game.

Most people from Gobbo's past don't want to talk about their personal proximity to her. Holes remain in her story, especially in her formative younger years. Some of them may never be filled. The story in this book is not finished, and we can only hope that publishing it will help bring other parts of the Gobbo enigma to light.

Finally, we like to think that the fact of this book is reassuring. The Gobbo story needs to be told for the oldest of reasons. She represented a justice system glitch that imprisoned people unfairly, defrauded judges, hampered murder investigations and may have cost lives.

The scandal was perpetrated by police officers who were sworn to uphold the law. The very exposure of their choices offers hope that those choices will never be repeated.

Anthony Dowsley and Patrick Carlyon, 2020

Part 1

The Rise and Fall of Informer 3838

Nicola Gobbo, The Real Story
1972-2013

1

Lady on the Ledge

2009

'I'm going to jump!'

The slim woman in her mid-thirties stood high on top of a building, screaming into her phone as the wind tousled her long blonde hair. She was running from her past, on a schedule that cost taxpayers $30,000 a month.

She was out of options. She could no longer juggle her deceptions. She had played both sides, the cops and the criminals. And both sides had turned on her.

The police wanted her to surrender her life and identity and go into protection. For her, such ordinary anonymity was unthinkable.

The alternative? A bullet in the head. That was what the Gangland criminals would want if the truth — *her* truth — came out.

She had befriended the kind of people who would put a body in a wheelie bin, or kill a competitor in front of his children. She was once wined and dined by these misogynists and murderers at any time of the day or night. She even slept with some of them. There was the drug runner who was always off his face, and the drug baron who worked on the next importation during breaks in his trial for the last importation.

But she was no gangster's moll, as many had assumed. Quite the opposite. She had helped put away the kings of Melbourne's underworld by pretending to defend them.

She was the undercover agent who had tilted Melbourne's drug war in Victoria Police's favour. And she'd broken all the rules to do it.

She was ethically mandated to protect her clients' confidences. Yet she didn't care about their interests. She didn't care about ethics. She wasn't a lawyer, except in name.

Nicola Gobbo was a defence barrister *and* a secret agent. She manoeuvred people like chess pieces in a game that they didn't know they were playing.

Gobbo told the police almost everything. She planned police stings against the clients who paid her to look after them. She convinced them to turn on their mates. She even vetted the police evidence against her clients — to make it stronger.

Informer 3838: one-stop shop. Licence to thrill, spill and bill. The woman who did what no defence lawyer had done before.

Yet Gobbo had always been different. She'd never quite fitted in. She was loud and opinionated, as one might expect of a barrister, but she was also the party girl who stood apart in her short skirts.

At her best, she was engaging and helpful. Eager to please. She had been driven to deception by scorn, fear and revulsion of her criminal clients, though self-preservation was never far away. At her worst, she was *Othello*'s Iago in a mini-skirt. A villain on no one's side but her own.

As Victoria Police Informer 3838, there was no right or wrong. Being 3838 offered her purpose. And power.

Gobbo's betrayals might have faded away in time. But she'd kept going, even as the death threats mounted.

It couldn't go on much longer, though. Gobbo was a spy, and spy stories end badly. If the baddies didn't get her, the truth would. She had cheated herself as well as everyone else.

This is why, as the story has been told (though Gobbo herself has denied it), she made a phone call to announce that she was standing on a high-rise ledge. Suicidal thoughts were overwhelming her. She felt suffocated by the claustrophobia and uncertainty.

No. She couldn't do it anymore.

'I'm going to jump!' she screamed again to the officer on the other end of the phone.

2

From Gobbo to G395

Nicola Gobbo, Student and Spy
1972-1998

It didn't have to go like this. Nicola Gobbo was gifted status by virtue of her unusual surname. Her uncle, Sir James Gobbo, was a Supreme Court judge, human rights advocate and Victoria's governor, an exemplar of diligence and dignity. 'Gobbo' should have been a lifelong passport to respect.

But this Gobbo was drawn to notoriety. Something was missing. She wasn't like the other Gobbos. The image she presented conflicted with her motives.

Investigating Gobbo's childhood feels like a form of archaeology, with clues to her early life buried like ancient artefacts.

She was born in Melbourne in November 1972, a Scorpio in the Chinese Year of the Rat. Her father, Allan, was first-generation Italian. His family claimed that they had brought the first espresso machine to Australia in the 1930s. Gobbo herself learned Italian and probably drew on her European heritage in later years. Parts of Melbourne's underworld were loosely divided into ethnicities such as Lebanese and Italian. In that world her family background, both for its cultural origins and legal reputation, bought her credibility.

Allan Gobbo worked at VicRoads. He and his second wife, Mary, a nurse, lived with their children in the affluent eastern suburb of Kew. In a 2019 TV interview, Gobbo herself emphasised the family bonds, describing her parents as 'hard-working' and 'old-fashioned'.

Gobbo told the ABC's *7.30* she was one of five children. She was close to her half-sister, Linda. Her younger full sister, Catherine, followed Gobbo into the law.

Their choice seemed almost fated, considering the achievements and reputation of Allan's brother, Sir James. Gobbo had wanted to be a lawyer since childhood, she wrote in 1996, because she had 'been instilled with a strong sense of social justice in a family with an established legal background'.

Gobbo's early life can be glimpsed only from afar. A family photo here, a school report there. Just enough to provide impressions of happiness and stability. Faded photos she supplied to the ABC depicted Melbourne suburbia and childhood pleasures. They're remarkable for their ordinariness. Summer days floating on a plastic tube in a backyard pool. Red stains around the mouth from eating watermelon. A beach snap, perhaps from a 1970s Gold Coast, alongside a man, presumably her father. In what appears to be a communion photo, she has her hands clasped, her dress starchy-white in keeping with Roman Catholic custom.

Gobbo is remembered as a 'big unit' at Genazzano College, a Catholic girls' school in Melbourne's leafy east, where she finished Year 12 in 1990. A school report, in which she was given an 'A', said Gobbo was 'reliable' and 'eager to please'. Gobbo liked footy, and regularly attended games of her VFL (AFL) club, Fitzroy, with a schoolmate. Decades later, her schoolfriends do not want to be publicly associated with her.

Her nickname was Smurf, after the tiny cartoon characters, yet she stood out in every class photo for her size, like a woman dressed as a girl. Despite the frenetic lifestyle she later adopted, and the unbearable stresses she endured, she remained large-framed throughout most of her adulthood.

She was always comfortable as the centre of attention. Take the time a fellow school student drew a lewd reference on a classroom blackboard about Gobbo's supposed sexual encounters with a celebrity. Gobbo rubbed the image out, but she seemed pleased about the tittering.

Gobbo was a polariser. You either played as her audience or you avoided her. 'I don't think she opened up to anyone about anything,' a fellow student would tell Carlyon.

By her final year she was a regular at nightclubs — probably using a fake ID to gain entry, like many other Genazzano girls. Melbourne was slumping into recession, and though many of their parents would lose long-held fortunes, the private-school kids of Melbourne's inner-eastern bubble didn't appear to care.

Clutches of Genazzano girls headed to Tok H, a Toorak hotspot, for $1 drinks on Thursday nights. (Carlyon, who went to a nearby boys' school, never met Gobbo there. He recalls bad karaoke and drunken pashes.)

Gobbo was more promiscuous than the others. At least she said she was. On Mondays she told schoolmates of intimate encounters with bouncers and celebrities at the city's Tunnel nightclub, from which patrons stumbled into the inky dawn.

These tawdry tales were the dark half of her double life; in the other, Gobbo was a prefect and house captain. She was also an exceptional student: in her final year she sometimes took over the Legal Studies classes at Genazzano College, mostly because she seemed better informed than the teacher.

Yet at the same time she faced a personal crisis: the death of her father, Allan. Gobbo might not have excelled at deep friendships, but many of her school peers attended the funeral. Allan Gobbo had survived five years after a cancer diagnosis gave him only a short time left. Throughout, Gobbo had feared her father had only days or weeks to live. She and her siblings bonded through trauma.

* * *

Gobbo's Year 12 marks were outstanding, yet not high enough to qualify for Law at the University of Melbourne — or so it's said.

Gobbo once compared university entry scores with a fellow first-year student destined for high political office. He pointed out that her score did not meet the university's requirements.

It's possible she applied for, and received, special consideration for her recent bereavement. But she offered her fellow student another reason for her acceptance to the prestigious university: 'My name is Gobbo.'

Law was an easy choice. She was proud of the Gobbo heritage, and a Law degree would be the basis for a public role in society. Gobbo had strong views on sport and politics; she would be heard no matter what forum she landed in.

She thrived on a happening university campus. There was a chocolate appreciation society and seven or eight pubs nearby.

The Clyde, in nearby Cardigan Street, bounced most weeknights; even impoverished students could guzzle $1 pots of beer. The Law fraternity initiated PTNs — Pleasant Thursday Nights. Gobbo sculled spirits in order to be seen doing so.

She was always there, the tall blonde with the 'pancake make-up'. One former Law student recalls his first sighting of Gobbo, when she walked into a room and announced: 'I'm Nicola Gobbo, I'm a nymphomaniac.' Then walked out again.

She didn't appear 'classy', another fellow student recalls. She didn't sound privileged, even if she projected an air of entitlement. She swore as if for effect. 'She was a show-off,' one of her peers would tell Carlyon. 'She always wanted you to know that she was a Gobbo.'

Gobbo went to Tunnel nightclub too, and she was there in 1991 when Collingwood footballer Darren Millane drank heavily, drove into a parked truck and died. His coronial inquest followed a funeral attended by 5000 or more grieving football fans. Gobbo gave evidence that Millane didn't appear to know where he was or what he was doing, in testimony accepted as the true course of events.

Here was Gobbo's first embrace of public notoriety. She was telling the world that she frequented all-night clubs and befriended footballers, a perch at odds with her strait-laced upbringing.

* * *

Academically, she took a while to find her way. In her first year at university, she withdrew from Economics 1a and failed Australia in the Global Economy, and switched from Commerce–Law to Arts–Law.

For her Law degree, Gobbo studied Criminology and a range of Criminal Law subjects, perhaps already certain of her future trajectory. She even served as Vice-President of the Law School. Among her fellow students were numerous future luminaries, including Peta Credlin, described as the country's most powerful woman during her time as Prime Minister Tony Abbott's chief of staff.

Gobbo had ambitions to become prime minister herself. Her star burned brightly — perhaps too brightly. She seemed daubed with the glow of a shiny future.

Immersing herself in the hotbed of student politics and its petty agendas, Gobbo ran for election as co-editor of the university's student newspaper, *Farrago*. She'd already done a four-week stint in the Business section of the *Herald and Weekly Times* after she finished school, where she was remembered as good company, always up for drinks — and for namedropping her uncle.

Editing *Farrago* was often seen as a stepping stone to journalism or political office: a natural stop for a girl who wanted to be prime minister. Gobbo ran on a 'Rescue *Farrago*' ticket, and was elected with three female Jewish peers.

She was later accused of breaching election regulations: perhaps the first time she was called upon to defend prohibited conduct. She explained that her *Farrago* ticket had been subjected to anti-Semitic harassment, and played the patronising victim card. 'In essence, my alleged breach of regulations amounted to nothing; perhaps the allegations were partly due to the frayed tempers and highly charged emotions of all involved,' she wrote in 1997 in an application to be accepted as a solicitor.

Co-editing *Farrago* was a real job: sixty to seventy hours a week. Gobbo wrote topical stories in the tone of a cub reporter, with sprinklings of analysis. Her newspaper photo featured a toothy smile, big earrings and big hair.

Like all student newspapers, *Farrago* attracted controversy for its political stances. At the time, Gobbo was a Labor Party supporter, at odds with the Kennett Government, which later appointed her uncle as governor. A letter she wrote as a Year 12 schoolgirl, decrying the

ALP's overthrow of Premier John Cain, had been published in the *Herald Sun*.

She sounded starstruck in a *Farrago* interview with New South Wales Labor leader Bob Carr. 'Carr is one MP who has maintained his integrity and commitment both to his party and his own ideals through many years of political involvement.'

But it wasn't all about politics. As Gobbo wrote in an article headlined 'The Place to Find a Well Hung Jury': 'If the dancing frenzy and amount of alcohol consumed are any indication of future legal prowess, then those at the 1993 Law Ball will constitute an impressive addition to the profession.'

While negotiating this whirl of socialising and student politics, Gobbo completed her degree, albeit with mainly average results. At least she nailed her final Law subject. Somewhat ironically, considering her future path in life, her only first-class honour in five years was in Legal Ethics and Professional Conduct.

She toyed with the idea of a thesis about police informing — and she was certainly well placed to address the subject. At the time, she was already pursuing a double life. She was a Law student *and* she was a police informer.

* * *

It was 1993 AFL Grand Final day, and Melbourne was talking about *that* goal. Michael Long bounced the ball four times, while weaving past opponents, to produce one of the most memorable moments in Essendon's premiership win over Carlton.

Nicola Gobbo had weightier concerns.

A third-year Law student at the University of Melbourne, she lived in nearby Carlton with her housemate, Brian Wilson. Wilson was a nightclub bouncer and drug trafficker, thought to have a sideline in guns. Dowsley and Carlyon have been told he was close to underworld drug king Mark Moran. He was the first bad man on Gobbo's lifelong list of bad men.

They met through the rock band INXS. Wilson was working as an after-hours security guard at the University of Melbourne when INXS performed there for the first time, a few years after the band released the single 'Suicide Blonde'.

Gobbo, as a *Farrago* reporter (and co-editor), was lined up to interview the lead singer, Michael Hutchence. It's unclear whether the interview happened, but the arrangement led to Wilson becoming Gobbo's housemate and property co-owner. She wanted someone to help pay the mortgage on her house, but she and Wilson also fell into a sexual relationship.

Sometime later, around August 1993, someone had tipped off the police about Wilson's illegal activities. After two weeks of surveillance, officers raided the Rathdowne Street home he and Gobbo shared, a single-fronted terrace squeezed between bigger properties.

A pungent aroma engulfed police officers when they entered late on the afternoon of Friday 3 September, three weeks before Grand Final day. A twenty-litre drum filled with marijuana heads sat in the lounge room. Wilson was home; he was handcuffed and told to sit.

Gobbo arrived almost two hours later. In the interim police had searched for amphetamines, checking all the usual places, finding almost nothing.

Sergeant Trevor Ashton, the officer leading the raid, spoke to Gobbo in her bedroom. He had discovered a cigarette packet in her chest of drawers containing a small amount of amphetamine.

Gobbo immediately directed him to air vents in the laundry. They were easy to miss. Secreted inside the vents were big bags of white powder, which Gobbo explained were Wilson's and not hers. Who knows if the police would have found the amphetamine without Gobbo's — as Ashton would put it in 2019 — 'willing' assistance?

Wilson was charged with drug trafficking, Gobbo with use and possession.

Now, this was a problem. A criminal conviction can be a life-changer for anyone, but especially so for an aspiring lawyer. If convicted, Gobbo might fail the 'character' requirements of the Legal Admissions Board. Her career would be cruelled before it began.

What was said and agreed to in Gobbo's conversations with police after her arrest in 1993 is unknown. The officers involved had little memory of the incident when cross-examined twenty-five years later.

At least one of them is still miffed that Gobbo was not charged with trafficking. Under the law, she was in possession of 1.4 kilograms — a trafficking quantity — of speed, worth $82,000, because the drug was found in the house she co-owned.

Sure of herself. That was former senior constable Michael Holding's take on Gobbo at the raid. He took an instant dislike to her. Cross-examined in 2019, he wondered about the right words, before settling on this: 'I thought she felt the process was like a game.'

What we do know is that Gobbo's future career path was mapped out by the time her police interview concluded at 2.03 am on Saturday, 4 September.

In December, Wilson was found guilty of trafficking and received a sentence of eight months in prison, which was suspended. Gobbo pleaded guilty to use and possession, and received no conviction. A good result: bothersome, but explainable to any law admissions board.

Afterwards, Trevor Ashton stayed in touch. Gobbo sold pies at the Melbourne Cricket Ground, high in the Great Southern Stand, and Ashton scaled the grandstand several times to speak to her when he was rostered to work at the ground.

Neither Gobbo nor Ashton could recall in 2019 why they stayed in contact at this time; she would say she was 'cooking chips' to pay the Carlton mortgage. But within a couple of years of her arrest, Gobbo was registered by Ashton as a police informer.

When cross-examined in 2019, Ashton's memories of this time were patchy. He could barely recall seeing Gobbo after her 1993 arrests, though he was forthcoming when shown his police paperwork. 'That's definitely my scribble,' he said, sounding surprised.

Gobbo's first incarnation as an informer was G395. The undated police informer registration form from mid-1995 describes her as 'very good' in terms of reliability. Her declared motives for informing were simple: she 'genuinely wants to assist police'.

She went out of her way to help, if the bare history is any measure. That same month she reported to police that a 'Gary's Milk Bar' was handling stolen cigarettes.

But 'Gary' was not her main target at the time. Rather, Gobbo seemed intent on getting Brian Wilson. Was she afraid of another conviction, or simply scared of him? She said later that Wilson was prone to drug-addled violence. The name of the police operation seemed fitting: 'Scorn'.

Police had launched a second investigation on Wilson on 3 April 1995 and were keen to discuss his alleged trafficking of guns and drugs. Ashton and his subordinate, Constable Tim Argall, met with Gobbo on 12 July 1995, and she updated police with information throughout that month. One of the officers who conducted the 1993 raid told the authors he recalled being amazed in mid-1995 to see Gobbo at the pub, merrily draped by detectives.

Scorn was officially launched in February 1996. Gobbo introduced Wilson to an undercover officer posing as a drug buyer. She was 'eager to participate', Argall would say in 2019, and 'when it came to using the covert operative she was excited about that'. She 'plucked a name [for him] and we had to run with it'. Gobbo was getting ahead of herself, taking control.

Then the operation was stopped. Wilson had sought to *buy* drugs, not supply them. He was not trying to get involved in trafficking. Gobbo's information had not proven useful.

Detective Senior Sergeant Jack Blayney, a superior to Argall, wrote that Gobbo was a 'loose cannon' who was 'making her own arrangements and not liaising with investigators'. His view — that Gobbo was unsuited to police informing — would go unnoticed for decades.

Wilson and Gobbo stopped sharing a residence at some point. He moved to Queensland, then New Zealand. In 2019, he did not want to hear about Gobbo's betrayal of him in 1995. That was a 'bad period of my life', he told the *Herald Sun*'s James Dowling. 'Some people learn from them, some don't.'

* * *

Even before Operation Scorn ended, Gobbo had been keeping herself busy elsewhere. Once again, she'd leaped by choice into the spotlight after she wrote an affidavit that became a national election headline.

On 28 February, three days before the 1996 federal election, Labor treasurer Ralph Willis fronted the media with a pair of letters — one purportedly written by Victorian Liberal Premier Jeff Kennett — as evidence of a Coalition plot to reduce State funding. The humiliating discovery that they were a hoax contributed to the resounding Labor defeat that saw John Howard's Liberal Party swept to power.

On 1 March, Labor supporter Gobbo made a statutory declaration to Federal Police, naming the person she believed had forged the letters. Scott Ryan, known as 'X' at the time, worked part-time for both Kennett and Deputy Opposition Leader Peter Costello. He denied the accusation and demanded to be interviewed by police so that he could clear his name, which he did. Ryan would later serve as a federal government minister and Senate president. Then *Herald Sun* journalist Andrew Probyn covered the story and later described the allegations against Ryan as a 'cack-handed [and] amateur political smear'. To this day, it is unknown who forged the letters.

A nobody, Gobbo had plonked herself in the middle of a nationwide political scandal. At the time, she was serving her twelve-month articled clerkship at a Melbourne commercial law firm. When the story became public she was engulfed by journalists — or so she told Constable Tim Argall when she decided to drag him into her melodrama.

On the morning of the 1996 election, she rang to tell him about a throng outside her Kew home. Argall told her to drive into the city. She parked near the Melbourne Central shopping complex. As Argall would later reveal: 'Nicola got out of her car and said that media were still following her — I did not see anyone following her and there did not appear to be any media vehicles or journalists in the area.'

Gobbo went dead as an informer for almost three years after Operation Scorn ended, but she remained friendly with Argall. Their relationship over the subsequent decade was typical of the smudged boundary between her professional and social lives. Argall was compelled to admit in 2019 that, after he and Ashton registered Gobbo as an informer, he slept with her. He explained their circa 1997 sexual encounter as a one-off romp; he could not recall how it came about.

Trevor Ashton didn't know about the Gobbo–Argall relationship, he would claim twenty-five years later, sounding shocked. He would have kicked Argall off the case if he had. Every young male officer is warned about breaching the 'Three Ps' principle — Piss, Property and Pussy.

* * *

Gobbo was admitted as a legal practitioner in April 1997. Her certificate read: 'And we believe her to be a fit and proper person to be admitted to practise as such barrister and solicitor.'

Yet her 4 February 1997 application to the Legal Admissions Board warrants a closer look: her sworn statement conflicts with police documents at the time of her 1993 arrest. Gobbo distorted the truth to become a lawyer.

She told the board she had been unaware in 1993 that Wilson was a drug user. But how does that sit with Wilson's marijuana-filled drum, described by one of the raid officers as 'just, like, in your face'?

She also told the board she spent about ninety hours a week on campus back then. 'As a result I was very rarely home at the same time as my housemate who did shift work as a security guard,' she said in her affidavit. 'This pattern continued for the four weeks we shared a house.'

Four weeks? Police records from 1996's Operation Scorn suggest otherwise. As does her 2020 testimony that she pitied Wilson and took him back in as a house guest in 1995, and that he co-owned the property.

Gobbo claimed in 1997 that police had told her she was being charged only because she was 'deemed liable on the basis of owning the house'. Again, this conflicts with Trevor Ashton's statement that he found drugs in *her* chest of drawers.

Gobbo wrote that her lawyer had advised her to plead guilty. She'd received a shock, she said, when she went to court in December 1993.

She suggested that she had been of media interest as the errant niece of a then Supreme Court judge. 'I was approached by a reporter outside court and I was afraid to have the matter ventilated in the papers,' her affidavit stated. 'I had nothing to do with the drugs on the premises and I had not asked my housemate about his activities. I certainly was not involved in any drug-related activities with him.'

She would not have pleaded guilty if she had had the episode over, she declared. 'I did so then as a result of advice received by my solicitor and the pressure of the media,' she wrote. 'My level of maturity and my judgment of others were also factors which led to my guilty plea.'

In a separate document addressed to the Chairman of the Board of Examiners for Barristers and Solicitors, Gobbo cited reports from a doctor and a criminal psychologist that 'indicate my naïve behaviour and poor judgment from this time'. Only four years later, she seemed to be saying, she had shed her naïveté and poor judgment. She was all grown up now.

'I can assure the members of the Board that this experience taught me a very valuable lesson and one which I know has provided me with a better understanding [of] the criminal justice system ...

'I can assure the members of the Board that upon being granted admission to practice, my integrity and honesty will not be compromised. In accordance with the trust and privilege vested in me by the Court, I will endeavour to be an upstanding and honourable member of the legal profession.'

Her sworn assertions were impossible to disprove. A case of what she might call 'plausible deniability'.

* * *

A seasoned criminal defence lawyer took Gobbo on fresh from the University of Melbourne, at a time when ecstasy and cocaine began flooding the Melbourne social scene and their suppliers started shooting each other.

He thought she was amazing; she treated him as a target.

3

Get Shorty

Nicola Gobbo, Law Graduate and Spy
1997-1999

Gobbo's first boss recalls the late 1990s sweetly. He chats to Dowsley and Carlyon in a café in Melbourne's legal district, next door to the building he is about to put up for sale for around $26 million. Not that he boasts about his wealth.

Parts of his story have been suppressed, along with his name. But let's call him 'Levi Diamond'. If he is ever cast in a movie, Danny DeVito should be the first call, despite Diamond's own view that DeVito is too short.

Diamond wears a short-sleeved shirt and striped tie. He sports bags under his eyes, his wrinkles offset by his mailbox-slit smile. He speaks of his employees like a shepherd discussing his flock. There is a twinkle about him, a kind of weary wisdom fed by decades as a criminal defence lawyer. A scholar of human nature, he's been shot at and stabbed, had his home firebombed and been attacked by a woman with a baseball bat. Twice, Diamond was suspended from practice. Twice, he was reinstated.

His clients have included some of the most charismatic shitbags in modern Australian criminal history. Aspiring drug baron Tony Mokbel was a regular in his office, along with his creepy brother Horty. John Higgs was here too. Higgs had set up his own bikie branch with a sideline in drug importation.

Gobbo met these criminals for the first time in Diamond's office from 1997 onwards.

Her friends and *Farrago* co-editors had arranged her first acquaintance with Diamond. They knew him through Jewish circles and suggested she meet with him to discuss career options. Gobbo was bored with the commercial bent of her articled clerk employment; Diamond did real estate and criminal law, which sounded more enticing. When they sat down, Diamond twigged to her surname and legal heritage. Her drug possession case came up during the chat, but Diamond dismissed it as a typical tale of a university kid being busted for low-level offences.

'I rang him, made a time to see him, and literally went there thinking he might have some suggestions on where to go and he offered me a job on the spot,' she would later recall.

The initial arrangement was a one-month trial. Yet Gobbo impressed him with her strong work ethic, even after he reminded her she was not being paid by the hour.

She showed instant talent for summarising briefs of evidence and identifying the best witnesses for a client's defence. Her research skills were brilliant; another lawyer likened them to reading an entire phone book and finding the two or three numbers that mattered. Soon she was managing minor criminal courtroom matters, such as motion hearings, without Diamond's direct supervision. She would strike out on her own as a barrister in twelve months' time; until she passed the bar exam she would remain a solicitor. The same eagerness to please noted in her school report a decade earlier underpinned her professional strengths.

Through Diamond, Gobbo was able to forge connections with high-flying legal peers early in her career. She 'instructed' cases as a solicitor to legendary barristers. She took inspiration from pioneering women who had become Queen's Counsel barristers, such as Lillian Lieder QC. She was impassioned and enthused, qualities already being noted by observers who assumed that she would ascend to become a Supreme Court judge.

Gobbo was openly ambitious, and thrilled by the variety of criminal cases Diamond dished out. Each day she woke up wondering who she would meet and where she would go. She was exposed to police briefs of evidence against her clients for the first time. She prided herself on exposing their flaws of logic — and the underlying faults of the police investigation. She learnt the difference between thorough and sloppy police work. Using the kind of language most would not expect to hear in the mouth of a solicitor, she called the officers responsible 'liars' and 'cocksuckers'.

If she was getting to know lawyers and cops, she was getting to know Diamond's criminal clients too. Tony Mokbel sweet-talked female staff at Diamond's office and presented them with gift cards one Christmas.

The beginnings of their association as lawyer and client were more vexed. She accompanied Tony Mokbel to court, as a junior solicitor, for a bail surety for his brother Horty. He stated that he solely owned a property, which he did not. He was charged with perjury, and Gobbo was called as a witness for the failed case against him.

It was the start of a long, and often fraught, relationship.

* * *

'Nicki' bristled with energy and vulnerability. Diamond had liked her immediately. He assumed the affection was reciprocated: at every office Christmas party, Gobbo beelined to Diamond for a dance.

He sounds wistful, many years later, like a parent discussing a prodigal daughter.

The new employee's work was exemplary, but the rest of her life played out like a soap opera for the entertainment of her colleagues. She revved a little black sports car through the Richmond laneways behind Diamond's then office, slotted it into the tightest of spaces, and climbed out as if she were scaling a wall.

She seldom turned up on time. She was often outside, fag dangling from her mouth. She was the court jester, never short of stories that began with: 'You wouldn't believe ...'

She was quirky too. That big brain of hers sometimes entertained strange lines of thought. She once told colleagues she was concerned that her microwave was bugged by police because of a flashing red light.

They were unsure how to receive this — why would police bug a junior solicitor's home?

Yet Diamond was beginning to fret. Lawyers traditionally kept a distance between themselves and their clients, lest their client relationships should get mistaken for friendships, but she seemed overly familiar with many of hers. Dangerous men, dangerous liaisons. At the same time, she drank with police, and even slept with some of them.

Gobbo was dropped off at work one morning in an unmarked police car. When Diamond left the office one evening, the same man in the same car was outside, waiting for her. The man, who Diamond later learned was a senior Victoria Police officer, shielded his face so as not to be seen.

Diamond spoke to Gobbo about a 'bad look' and 'crossed lines'. He told her to avoid screwing cops and criminals. She would get burned, he explained, in avuncular advice steeped in long experience. Gobbo countered that she knew what she was doing.

She used profanities that flushed Diamond's fleshy cheeks. More subtle were other traits. The wheedling. The disregard for rules. Diamond still shakes his head. He describes Gobbo, with affection, as 'immature', 'short-tempered' and 'irrational'. She was a 'wild child'.

He could see all that, but he never understood the toll Gobbo's choices were taking on her. He never understood her visceral responses to police. They didn't make sense, given her romantic associations with police officers.

He recalls how he once shook the hand of Wayne Strawhorn, a Drug Squad detective who, at the same time, was investigating Diamond — with Gobbo's secret assistance. Gobbo spoke to Diamond afterwards of going to the bathroom to throw up.

She deceived him, as she did everyone else. She was already falling into unwise relationships that strained both her professional and personal wellbeing. Knowing how she suffered for it doesn't make it any better.

Diamond feels cheated by his misjudgments, disarmed of his instincts.

'I thought I knew her but I didn't,' he says.

* * *

Nicola Gobbo had tried and failed as a police informer almost three years earlier. Now she was secretly presenting herself for another stint.

She was trying to jail her boss. According to her, he was laundering money.

Detectives from Gobbo's second informing period speak of her eagerness to jail Diamond. She urged police to check certain properties and analyse a trust account.

They argue they were led by the hand of an agent provocateur. They say they applied no pressure.

She recalled it differently in her diary from the time. In *her* version, which carries some weight as a contemporaneous, and private, account, she wasn't a scorpion, but a cornered chicken.

In childlike loops, she wrote about a mid-1998 meeting with two detectives. They told her that her name was on incriminating tapes. (Exactly what was on the tapes that implicated her remains a mystery.) One diary entry rings with authenticity. 'Mud sticks, get a raincoat soon,' Gobbo wrote that detectives told her.

The 'raincoat' was an offer of protection. She could shield herself from prosecution if she assisted the investigation into her boss.

One of those detectives was Senior Sergeant Wayne Strawhorn, a feared drug buster within Victoria Police. Gobbo regarded him as 'all-powerful' and intimidating. He contacted her in 1998 because he believed Diamond was laundering money for client John Higgs. Gobbo would claim in 2020 that she felt Strawhorn manipulated her by taking advantage of her perceived proximity to her boss. Diamond has always denied the allegations and has never been charged with any offence.

Diamond annoyed detectives. As Gobbo would later, he had cornered the market for representing suspected drug traffickers. He was often the lawyer for most or all of the suspects charged in major drug raids at the time.

Gobbo and Strawhorn met repeatedly at a South Melbourne coffee shop. He grilled her for information and she went along with the questioning. Yet Gobbo would later assert that she told Diamond about Strawhorn's suspicions against him. According to Diamond, he sent Strawhorn a fax demanding that he leave Gobbo alone.

In isolation, her words seem plausible. Strawhorn was undoubtedly a 'boogie man' obsessed with fighting crime. He might have coerced Gobbo's cooperation. But her claim to compulsion gets muddied by separate but related facts.

A month or so before the purported offer of a police 'raincoat', Gobbo rang the Australian Federal Police. She asked about the AFP's recruiting policies. Two AFP officers met her the following day, 14 May 1998. In keeping with Gobbo's propensity to blend the social and professional, the 7 pm office meeting moved on to the Celtic Club pub and concluded at about midnight.

According to the officers, Gobbo raised issues of morality and ethics relating to police and lawyers. She stated that she believed her home was bugged by police. She wanted to talk about a tax evasion charge against Horty Mokbel that would later lead to that first unusual encounter with brother Tony. (Horty would end up beating the charges.) She also offered information about a conspiracy-to-defraud case against a wealthy Jewish family.

The AFP officers concluded Gobbo had no information of substance. They dismissed her as 'untrustworthy'. Yet Gobbo kept calling them. She kept offering herself up as a police informer because she could not 'cope', as she put it, with the ethical issues of her circumstances. She was drastically uncomfortable with what she perceived was the wrongdoing around her.

Just as she had as a third-year Law student, Gobbo was again seeking to inform — and trash the ethics of her profession — six months before she was admitted to the Bar as a barrister and at a time when she was being held up in public as a promising light of legal excellence.

Strawhorn was the first of four Svengali-like detectives in her longer period of assisting police whom she named in 2020. She would say Strawhorn took advantage of her naïveté and paranoia. So much for her claims of maturity the year before, in her application to be accepted as a lawyer.

Her relationship with Strawhorn started a pattern she later spoke about to her psychologist. She felt these detectives used her to 'fish' for jigsaw pieces in investigations. She sought to 'please them' at the time, not realising the extent to which she was being used. 'And as pathetic as that sounds for me to admit … I think that's the best way to put it,' she would say in 2020.

She sounded enthused at one meeting with detectives five months after the 'raincoat' meeting, suggesting four avenues of investigation for them to pursue.

But one officer was not impressed. Detective Senior Constable Chris Lim expressed concerns similar to those of Detective Senior Sergeant Jack Blayney three years earlier. Lim felt Gobbo was 'too overt' in her desire to provide information. She was known to have had inappropriate relationships with police officers, and, according to one police report, to be in possession of drugs belonging to a client.

This was five years after she was caught in possession of hard drugs at her Carlton home and a few months after she was accepted as a barrister. And yet she was on the police radar for carrying drugs?

Lim dismissed her as unsuited to police informing. Yet his opinion, like those of Blayney in 1995, and the AFP officers she had met with more recently, seemed to be ignored.

Gobbo spoke to Drug Squad officers throughout much of 1998. Strawhorn was present at a meeting the following May, at the Emerald Hotel in South Melbourne. Jeff Pope, a young detective from the Asset Recovery Squad (part of the Major Fraud Squad), came along too. The group discussed the criminal allegations against Diamond.

The Emerald was known for quality pub grub in the emerging dining market of the era. At this hub of horse-racing figures, Gobbo had a regular courtyard table where she could smoke.

The next day, Pope applied to register Gobbo as a human source. It appears that he was unaware of Gobbo's previous informing in 1995, though Gobbo herself says she did not know that until almost twenty-five years later. No concerns about a potential conflict with the ethical demands of her profession were noted on the application.

Once Informer G395, Gobbo was now Informer MFG13.

As Pope would reveal in 2019, he spoke to Gobbo every day for the first two weeks of June 1999. Their chatter extended to football, politics and the police. Then, as now, Gobbo voiced strong views on many matters.

There was a four-hour get-together in the inner Melbourne suburb of Armadale, at which she promised to provide incriminating computer disks to substantiate the criminal claims against her boss. She offered to chat with a client of Diamond's suspected of involvement in the alleged money laundering.

She also pushed the boundaries of the relationship. She asked Pope to help vary a restraining order for one of her other clients. She also sent him notes for his Law degree studies.

Yet by November 1999, Gobbo's informer role had fizzled. Pope dismissed her information as of 'no value', and she was deactivated. Diamond was no longer to be investigated. Naturally, Diamond argues there was nothing to investigate. It would be another sixteen years before he learned that she had assisted in a criminal investigation against him.

Pope, by his account, received a call from Gobbo in 2000 after an 'odd' drug raid in Abbotsford. The property contained no drugs, cash or drug paraphernalia. Gobbo told Pope that he didn't know what he 'had stumbled into'.

How did she know that Pope had attended the property? She was just twenty-seven, not long out of university, but she was already omnipotent, an outsider on the inside.

Pope had an unplanned meeting with Gobbo in 2000. They ran into each other at court, and went for coffee at the nearby Metropolitan Hotel.

Gobbo was getting ahead, she told Pope. She was about to go on a holiday to Hawaii — but she would pay for the 'right companion' to come along.

Pope declined the purported offer, which Gobbo contends was never put to him. Whether his or her version is accurate is a matter of guesswork. 'At the end of our conversation she asked whether our

34

relationship was ever likely to develop into something more meaningful,' Pope would say in 2019. 'I said "no" as I was happily married. As I recall that was the end of the conversation.'

* * *

Gobbo was indeed getting ahead by this stage.

In early 1999, just before the escalating Gangland feud exploded into bloody life, Gobbo was being toasted in the news pages of the *Herald Sun*. At twenty-six, she was admitted as one of the youngest female barristers in Victoria's history. Gobbo was poised to perpetuate family pride. She seemed set to emulate Lieder, who along with Betty King QC (later to become the Gangland judge) was one of the first women to 'take silk' in Victoria. Gobbo stood as an emblem of a changing world, one that was finally giving women overdue recognition. She was a role model. As she had fêted Lieder, would younger female lawyers thank Nicola Gobbo for blazing a path?

Diamond's favourite ex-employee was now a barrister he briefed for criminal clients. As a solicitor, she had learned the grunt work of painstaking research and paper trails. Now she could appear in court, cross-examining witnesses and excoriating the police officers she had privately railed against.

Barristers are generally precluded from working in partnership with other barristers or solicitors. They work from 'chambers' shared with other independent barristers. Yet Gobbo had a ready list of prospective clients after only a year of working under Diamond — his.

She was fearless. On the fast track.

Gone was the little black car she had driven to Diamond's office; now she drove a luxury sports vehicle — fast. She wore mini skirts. She embraced the trappings of her lucrative line of work.

Wheat Restaurant and Bar in Lonsdale Street, in the heart of Melbourne's legal district, became a second office for Gobbo. She smoked on the balcony there with a phone permanently attached to her ear.

She also gravitated to South Melbourne pubs — like the Emerald — that took food and prices seriously, and to Melbourne's best Italian restaurants in Carlton and Fitzroy, which had gifted the metropolis its preoccupation with gastronomy and wine.

Gobbo was the master of the drop-in drink — perhaps at Mint, which buzzed with lawyers on Friday afternoons, or across William Street at the Metropolitan.

She represented major drug criminals because they could afford her. She chased their business and socialised with them regularly. The young woman who preferred to wear Chanel's Allure or Calvin Klein's Eternity was roughly earning about $250,000 a year.

* * *

Criminal lawyers of Gobbo's ilk are enveloped by the depraved and the disturbed. The terms of engagement are well understood.

The scruffy delinquents who materialise at their wood-panelled offices are usually guilty of the criminal charges against them.

A criminal trial is not simply a test of guilt or otherwise; the onus is entirely on the prosecution — usually the police and the Office of Public Prosecutions — to prove guilt beyond reasonable doubt. Defence barristers like Gobbo seek to expose holes of logic or fact in the police cases against their clients.

By the time of her chance meeting with Pope in 2000, Nicola Gobbo's freakiest clients were drawing journalists to the courtroom.

Gobbo defended a bird breeder who smuggled parrot eggs in his underpants.

For a drunk driver, Gobbo argued that her client thought he had been drinking light beer.

For a pensioner busted with 1100 marijuana plants in his backyard, she claimed the man had sprinkled seeds from a jar he'd found in the garage.

Gobbo told a court that a woman who helped her paralysed partner commit a sexual assault deserved compassion because she'd lost babies soon after giving birth.

A client in an international prostitution scheme was a 'dupe'. Gobbo's legal wrangling in this case repelled another barrister involved,

Sharon Cure, who wondered at Gobbo's ethics at the time. Gobbo and Cure would clash in the years ahead.

Gobbo came to be feared by police officers whom she cross-examined. She might have socialised with them outside the courtroom, but inside she projected contempt for them. Renowned homicide detective Charlie Bezzina never questioned her ability. 'She was good on her feet' was how Bezzina would describe her courtroom style to the authors in 2018.

Detective Sergeant Paul Dale of the Major Drug Investigation Division, soon to be a controversial figure, was similarly impressed by Gobbo's outward professionalism. She was 'Amazonian', he would say in his 2013 book *Disgraced?*. 'Long blonde hair, short skirts, short tops with plenty of breast showing …' Gobbo was an excellent lawyer in part because she excelled in studying human nature. 'I think she loved the limelight that came with dealing with both the major criminals and detectives who caught them,' Dale would observe.

Outside the courtroom, though, things were trickier. Her name in police and legal circles differed from her public profile as a thrusting female lawyer. Her path was already marked by unorthodoxy, and her reputation was suffering.

Melbourne may be a thriving metropolis of European-style elegance, but it can also be mistaken for a village of a few million people. Colder than the northern states, more buttoned-up, Melbourne is the preserve of the quiet word. Real power is mostly hidden, wielded by few and dispensed with a nod or a whisper.

Inspired by the likes of Betty King, Gobbo harboured thoughts of becoming a judge, but her choices from the start of her career had precluded her from judicial promotion.

The story goes that two magistrates advised Gobbo her criminal associations risked costing her a future appointment to the bench. Her profile was rising but so was the whiff of wrongness about her. She was thought to be too close to her clients. As a former judge now puts it, she was dismissed (mistakenly) as a 'gangster's moll'.

Colleagues later disdained Gobbo's pretensions of a seat on the bench. She didn't work hard enough, one would tell the authors. The law is more than coffees, phone calls and exchanges of gossip.

Not many of her fellow barristers have kind words to say about Gobbo. Her 'radioactive' aura, says a female colleague, was coupled with a generous use of fake tan. Many women avoided her.

A journalist recalls her at the bar of the Celtic Club, where the carpet clung to the soles of your shoes. She was alone, shouting drinks and 'clearly desperate', like a lonely girl at the school prom.

Dale remembers seeing Gobbo at a Christmas party in another city bar: 'She was very drunk, very loud and the centre of attention … This appeared to be her personality at the time, larger than life … She was like that at police social gatherings as well as when in her own environment.'

A politically incorrect underworld source from the time says: 'What caught my eye was the way she dressed and the way she presented herself. She was cheap and easy. I thought there was more than meets the eye. And she thought she was untouchable because of her blue-blood family.'

Yet her uncle Sir James heard the rumours. Gobbo was spotted in the street, crying uncontrollably, after an annual blessing for the legal fraternity, called Red Mass, at Melbourne's St Patrick's Cathedral in the early 2000s. One of Australia's finest barristers stopped his car and offered her a lift. She told him that Sir James had turned his back on her at the event. It mattered: for the past decade, Nicola Gobbo had name-dropped her uncle at every opportunity.

Such moments of humiliation were the price for the life she had chosen. Her networking with undesirables and fraternising with police had cast her as unseemly.

But Sir James knew little of the deeper truth. No one did.

An episode tracing to Gangland's earliest rumblings offers insight into the double life she was leading by this point.

Detective Senior Constable Stephen Campbell was one of four officers on an operation at the St Kilda Marina in 1999 who were later charged for trafficking marijuana. The story went that the officers were tipped off about a drug deal by the man who was picking up the drugs. The officers were later accused of having stolen the thirteen kilograms of marijuana before the deal was done.

The crook who tipped them off can't be named, but let's call him Pistol Pete. He was also charged over the drugs, and later convicted. He made a statement implicating the four officers, and became a key witness in the unsuccessful prosecution against them.

Nicola Gobbo represented Pistol Pete — but she also slept with Campbell over two distinct periods, around 1999 and 2001.

By the time the case went to court in 2005, Campbell and Gobbo were still friends. He and his fellow officers would be found not guilty, after Pistol Pete reneged on his statement.

He had no idea that his lawyer was close to Campbell throughout this time. He said in 2019 that he would have 'sacked her on the spot' if he had.

Pistol Pete had assumed that his lawyer was working in his best interests. He later declared that Gobbo gave 'a whole new meaning to barristers dicking police'.

Most lawyers don't act this way. For them, controversy is contained to their clients.

The legal system is a fluid beast. Its fundamentals were developed over centuries, but, like language, it is always evolving. Lawyers can be expected to push boundaries in pursuit of their cause, but there is no latitude for them to behave outside the rules. They are policed by ethics boards, and they become scholars in what they can and cannot do.

Protections are enshrined in the system. If you are charged with a crime, you consult with a solicitor. If the case is serious enough to go to court, the solicitor will brief a barrister, such as Gobbo, to represent you. They cannot take your case if they are conflicted — say, if they represent another client whose best interests do not match yours.

A 2000 case in Queensland known as *The Queen v Michael Carl Szabo* depicts the rigours of the profession. In *Szabo*, a defence lawyer did not disclose to his client his recent romantic relationship with the prosecutor — which resumed shortly after the trial. When it was revealed, the guilty verdict was set aside and another trial was ordered, even though the defence lawyer was thought to have presented a competent case for his client.

Criminal barristers play an adversarial role aimed at identifying flaws in the case against you. They cross-examine police officers and other witnesses. They also seek to subpoena unpresented documents that may help your defence.

Sometimes, when the prosecution case is very strong, your barrister may advise you to plead guilty to some charges to reduce your overall sentence. Typically, the prosecution files as many charges as it can identify, then a plea-bargaining process begins. In exchange for pleading guilty to some charges — thereby expediting the justice process — the prosecution may drop other charges. This process is bamboozling to the average defendant, who is generally reliant on the advice of their barrister. It helps explain why many defence barristers wheel whole suitcases filled with documents to and from courtrooms. They are fighting battles on behalf of you, the client, that you often cannot fathom.

You are entitled to speak to your solicitor and barrister 'in confidence'. The conversations are shielded by 'legal professional privilege'. They cannot be monitored by police. Apart from a few narrow exceptions, your lawyer cannot repeat incriminating information about you to anyone. He or she is ethically bound to provide independent advice that is in your best interests. For the system to work, you must trust in your lawyer's unfettered representation of you.

These are the general rules that explain why Gobbo's choices would repulse the entire legal fraternity.

The Law Institute of Victoria's Professional Conduct and Practice Rule 1.1 states: 'A practitioner must, in the course of engaging in legal practice, act honestly and fairly in clients' best interests and maintain clients' confidences.'

Sounds simple enough. Four things: honesty, fairness, client welfare and confidentiality. But Gobbo must have missed the memo.

She did not provide independent advice. She did not uphold the confidentiality of her arrested clients. She did not even act as a barrister should, leaving the everyday work to the solicitors who briefed her. She turned up at police stations after her clients were arrested, a proximity that is a solicitor's domain. Her fingerprints smudged every aspect of her clients' cases. And each time she put police interests ahead of theirs, she was in breach of her sworn duties to both her clients and the court.

Pistol Pete's account offered only an inkling of Gobbo's bigger deceptions. Around the time he was caught with thirteen kilograms of marijuana, Gobbo had already graduated to become a confidante to the underworld's biggest names.

Melbourne's Gangland War was triggered when three punks met in a nothing park, and one punk shot another punk in the guts.

4
A Shot in the Park

The Gangland War Erupts
1999-2010

The park where the Gangland War began is squeezed between houses in the suburb of Gladstone Park, like a planning afterthought. There are no signs, no tour groups.

Here, drug baron Jason Moran *did not* kill wannabe drug baron Carl Williams on 13 October 1999. Instead, he wanted to remind Williams, in his Mambo shirt and thongs, of his place.

There was history between them. Jason Moran and Williams had recently scuffled after a friend of Williams had failed to return a piano belonging to Moran. Williams had also taken up with Roberta, the wife of Moran associate Dean Stephens. To this day, Roberta Williams says Carl saved her from Stephens.

But that's not why they were in the park. They were there because Jason and his half-brother, Mark, were upset about a delivery of pills from Williams that had crumbled, a disputed pill press, and Williams's undercutting of the Moran price of ecstasy tablets. They wanted $400,000 whereas Williams believed Mark Moran owed him $1 million.

Dead men cannot pay. So Jason whipped out a .22 Derringer and shot Williams in the stomach instead of the head.

'We want that bullet back, you fucking dog,' one of the Moran brothers reportedly said.

The aftermath of the Williams–Moran encounter heightened its oddness. The three men drove — in the same car — back to where they had met earlier at a nearby shopping centre. A wounded Williams had turned twenty-nine that day, and came home to find his mother, Barbara, had baked a chocolate birthday cake.

He reluctantly went to hospital five hours later, where he invoked the criminals' code of silence, and told police he'd been knocked out while on a walk and had woken up with a pain in his stomach. He couldn't remember a thing, he said.

Yet Jason Moran had made a fatal mistake by not listening to brother Mark, who had urged him to kill Williams. After this encounter in a park with no name, a grudge would morph into a vendetta and launch an unprecedented bloodbath.

* * *

Moran had underestimated Williams. He'd inadvertently started a Gangland war in which thirty or more people would be killed, while countless police officers built careers on responding to the community's increasing demands for action.

Gangland lacked the codes of Italian mob warfare. Gangland was all about Victoria's rocketing recreational drugs market.

Over the previous decade, ecstasy (MDMA) and speed (methamphetamine) had begun flooding the Melbourne party scene. Everywhere you turned, otherwise law-abiding citizens were throwing down pills for a fun night out. Most young adults of the era seemed to try ecstasy at least once (though Dowsley claims that he did not).

By 1990, Melbourne was known as the amphetamine capital of Australia. Levi Diamond's client John Higgs was behind much of the importation and production during this time. Higgs was thought to have got his start from Hells Angel bikie Peter Hill, who learned how to make speed on a trip to America and sold the recipe to him for $1000. (Hill was eventually convicted of drug crimes.)

The genesis of the underworld conflict is often traced to the 1996 arrest of Higgs, considered the dominant player in drug trafficking since the previous decade. An informer file linked to Higgs and his syndicate was stolen from the Victoria Police Drug Squad in early 1997, leading to questions about corrupt cops and the force's ability to protect high-risk sources. Higgs's subsequent downfall is said to have created a vacuum of power in the underworld swamp.

Williams believed there was enough demand for ecstasy and speed for *all* the main drug traffickers to get rich. They could have shared drug cooks and cooperated on importations while avoiding petty grudges. Williams's Pollyanna thinking had been sound, at least in theory. But the newbie had underestimated the greed and ambition of Melbourne's more practised drug warlords. The generals staked out their territories, and nominated their enemies, but their soldiers sometimes changed sides.

Gangland was sparked in October 1999, but a brutal drug trade had flourished for generations, hidden in plain sight from Victoria Police. Blood had long splattered the Melbourne wharves and produce markets in explosions of anger and brutal power plays, yet no one ever saw a thing.

Police's inability to crack the underworld's code of silence dated back to 1958, when Freddie 'the Frog' Harrison was killed on the docks, and thirty-odd witnesses, including a bystander splashed in Harrison's blood, could not identify the killer. Many of the men said they were in the toilet at the time of the murder — a two-man toilet, mind.

Gangland was just an amplification of a previously unseen battlefield. Vaulting egos collided with expedience: killing your opponent grew to be the easy option.

History favoured the killers. Hampered by the criminals' refusal to assist, police almost never solved underworld murders.

* * *

In any rundown of Gangland's major players, it's best to start with the Moran family. Mark Moran trailblazed the designer pill industry in the 1990s, and the Morans controlled much of Melbourne's drug trade during that decade before the upstart competitors emerged. He, along with half-brother Jason and Jason's father Lewis, were underworld royalty, their pedigree tracing to the Melbourne docks, and Lewis's membership of the Painters and Dockers Union in the 1960s.

The Painters and Dockers Union controlled the Melbourne waterfront for generations after World War II. Major drug rackets, as well as prostitution and extortion cartels, were birthed over coffees in Port Melbourne cafés. Under the umbrella of union strength, powerbrokers decided what drugs could get through the port: a lucrative sideline that enabled dockworkers to drive flash cars — and always aroused internal tensions. 'We catch and kill our own,' union secretary Jack 'Putty Nose' Nicholls once said.

The Morans inherited the Painters and Dockers stranglehold on drugs in Melbourne, especially speed.

Brothers Brian and Les Kane, both underworld docks enforcers, were murdered a full two decades before the Gangland War erupted. Les Kane's daughter, Trish, hooked up with a private-school boy when he was fifteen and they later married. That schoolboy was Jason Moran.

Jason Moran was a thug who carried a gun before he learned to drive. Moran fired so many bullets into other people's legs that a medical condition was coined — the 'Moran limp'. In death in 2003, he was described as a gentleman 'tragically taken from us'.

The Morans were loosely associated with Victor Peirce and Graham Kinniburgh. Kinniburgh called himself a 'retired dock worker', though his safecracking nous better explains his affluent address and kids' expensive schooling. Both Kinniburgh and Peirce were shot dead during the Gangland War.

* * *

The Mokbels were sometimes called 'the Village People', because of their lack of education and origins in rural Lebanon.

Like the matriarchs of many traditional migrant families, their mother, Lora, spoke little English. She was a woman of faith, and would regularly genuflect to the mounted crucifixes in her home.

Lora Mokbel thought her boys were wonderful. 'I promise, I promise, Tony is a very good boy,' she would tell Dowsley in 2012.

But Tony was a very naughty boy. All her sons were. Three Mokbel brothers ran separate drug operations in loose concert. They chased, delivered and manufactured, a hallmark of their operations being the exchange of drugs wrapped as presents. The low-key Grove Café in Brunswick was their preferred haunt.

Each brother had a nickname. Third son Tony's was 'L' or 'Lord Mayor'.

'Fat Tony', as he came to be known, had arrived with his parents from Lebanon (via Kuwait) in 1974, aged eight, and would trail his mother to her meat factory job at 4.30 am each day. He couldn't speak English at first, and later said he compensated by being the class clown. He remained a slow reader and writer, but it didn't matter much: everyone grasped the language of fear.

His father died on his fifteenth birthday. He later said that that was when he became 'dirty on the world'. He stopped going to school after his father's fatal heart attack. The obvious theory behind why Tony and his brothers — Milad, Horty and Kabalan — eventually turned to a life of crime is that they lacked authority and did as they pleased.

As a teenager, Tony gambled, a characteristic that would stamp his criminal grandness. He found success with a suburban pizza business, but gambling debts were said to inspire his criminal career. He was shrewd, at least in business, and acquired interests in fashion, property development and horse-racing. His on-track visits with his entourage earned them the label of 'the Tracksuit Gang'. Mokbel coveted a veneer of legitimacy, yet his orthodox pursuits were funded with illicit drugs.

Mokbel first flashed brightly into the police's sights in 1990 when he tried to bribe a County Court judge to help a mate on drug charges. The episode suggested his naïveté, a disregard for rules and a belief that everyone could be bought.

Mokbel turned to methamphetamine production, until listening devices picked him up in incriminating discussions in the 1990s. He had his guilty verdict overturned in 1998, with a curious defence: although he had agreed to produce the drugs, it could not be proven that he had sought to sell them.

It became clear that Mokbel was making tens of millions of dollars from drug imports and production. He was raided and charged in August 2001, but it was years before the charges were heard in court and he was pronounced guilty.

Milad Mokbel was the sausage-fingered younger brother who idolised Tony. He was methodical and clever, said one observer. According to another, he was overbearing and cheap. Tony had tried to dissuade Milad from trafficking heavier drugs such as speed, so Milad attempted to keep his forays secret. Milad was trafficking drugs from at least 2002 and was later convicted.

Second-eldest brother Horty Mokbel was trafficking speed earlier than Milad. As was eldest brother Kabalan, who was convicted of delivering heavy-duty drugs connected with a methamphetamine laboratory discovered by police in 2001 in Rye, on the Mornington Peninsula. Some of the Mokbels, as well as Carl Williams and another drug trafficker, Nik Radev, were suspected of investing in this laboratory. Such unlikely cooperation between sniping Gangland groupings shows that — as Williams had hoped — the lure of money could at times overcome historical tensions.

The episode also underscored the absurd profits of illicit drug production and trafficking. The Rye set-up was one of many pop-up labs of the era producing ecstasy and speed. Drug production was a risky business, and not only because of the law. Precursor chemicals costing hundreds of thousands of dollars could be turned into drugs worth tens of millions of dollars.

Such illicit alchemy required expertise, lest the investment get destroyed by poor cooking techniques. Ecstasy pills were carefully measured for quality by the market. Pills stamped with the Mitsubishi logo, for example, were known to be reliably effective 'pingers' by their upwardly mobile constituency. The young and educated law abiders rarely dwelled on the grotty origins of their happy pills, though some of them heard that Mokbel's pills were high-grade.

Mokbel commandeered the best drug cooks. They were coveted by the drug lords, when they were not being threatened by them, and could earn up to $80,000 a week.

Tony didn't inflict violence as casually as ordering hamburgers, like some Gangland figures. Rather, he used money to win people over to his point of view. His random generosity generated a tribe of sycophants, yet he cared little for the passing parade. They were hookers and hangers-on, there to be used until they lost their usefulness.

Tony's crazy-arsed audacity made people laugh. He drove a Ferrari with 'R U DARE' number plates. He was incorrigible, inveterate and ripe for parody. Jail stretches to him were like droughts to farmers: an unfortunate but accepted part of life. He spoke of the need to 'die with pride' when he was arrested in 2007. Or, as his role model, TV character Tony Soprano, once said: 'I find I have to be the sad clown: laughing on the outside, crying on the inside.'

'[W]e were all mates,' Tony told an *Australian* reporter in 2007 in describing Gangland. 'It started over a silly thing and suddenly there were just bodies falling all around me.'

* * *

Mick Gatto headed the Carlton Crew. He was a kind of third general who would stay standing after Carl Williams and Tony Mokbel toppled. Fond of cigars, Gatto bore the physical foreboding of a former professional heavyweight boxer, fine clothes hanging from a bear's frame. He avoided the darkly comical mayhem that surrounded Williams and Mokbel and garnered them constant media headlines.

Other members of the Carlton Crew attracted headlines, though. Gatto's predecessor at the top of the hierarchy, Alphonse Gangitano, had been a standover man who needed violence the way the rest of us need air. He had a penchant for literature and listed his occupation as 'gentleman' on his will. He used to hang out with Jason Moran — that was, until Moran allegedly killed Gangitano in early 1998, for reasons that remain unclear. Gangitano died in his underpants in his laundry.

This was how it went in Melbourne's underworld. Tribal disputes over drugs or debts or perceived slights ended in dead bodies — and the tossing of a gun off the West Gate Bridge. Gangitano's 1998 death was an unofficial entrée for a Gangland spree of caricatured notoriety

Gangitano now resides under statues of Jesus and Mary, his headstone so large that it completely overshadows his slab of gravesite marble. Ostentatious resting places became another Gangland quirk.

His successor, 'professional mediator' Gatto, had other worries. Tony Mokbel had been beaten up by bikies in a meeting arranged by Gatto in 2002. Mokbel was supposed to apologise for calling the Coffin Cheaters bikies 'dogs', but he ended up being gang-kicked as he lay on the ground. Shamed by the bruising, he hid from public view for a time and wore sunglasses for weeks. Mokbel blamed Gatto's crew for the beating, in what grew to be a significant Gangland grudge.

The enmity between Mokbel and Gatto was also stirred by Mokbel's flourishing friendship with Carl Williams, which began around the same time. They were allied by overlapping business pursuits, and Williams would write letters to the Mokbels until his death. Williams, who produced speed and also bought it from Mokbel, detested Gatto. Williams undercut the market, but his alliance with Mokbel stayed productive.

Mokbel had his own thoughts about how Gangland might finally end. 'It won't be over until that fat cunt is dead,' he said of Gatto in 2004.

Yet Gatto would be the only major figure to survive the War and thrive.

* * *

The tinderbox of Gangland was an unlikely exemplar of multiculturalism. Lebanese mixed with Russians and the Mafia, as well as Turks and 'Skip' upstarts such as Carl Williams and his father George. Crews morphed according to politics and power.

The Sunshine Crew, for instance, came to be hitched to the Williamses. Yet its leader, Andrew 'Benji' Veniamin, who'd almost certainly killed his predecessor Paul Kallipolitis, was long linked to Gatto, who would kill him in 2004. Most of the Sunshine Crew members had been childhood friends. The crew also later included Gangland heavyweight Rocco Arico.

Veniamin, a former kickboxer with a pit-bull temper, probably killed six people for money, yet he wore the flashy sunglasses and other accessories of someone who wanted to be noticed. He was mindful of the public fascination for Gangland.

As were Gatto and Judith Moran, the mother of Jason and Mark. They were among the underworld figures to later publish their thoughts in books. Gatto would even sign autographs in the street.

'I find it an increasingly strange place where people like Mick Gatto can become social commentators,' Victoria Police Assistant Commissioner Simon Overland said. 'These are not nice people. They are not celebrities. They should not be treated like celebrities.'

* * *

The Gangland War escalated quickly after Williams's stomach wound. This family feud lacked the pathos of Capulet v Montague, but Williams v Moran was just as murderous.

Jason Moran's choice had granted Williams another decade of life: ample time for Williams to kill him, his brother Mark, his father Lewis, and up to seven others whose continuing existence was bad for Williams's business.

At the time of his shooting in 1999, Carl was an ambitious bogan of twenty-nine going on fifteen. He still lived with his mum Barbara and dad George. Older brother Shane, known as Pear, had died of a heroin overdose two years earlier. In tribute, Carl Williams vowed never to traffic heroin.

Father and son bonded after Pear's death, and together they graduated into a Gangland crime outfit. George was later said to 'pull the strings' of the operation. He had grown up as a pool shark, and had been blinded in one eye in a pub fight. He had moved his family to Broadmeadows, a kind of Struggle Street of unemployment where many of Carl's schoolmates later joined him in jail.

The Williamses were close-knit, even though George and Barbara had drifted as a couple. After she moved out of the family home in Broadmeadows, her sister moved in as George's new romantic partner. When Barbara died in 2008 of a drug overdose, her son described her as his 'pillar of strength', whom he'd called on the phone each morning.

Carl was considered soft as a kid, but he followed his brother into drug trafficking after leaving Broadmeadows West Technical College in Year 11. He had hoped to be a policeman, until he was clocked over the head with a telephone book in a police station.

When he fell in with the Morans, Carl delivered drugs and did dogsbody duties. Carl was friends with his bosses; he went to the races with them on days out. He was busted in a speed lab in his twenties and served a brief stretch in jail. His drive to drug trafficking was largely driven by his aversion to hard work. He lived on fast food and hair product.

Police knew little about Williams when Jason Moran shot him in the stomach in 1999. They belatedly realised that his shitkicker status was misplaced. Williams was wily and manipulative. In just a few years, he had nurtured his own enterprises and loomed as a serious player in the Melbourne drug trade. He showed little respect for police, a common trait throughout Gangland. The law was a nuisance, not a handbrake. So Williams started killing people.

Psychos for hire aren't usually known for their insights. Yet an armed robber and hitman who befriended Carl Williams in prison had a simple explanation for the Gangland death count. Williams was a 'very kind person before he was shot', he said. After that, Williams's 'whole demeanour changed'.

Carl Williams's burgeoning relationship with Roberta Mercieca (later Williams) fostered his desire to cleanse the playing field of old-time crooks, such as the Morans. He and Roberta married in 2001, despite a 2000 Christmas Day incident when a pregnant Roberta confronted Carl over an affair with another woman and he fired several shots at her. A couple of months after their daughter, Dhakota, was born in March 2001, Carl was charged with drug offences after an undercover sting. While remanded on these charges, Carl Williams befriended Tony Mokbel in prison.

Williams appeared to obey few underworld codes. He presented as a loving son, a devoted husband and a doting dad, but also as an odd blend of apathy and violence. He looked like a teddy bear with hard eyes. His goofy expression hid a reptilian heart.

He anointed himself as 'the Premier'. He drove a war that resembled a spectator sport for ghouls. The soldiers wore Gucci watches, drove expensive black cars and mangled pronouns. They thrived then died in a macabre spectacle of bad blokes whacking other bad blokes.

Men died for being too close or too distant, for owing money or being owed, because of lifelong feuds or passing rages. Loyalties and suspicions collided with paybacks and rip-offs in a haze of drug-induced paranoia. The victims' wives, bowing to the accepted Gangland narrative, publicly called for revenge.

Those close to Williams say he didn't pull the trigger on Mark Moran, killed outside his home on 15 June 2000. Williams took pride in not carrying a firearm, but he was the chief suspect despite his insistence that CCTV footage from a bottle shop showed he could not have committed the hit himself.

The killing was originally considered revenge for the death of fruiterer Frank Benvenuto. When Benvenuto, the local Calabrian mafia head, was gunned down in his bayside Melbourne driveway in 2000, he was on the phone to his standover man, Victor Peirce. For years, police suspected that he had told Peirce the name of his killer.

A career hitman, Rod 'the Duke' Collins was a suspect among many. Melbourne's then busiest hitman, Benji Veniamin, placed a tribute to Mark Moran in the *Herald Sun*: 'You are a true sincere gentleman never to be forgotten.'

Veniamin was said to be the shooter when Victor Peirce was shot dead in his car in Port Melbourne on 1 May 2002. Few people mourned Peirce's loss. He was notorious for being tried and acquitted for the killing of two police officers, Steven Tynan and Damian Eyre, in Walsh

Street, South Yarra, in 1988. When Peirce's family placed flowers at his Port Melbourne murder scene, onlookers tossed them into a nearby bin.

Police explored many theories. One version said Peirce was killed because he knew who had shot Frank Benvenuto in 2000. This theory also linked Peirce's murder to the deaths of standover man Dino Dibra in 2000, and drug trafficker Paul Kallipolitis in 2002. The common link was the suspected killer, Veniamin.

The shootings mounted. Nik Radev, a drug manufacturer who preferred using torture to talking to get his way, wanted the services of one of Mokbel's drug cooks. When Radev stepped out of his black Mercedes in Coburg on 15 April 2003, he was shot seven times. Williams was thought to have ordered the hit because Radev was bullying his way to Gangland significance.

Radev enjoyed one consolation: he died wearing a Versace suit and a $20,000 watch. Not bad for a man whose official work history amounted to an eight-month stint in a fish-and-chip shop in the 1980s.

* * *

Assistant Commissioner Simon Overland once said that 'organised crime never ends'. Likewise, the police would never tire in their pursuit of these career criminals.

'The message is you can get away with things for a period of time, but eventually we'll catch up with you,' he told *The Age* in 2004.

The longer history bears out Overland's observation.

Gobbo represented Carl Williams. And Tony Mokbel. And Mokbel's crew. She advised Mick Gatto. And Faruk Orman, the alleged getaway driver in the Peirce killing.

She was also close to police officers such as Stephen Campbell and Paul Dale. She was playing all sides: the cops and the crims, and the lawyers who represented the glue between them.

She knew all of the Gangland players, good and bad. She chortled at their jokes, babysat their kids, and woke up next to them.

And they didn't know her at all. No one did.

Least of all herself.

5

The Stuff of Myths and Legends

Task Force Purana
2003-2004

Until mid-2003, ordinary Melburnians sized up Gangland's likely prospects — and targets — as they might horses in a form guide. It inspired little more than a ghoulish voyeurism. Was the killing of the bad *really* all bad?

But the murder of Jason Moran on 21 June 2003 changed all that.

Moran was known just as 'Jason'. In the Gangland ooze of nicknames, a one-name title denoted high status.

Yet despite this position, and a widespread fear of 'the Moran limp', Mark Moran's death in June 2000 had exposed his half-brother. Carl Williams later boasted that he told Jason while they were in prison together: 'I got that bullet out and had it put in your brother.'

By 2003, Jason Moran's warning to Williams in October 1999 loomed as a death warrant. For a time Moran got lucky: he and Williams kept getting jailed, as if clocking on for alternating shifts. As Jason entered, Carl left, and vice versa.

Soon, though, Williams was offering $200,000 for Moran's death. He and the shooter conjured odd plans, like surprising Moran by jumping out of a car boot. In another scheme, the killer was to don a wig and pretend to be a mother pushing a pram. Williams also fantasised about killing Jason at his half-brother's gravesite on the anniversary of Mark's death.

They schemed for months, then botched their choice of venue.

On a Saturday morning in Essendon North, surrounded by other junior footy mums and dads, Moran sat in a light-blue Mitsubishi van with a friend, criminal Pasquale 'Little Pat' Barbaro (not to be confused with a Calabrian crime boss who appears later in the book). Five kids, including Moran's six-year-old twins, sat in the back. Moran had just been diagnosed with testicular cancer. He had a gun down his pants.

Let's call the killer 'the Assassin'. When he appeared at the driver's window, Moran might have glimpsed a blur of gloves and a balaclava. Then he was blasted with a shotgun and slumped forward.

The Assassin wasn't finished. He used a long-handled revolver to shoot Barbaro while the kids in the back looked on.

Such unchecked retribution put innocents in danger. The public was glimpsing a twilight world where hitmen roamed freely and their masters plotted.

Suddenly, the public mood shifted from morbid fascination to fear and anger. The citizens of 'the world's most liveable city', as Melbourne is commonly known, demanded an end to the bloodshed.

* * *

Gangland was a problem for Victoria Police, but an opportunity too. Police had faltered on organised crime in the late 1990s. Investigations had dried up, intelligence became dated and resources were misdirected.

There were several reasons for this, but the most damning was endemic police corruption.

A myth of clean cops had flourished in Victoria ever since an abortion protection racket was uncovered in 1970. Senior police officers stood accused of extorting massive bribes from Collins Street medical specialists. Homicide chief Inspector Jack Ford, the traffic branch head Superintendent Jack Mathews, and former detective constable Martin Jacobson were given lengthy jail terms. 'By your conduct, you have severely shaken the community's confidence in the Victoria Police

Force and, inevitably, I think the morale of the force itself must have suffered,' the sentencing judge told the men.

The line went that the convictions meant the bad apples had been purged. Yet the truth behind the shiny façade was very different.

The Drug Squad acquired a reputation for playing by its own rules. It had lapsed into corruption in the mid-1990s in part because of poor oversight. By the turn of the twenty-first century, it was another relic of the past, where the ends came to justify the means, and once-fine officers slid into dark places.

The Drug Squad's Chemical Diversion Desk sold precursor chemicals on an undercover basis to drug suppliers, then tracked who used the chemicals to produce ecstasy and speed. The targets were big fish.

Sometimes, though, detectives lost track of the chemicals they supplied. There was a relentless temptation to profit from a largely unmonitored program. This behaviour remained unchecked for at least five years.

In December 2000, someone from a chemical company contacted Victoria Police's Crime Department with troubling reports about the Chemical Diversion Desk's transactions. This led to Operation Hemi.

Hemi investigated allegations that Drug Squad members had made unauthorised purchases of chemicals and drugs of dependence from a pharmaceutical company. In July 2001, former detective senior constable Stephen Paton was arrested, along with Detective Sergeant Malcolm Rosenes and three civilian offenders.

Paton had even set up his own chemical company in order to make the unauthorised purchases, which he later sold to criminals. He was charged with trafficking pseudoephedrine, a precursor for making speed. His supervisor, Rosenes, was working as a go-between for an ecstasy supplier and an Israeli drug syndicate. He was charged with trafficking ecstasy and cocaine.

* * *

On 25 November 1999, six weeks after being shot by Jason Moran, Carl Williams was roused from sleep by police inside a housing commission property in Broadmeadows. A press was punching pills in another room. Clad in a red Mambo shirt, Williams pulled the covers over his head and hid in his bed. His father George was found in a second bedroom with a loaded pistol. Police had turned up to serve arrest warrants on other people; instead, they stumbled onto 30,000 pills and nearly seven kilos of speed, later valued at $20 million.

The Drug Squad was called, and Rosenes and Paton turned up to investigate. The case against Williams junior and senior was delayed, on the say-so of the Supreme Court, until the charges against Rosenes and Paton were heard. Both Rosenes and Paton were convicted. Williams was granted bail after being held on remand for more than a year on these and subsequent drugs charges. In 2004, the 1999 charges were dropped altogether.

Rosenes and Paton did not corrupt this particular investigation. But they typified a cultural rot within Victoria Police. They were proof that police needed controls to avoid the temptations of human nature.

Corrupt Drug Squad cops were motivated by the same sort of greed as Gangland lords. Only the naïve put good and bad at the ends of a spectrum.

After Stephen Paton received a six-year sentence, he told *The Age*'s John Silvester: 'We were locking up crooks. You just forget where the line is.'

* * *

In early 2001, Christine Nixon — then a New South Wales assistant police commissioner — was interviewed for the role of Victorian chief commissioner by a panel that included Premier Steve Bracks. She told them that she doubted Victoria Police were as clean as they appeared. She would later label the Drug Squad's Chemical Diversion Desk 'a major drug dealer'.

A month after Operation Hemi concluded in July 2001, Nixon instigated the so-called Purton Review, which found major problems with informer handling within the Drug Squad. She shut down the department in November 2001 and replaced it with the Major Drug

Investigation Division (MDID). The Chemical Diversion Desk was a thing of the past. There would be random drug and alcohol tests and greater oversight of informer use, Nixon declared. But the overhaul was flawed. Old Drug Squad officers successfully applied to join the MDID, and some of them were dirty cops.

* * *

The review also recommended that police set up a task force to continue investigating bent drug cops. The result was Operation Ceja, which ran from 2002 to 2007.

Some former Drug Squad officers now being implicated in crimes were among the same officers Nicola Gobbo had been informing to a few years earlier.

Detective Senior Sergeant Wayne Strawhorn — who had investigated Diamond on the strength of Gobbo's information — embodied the crossed lines.

Over a decade, Strawhorn fashioned a legendary status within the Drug Squad. He became celebrated for bringing down high-profile drug importers. He seemed immune to material trappings. He had few obvious kinks.

Then he was arrested in March 2003, and charged with supplying two kilos of pseudoephedrine to Mark Moran.

Strawhorn was sentenced to seven years' jail after three trials. He had used the 'noble cause' defence, yet his sentencing judge unambiguously declared: 'Members of the police force are not above the law and it is simply no excuse that your serious breach of the law may have resulted from some misguided belief that the end justified the means.'

* * *

The droppings of the former Drug Squad littered the Gangland landscape. Bad cops meant bad men got bail, and were free to go on trading drugs and shooting each other.

In this environment, Gobbo was becoming known as 'the Bail Queen', a pro at getting suspects freed until their cases were heard. She took advantage of the growing stench of corruption that surrounded the members of the old Drug Squad.

'She was staunch in arguing that cops are corrupt and she was a staunch defence barrister,' detective Charlie Bezzina would say in 2018.

Paul Dale later recounted his impressions of Gobbo during this period: 'When Nicola came into the St Kilda Road MDID offices, she'd seek out a sergeant, because she knew that she needed to talk to people of rank. She also had contact with detectives at the Ethical Standards Department (ESD) because some of her clients had given information against corrupt police. And when the detectives from the old Drug Squad had corruption allegations levelled against them, Nicola Gobbo would march her clients off to bail hearings and tell the court that because of allegations of corruption, her clients might not come to trial for years.'

* * *

As Nixon called it, the Gangland War was a turf skirmish about pill presses and territory, about drug traffickers with hitmen on speed dial. They had a head start. None of the dozen or so Gangland killings up to 2003 had been solved.

In January 2003, just months before the shooting of Jason Moran changed the rules for everyone, Nixon recruited an old colleague to head up the Gangland investigation.

As an earnest young Australian Federal Police (AFP) officer, Simon Overland had worked on the vexed investigation into the 1989 murder of AFP Assistant Commissioner Col Winchester. Through that he had come to know Christine Nixon of New South Wales Police.

Overland felt modern, like a politician on the rise. People gravitated to him when he entered a room. He wore boots, rather than brass police shoes: a choice that bolstered his already imposing height. As Assistant Commissioner (Crime), Overland became the public face of Victoria Police's Gangland fightback, and Nixon came to rely on him more than any other subordinate.

Overland was a complex figure. One of his senior Gangland investigators would tell Dowsley and Carlyon he found him 'thin-skinned' and 'paranoid'. 'Anyone with investigative prowess that challenged him — he would take a set against you.'

Carlyon would also interview Overland himself in 2011. Overland cited Atticus Finch, and his noble pursuit of justice in *To Kill a Mockingbird*, as an inspiration. Yet he was also prepared to win a just war using unorthodox methods. As Colonel Nathan R. Jessup said in the film *A Few Good Men*, the people 'can't handle the truth'. All we, the public, had to do was stay ignorant and be grateful.

At the time, homicide was broken into investigative crews, each supervised by a senior sergeant. They took turns to be on call, then were replaced by the next crew when another murder took place. The system produced independent and highly motivated crews that were able to give all their attention to individual cases. The shortcoming was that the bigger story was being missed. Each of the Gangland murders was being investigated in isolation.

In 2003, three crews realised that they had the same chief suspect for three separate murders. Senior Sergeant Phil Swindells , who led one of these three crews, began pushing for a Gangland task force. Overland gave the new operation his approval.

The task force, which began in May 2003, was called Rimer to begin with, a random name thrown up by the computer. It was soon reincarnated as Purana, which refers to a class of Hindu sacred writings comprised of popular myths and legends.

Hothead Benji Veniamin was the starting point. At this time, Veniamin was thought to have killed Dino Dibra, Paul Kallipolitis and Nik Radev. But building a dossier of information would take months and more deaths.

Commentators have since asked whether earlier police insight into Gangland might have quelled a raging war before more died. The success of Purana highlighted the deficiencies of earlier police models.

A closed shop, Purana quickly grew to fifty-three staff, broken into nine investigating groups. The task force was led by a rotation of senior officers over the course of the Gangland War. Swindells headed Purana until Inspector Andrew Allen took over in August 2003.

One of his replacements was Jim O'Brien, a thirty-year veteran who headed Purana from 2005 to 2007. O'Brien loathed Tony Mokbel in particular. He was so proud of the task force's work that he lobbied for a Purana medal. He rotated in the role with Gavan Ryan, who led the task force's culture of modernity until 2008 as 'an angry enforcer of professional integrity', according to ABC journalist Chris Masters.

Members of the elite squad took to wearing striped ties as a kind of uniform of excellence. Theirs was a show of camaraderie in a righteous cause, as if nodding to Eliot Ness and his 'Untouchables'.

There would be no early successes, however. Nixon would describe Purana's first year as an 'uphill, sometimes demoralising slog' in her 2011 autobiography *Fair Cop*. Purana sought to build 'the picture and the intelligence from the ground up, bit by bit, trying to chip away at the code of silence protecting the killers, all the while being second-guessed and undermined by commentators and even other police,' Nixon wrote. 'And all the while the murders continued.' Police even called in Essendon football coach Kevin Sheedy for a motivational speech.

The speech appeared to work. The task force became so successful that it remained active long after the 2010 death of Carl Williams, the unofficial bookend to the Gangland story.

Ultimately, Purana would grow to more than 100 staff, including analysts and surveillance and support crews working up to sixteen hours a day. It logged 836,173 phone calls, listened on devices for 53,000 hours, and undertook 22,000 hours of physical surveillance.

By the end of the war, Purana had seized more than $60 million of criminal assets. It had put Williams and Mokbel away, as well as many of the hitmen paid thousands of dollars to take a life. Purana would make names for police officers like Stuart Bateson, whose pursuit of Carl Williams was considered (favourably) as obsessive. He too would receive an Australian Police Medal. His chummy charisma underpinned his doggedness.

Bateson had been earlier seconded to the Lorimer Task Force, which had successfully investigated the shooting of police officers Gary Silk and Rodney Miller in 1998. But by war's end, Purana had replaced Lorimer Task Force as Victoria Police's internal benchmark of greatness.

The figures on both sides of the Gangland War also achieved nationwide fame when Series One of the *Underbelly* franchise — based on a book by journalists John Silvester and Andrew Rule — premiered to popular and critical acclaim in 2008 (though not seen in its entirety in Victoria till 2011 due to Supreme Court suppressions). All the major players of Gangland featured in a stylised version of real events, with Bateson becoming a composite character played with charming cockiness by Rodger Corser.

Crown Prosecutor Geoff Horgan, who put many of the baddies away, would call Purana the 'most important criminal investigation that Victoria Police produced'.

Nixon herself would write in her autobiography that 'Purana, overseen by Simon Overland, pioneered some radical, multi-dimensional investigative techniques in Victoria, drawing together police intelligence, financial profiling, criminal profiling, family histories and more to build sophisticated dossiers on each of the murder victims.'

Yet both of them overlooked the most critical tool in Purana's success. The history has to be rewritten. Task Force Purana's investigation had a taint.

The taint was Nicola Gobbo.

* * *

By the early 2000s, Gobbo was leading the kind of double life she'd rehearsed at school. Back then, it was sex and celebrities; now, it was guns and gangsters. Not long after Jason Moran was killed, Gobbo raised her risk-taking to a whole new level. This led to her first encounter with the Purana Task Force.

She was attracting new clients, such as Carl Williams's father George. Soon came the celebrated Tony Mokbel bail case in 2002, which propelled Gobbo's public profile.

Gobbo was a someone beyond police and crime circles, a growing fixture in the gossip and commentary pages of the Melbourne newspapers. She was becoming public property, an attention-grabber for clients such as an alleged drug runner who had an iguana called Godzilla and a python called Cuddles.

In a *Herald Sun* profile published 8 December 2003, entitled 'Million-Dollar Eagle Flies High', she was described as 'a formidable presence in impossibly short skirts' who was fast becoming 'a legal celebrity'. She called her father Allan her biggest influence: 'He was someone who always helped people and never asked for anything in return. And that's probably the biggest thing he's instilled in me.' Gobbo was described by one of her siblings 'as a one-person Salvation Army'.

'She spends time at weekends visiting clients in prison or on remand,' the newspaper's John Ferguson wrote. 'However, she has managed to rile some of those in the police force who pay professionally when she succeeds.'

Gobbo told Ferguson she had friends who were police officers. 'I have clients who are police, former police who are clients,' she said. 'Those that are professional in what they do … it's not an antagonistic relationship at all.'

When she placed her beachside apartment in Middle Park on sale in October 2002, *The Age* reported it. In September 2002, *The Sunday Age* covered her trip to Bali in a gossip column story that began: 'Chalk up another amazing performance by Melbourne barrister Nicola Gobbo.' 'Nic' had gone there with a girlfriend. They spent 1.2 million rupiahs shouting beers for American sailors at their hotel bar. 'It was a long night,' a source said. There's a strong chance the source was Gobbo herself.

A few months later, in the lead-up to the November 2002 Victorian State election, a debate was held between the major candidates, Robert Doyle and Steve Bracks. It prompted *The Age* to seek expert responses — from 3AW's Neil Mitchell, the ABC's Virginia Trioli, a political scientist, and 'barrister' Nicola Gobbo.

'It gave Victorians an opportunity to decide whether to trust a Liberal Party leader who offers no original thought and whose answers were evasive and lacking in substance,' Labor supporter Gobbo declared.

'The Bail Queen' was becoming a celebrity, just like the Gangland clients she represented. And the higher the death toll climbed, the more their status rose.

* * *

Then Gobbo was asked to appear for Mokbel and Williams's rival Lewis Moran at a bail application over drug-trafficking charges. It was July 2003, a month after Jason Moran's execution at a kids' football clinic. Mokbel and Williams ordered her not to accept the job.

Yet she did appear on Moran's behalf, successfully. In court, Gobbo argued that the children of murdered half-brothers Mark and Jason Moran needed a father figure. Police protested that Lewis Moran, if freed, might try to avenge Jason's and Mark's killings. But Moran got bail.

Later the same week, Gobbo received a visit from Benji Veniamin. He was there to menace her, at Williams's behest, for assisting an enemy player.

'He screamed and threatened me,' she later said in a sworn affidavit. '"You are part of our crew. You were told not to go anywhere near Moran, and you did it anyway. How dare you do what we told you not to do. Tony's not happy with you. Carl is not happy with you. You're a fucking dog."'

Yet Gobbo was not to be put off. She was never someone to bow to unreasonable threats. She would willingly place herself in danger, as if confident that forces beyond her control would save her when required. She appeared again for Moran the following week.

Afterwards she was approached by Swindells on the Melbourne Magistrates' Court steps, a backdrop for many unscheduled meetings between police officers and Gobbo. The pair chatted amid criminals, belligerents, media photographers and police officers.

The Purana Task Force had been launched just a few months earlier. Police intelligence had picked up the threat against Gobbo. Swindells told Gobbo to be careful because Veniamin was a 'dangerous individual'.

The chat with Swindells led to talks with Bateson, one of his officers at the time. She was already acquainted with Bateson through representing suspects in the Jason Moran hit, and she and Bateson would work closely in getting convictions, in events described in the following chapters.

Gobbo was still two years away from being registered again as a police informer. But she was soon informing anyway, to Bateson. She had been a lawyer for six years, and she had been informing both on and off the books for six years.

The triggers for her duplicities ahead seem obvious enough: no one forgets a hitman like Veniamin outside their home. But her loyalties were professionally mandated. She was selling out her own side in a choice no other lawyer would contemplate.

She rang Bateson repeatedly and met him for coffee at the Emerald Hotel to feed him secrets about her clients. She threw in legal colleagues too, for purportedly helping Williams and other Gangland heavyweights avoid prosecution. She accused these peers of perverting the course of justice, bowing to the demands of their kingpin clients by protecting them at the expense of their underlings.

It seems unfair to name these lawyer targets given they were never charged, but they commanded similar profiles to Gobbo's at the time. Bateson (rightly) suspected Gobbo herself of similar misconduct.

He manipulated her to glean information, she would claim in 2019, but he was more professional — or 'gentlemanly' — than Strawhorn. 'We did start off, when I say start off, when I first had dealings with Stuart he made it clear that he … didn't trust me, didn't approve of me,' she said. 'He specifically told [me] that I was having a sexual relationship with Carl Williams, which was ridiculous and absurd … I wouldn't say [Bateson] was a fan of mine at the beginning.'

(Gobbo has had many years to contemplate this relationship, as she has the relationships with Strawhorn and other police handlers, official or otherwise.)

'I can look back now with hindsight, a wonderful thing as it is, and — like what possessed me to have all of those conversations with him and why did, why did I feel the need to basically purge my soul to someone ... who claimed that he did but didn't have my interests at heart,' she wondered.

* * *

Meanwhile, Gangland machinations rumbled, keeping Gobbo and other lawyers busy.

Willie Thompson, a drug dealer and gym junkie, was officially listed as a 'lollipop vendor'. In reality, he was linked to the Morans and Nik Radev. He was killed in his convertible on 21 July 2003, a month after Jason Moran. The hit, outside his southeast Melbourne gym, was a messy job, with bullets lodging in nearby buildings. It was a clue to the rising recklessness.

Thompson, a school friend of Tony Mokbel, was thought to have been killed on the orders of Williams over a drug trade dispute.

In a subsequent catch-up at Red Rooster, it was believed that Mokbel asked Williams to kill Thompson's killer. Williams brokered a deal to kill his nominated patsy for the Thompson hit, Michael Marshall, officially a hot-dog vendor but likely a drug dealer. Williams deployed his hitmen on 25 October.

Marshall's shooter would later claim that he didn't see Marshall's five-year-old as he pumped four or five bullets into the father's head. 'Someone shot Daddy!' the boy cried, running inside to his mother.

In Gangland, one death begat the next. A Purana cop chatted with a Gangland figure, purportedly asking him to stop leaving bodies in the street. The charred remains of the next Gangland victim, Mark Mallia, were found in a wheelie bin stuffed down a drain on 18 August 2003. He was killed on the orders of Williams.

Mallia had worked for Radev before Radev was killed. One theory behind his murder goes that he had rattled Williams by asking questions about Radev's death at a seafood lunch at Crown Casino. Williams decided that Mallia had to die. Mallia was tortured with a soldering iron in a garage before being killed.

Even some of the giants were starting to feel threatened. In early 2004, Mick Gatto brokered a flimsy truce with Williams after Gatto's mate, Graham Kinniburgh, was gunned down in his Kew driveway after midnight on 13 December 2003. Gatto assumed that Williams had ordered Kinniburgh's death, and had heard of a contract on his own head.

Their exchange was caught on a Crown Casino security video, and experts deciphered the chat.

'If anything comes my way then I'll send somebody to you,' Gatto told Williams. 'I'll be careful with you, be careful with me. I believe you, you believe me, now we're even. That's a warning. It's not my war.'

Ironically, though, it was Gatto who inadvertently made the war's next move. The shooting of hitman Benji Veniamin at a Carlton restaurant on 23 March relieved everyone who feared the little hitman — including Gobbo. According to Gatto's version, Veniamin pulled a gun on him, then Gatto tried to wrestle the gun from Veniamin's hand. During the struggle for control of the gun, five shots were fired. Three bullets hit Veniamin — one in his head and two through his neck. Gatto's account was accepted in a jury finding of self-defence.

Yet Gatto was haunted by memories of the gurgling and the splatter. He was no Macbeth, but he later had a Banquo-esque moment, which he recounted in his 2010 book. He woke one night choking, convinced that a ghostly Veniamin had returned to throttle him.

Police had already linked Benji to the murders of Dino Dibra, Paul Kallipolitis and Nik Radev, but they would eventually suspect he also killed Frank Benvenuto, Victor Peirce, Graham Kinniburgh and Mark Mallia. He was dead before police could charge him with a single murder.

* * *

As Benji Veniamin expired inside a Carlton pizzeria, Gobbo was still eighteen months away from being re-registered as a police informer. But her perplexing place in events leading up to the tragic double murder of Terry and Christine Hodson revealed she was already as big a liar as any Gangland hitman. The Hodson murders proved just how out of her depth she was.

6

A Dog's Tale

Terry Hodson, Family Man
2001-2004

Terry Hodson was a doting grandfather who loved his wife's home cooking. He and Christine had been teenage sweethearts and came from the same Staffordshire village.

Their East Kew home, just down the road from the Harp Road Police Station, was filled with family photos. A BMW gleamed in their garage. There were many BMWs in this wealthy nook of Melbourne's east. But not so many gun-toting drug dealers.

Terry Hodson was a survivor. He'd left school at fourteen, and met Christine when he was on a work site. Later, he'd run a car yard, but ended up in jail when a deal went sour. He'd escaped and eventually moved to Melbourne, and now, in his fifties, veered towards Arfur Daley stylings.

He thrived on Scotch and coke — cocaine, that is. He nicknamed his grandson 'Villain' and his gun 'Roscoe'. Two of his children, Mandy and Andrew, sold drugs for him.

Cops liked him, even when they were charging him. 'Chrissy', as cops called her, was a devoted wife. 'If you didn't know who they were, you'd think, "Well, they're quite nice people",' an investigator would tell Dowsley and Carlyon.

Hodson was small-time compared with the drug barons he informed against. He was mostly unknown past the TAB pub a few hundred

68

metres from his home. Until he was executed, that is, alongside Chrissy, in front of the TV in May 2004.

Ex-chief commissioner Christine Nixon agreed in 2011 that their killings remain the 'greatest stain' on Victoria Police's reputation. And one of the saddest unsolved mysteries.

Not many murders boast so many facts and so few answers. The longer story of the Hodson killings has taken years to be told. Even now, their case, like any that involves Nicola Gobbo, flounders in conflicting notions that muddle the obvious starting points.

* * *

Dowsley and Carlyon have spent countless hours holding the details of the Hodson case up to the light. They feel deeply for the Hodson children, who relied on Dowsley to fill them in on Gobbo's proximity to their parents in life and in death. The two Hodson daughters, Mandy and Nikki, are grateful to Dowsley for his unfettered pursuit of the truth. He, like the fictional LA detective Harry Bosch, has a singular approach: 'Everybody counts or nobody counts.'

The Hodsons weren't clean, but they were a loving family. It happened to the Hodsons, but it could have happened to any of us.

It is an involved story. The following is intended to guide the reader through the murk.

In the Hodson vortex, some of the cops were the crooks, and the crooks were the victims. The informer informed on his informer handlers. The informer, who became the victim, was under protection when a police officer was suspected of having him killed. The police officer's murder charge was dropped when a witness against him was killed in protection.

Make sense? It's not supposed to. No one except the killer or killers know/s what happened.

The Hodson case featured more double crosses than a sewing bee, and plenty of stitch-ups. Nothing was as it appeared, largely because the loudest voices in this tragedy would almost all be discredited.

Nicola Gobbo was prominent among them.

* * *

This tale began when two of the Hodson children, Andrew and Mandy, were charged with drug offences in 2001. Mandy — nicknamed Dimples by her father — had discovered hard drugs on her twenty-third birthday, when Terry gave her speed.

He turned police informer to help his kids. He couldn't bear the thought of his daughter in a prison cell.

Terry Hodson — Informer 4/390 — was handled by Detective Senior Constable David Miechel, who had arrested Andrew and Mandy. Miechel would soon be working under Detective Sergeant Paul Dale at the Major Drug Investigation Division (MDID).

Nothing about Dale said average, except his country upbringing playing footy, and dreaming of bright lights, in Yackandandah in Victoria's north. Hodson later told police that Dale was always complaining about a lack of money. Dale denies he once asked Hodson for a gun, as Hodson claimed, and for ecstasy pills so he could try them with his girlfriend.

Dale was thought of as a charmer, a man's man and a ladies' man too. He was always good for a beer, with both cops and crooks. He wasn't an elite detective, but he was pretty cunning.

Dave Miechel sported a ponytail and rode a motorbike. As a kid on the Murray River, he hung out with the nerds at school. The first surprise for classmates was when he grew up to be a detective. A bigger shock was when he turned out to be a dirty one. When asked 'What's the best advice or motto to live by?' on a school reunion questionnaire, Miechel wrote: 'Deny, deny, deny. Demand proof.'

Miechel has since been dismissed as a corrupt cop who ignored Chief Commissioner Christine Nixon's clean-sweep missive. The embodiment of greed and deceit, Miechel is now thought to have threatened, harassed and profited for years under the cover of a police badge.

Miechel was secretive in ways that put fellow officers off. He was especially secretive about his love interest, Mandy Hodson. Obviously he shouldn't have been sleeping with a suspect who was also the daughter of his informer.

The lines got even more blurred. In return for informing, Terry Hodson was allowed to deal drugs from his home. He basically had a green light to break the law.

Police superiors knew Miechel was too close to the Hodsons. The other Hodson daughter, Nikki Komiazyk, knew it too: she says that when her partner, Peter Reed, was about to be raided at home, Miechel tipped her off beforehand.

Terry Hodson's relationship with his handlers breached virtually every tenet of informer management. Informer misuse, incompetence and the withholding of intelligence from other police would all fuel the Hodson tragedy ahead.

The State of Victoria still owes the Hodson kids the truth, if not more. The system failed their parents. Those who played outside of the rules have never been held to account.

The Hodson scandal has been told many times, but no telling has properly included Gobbo's place in it — until now. Her role in events before and after the killings defies the sympathy that might apply elsewhere in her story.

A naïve manipulator doomed to regret her improper proximity to the Hodson killings? This is the kindest possible take on Gobbo's role, and it's probably *too* kind.

* * *

Terry Hodson was a prolific informer. He ratted out his enemies and his customers and his friends. Like Gobbo, he treated informing as a game.

Not that his targets wanted to play.

Take Carlyon's suburban cricket team-mate, a former private-school kid who turned to drug dealing. He was picked up in a freeway chase after he bought thousands of ecstasy pills from Hodson, took legal advice from Nicola Gobbo, and spent several years in a country prison thanks to his 'friend' Hodson, who had snitched on him.

High demand for pills meant good times for Hodson. But he grew addicted to the adrenaline of his double life. When the MDID could not find $20,000 so he could make an undercover purchase of pills, he paid for the drugs himself. That he later sold the pills at great profit suggests the glaring deficiencies of police oversight at the time.

Yet Hodson's enthusiasm for informing also endangered him. Even nobodies like Carlyon's drug-dealing cricket mate expressed a desire to kill him.

Hodson's informer number kept turning up in police briefs against the drug criminals. Nicola Gobbo, who worked for many of the accused, figured out that Informer 4/390 was Hodson. She fished for information from Miechel outside court one day, and her curiosity prompted an urgent informer number change.

But identifying the exact starting point of Hodson's collision course with death is fraught. The prevailing version of events is based on Hodson's own words to anti-corruption police. His story implicates Paul Dale, who was charged with several crimes but never convicted of any. Dale has always maintained his innocence.

Hodson would speak to police of a chicken salad lunch with his handlers Dale and Miechel at Romeo's, an Italian restaurant in uppity Toorak, on 8 September 2003. There, he alleged, the trio conjured up plans to burgle an illegal drug storage house in Dublin Street, East Oakleigh, a suburb in Melbourne's southeast.

Dale, Miechel and Hodson purchased burner phones under false names to communicate. It would be an 'easy job', Hodson said he was told, because Dale's police unit had the drug residence under surveillance.

The burglary stank of diabolical perfection. The burglars knew what was in the house and when it would be unoccupied. They knew the gaps in the police oversight, because they *were* the oversight.

On the night of the burglary, 27 September 2003, Melbourne was distracted: earlier that day, the Brisbane Lions had won the AFL flag for the third time in a row.

Three previous burglary attempts had been aborted because tenants were home. Though Dale had turned up on these earlier occasions, according to Hodson, he pulled out on the night it actually took place, supposedly because he was tied up with guests at home. As a result, Hodson said, he and Miechel squabbled about Dale's cut.

That night, Hodson was buzzing after snorting cocaine from a vial he was carrying. (One suspects he always carried a vial.) He and Miechel basted themselves in 'Stop' dog repellent to deter the guard dog in the house, and lit cigarettes for the police surveillance camera, hoping this might throw off investigators later, as neither smoked.

Miechel, dressed in black, smashed the front light and charged the front door with his shoulder. A neighbour heard the breaking glass and called police.

The pair rushed into different rooms of the house and rifled through drawers and cupboards. Hodson saw a blinking light in a bedroom and fretted that a silent alarm had been tripped. But the burglars appeared to be in luck. They grabbed plastic bags stuffed with drugs and cash.

To this day, controversy swirls around the size of the haul. One of the drug tenants alleged that $750,000 cash was taken. It remains unaccounted for, leading to suggestions that Miechel never admitted any wrongdoing because he knew he would receive a cut of the massive takings later on.

They tossed bags of drugs over the back fence of the property before separating, then met at a nearby school and watched a police car cruise by. Hodson correctly assumed that someone had heard the disturbance and notified the police.

Miechel dashed back to get the stash.

Here, it all went wrong.

Despite the dog repellent, Miechel was bitten on the arse by police dog Silky after he was found up a tree. Hodson gave himself up when a police dog rushed him in his nearby hiding place.

Police later described the burglary arrests as a triumph of Neighbourhood Watch. They were also a new low in a flourishing chapter of Victoria Police corruption.

Miechel's dog bite led to a limp, and warranted a trip in an ambulance and skin-graft operations.

He rang Dale after his arrest with an ambo's phone. Dale's movements over these first hours and weeks after the burglary would be probed for years to come.

Dale turned up later the same night at Room 104 of the Freemasons Hospital in Melbourne's inner east, not far from the MCG and its surrounding pubs, filled with sad Collingwood fans. His visit to Miechel's bedside was unsanctioned and unsupervised.

He rang his superior, MDID head and later Purana Task Force leader Detective Senior Sergeant Jim O'Brien, at 9.32 pm. O'Brien would say in 2019 that he thought Dale's explanation of events sounded like 'rubbish'.

Dale went straight from the hospital to the MDID offices on the twelfth floor of the St Kilda Road Police Complex. Investigators came to believe — and Dale later denied — that while there he stole a confidential dossier that became known as the Blue File.

The Blue File contained thirty-one of Hodson's information reports to police. There were many 'blue files' at the MDID, stuffed into a clutter of safes and filing cabinets. Yet security was so poor that the office cleaner could have lifted a file from one of the unlocked filing cabinets.

Hodson's 'highly protected' blue file, which contained the names of those he had betrayed, was soon circulating throughout the underworld.

No one else bar Dale had reason to pinch the file, investigators later argued. Its possession offered Dale leverage against Hodson. 'Dale had the opportunity to steal the blue file and, if he was involved in the break-in, he had a motive to do so,' retired judge Tony Fitzgerald QC would argue in a 2005 report on behalf of the Victorian Office of Police Integrity. Fitzgerald would find 'no evidence that any other person did so or any sufficient basis for suspecting any other person'.

Dale was left out of a departmental crisis meeting on the Monday, two days after the burglary, then he was seen at his desk ripping pages out of his police day book. Forensic tests later showed he rewrote the entries in his day book for 27 September, the night of the burglary.

Dale took lengthy sick leave in the week afterward. He was in the frame for the burglary and he knew it. He would fight for his job for years, but within months of the burglary he was working on a construction site. The once-decorated detective was now digging ditches.

Terry Hodson, meanwhile, was considering his options.

He had been caught red-handed at the Dublin Street burglary, but there was an out. He could snitch on dirty cops and save himself a long jail sentence.

He took a tentative step towards cooperating with detectives by leading them to Miechel's motorbike in the post-dawn hours after the burglary. He hinted at a willingness to help.

But he needed a lawyer. Inspector Peter De Santo, of the police Ethical Standards Department (ESD), found one for him: Nicola Gobbo.

De Santo had the thrusting obstinacy of an old-time corruption-buster. He knew Gobbo well. Two years earlier, Gobbo had represented Andrew Hodson over charges of drug dealing and armed robbery.

De Santo had spoken to Andrew and Gobbo about corrupt officers within the Drug Squad. He wanted to talk to Gobbo again, now that Andrew's father was embroiled in the Dublin Street burglary.

He and Gobbo had stayed in touch. When De Santo had sought secret information in the intervening years, he'd called her, and she had provided it. Their chats had constituted another unofficial instance of Gobbo's informing: Wayne Strawhorn, Stuart Bateson, and De Santo, the detective investigating Strawhorn.

De Santo 'scared' her, she would say in 2019. He was a 'master of deception' who gathered insights like 'moving chess pieces'. He was not a bully, she told the royal commission. '[H]e would do it in a very professional way but he was, um, conniving is probably the best way to put it, he was, he was a scary bloke.'

A few days after the Dublin Street burglary, De Santo called Gobbo, to get to Andrew, to get to his father. He wanted Terry Hodson's evidence. He needed the informer-turned-burglar to inform on his police handlers, Miechel and Dale.

Within a week, Hodson implicated Dale as a co-conspirator in the burglary.

Either Hodson was recounting a detailed version of true events, or he was a very good liar. Police accepted his account.

De Santo was just doing his job, and doing it thoroughly. Yet De Santo's choice of Gobbo as Hodson's lawyer had already triggered deceits that would culminate in Hodson's death. By the time Hodson officially named Dale as a big-time burglar, Dale was pursuing a budding friend and drinking partner: Nicola Gobbo.

* * *

Dale and Gobbo were once foes. They had first become acquainted through courtroom tussles. Gobbo once excoriated Dale in the witness box, in a display of belligerence so pronounced it was reported in the newspapers. They were on poor terms, until one night when, according to Dale, they drank with a group at a South Melbourne pub, before the crowd piled into her Mercedes coupé and went to the casino.

In the aftermath of the Dublin Street burglary, Gobbo positioned herself at the centre of the conflicting agendas of Dale and De Santo. She was playing both sides. Whoever won the battle stood to gain the critical prize of Terry Hodson's loyalty.

The devil shelters in the details, and what happened next is involved. To this day, it remains unclear why Gobbo interfered the way she did, and whose side she was on.

Let's retrace the steps.

On Sunday, the morning after the burglary, Dale rang Gobbo about Azzam (Adam) Ahmed, who oversaw the drug-house operation, Abbey Haynes, the drug house sitter, and Colleen O'Reilly, a drug mule, who had all been arrested by Dale's crew. They wanted to talk to Gobbo about representing them.

On Tuesday, De Santo rang Gobbo. He had a job for his unofficial informer. She already had intelligence for him: Hodson had intimated to her that Dale was involved.

On Wednesday, she met with Terry and Andrew Hodson at the Celtic Club in Melbourne's legal precinct, pretending to act as a lawyer, but in fact acting as a police agent. As Andrew Hodson would recall later, Gobbo was 'fishing for information' from his father. Terry Hodson's paranoia was high and he appeared stoned. Her notes of the meeting reiterated her earlier intelligence about Dale. She was told Dale was 'off' — corrupt — as was the Drug Squad hierarchy.

On Saturday, Hodson rang De Santo. He had received an anonymous phone call. He believed the caller was Dale. Hodson was urged to 'stick together' with Dale and Miechel. There was 'no need to get into bed with anyone', and the caller promised 'you'll be looked after'. Hodson took the call as a coded warning not to roll on Dale.

Hodson told De Santo something else too: that 'the blonde lady [Gobbo] is sleeping with the three-striper [Sergeant Paul Dale]'.

On 9 October, while her client engaged with Ethical Standards investigators, Gobbo accepted a drinks invitation from Dale. They went to O'Connell's, a South Melbourne pub, and got blind drunk. She brought along a file of criminal conspiracy cases because he was fretting about his situation.

There was a lustful attraction that night, Gobbo would later admit, coupled with paranoia: Dale feared that she was wearing a wire. They kissed at the bar before going home together. She blacked out. But she said that this night was the first time they slept together.

Here's the question. Why would she meet a cop who had arrested her clients from the Oakleigh drug house and was also a suspect in stealing from them? Worse, why would she sleep with a man Terry Hodson, her latest client, had told her was 'off'? She knew that Hodson was providing evidence to De Santo that could jail Dale for a decade or more.

Gobbo had no good reason to catch up with Dale, but lots of bad ones. They kept catching up, on and off, for years.

When Gobbo and Dale got together for a second time about three weeks after the burglary, over coffee, Dale diarised the meeting as a catch-up with his lawyer. She would describe the meeting in a 2009 statement to police as an attempt by Dale to glean information about what Hodson had revealed to police. Police came to believe that her assessment was correct.

'Paul spoke to me and was desperate to find out whether Terry had made a statement implicating Paul in the burglary,' Gobbo would say. 'I didn't know and I told Paul this. I did not inform Paul about my contact with ESD on Terry's behalf.'

She would tell police she had advised Dale to get an Orange-brand phone — which investigators believed was code for a burner phone — in October 2003.

Gobbo's statement would not describe the nature of her catch-ups with Dale after the first 'entirely social' meeting in October. Or explain why she and Dale used burner phones, hers given to her by drug-house client Adam Ahmed and registered under Russian names. This was another red flag. Lawyers should never need to use burner phones; their client conversations, overheard or not, are privileged and cannot be used in evidence. Anyone using a burner phone, from criminals to cheaters, has bad motives for doing so.

Gobbo's conflicts were outrageous. She was Hodson's lawyer, at the behest of Victoria Police. She was volunteering to be Dale's legal advisor, thereby endangering Hodson. She was also the lawyer for all of the criminals who ran the Oakleigh drug house: Adam Ahmed, Abbey Haynes and Colleen O'Reilly. Behind them was Gobbo's biggest client of all, Tony Mokbel.

She could not serve this spread of clients without compromising the interests of some of them. In hindsight, it seems remarkable that these conflicts were not identified by a judge or professional body at the time. Gobbo appeared free to make up the rules as she went, and she would continue to do so in the years ahead.

Hodson, too, was making it up as he went along. He was a conman, and you can't con a conman. He talked to Gobbo, whom he dubbed 'the Big Lady', to try to get messages through to Dale, whom he feared.

Hodson is thought to have worn a wire under his white overalls for a meeting with Gobbo at Dominos Café in the city's legal district on 30 October. Gobbo would recall that Hodson offered her cash and cocaine during the chat. Nothing much came of it.

Gobbo saw De Santo by chance on 4 November at the Melbourne Cup, where the Flemington crowd topped 120,000. In the Members Enclosure champagne bar, soon after Makybe Diva won the race, Gobbo fed De Santo allegations that Dale and Hodson were 'trafficking prior to the [Dublin Street] incident'.

Gobbo's choices did not make sense. She was speaking more and more to Dale on burner phones, and she was teasing his would-be nemesis, De Santo, with incriminating claims about him.

A few weeks later, Gobbo chased Dale for a drink for her birthday. She met him on another night to quell his paranoia. He feared criminal charges, but Gobbo would say that Dale also feared that Tony Mokbel might kill him first over the stolen drugs.

On 5 December 2003, after two months of fretting, Dale, Miechel and Hodson were arrested and charged with the Dublin Street burglary. Victoria Police, with Hodson's detailed evidence, were ready to present a case against two of their own.

Although Hodson was cutting a deal, Gobbo was still meddling. She visited Dale in prison soon after his arrest, and again a week later. She would tell police in 2009 that the second visit was the only time she spoke to Dale in a 'strictly professional capacity'.

Yet she exchanged documents with Dale in the coming weeks after he got bail. He gave her his 'hand-up brief', the evidence gathered against him by investigators. In return, she provided him with the hand-up briefs of her other clients in the case — Adam Ahmed, Abbey Haynes and Colleen O'Reilly. She later said that she wanted to help her clients through these exchanges, and that Dale agreed to this.

Why would Dale want to assist scumbag drug suspects? They were comparing notes to find the investigation flaws.

She later told investigators that during the prison visits Dale said he wanted to see Carl Williams and Tony Mokbel. So much for Dale's right to confidentiality from a professional legal advisor.

Williams loomed in the background. For Gobbo was also fraternising with her *other* big client in this catastrophe of impropriety.

* * *

Investigators would accuse Dale of dabbling in the dark side from 2001, by courting a Williams associate so he could get to Williams, who then paid Dale for tip-offs.

Paul Dale still says he knew nothing of the Dublin Street burglary plot, though he has never explained the absence of specialist surveillance police at the location of the house on the weekend when it was burgled. He wrote an outraged autobiography about a wronged cop in 2013. The book was a potted tale: he overlooked his use of burner phones, which he said in court were for extramarital affairs. But the fact remains that Dale is a free man and has never been convicted of a single crime.

In statements from 2007 — most of which police were able to corroborate — Williams would claim a relationship with Dale dating back to 2002. He said that he and Dale walked laps in an inner northern Melbourne public pool to avoid eavesdropping police. A decade later, George Williams would support his son's claim in open court. Dale, of course, has denied any improper links with either Carl Williams or Tony Mokbel, and police have never proven them.

Gobbo's 2009 statement to police did not explain why she helped Dale communicate with Williams in the months preceding the Hodsons' deaths. In her statement, she described a catch-up on 2 May 2004. Phone records would show that Gobbo and Dale tried to communicate forty-six times that day. Gobbo fished Dale out of one Richmond pub and they went to another. He rang Carl Williams four times from 9.36 pm. He got through to George Williams and said: 'Tell Carl to ring Nicola. He's a fucking useless prick.'

Gobbo met with Williams on 5 May at Café Martini in Lonsdale Street. The meeting was observed by detectives, but they couldn't know that Gobbo was passing on a message: Dale wanted Williams to call him.

Williams would say in 2007 that he called Dale's burner phone from a payphone at the Watergardens Shopping Centre the next day. The fact of the call would be verified by police. The pair were thought to meet later that day in the northwest Melbourne suburb of Hillside. This was just nine days before the Hodsons were killed.

Dale would deny the meeting took place. Police would retrace George Williams's car, which had a tracker on it, to a location near Dale's temporary place of work on a construction site, supporting Williams's 2007 assertions.

According to Williams, he and Dale walked near a building site. Dale told Williams that he had hired a hitman to kill Terry Hodson some time earlier, but the job had not been done. Dale needed Hodson dead before Hodson testified against him for the Dublin Street burglary. Williams agreed to arrange a replacement hitman for $150,000. The chat ended when Dale went to pick up one of his children from daycare or kindergarten.

The next day, Williams contacted Rodney Collins, the ghastliest of killers-for-hire. Even photos of Collins give off a stench. Bystanders were sometimes also killed during his paid hits, loose ends to be dispatched. Collins tended to kill the partners of the men he was hired to hit, in a kind of two-for-one zeal. When he went to kill Dorothy Abbey in her lounge room in 1987 after murdering her husband, he found he had run out of bullets, so he used a kitchen knife to slash her throat.

Later that day, Williams and Collins caught up at a city restaurant, Windows. Tony Mokbel, sporting a cap, joined the group.

His presence here represents another direct link to the Hodson story. Police would determine that it was Mokbel who distributed the Blue File allegedly stolen by Paul Dale to Gangland figures on 28 February 2004. And they would theorise that Mokbel had received it from Nicola Gobbo. Police discovered that the Blue File was faxed from Taiba Stables — linked to Mokbel — to underworld figure Mark Smith in Queensland.

Dale had caught up with Gobbo in February. He talked to Williams on Gobbo's phone on 27 February 2004. And a phone call between Gobbo and Mokbel was later said to have been intercepted by the Australian Federal Police that same month. During that call, Gobbo supposedly told Mokbel that their mutual friend 'Pauline' had been in touch about documents for Mokbel. Victoria Police would come to believe that 'Pauline' was Paul Dale, and that the 'documents' were the

Blue File. Of course, Dale maintains his innocence and says that he was set up by Williams and other criminals to whom lying is second nature.

The Gobbo–Mokbel phone intercept was vital. In a submission for a coronial inquest into the Hodsons' deaths ten years after they were killed, police argued that the phone call and Mokbel's possession of the Blue File confirmed the nefarious motives of a dirty cop.

Their theory implied that, in handing over the Blue File to Mokbel, Gobbo had knowingly endangered her client Terry Hodson.

Victoria Police would say they only became aware of the AFP-intercepted recording in 2010, six years after it took place. And here's something stranger. Investigators couldn't get their evidence straight. At the coronial inquest's conclusion, Victoria Police withdrew the purported Gobbo–Mokbel phone call as evidence. They would argue, using logic lifted from Monty Python, that there was now no evidence that this evidence existed. One investigator was adamant that the phone call had taken place. Another detective was equally convinced that it had not. It may exist or it may not, but it has never been produced.

The Hodson children say police never told their father that the Blue File, containing the information reports laying bare his numerous betrayals of hardened criminals, was handed out to the very people he betrayed. Even if Dale didn't want him dead, plenty of others did. Gobbo has denied she passed it on, but the dreadful truth was that the document doubled as a death sentence after it was stolen from MDID offices and delivered to Tony Mokbel. What we don't know is how it got there.

Hodson never knew the size of the bullseye on the back of his head — or that his own lawyer had linked herself into the chain of his demise. In December 2003, soon after he was charged, he had left Gobbo for another lawyer, Dowsley's friend Rob Stary, who secured a deal in which Hodson would serve no jail time for the Dublin Street burglary in exchange for rolling on Dale and Miechel.

Hodson then inexplicably took back Gobbo, the meddler he did not trust, as his legal representative before April 2004. This decision was one of his last.

7

Dead Man Walking

Fallout from a Double Murder
2004-2007

Andrew Hodson had a 'weird feeling' on the morning of Sunday, 16 May 2004. When he drove past his parents' place, the garage door was down: big night, he assumed.

He returned later that day, a side-stop on his way to buy cigarettes. Sister Mandy's car was already there.

Drawn by her shriek, he rushed into the TV room. He touched his mother and father, who were stone-cold. He whispered their names, over and over.

Mandy would later recall the scene in sepia tones. On her way in she had seen her father through the window, lying on the floor, and had thought he was playing a joke. When she found them, she went straight into the kitchen and snorted a line of cocaine to steady herself.

Terry and Christine did not expect to be ambushed the way they were. Drinks lay undisturbed on a stand. Christine wore pink moccasins, Terry trakky daks. Both were found to have drugs in their systems. Terry had a cigarette locked between his stiffened fingers, and a spent bullet cartridge on the back of his head.

Mandy now believes her mother was shot first so that her father would suffer from the knowledge in his final moments.

* * *

Over lines of coke, the Hodson family had chatted about the September 2003 burglary soon after it took place.

Mandy would tell Dowsley and Carlyon that she punched her father when she heard what he'd done: 'I just looked Dad straight in the face and said, "You and Dave still went through with it even after Dale called at the eleventh hour and said he had a dinner party?" I said to him, "Oh, youse are fucked."'

Her father had broken his own rule: don't let greed into the equation.

Internal investigators had wanted the family in witness protection. The youngest child Nikki, nursing a baby, had railed against upending her life. She wouldn't do it.

Her stance still haunts her. Her father had opted against witness protection because he wanted the family together.

Andrew Hodson's first phone call when he saw the bodies was to Gobbo. She gave him Inspector Peter De Santo's number.

'Fucking Dale's done it,' he told De Santo.

De Santo was told that his boss, Assistant Commissioner Simon Overland, did not want him to attend the crime scene. Overland feared the media would see De Santo and link the murder to police corruption. De Santo fought the order and braved the chaos of cops and media.

Andrew Hodson didn't care about TV cameras. He sobbed as he crossed the road to embrace De Santo.

* * *

Detective Senior Sergeant Charlie Bezzina spotted the joint in the ashtray, the bodies side by side. He got to the hidden chemicals and the missing .45 pistol later.

The Hodsons' murder had been a methodical hit. There was no upturned furniture, no signs of struggle. Even the gold straw Terry Hodson used to snort cocaine sat in its usual place.

There were conflicting theories about the point of entry. Scuff marks on a trellis suggested the murderer had taken his victims by surprise. But nothing showed a home break-in, feeding the belief that Terry

Hodson knew his killer. The neatness of the kills reduced the number of possible suspects to a handful.

Hodson had broadcast his upgraded security to the underworld. He had organised it himself, including two German shepherds and a home-made CCTV system.

One night in the lead-up to the killings, a bottle was hurled down the Hodsons' driveway. Of more concern, a security sensor had been tampered with. 'Murray, it's started, I'm a dead man walking,' Hodson had told Murray Gregor from the Ethical Standards Department (ESD) when the detective inspected the sensor.

Police wanted the Hodsons safe, but they didn't want to have to spend money setting up surveillance to protect them. Some believe that their tight-arsed approach helped get the Hodsons killed, and that they should have done far more. The failing brought into question Victoria Police's ability to protect other witnesses and informers.

The police found the dogs beaten and locked in the garage, and the video tape of the premises had gone missing, presumably pocketed by the killer.

Bezzina was appalled by the ESD's lack of care for Hodson's safety. He told ESD officers at the crime scene that the inadequate protections were a 'clusterfuck'.

Paul Dale firmed up as a suspect at once. He had been charged over the Dublin Street burglary six months earlier; now the star witness in the case against him was dead. Bezzina arrested Dale at his Coburg home the following morning, Monday, at dawn. Dale explained that dozens could vouch for his whereabouts over the previous couple of days: he had been in Bendigo on a blokey weekend. (Gobbo later said she had declined his invitation to attend.) Dale was precise with details, and Bezzina wondered if he was 'over-alibied'.

Williams later alleged that he arranged for Dale to deliver the $150,000 payment to a wheelie bin at the home of Williams's mother Barbara. Williams spoke to killer-for-hire Rodney Collins three days after the Hodson deaths. They correctly suspected Williams's phone was bugged: in what police took to be code, Collins boasted that he loved cold weather because it kept the 'gigs' (witnesses) away. He said something had been 'overlooked', taken to be a reference to the surveillance cameras he discovered after entering the Hodson property.

* * *

At his home on Monday morning, Victorian Premier Steve Bracks was apprised of the 'shocking incident', as he would publicly call the Hodson killings.

Bracks's confidence in his police force was shaken, he later wrote in his autobiography, *A Premier's State*. Two people killed in police protection, possibly by a dirty cop?

Bracks asked bureaucrats to prepare for a royal commission. Gangland killings were a political bedsore in a State where law and order always featured highly on the list of election priorities. Just under a year earlier, Jason Moran's and Pasquale Barbaro's deaths, in front of children, had shifted underworld excesses onto Main Street. The Hodson killings were treated as Gangland-related deaths numbers eleven and twelve in the short period since.

Victoria Police had briefed Bracks's Department of Premier and Cabinet by the afternoon. Bracks was struck by their foresight. It had not been conveyed to them that Bracks was considering a royal commission, yet police had already prepared their arguments against launching one.

Just like the aftermath of the Jason Moran murder, Chief Commissioner Nixon knew the current moment was crucial. Amid the tragedy, and the jibes about police corruption, lay possibilities. Overland, her right-hand man, had helped set up the Australian Crime Commission (ACC) — a coercive forum with extraordinary powers to question witnesses — just before coming to Victoria Police. That experience inspired their thinking when they went to their political masters with a list of requests within weeks of the Hodson killings. The pair laid out a blueprint that would eventually lead to Gangland arrests — and a new police culture condemned for its lack of transparency.

After listening to their ideas, Bracks opted against a royal commission. Instead, he created the Office of Police Integrity (OPI), an independent body for investigating police officers. As Nixon would note in *Fair Cop*, like the ACC it wielded 'coercive powers — that is, the authority to compel witnesses, usually in secret, to answer questions and to tell no one'. So did another new coercive body set up to tackle organised crime: the Office of the Chief Examiner (OCE). It was able to unravel the tangled links binding the main players in Melbourne's underworld by forcing them to provide information under threat of perjury or contempt.

ACC, OPI and OCE examinations would often run parallel to police murder or drug investigations, and all these examinations have inspired questions about the appropriate separation of authority. Both the OPI and the OCE would be dubbed 'star chambers', a term that harks back to the fifteenth-century royal English court of the same name, which came to be known for its secret sessions without a jury, and the arbitrary use and abuse of power.

The OPI was formally established in November 2004. Its deputy commissioner, Graham Ashton, was the son of a butcher, and a former Australian Federal Police colleague of Overland. He would conduct many of the secret interviews himself, and as early as 2004 he was asking questions about the links between Nicola Gobbo and the Hodson killings.

Not only had Nixon avoided a royal commission, she had also won more resources for Gangland investigations, and the legislative power to seize assets — which would yield about $60 million from Gangland figures over subsequent years. 'Had I just become an immeasurably powerful woman, or a hugely burdened one?' she wondered in her autobiography.

What she did not do at this time was dedicate a task force to solving the Hodson murders. It's odd that the official investigation was left with Bezzina and his on-call Homicide Squad crew, given both the ESD and Purana boasted intelligence that was critical to the case. Under Bezzina's control, the Hodson investigation had to be slotted in around whatever other unexplained deaths occurred in Victoria.

* * *

Murder investigations are not always as they are depicted on TV. Interviews accumulate, yielding little information. Suspects are eliminated. Enthusiasm sags. Bezzina's investigation of the Hodson murders gradually turned into a box-ticking procedure, as difficult crimes often are. Bezzina was reduced to figuring out what *did not* happen in an attempt to isolate what *did*.

He interviewed Dale only once — the morning after the murders — because he lacked the relevant information to question him further. Weekly briefings with command slowed to monthly meetings.

He interviewed Nicola Gobbo a few months after the killings. He treated the chat as a mere formality, he would tell Dowsley and Carlyon in 2018. By then he barely remembered the encounter.

Gobbo was brash in her responses, despite her initial displeasure that the interview was being video-recorded. She sounded offhand, as if she had somewhere else to be. She was performing.

Sure, she knew Terry Hodson was an informer, she said to Bezzina. Tony Mokbel had told her in 2002. Yes, she had told criminals this fact before his death. (Hodson himself had had no idea that his life was being jeopardised by unguarded courtroom chatter.)

As a lawyer who used burner phones and had close connections with Tony Mokbel, Gobbo had a lot to hide. She employed the same tactic of deflection with Bezzina that she would later use with many others (including Dowsley). She told him she had tired of criminal law and Tony Mokbel, who used her.

She deliberately threw Bezzina bait to seek to steer his professional gaze elsewhere. The 'talk of Melbourne' was that her other client Andrew Hodson had been involved in his parents' deaths, Gobbo explained. Something to do with a missing gun, crime-scene tampering, and the apparent lack of resistance from Terry and Christine. '[O]ne has to ask how someone would get in there,' she said knowingly. She explained how father and son had fallen out after Tony Mokbel showed Andrew written evidence that Terry was informing. Andrew was considered a hothead who had motive.

She was deliberately misleading the investigators; she falsely stated she had had dinner with Andrew on the night his parents died. Bezzina and his crew would spend years probing Andrew in a wasted effort, in part because Gobbo sent them down the wrong rabbit hole.

* * *

Four years later, in July and August 2007, Gobbo's dodgy past involvement with the Hodsons finally bit back. She was called to appear as a witness at a secret OPI inquiry into the Hodson killings headed by Tony Fitzgerald QC. A witness statement from Carl Williams had named police officer Paul Dale as the Hodson killer and sparked a fresh (and secretive) police investigation.

Fitzgerald was already across the case. In 2005, he had looked into the theft of the Blue File for the OPI.

Gobbo stood to confront serious questions she had deftly avoided for three years. Understandably, she panicked. The chaos of yesterday was feeding the chaos of tomorrow.

By this point Gobbo was officially informing to police for her third stint. An OPI examination could expose her informer history to the underworld. She was only ever one successful subpoena away from a bullet.

Gobbo's handlers spitballed scenarios to protect their golden goose. She spoke of walking out of the hearing if dangerous questions arose. But she couldn't: uncooperative witnesses at OPI hearings could be jailed on the spot.

Police discussions went as high as Assistant Commissioner Overland. He gave his assurance that the OPI would be made aware 'of her status', and presumably would spare her questions that revealed her informer role.

Plausible deniability worked well with the crooks. But lying under oath is a crime. Gobbo had a problem in the OPI witness box. Within minutes, she was asked which police officers she knew. If she listed her specialised police handlers, it would be plain she was an informer. She rushed from the hearing, in tears, to consult Purana head, Detective Inspector Gavan Ryan, who was watching events on a camera in a nearby office.

Soon, Fitzgerald was pointing out 'untruths' in her evidence.

'Various of your relationships, particularly during that period [2004], are of considerable interest; and you could expect to be asked more about aspects of those things, and you might think that you could be more forthcoming and more accurate than on the last occasion,' Fitzgerald told Gobbo in an August 2007 sitting.

In describing Gobbo's earlier evidence, he said: 'I tell you that just as you took an oath on this occasion, you took an oath on the last occasion; and it's sufficient that I say I think that, I believe that you neither told the whole truth and that indeed in some instances you told untruths ...'

Despite Overland's assertion, it appears Fitzgerald was never informed about Gobbo's informer status. He told her in the hearing: 'Do I think that you are, if charged, at risk? The answer's yes.'

Dates were touted for Gobbo to appear at another OPI hearing, but it did not take place. It's odd that a witness accused of lying under oath was not recalled. Gobbo was not charged with perjury. Her informing was not revealed.

Why wasn't Gobbo held to account? The answer matters. Her insights into the Hodson killings — and the extent of her possible involvement — remain unknown to this day.

* * *

By 2007, Bezzina felt let down. He was a celebrated cop whose presence on the Hodson case had lent it gravitas. He had reported regularly to Overland.

Yet he would tell Dowsley and Carlyon that his homicide investigation was 'window dressing' that allowed other departments the latitude to pursue their own agendas. He believes to this day that Overland was running his own investigation behind his back. Perceptions persist that Bezzina's investigation, unbeknownst to him, was an exercise in spin aimed at distracting focus from these other machinations. Harry Bosch, the fictional LA detective in the Michael Connelly series, has a name for the game-playing and byzantine politics to which Bezzina fell victim: 'high jingo'.

This was something like Bezzina's 150th case over seventeen years in the Homicide Squad. It was, he would say in 2018, the 'clusterfuck' that precipitated the end of his police career.

Bezzina and Overland fell out over the case. 'We — being the homicide team leaders — we were a thorn in [Overland's] side because we would stand up to him,' Bezzina would say in the wtiness box in 2019. In 2007, Overland ordered that Bezzina be transferred out of the Homicide Squad to take a non-operational role. He quit this role after a week and took extended leave before retiring in 2009.

He had been told by Overland: 'I knew you wouldn't solve it.'

Overland was right. Bezzina never had a chance. Too many Victoria Police officers made certain of that. Vital clues about the Hodson murders were kept from him. Bezzina did not know that his murder victim's lawyer, Nicola Gobbo, had been speaking on burner phones with his chief murder suspect, Paul Dale. In 2005, Bezzina had waited for a call from the OPI's Tony Fitzgerald QC about the disappearance of Hodson's Blue File. The call never came.

Bezzina was unaware of Dale's attempts to call Williams in the days before the Hodsons were killed, or the fact that the calls were taped. If this critical intelligence had been acted upon *before* the Hodson deaths, it's possible Terry and Christine could have been saved. And if Purana had shared the tapes with Bezzina, it might have cracked open the investigation within days. Instead, the tapes were given by Purana to a subsequent task force, Petra, a full three years after the Hodson deaths.

Nor did Bezzina know that the Dublin Street drug-house sitter, Abbey Haynes, had been speaking to other police. Haynes's third statement would open up new possibilities in the increasingly vexed investigation. Haynes would say she was told beforehand that Terry Hodson would be killed.

She worked for Adam Ahmed, who looked after the Dublin Street drug house for his boss, Tony Mokbel. Ahmed and Haynes had a casual sexual relationship in early 2004. They faced charges after the drug-house burglary, but at the time of the Hodsons' murders both were out on bail and manufacturing ecstasy pills.

In her statement, Haynes would say that two weeks before the killings, 'Adam told me that something was going to happen to Terence Hodson ... Adam never mentioned Christine's name at all ... I can't recall the exact words he used but I was left in no doubt that there was an intention to kill Terence Hodson.'

They spoke about the same subject a day or two before the murders. Ahmed told Haynes to go out on the Saturday night. 'He told me to make sure that I was seen by people,' she would tell police. 'I didn't ask Adam why he told me to be out. I suspected that he was telling me to be out and be seen because there was an intention to kill Terry Hodson that night.'

Late on the night of the murder, Haynes went to a nightclub in Albert Park. Ahmed called her after she got home, some time after 2 am. 'Adam said, "You know what we talked about a little while ago, it's happened" or "it's done". I can't remember his exact words but it was words similar to that.'

For the record, Ahmed would deny Haynes's claims. He would explain that he had suspected Terry Hodson *might* be killed 'because it was obvious to me that he was working with police'.

Yet Haynes had no known reason to lie in her statement. The revelation offered no benefit to her.

If we assume, for a moment, that Haynes's statement was accurate, we can surmise that a circle of people knew of the impending murder of Terry Hodson. That group might have included Tony Mokbel and Carl Williams.

Haynes said that Dale might have been on the take from Mokbel. 'The European' — a criminal-turned-snitch who will feature in coming chapters — would tell police in 2005 that Mokbel paid $50,000 for Hodson's death on behalf of Dale. Dale therefore owed Mokbel 'big time'. These claims are like so many others in an unsolved case — speculations built on speculations.

The question is: who told Ahmed the hit was about to take place? Was it Mokbel? Or Williams? Or was it Ahmed's lawyer, Nicola Gobbo?

Facts overlooked until now support (but do not prove) the supposition that Gobbo knew Hodson's life was going to end. On the night of 15 May, when the murders took place, Nicola Gobbo was dining in Melbourne's Chinatown — with Adam Ahmed.

Did he talk about the $1.3 million worth of drugs and cash stolen from him by her other client Terry Hodson? Did she talk about Hodson's hopes for a $1 million reward for snitching on his alleged Dublin Street burglary accomplices? Did the pair discuss the murders about to happen in Kew over honey chicken and fried rice?

'You couldn't rule it out,' a police investigator now says. 'It seems logical to me that it's a possibility that Gobbo had some cursory involvement. She was a fixer. She put people together to sort things out.'

At the time of the murders, she was mostly fixing things for Tony Mokbel. But no one understood the toll Mokbel's demands were taking on her — or the unthinkable step she would soon take as a result.

8

An Indecent Proposal

Nicola Gobbo Becomes Informer 3838
1997-2005

The shifting dynamic between Gobbo and Tony Mokbel drives the unusual story of the defence barrister who became a police infomer. The pair first met when she worked for Levi Diamond in the late 1990s. She appeared as a witness against Mokbel; a few years later, Mokbel was her biggest client.

In August 2001, Mokbel was accused of importing more than half a tonne of ephedrine to produce $2 billion worth of street drugs. He kept getting rejected for bail — until he got a lucky break: two officers from the former Drug Squad were charged with trafficking (and later convicted).

In early 2002, Gobbo walked into Mokbel's maximum-security prison and asked him for his business. Barristers don't normally hawk for clients in prisons — but in this case, her moxie paid off. Her speciality was exploiting corruption within the force to get bail for her top clients, and her secretive informer relationship with the ESD's Peter De Santo, who had charged the two bent cops the previous year, proved handy. She used De Santo's evidence to successfully argue the case for Mokbel's release.

After handing over $1 million in bail money, Mokbel became a free man on Valentine's Day 2002. He kissed Gobbo on the cheek outside court before they streaked away in a black car. Because of ongoing police corruption trials, he didn't face a preliminary hearing until 2005, when Melbourne was steeped in extreme violence over the control of the drug market, leading to plenty more work for Gobbo.

Gobbo had been dining weekly with the three other Mokbel brothers to discuss Tony's remand; after he was bailed, she dined with *him* regularly too. She was part of the Mokbel crew, as she would be part of the Williams crew and the Carlton Crew. She was used as 'camouflage' during their criminal discussions to provide confidentiality cover from investigating police. Gobbo was entrenched in the Gangland hierarchy long before Gangland exploded. She not only liked these men, but she also liked to be liked by them.

As eager as she was to please, the pressure from Mokbel was also immense. He compelled her to breach her ethics by employing her to represent his underlings when they got arrested — not to help them, but to ensure that they did not incriminate him.

Yet Mokbel, Gobbo would say in 2020, had 'some redeeming features'. He preferred cash — and spending it — to violence. But he was still a drug baron and, like all drug barons, he didn't play by civilised rules. Violence certainly wasn't a foreign instinct. As he later told Gobbo, he skinned informers alive, along with their children.

* * *

Gobbo slept in one Saturday in July 2004. She could not shake a headache after waking up.

The phone rang. She answered, but she couldn't form words to talk. When she tried getting out of bed, she collapsed. She was hysterical and had no idea what was happening.

She sent a text message to get help. Her client — and burner-phone provider — Adam Ahmed took her to a hospital emergency department, where she passed out.

When she woke, she learned that she'd had a stroke. A neurologist told her, 'I understand you're a barrister. I hope you'll be able to speak again.'

She was just thirty-one.

Any young person who has a stroke shrinks at mortality's brush. They are told facts normally reserved for the old or infirm. Cardiologists and neurologists explain the dynamics of the heart and the brain. In some cases, they test for a congenital heart abnormality known as a patent foramen ovale (PFO). A PFO is a hole between the right and left atriums of the heart that did not seal over properly at birth, and allows blood to spill into the head. In young people, it's commonly associated with strokes. About one in four people has a PFO, and most of them never know. The condition can be repaired with keyhole surgery, and we know that Gobbo underwent heart surgery. (Carlyon had PFO surgery in 2011, after a mini-stroke while putting socks on his eighteen-month-old son. He knows how preoccupying the loss of control can feel.)

Gobbo regained her speech within two days, though she would be permanently plagued with pain in the joint connecting the jaw to the skull. For years, she would take morphine and oxycodone ('hillbilly heroin'), and would wake some mornings groggy from a range of other heavy-duty medications. Before she got up she would speak out loud, to check that she had not had another stroke in the night.

As she would tell *The Age* in 2008, banks of her memory were erased by the stroke. She was forced to rely on the recollections of her younger sister about her childhood.

* * *

'Every criminal' in Melbourne visited her in hospital, including the Mokbel brothers. In a quieter moment, she rang her unofficial police handler, Stuart Bateson. Gangland stopped for no one.

Detectives from two different police units considered trying to recruit Gobbo from her hospital bed in 2004. The idea never went anywhere. But it explains the precarious position Gobbo was in during her pre-registration years. She was suspected of legal misdoings at the same time as she was unofficially informing to a succession of detectives. Life-threatening condition or not, she was susceptible to police pressure.

The Homicide Squad compiled a Gobbo profile at about this time. In the brutal language of police officialese, Gobbo was described as 'solid' of build and 'ruddy' of complexion.

The report showed considerable insight. 'It is suspected that GOBBO has detailed knowledge of the affairs of persons like MOKBEL and WILLIAMS but is unwilling to tell police exactly what the information she holds is, possibly due to her fear of these identities,' the profile read. 'Another reason is that she will play one side off against the other in order to gain benefit for herself.'

* * *

Gobbo later blamed stress for what had happened to her. The stroke 'changed my life', she would say. She later observed that the timing of her stroke could have been 'fortunate'. The medical emergency offered an unexpected way out of her increasingly troubled roles as lawyer and puppeteer, an ideal excuse for her to walk away from all her troubles. No one could dispute a medical impairment.

But she didn't walk away. She was back in court within weeks. She was addicted to her double life, even if she suffered for her choices.

No one needs a doctor to tell them that death threats heighten anxiety, and there would be dozens over the coming years. We don't know Gobbo's fuller medical history, but we do know extreme anxiety came to disable her. Her neuralgia was exacerbated by tension and uncertainty. She developed stress-related skin lesions and had several hospital stays for concurrent conditions. Fear would nestle as her closest companion.

The Hodson killings, just two months before her stroke, had rightly unnerved her. When Bezzina interviewed her, she told him that she had received a death threat. Bezzina replied that she was 'amongst it', which he later explained as meaning she was 'running with the foxes and hunting with the hounds'.

* * *

Gobbo's stroke brought many changes, but it did not soften the demands of her clients. It's unclear when she slept through these years.

She met clients late in the evening, yet masqueraded as a conventional barrister during the day.

Police surveillance spotted Mokbel and his lawyer in late-night catch-ups. She moved into a Port Melbourne apartment block around the corner from Mokbel's penthouse. The residences shared an underground carpark. One day in court, in late 2004, she overheard a police prosecutor speaking of her alleged tryst with Tony Mokbel. She threatened to sue him for defamation. He replied that if she did, he would play the court an audio tape of her having sex with Mokbel.

She later denied that they ever spent time overnight in each other's apartments. But choosing to live right near a man whom she derided for the pressures he placed upon her is another puzzling contradiction. Was Gobbo playing at being a full-time spy? More likely, she just liked being close.

During this time, Gobbo was telling Stuart Bateson about various Gangland heavies and their purported crimes. Yet there is nothing to suggest she was informing against her biggest meal ticket, Tony Mokbel — not yet, anyway. Mokbel's legal woes were an ongoing topic of discussion between lawyer and client; he rang Gobbo multiple times a day. She thought he was a 'very sensible individual'.

Something changed from about March 2005. Mokbel began using a new solicitor for his affairs, Zarah Garde-Wilson.

As criminal lawyers, Gobbo and Garde-Wilson boasted competing profiles during the Gangland years. The women collided often, though Garde-Wilson attracted more attention. She was glamorous; Gobbo was not. Garde-Wilson frequently posed for photos with her pet snake, Chivas. She'd also been the partner of Gangland figure Lewis Caine, who was killed in the back seat of a car. Her name appeared as both a solicitor and defendant at the time. She was a country girl who became a Gangland siren. In one of her many magazine profiles, an anonymous source criticised Garde-Wilson for crossing accepted lines. The source was Gobbo.

Gobbo later claimed that after taking on Garde-Wilson, Mokbel went from being reasonable to 'belligerently fighting back every single thing'. He was not relying on Gobbo as he once had. He was listening to someone else, who was young and attractive. Gobbo felt sidelined. She would tell the royal commission she was concerned about the fact that Mokbel's instructions had become 'insane'.

Her client had defected and was listening to someone else. Gobbo had to be 'wanted and valued and needed' by the likes of Tony Mokbel. Her need to shed the 'Mokbel monkey', as she would call it, appears to have been partly driven by jealousy. That said, there is no doubt she was also increasingly terrified of him.

* * *

Nothing had changed. Twelve months after her stroke, Gobbo was being compelled to make the same unethical choices for Mokbel as she had before her turn. She walked to the Melbourne courts one day, hoping to be hit by a car or tram. Gobbo felt so trapped that she did the unthinkable. Early on 31 August 2005, Gobbo rang Detective Senior Constable Paul Rowe and began confessing.

Rowe later became a public emblem of anguish due to his involvement in the 2012 murder investigation of Jill Meagher. But at this stage he was part of the Major Drug Investigation Division (MDID).

Gobbo rang him out of the blue. Rowe had been investigating a Gobbo client and Mokbel acolyte, 'Mr Beautiful', who was charged with (and later convicted of) trafficking ecstasy. She and Rowe were due to appear on opposing sides of the courtroom later that morning.

Rowe knew Gobbo's reputation. His boss, Jim O'Brien, had received complaints from his subordinates about her behaviour. O'Brien had considered trying to tap her phone.

The MDID suspected that she represented Mokbel's associates, on Mokbel's orders, to ensure they didn't roll on him to police. Putting her clients' interests behind Mokbel's invited questions of perverting the course of justice. Such lawyer misconduct is criminal.

Gobbo's phone call, Rowe later agreed, was 'quite extraordinary'. She confirmed that police suspicions were well placed — but didn't go far enough. She admitted she was not acting in the best interests of Mr

Beautiful and other underlings to protect Tony Mokbel — in effect, that she was running a protection racket for a drug baron.

She had read Mr Beautiful's record of interview with police. Mokbel was named in it. She would be imperilled, as Mokbel's legal fixer, if the mention came out in court and Mokbel heard about it. Mr Beautiful, a handsome man on whom Gobbo later became fixated, would be forced to take the fall because Mokbel had terrified Gobbo into submission.

Rowe agreed to meet Gobbo at the Melbourne Magistrates' Court that morning. Superiors, including O'Brien, advised him to record the conversation. A tape of Gobbo's claims would amount to an admission of guilt.

Tears rolling down her cheeks, Gobbo spoke to Rowe for five minutes or less. People walked past, including Gobbo's close colleagues, unaware that this odd exchange would transform the Gangland War and lead to a royal commission.

In the course of those five minutes, Gobbo confirmed that she regularly gathered information for Mokbel's benefit, under duress, to the detriment of his associates.

'The fact that lines were being blurred is not a massive surprise,' Rowe would tell the royal commission in 2019. But the fact that Gobbo was telling him was an 'unbelievably unexpected situation'.

'She was just really stressed,' Rowe emphasised. 'Just under enormous pressure. You could see it on her face as she spoke.'

Gobbo sought a 'hand of friendship'. She didn't want to represent Mokbel's associate that day in court. 'She was 100 per cent looking for a way out of that environment,' Rowe claimed.

So the police made her an 'offer'.

Rowe agreed to meet Gobbo again later that same day. He and his superior officer, Detective Sergeant Steve Mansell, took Gobbo for a drive around Footscray Market. The conversation was again recorded and lasted about an hour.

Gobbo told Rowe and Mansell that most of Mokbel's assets were concealed and that he laundered money. She talked and they listened, in what played out like a counselling session.

Gobbo was admitting wrongdoing, but she wanted help from police in return for her candour. She did not want to walk away from her criminal law career; it wasn't an option. She wanted to be rid of Tony Mokbel without losing her business or her name — or suffering a more dramatic fate. So she sought a solution that no defence lawyer should consider.

She was uniquely placed to feed police information that would implicate Mokbel. All she had to do was breach her professional ethics and hide her betrayals, lest she be killed for her deception.

Gobbo was willing to play both sides. She had done so since 1995 with a string of police officers, from Tim Argall to Stuart Bateson. And she would do so for the rest of her legal career.

The detectives made their pitch. Mansell invited her to 'get on board' — that is, to become a police informer, for what would be the third time — unaware that she had already been informing, officially and unofficially, for a decade.

She grasped the risks. 'If anyone finds out about this, I will be murdered,' she said.

Mansell agreed. Yes, the arrangement would have to be managed carefully.

Legal considerations were not discussed. A defence barrister who was also an informer was an obvious challenge. 'It's not like we had to articulate it to each other,' Rowe would say in 2019.

He admitted that he viewed the chat as a disclosure about a crime, not the pivot for an unprecedented relationship that ran the risk of tainting every conviction it brought about. How could the force possibly ignore information that indicted drug traffickers? Damned if they did, damned if they didn't.

* * *

Rowe has since dismissed any idea that Gobbo's coming forward was a grand scheme to embark on an informing career. But he didn't know her informer history, and no one checked. For Gobbo, the only fix for feeling low was more danger. She yearned for the attention and the power of providing secret information. It made her feel important.

Gobbo later likened this era of her informing to community service. Yet she wasn't inspired by a desire to clean the streets. Her choices were driven by self-preservation. She could see no other way except playing both sides. As she once told her client Terry Hodson: 'When you're walking on a tight rope, the only way to stop from falling is to play both sides against the middle.'

But was there even more to it than that? Gobbo had privately decided to help police twelve months earlier, when she'd started informing unofficially to Bateson. He followed Argall, Strawhorn, Pope and De Santo. In 2020, Gobbo would describe her informer registration in 2005 as inevitable: it had been a question of when, not if.

Bateson's Purana superior, Inspector Gavan Ryan, had been suspicious when his detective began speaking to Gobbo at the end of 2003. Ryan had wondered if Gobbo was seeking to be a double agent for the criminals and briefly put her under police surveillance at about the start of 2004.

His concerns were shared by the head of the Ethical Standards Department, Superintendent Stephen Fontana. In labelling her as 'unreliable', Fontana joined a growing list of senior police officers who had condemned Gobbo's use. The doubters had included Senior Sergeant Jack Blayney in 1995 and Detective Senior Constable Chris Lim in 1998; by 2010, they included the Deputy Chief Commissioner, Sir Ken Jones.

* * *

On 16 September 2005, two weeks after she first phoned Rowe, Gobbo went on another drive with Rowe and Mansell. She was meeting Senior Sergeant 'Sandy White' and one of his subordinates, 'Peter Smith'. White was the head of the newly formed Source Development Unit (SDU), which handled high-risk informers.

The unit was established as a direct consequence of the Hodson killings, the latest tragedy in the blighted history of Victoria Police's informer management. The woman who played the circus ringleader in the lead-up to the Hodson deaths, Nicola Gobbo, was about to become the SDU's first big recruit.

The car made left and right turns through the tree-lined streets of Middle Park, a pocket of Melbourne preferred by wealthy barristers, including Gobbo at one time prior. The two officers kept their eyes on the side and rear-view mirrors to ensure they were not being followed as they passed the Victorian-era houses with their elaborate leadlight windows.

As the car snaked the few kilometres to Southbank, where new apartment highrises blocked the light, Rowe and Mansell told Gobbo they were being deliberately cautious. 'They said to me it was for my own safety, so that they could ascertain that I wasn't being followed,' Gobbo would tell a closed courtroom in 2017. 'But I also thought that it was because they wanted to make sure I wasn't setting them up.'

She felt sick in the stomach. 'It's all this build-up to "We're going to pick you up and take you somewhere safe, no one will see, you've gotta not be followed", and yet we end up in a building about thirty metres from where Tony Mokbel was living,' she said.

* * *

The SDU was an elite, highly secretive unit, made up of officers ranked sergeant or above. They used police jargon about 'sterile corridors' (protecting the source's identity from police investigators) and the delightfully oxymoronic 'partial sterile corridors'.

Sandy White would later be decorated for his work with an Australian Police Medal. He was old-school, a cop for more than three decades, the kind who Gobbo suspected had few interests outside of the police force. White's dedication to his work, like Gobbo's previous handlers, inspired her misplaced need to impress him.

Her meeting with White and Smith took place in a hotel room opposite the *Herald Sun* offices on City Road. Gobbo declined offers of tea, coffee and red wine. She offered White a potted summary of her unofficial assistance to Victoria Police in the past. She explained that she had been in grave danger for a long time.

'You need to trust us fully, but we cannot entirely trust you, because of the nature of the relationship,' White told Gobbo. 'Trust is something that is earned.'

The terms of engagement they struck sound naïve now, almost wistful. The lynchpins of their unholy agreement would be shattered within months. For White and his superiors, a noble end justified an indecent proposal.

Gobbo did not want the meeting recorded, because she knew physical evidence could expose her in a courtroom. White told her their conversation wouldn't be taped, but he lied. He had already pressed the 'record' button.

He told her she would never be called as a witness: a major career hurdle for a defence barrister and deadly for a police informer. But he was wrong. Later, she *was* called as a witness.

He said her intelligence would be shared within Victoria Police without her being identified. Yet she would be identified, again and again, when her information was passed to investigators.

White said police reports relating to her informing could be hidden from judicial processes. It would be their little secret. Gobbo was supposedly being offered an invisibility cloak to hide her informing from the criminals and the justice system. Yet she stood to be disrobed, again and again.

White told her that Victoria Police would claim PII, or public interest immunity, to conceal her identity in legal documents. PII is a life-and-death measure judges grapple with all the time. Police often claim PII to protect their informers' identities. In criminal cases, judges must weigh up the exposure of a source's name, and subsequent risk of harm, against the need for an open trial.

Gobbo grasped PII, because she had fought for the right to see confidential documents, protected by PII, as a defence lawyer on behalf of clients. She knew that PII was hardly failsafe, especially when the same informer repeatedly gave police information. She herself had figured out Terry Hodson's double-agent role when his informer number kept appearing in court documents.

From the beginning, Gobbo had no illusions, yet she still went ahead with it. She was wedded to her double life, in part because she could see no other way, but also because she thirsted for the excitement:

'If this gets out, say nice things at my eulogy, because I will be gone — and enjoy the royal commission,' she said.

She was given informer number 3838. Whispers endure (though it seems unlikely) that the designation was a lewd reference to her bust size.

Within days, Assistant Commissioner Simon Overland and a subordinate, Superintendent Tony Biggin, met to discuss their new recruit. Again, there is no evidence that the question of ethics was raised in the meeting. Gobbo was to be used as a release valve, dampening the political pressure police were under to solve Gangland crimes.

Both lawyers by training, Overland and Gobbo never met, despite widespread claims of clandestine chats. Yet she would become his secret weapon — a kind of Jason Bourne who would eventually turn on the power that built and then discarded her.

* * *

Gobbo generated five slabs of invaluable intelligence at that first meeting with White and Smith. Her fears drenched the discussion. She 'was worried about having another stroke at this rate'. Yet in the first three months after Informer 3838 was registered, police completed 183 reports based on her information: almost two a day, every day.

Sandy White had travelled to Britain and Canada to research informer models and protocols. He took pride in his unit as a new and better way. Everything was recorded, if hidden from scrutiny at the time.

Between 2005 and 2009, she had more than 100 meetings with her handlers that were recorded on audio tapes. Her handlers took notes during her constant phone calls, which were summarised as information contact reports.

The SDU was a one-off; so was Gobbo. Urgent intelligence was assessed and disseminated immediately as so-called 'hot briefs'. Because she produced so much information, some of her handlers got months behind writing up the reports.

Who could blame them? The pace was frenetic. Gobbo didn't stop. No detail appeared to defy her gaze; she was a brainbox of facts and observations. One Gobbo information report even described another lawyer as sporting a $2500 Versace tracksuit.

Gobbo would spend hours on the phone with handlers, who were rotated like frontline soldiers for rest breaks. Their official jottings would be as telling for what they did *not* say as what they did. How Gobbo got her information was often glossed over, as if her handlers did not know, or did not care to know. Did she wear a hairpin wire, as rumoured, for pillow talk? It sounds far-fetched, but police records do not say.

Gobbo provided far more than drug-lab sites and phone numbers. She told police who was fighting who and why. She identified the weak links to exploit. Her dedication scuttled any pretence of client loyalty or confidentiality.

Yet it seems likely that Gobbo's information flow went both ways: to the cops, and to the criminals. It had to, otherwise Gobbo would have been killed. She built trust through sharing information with police. It makes sense that she also ingratiated herself with criminals by alerting them to police targets and activities. Police had already expressed fears that Gobbo the police informer could, in fact, become Gobbo the double agent working for the baddies. White was wary of giving her information she did not need to know. Yet she spoke directly at times to Purana investigators so that her informer activities were not mistaken for conspiring to commit crimes.

Gobbo would call her handlers up to nine times a day from her secret phone dedicated to this purpose. Her 'Bat Phone' lived in her handbag. Sometimes, she ended calls abruptly because the mark of her informing had turned up for coffee or a drink.

These calls produced the information reports that are Gobbo's story, as told to the police who listened, cajoled and 'tasked' her.

* * *

Nicola Gobbo was springloaded with ideas on the day she arrived for her first meeting with White and Smith. She'd given the role a lot of thought over many months. She'd wanted to jail her biggest client and chief irritant, Tony Mokbel, for a long time.

Victoria Police wanted Mokbel badly. He was the Teflon-coated white whale, the smart-arse who dismissed detectives as 'muppets'. One of White's first requests at this initial meeting in the hotel room was: 'Tell me everything you know about Tony Mokbel.'

So she did, with a preamble: her relationship with Mokbel and her betrayal of him would make 'the greatest story', she suggested.

'That's the book we're never going to write,' Smith replied.

Gobbo described Tony Mokbel's sense of invincibility: '3838 believes nothing will ever happen to MOKBEL because everyone knows that if you kill Tony, the brothers will kill you,' the handlers' report read.

It would be 'fantastic', she explained, if police arrested Mokbel. But the charges had to be so serious that he couldn't get bail.

'He's not going to fight a trial from within custody because his access to be able to speak to people is massively cut off,' she told her handlers. 'I mean, you will monitor every call, every visit, he'll be in [a high-security unit], presumably … He would plead. Things would change. God, it would relieve so much pressure off me.' (The last sentence is telling, putting paid to her later claims of altruism.)

Five minutes later, her handlers deferred to her sense of importance. They admitted that Gobbo knew far more about Mokbel's criminality than they could. Only the day before, she told them, Mokbel had decided he might bribe police officers. 'He thinks all police officers are a joke … He continually tries to make you think he's got police in the back pocket. Continuously.'

Gobbo was a talking catalogue of Mokbel's criminal history. He ate too much when he was stressed. He thought he was 'Tony Soprano'. Without Gobbo, how would police know that Milad Mokbel was sleeping with the sister of a police officer and getting confidential information from his lover?

Gobbo spoke to Tony Mokbel almost every day and dutifully reported details of each conversation to her handlers. She billed Mokbel for it, too: $84,000 in legal fees over the four months until March 2006.

The chasm between Gobbo's distaste for a target and her shows of subjugation to them was most gaping in the case of Mokbel. Police wondered at the continued late-night catch-ups between the pair, as well as Gobbo's ongoing protection of the 'Lord Mayor' at the legal expense of his acolytes. As much as ever, she was one of Mokbel's crew.

Yet Gobbo despised him by now. 'Tony Mokbel is basically stupid and doesn't listen to 3838 advice,' her handlers later wrote. 'Example, he was summonsed to the ATO [Australian Tax Office]. 3838 told him not to answer questions but he said no, they're all idiots, answered questions and now he has been hit with a tax bill of $4.5 million.'

* * *

On her very first day as an informer, Gobbo floated the perfect way to nab Mokbel. One of Mokbel's crew, she said, 'could have sold all of them, put everyone in jail for a long time'. But he hadn't. Perhaps he would, Gobbo suggested, with a push.

A police operation, Posse, relied almost entirely on her insights. It sought to marginalise the Mokbels and disrupt their associates.

Detectives heeded her advice and fingered this crew member as the wobbly link in the criminal chain of control. And when this link broke, it would scuttle the Mokbel empire.

9

Breaking Sad

Bringing Down the Mokbels
2005-2006

Tony Mokbel looked and sounded like a soft touch.

His associates knew differently.

Mokbel's inner sanctum — let's call them the Chemical Brothers — included Tony's brothers, and a wider gang of drug dealers, cooks, crooks and standover men. Walter White, the *Breaking Bad* character, was still years away, but the Chemical Brothers were masquerading as his real-life prototypes. They conjured the highest-quality drugs. Their product pulsed through Melbourne's nightclub scene and beyond.

But being a Chemical Brother could be seriously stressful. They had to somehow survive the hazards of their calling — guns to the head, drives in car boots and an alarming tendency to use what they trafficked. Their trade was a balancing act of secrets, strip club exchanges and glass containers. One Chemical Brother had been asked to repay $5 million that one of his paymasters, Nik Radev, said he now owed him. That supposed debt was thought to be the reason why Radev was killed by Gangland chiefs in 2003.

There were other similarities between Walter White and the Chemical Brothers. One, when he was off the clock, was a family man. Another did the White story in reverse — he later gave up drug production to go into teaching.

Pseudonyms must be used to describe these men and the roles they played for Mokbel.

'Mr Average' was a skilful criminal who resented his chosen trade. By now, he worked mainly for the Mokbels, but he didn't care for them. He was softer than his bosses. 'Mr Money' did the numbers and 'Mr Beautiful' pressed the pills. 'The Apprentice', as with *Breaking Bad*'s Jesse Pinkman, wanted to learn all the techniques of the trade from the associates, such as how to launder money in betting binges at casinos, how to cook chemicals and how to stay alive.

The Chemical Brothers propelled the big profits. Mokbel fought off his competitors to employ their skills. Like every self-respecting drug lord, he relied upon local and international arms for supply, and Rob Karam was his man at the docks.

The Chemical Brothers were involved in the odd car chase and shootout with criminals, but they were ordinary too. One shopped at Bunnings, much like a suburban dad attending to the back deck. He was a regular at Crown Casino's Mahogany Room who also fretted about paying his bills.

As part of Mokbel's crew, Nicola Gobbo naturally became familiar with the Chemical Brothers — in some cases, very familiar. She flirted with several of them. One had known Nicola Gobbo for a few years, since she first represented him on drug-related charges. But by 2005, professional pretences had washed away. They now spoke about the 'what ifs' of a relationship. She saw his doctor about rehab on his behalf. She teased him by complaining of a lack of sex.

Throughout the manic final months of 2005, she made herself useful to the crew in any way she could. She babysat their kids and exchanged Easter eggs with them; once, when a Chemical Brother became indisposed, she took his kids to a shopping centre to keep them occupied. She always answered their calls. We cannot hear their conversations, but she played the role of confidante, sounding board and advisor.

Like the other Chemical Brothers, Mr Average came to rely on Gobbo. He was in and out and up and down, but he always gravitated to the one person he trusted. What Mr Average didn't know was that his life was trickier than he figured.

Gobbo was betraying him.

* * *

Gobbo's feelings for the Chemical Brothers defied easy categorisation. She nominated Mr Average to police as the Mokbels' one-way ticket to prison; the one downside was that her friend would be sacrificed in the pursuit. She was capable of condemning him but feeling sorry for him too. He was the latest in a line tracing back to her housemate and boss in the 1990s. Her head and her heart sat in opposing camps.

By early 2006, she found interactions with him 'difficult and draining', but she declined a police invitation to stop informing — the first of many. But she wondered how long her 'cock-tease' approach could last. (Both have since said their flirting never went beyond chatter.)

She also continued to mine the other Chemical Brothers for information. She learned more about the origins of illicit drugs than any lawyer needs to know. She recited terms such as ketone and hydriotic acid to her police handlers with ease.

The Chemical Brothers described making meth as others describe art. It's a tricky business, and even the best sometimes came close to perishing in lab explosions, which were inevitable from time to time. In 2001, a neighbour who asked why one of the Chemical Brothers was bolting from his house was told 'You'll find out,' moments before a suburban explosion. They also had to contend with noxious gases — Mokbel's pop-up labs sometimes relied upon garden hoses threaded down toilets to expel the fumes. No wonder they were often described as being 'off [their] heads'.

Gobbo's handlers reminded her about the need to maintain professional relationships with criminals. But she didn't — or couldn't. After almost a decade as a lawyer, she thrived on pushing the boundaries with clients. Now, as 3838, she toted an unofficial licence to do so.

She knew some of the Chemical Brothers had tired of the Mokbels' use of them. Tony Mokbel was paranoid. Once, he 'sent someone along to watch [a cook], to make sure [the hired help] didn't skim anything off the top for himself', Gobbo would testify in a closed court in 2017. 'The person that he sent ... actually died during the cook, and [the help] had to deal with the dead body. So he was — he was angry, resentful.'

Bitterness inspired one of the henchmen to give Gobbo a copy of *Leap of Faith*, a Steve Martin comedy film about a crooked faith healer. 'He's a shocking criminal,' Gobbo told her handlers of Steve Martin's character. 'Dishonest, lying piece of human waste who becomes this kind of preaching evangelist ... And the reason [the henchman] gives it to me is, he says, "I found this movie and it's exactly how Tony Mokbel is. He has all these people under his spell and they believe him and do exactly what he says, and they don't — they don't question him."'

Gobbo was now passing on the intricate details of major crimes, such as exchanges of chemicals in a McDonald's carpark. She described Gangland's jungle floor of grudges and schemes. Who trusted whom and who did not. Who was funding the meth cooks.

Such unfettered detail was invaluable to investigators. They played cat-and-mouse with criminals long trained to avoid police detection. The Chemical Brothers swapped cars as readily as they changed phones. They knew about mobile phone triangulation, which pinpoints a person's whereabouts, and other investigative tactics that police seek to cloak.

What they did not know about was Nicola Gobbo.

* * *

Gobbo had been eager to please her handlers White and Smith at their first meeting. She suggested that an MDID detective, Sergeant Dale Flynn, could appear at Gobbo's regular hangout, the Emerald Hotel, where she would be drinking with a Mokbel associate. Let the man down a few scotches first, she suggested. *Then* he might talk to Flynn.

She discussed delaying the date of one of the Chemical Brothers' sentencing for earlier charges to ensure an upcoming police sting could go uninterrupted. It's no small thing to lie to a judge about your reasons for an adjournment. The way Gobbo put it, it sounded like a doddle. She had bigger considerations, such as getting the Mokbels 'out of my life'.

By December 2005, Gobbo had a specific tip for her handlers to bring down Mokbel's empire. She was targeting the underlings. Investigators circled, but no arrests were made.

Gobbo attended the Mokbels' New Year's Eve party, where Tony had his own fireworks alongside the city's multi-million-dollar display. She was close to all the Mokbel crowd, and especially close to some of them.

Police surveillance spotted Gobbo taking delivery of a red briefcase from one of the men, and it's thought that investigators suspected she might be committing crimes. Another time, she met an associate late in the evening outside the Supper Club in the city for the exchange of what was described in a later court case as a 'small item'.

By early 2006, Gobbo was trying again, telling police about drug deals worth millions. Shortly after, her intimate proximities gave her hallowed status (and unfettered access) when Melbourne's underworld was invited to a birthday party for one of the Chemical Brothers.

The celebration was a leave pass. An excuse to forget. The past few months had been rough for the birthday boy. He was in poor health, in another Walter White touch, and wondered how long he had to live.

Life was tough for the other Chemical Brothers too. Some were about to enter rehab and were regularly visiting psychiatrists for personality disorders. Some faced decades in jail for earlier offences. They had bought 21st birthday presents for their primary school-aged kids, knowing that they would not be there. The party loomed as a kind of Last Supper for the most unchristian of characters. Even the media were tipped off about it.

Milad Mokbel was among the 150 or so people who gathered at upmarket Wheat. Usually a venue for lawyers, that night it was overrun by hardnuts and headkickers.

Drug importer Rob Karam was there too, taking time out from fighting massive drug charges. He chatted with Fedele 'Fred the Bear' D'Amico. The pair hadn't fallen out — yet. A nightclub owner with Valentino stylings, D'Amico would survive two murder plots, including one that Karam would be questioned about. D'Amico would be a preliminary suspect in what later became the biggest ecstasy haul ever, but he would not be charged.

Tony Mokbel himself was a no-show, perhaps preoccupied with his own fate. In nine days' time — for reasons that will be revealed in a later chapter — he would dematerialise and trigger Australia's most unusual manhunt.

Expense was not an issue in organising the party. But the birthday boy didn't pay for his party upfront. He always seemed to be short. Instead, the $17,000 café bill was put on Gobbo's Visa card.

Nor did the birthday boy accept the RSVPs. Gobbo looked after those too. He had wanted topless waitresses at his party, but she had told him no.

Gobbo was a natural-born hostess. She won the dance competition and gave a speech. In a photo taken on the night, a Mokbel associate can be seen cupping her breasts, 'off his head on gear', as Gobbo later described him.

In taking on the role of chief organiser, Gobbo wasn't just being helpful. She had arranged the RSVPs so she could pass on the names of the attendees to her handlers. Police surveillance noted each arrival and departure. Gobbo was their spy on the inside. She borrowed a police camera to photograph the baddies under the pretence of taking happy snaps.

Gobbo was thriving in these early days of her 3838 subterfuge. Weeks before the party, she had rung her handlers from a restaurant bathroom after she ate with two drug-running associates, presumably unable to wait to pass on intelligence. She had also suggested that an undercover agent could play her boyfriend for the birthday party, so that he too could get intimate with Melbourne's baddest. Police had at first embraced her idea of a covert agent — as the DJ — but ultimately decided against it.

The different parts of Gobbo's life had no cohesion by this point. As a conventional lawyer, she'd been invited to the sixtieth birthday of Robert Richter QC the previous month. As a rogue lawyer, she met Tony Mokbel in parks. Police couldn't listen in parks.

She dined with crime lords who compared the selling points of their prostitutes. They preened and plotted, the next deal the subject of every exchange. Sometimes their wives and mistresses came along. Gobbo strained for snippets of *their* chatter too.

One of Gobbo's handlers later called her 'the Octopus': her tentacles reached to the most unlikely of places.

* * *

Gobbo was told in confidence about a $4 million cook involving two Mokbels and another group headed by Mario Condello, a solicitor who had chosen a life of crime. The Carlton Crew's money man, who was a loan shark and into art scams, Condello was shot dead outside his Brighton East home in an unsolved crime in February 2006.

She was also told about a lab in Preston, around the corner from Regent Street. Her growing list of tips was guiding investigators towards an impending sting.

At the same time, the Chemical Brothers' paranoia was swelling. One of the associates was alternating between three cars, including a Mercedes with a secret compartment for storing guns. He confronted the driver of a Mitsubishi Magna that followed him to a service station.

Mr Average turned up to Gobbo's office, shaken, a few weeks after the birthday party. 'We're fucking burnt,' he told her.

Mr Average had spotted police surveillance cars near Milad Mokbel's home. He and the Apprentice drove into carparks and laneways and around the block to shake their tails. He compiled a list, identifying three police cars from the Purana Task Force.

Gobbo sought to quell his panic. If detectives were following him, she argued, it meant they didn't know where the drugs were. Yet she inwardly seethed. She was exasperated by 'police incompetence', she told her handlers. She couldn't believe the Purana detectives had been so obvious.

The timing of the planned sting was shifting from day to day, hour to hour. Her handlers tasked her to gain as much intelligence as she could, to provide updates on the associates' whereabouts. When she furnished them with specific details of a drug lab, they tracked a car used by one of Mokbel's men from a strip club to an address near a primary school, not far from the park where Jason Moran was killed less than three years earlier. The selection of a lab site so close to a school would divide the Chemical Brothers.

Gobbo was told that the Chemical Brothers might be 'pissing blood' because of their heavy workload with dangerous chemicals. But the cooks were delayed so that the crew could spend Easter with their families. They couldn't know that they were enjoying their last days of freedom.

A subtext runs through the police information reports at this time. Gobbo was juggling guilt and excitement. She told her handlers that she was informing to ease her conscience for having helped criminals in the past. But when they raised conflict issues about her desire to represent the same criminals after their arrest, she replied: 'What conflict?'

* * *

Police had conducted a review of their star recruit soon after Gobbo began informing in 2005. Her Informer Registration/Reactivation Application was updated in April 2006, not long before the Mokbel crew members were arrested. There were no other written reviews of Gobbo's work as Informer 3838, apart from so-called 'SWOT analyses' (strengths, weaknesses, opportunities and threats) from time to time on specific issues.

The review concluded that many police officers knew of Gobbo's secret role. 'Unidentified close work associates' of those police officers might also know, as well as members of the Australian Federal Police.

Within months, dozens of detectives were folded into the Gobbo subterfuge, and eventually 100 or more police officers would know about her unethical assistance. The risk of 'exposure' — officialese for 'murder' — through 'casual conversation, or otherwise' was considered high.

Gobbo's intimate relationships with police officers and her enjoyment of 'the company of male police officers' posed a 'high' risk too.

Of 'significant' risk was Gobbo's reaction when police did not act on her intelligence: 'a feeling of frustration may cause the Source to take unknown radical action in order to rid herself of contact with these people'.

The overall risk of her use was considered 'high'. Yet the review found that 3838 was both 'strategically and tactically viable'.

The conclusion sounds absurd now, as it was then. The more intelligence Gobbo provided, the bigger the chance she would end up in a body bag.

* * *

Police raided the drug lab in April as the lone bugler warmed up for his annual solo performance at Melbourne's Shrine of Remembrance dawn service. Two Chemical Brothers were the first to be arrested, and both would be represented by Gobbo.

A version of the raid story has been well told over the years, a tale seemingly steeped in good fortune. Yet the police account omitted the fact that luck played almost no part.

The story goes like this: a Purana detective was walking with his daughter. She heard a faint drilling sound, which turned out to be coming from the meth lab. The fluke find sounds highly unlikely in the absence of a starting point, which we now know to be Gobbo's tip-off.

Gobbo was both elated and saddened when she heard about the arrests. The right thing also felt like the wrong thing. Here was a job done — and hello to a new set of dangers. She thrilled at the gravity of the situation. She asked her handler before meeting her clients in need: 'Who's next?'

One of the Chemical Brothers offered a no-comment interview to investigators, who asked twenty-nine questions in the space of five minutes. But the detectives didn't need him to cooperate in this first interview. They had a back-up plan. She was hovering in the courtyard of the nearby Emerald Hotel, awaiting her cue.

Gobbo and her handlers had spoken beforehand about her client's inevitable desire to speak to her after his arrest. She argued that she had to turn up for him because her absence would trigger his suspicions. Self-preservation meant more to her than ethics.

Gobbo was told to ignore her handlers when she arrived at the police station. She had incriminated the Chemical Brothers: now, in phase two, she would convince one of them to roll on his mates and set off a chain reaction. Much planning preceded the event; Gobbo and police had discussed the profile she'd compiled over the past seven months, even the type of cigarettes that should be offered.

'Winnie Blues?' her handlers inquired.

Gobbo said it didn't matter. Just not menthol.

Gobbo got the call late in the afternoon. She met with her client for about an hour. They sat at a basic table with two chairs. Client and lawyer held hands as she cried over his arrest. The condemned was comforting his executioner. He worried that she would be criminally implicated in his crimes. The irony was that he wanted to protect the woman who had orchestrated his arrest.

Many years later, the duped client described the scene: 'She looked so distressed. She was shaking her head from side to side saying: "No, I can't fix this ..."

'I told her not to worry ... She said, "They know everything."'

Of course they did. Because she had told them everything.

The man would say Gobbo advised him he would do thirty years' jail. She was very convincing; the best result he could hope for, she said, would be twenty-three years. He owed the Mokbels nothing. His family would lose everything. He had to roll for himself and for them.

'I couldn't fathom the idea,' he would say later.

Gobbo, the actress, thrived in the role of sympathetic friend. 'She told me I needed to make a deal. "Let me go speak with them and sort something out ..."'

Gobbo walked out of the room and repeated the conversation she'd had with her client to her handler, in what was a gross legal breach. She left the police station, but the arrested man asked for her to return soon afterwards.

He and Gobbo later walked into the midst of a 'pizza party', as she would call it, in the boardroom of Purana headquarters on the fourteenth floor of the St Kilda Road Police Complex. She and her handler Peter Smith pretended not to know each other.

Detective Sergeant Dale Flynn spoke privately with the client and Gobbo in another room for two hours. It was called 'the pitch' and Flynn said it was 'simple'. The client was shown photos of his family and asked if he cared to see them in the next few decades.

Flynn took no notes: an odd choice, since police routinely notate everything from trivial phone calls to pivotal moments. By the meeting's end, the client had changed his mind. Offered an out, he accepted. All he had to do was risk his life and roll on the Mokbels.

Flynn would tell the royal commission in 2019 that it was Gobbo who persuaded the Chemical Brother to roll on the Mokbels during this discussion. The client himself would say that he would never have rolled if Gobbo had not returned to the station and encouraged him to do so. She wouldn't dispute the claim.

The doomed man then sat down with Flynn and Detective Senior Constable Paul Rowe, who had helped recruit Gobbo as an informer seven months earlier. It was 9.08 pm. Breaks for coffees and (non-menthol) cigarettes slowed the process, so that it was 11.27 pm before the interview ended.

Police asked the client a total of 456 questions. He told them he worked his 'arse off for very little', and that the Mokbels owed him a lot of money. Yes, he would help sting his associates. He would plead guilty and swap sides.

Gobbo slept poorly that night. She thought she was going to be killed once the Mokbels found out about the arrests. As their fixer–lawyer, she was supposed to warn them whenever a henchman was arrested by police.

Her satisfaction over the arrest was also dimmed by guilt. 'We have been victims of the same disease,' one of the Chemical Brothers had once told her, referring to the Mokbels. 'The general ethics of all this is fucked,' she'd told her handlers prior to the arrest.

Yet her empathy was limited. One of the arrested men told her that the police had overlooked hidden guns in their raid that day. She alerted them to their oversight. They retrieved the guns and laid firearms charges.

This isolated detail stands as one of the most clear-cut breaches of legal professional privilege in Gobbo's years of informing. International legal precedents are uniform in this regard. If police act on legally privileged information, prosecutions should always fall over.

By the next night, Gobbo sought praise from her handlers. She wanted thanks for her key role in dismantling a drug empire. She had located the drug lab for police, then persuaded one of those arrested at the lab to give up his bosses.

* * *

The morning after her client's arrest, Gobbo's biggest sting was already in motion. Her client was sent to work in his new role of criminal informer. He checked in with the Apprentice to maintain a pretence of normality. Their chat would directly lead to that man going to jail.

The snitch then met Milad Mokbel at the Grove Café in Melbourne's inner north to discuss prospective (fictional) meth deals. He wore a wire to record the conversation.

The day after, he met Mr Beautiful at an Avondale Heights carwash in north-west Melbourne, probably the one that Gobbo co-owned. She had bought into it in recent months, and her investment had delivered wads of cash that would be spotted in both her car and her home. Carwashes are good places for criminals to talk — the roar of the carwash water drowns out bugs — and therefore they are bad places for lawyers to be seen to invest their money. That day, however, the snitch again wore a wire, which picked up his discussion with his drug colleague about a pill press and ecstasy manufacture.

His work was not yet done. Next he arranged to meet Milad Mokbel again. He was the bigger prize. On Anzac Day 2006, the snitch turned up at Milad's home with fake drugs wrapped up as a present, in typical Mokbel style. Both men were arrested as they left the house, the snitch as show.

* * *

The snitching associate had chosen his path. After doing the police's bidding and nailing his criminal mates, he was remanded. His reward would be a remarkably short sentence.

But he didn't feel lucky. He would spend many hours drafting statements against his former mates and appearing in courtrooms where his character and reliability were trashed. In jail, the man had no friends or money. On the outside, the families of the Chemical Brothers squabbled over the snitch. He was labelled 'a dog'.

Gobbo began funding him in prison with about $190 a month. She wanted him to have a doona and pillow. The expenses would eventually reach $20,000, much of it paid by Victoria Police when Gobbo asked them to take over the payments. It wasn't much, if you accept the associate's sensational claim that he gave Gobbo $250,000 or more for safekeeping prior to his arrest (which she vehemently denied).

If he was going mad, so was Gobbo. For six months she had conspired with police to arrest and charge the Mokbel crew members. She'd listened to her clients' fears, absorbed their threats, and accepted their legal fees. She was sad about her dwindling income. She had helped imprison some of her best clients, who weren't the most prompt of payers even in good times.

But now that they were locked up and awaiting trial, the risks to Gobbo only compounded.

The Office of Police Integrity (OPI) wanted to speak to her in early 2006. OPI assistant director Graham Ashton believed Gobbo's evidence would be important to a new probe about the leaking of Terry Hodson's informer history. She was to be the main event, alongside chief Hodson murder suspect Paul Dale and their mutual friend, Detective Tim Argall, at a July hearing to be chaired by Tony Fitzgerald QC.

Gobbo was rocked by the prospect, as were her police handlers. Legal examination by the OPI could expose her secret informing. She would face the same risks again and again in all judicial forums in which she was called to give evidence.

Internal police discussions focused on shielding Gobbo from the witness box.

As her controller Sandy White understood it, Overland was to speak to Ashton about having Gobbo excused. Superintendent Tony Biggin wrote in his police diary at the time that Overland did not think it was in the public interest for Gobbo to participate in a hearing.

Ashton would recall these events differently in 2019, although his recollections were hazy. He couldn't explain why the OPI investigation was aborted in 2006. He maintained that he did not know that Gobbo was a police informer until the following year, when Gobbo *was* compelled to appear at an OPI hearing about the Hodson murders and was accused of lying in the witness box. Ashton rejected any implication that Overland had convinced him to drop the 2006 OPI hearing.

* * *

In the week after the Mokbel-related arrests, an incensed Horty Mokbel told Gobbo that the betrayer 'is a dog and soon to be a dead man'. Horty hoped that Gobbo 'had not fucked' this man. He had no information, just suspicions, and Gobbo maintained a calm front.

A week later, according to a police information report tendered in court, she said that Horty materialised in her office and grabbed her by the throat.

He openly accused her of informing. Gobbo had a watertight cover: she had been criminally suspected by police for her past 'enabling' of the Mokbels. She was on the Mokbels' side.

It was a deft answer under pressure, and Horty removed his hand. He was testing her, caveman-style. But he wasn't totally convinced. In leaving, he said he would not speak to Gobbo again unless she was 'naked'. He wanted to be certain she was not wearing a wire.

Ten days later, she advised the snitch on 'how to make him bullet proof' under cross-examination. '3838 to check [the associate's] statements and still wants to negotiate the best position for [him] as a client, regardless of how he got into that position,' an information report read.

Her home doorbell rang for the first time in twelve months. She wasn't home very often, usually only to catch a few hours of sleep. No one was at the door when she looked.

Five days later, the tyres on her BMW were flat.

Horty Mokbel asked if her apartment was for sale, which she took as a coded warning that he knew where she lived. In a police information report, it was noted that Purana police had got word that one of Carl Williams's mates was 'mouthing off' in prison about her.

According to police information reports tendered in court, Roberta Williams was saying Gobbo could be 'knocked'. She rang to tell Gobbo to 'keep fucking [the snitch]'.

Gobbo receded into despair. Stress gushed from a myriad of sources. She feared her informer secret was already becoming common knowledge. 'Upset is not the word,' she told a handler, who wrote: '3838 believes is in worse position b/c of trying to do the right thing. 3838 obviously very upset and crying uncontrollably.'

She spoke to her handlers about ending the information flow. She was feeling the burden of 'these people'. '3838 thinks only way to stop is gradually as people get arrested they will drop off, but 3838 whingeing about how much time things take. 3838 adv[ised] to get more sleep.'

Her handlers had suggested she slow her informing at various times in these opening months, but they'd never actually stopped her. Deluged with almost as many demands as pieces of information, they had become more than conduits. They were concerned for their secret weapon.

It seems stress was bringing on drastic health changes; Gobbo had always blamed stress for her stroke in 2004. Now, a doctor had found a small lump in her breast, though he believed it could be treated with antibiotics. She had checked in with her heart surgeon. She was losing weight, fast, and not because she subscribed to the first two of the three Cs of weight loss — coffee, cigarettes and cocaine. She shed more than forty kilograms rapidly, and she visited a succession of doctors about cancer fears.

There were her emotional concerns too. She turned down a police offer of a psychiatrist, stating that 'talking to handlers helped'. She was adamant that her informing was stress relief rather than stressful.

Another report from as far back as February 2006 indicated that Gobbo was worried her controller Sandy White was not impressed by her. Here were the beginnings of an unhealthy symbiosis: she needed to be validated by White, her 'father figure'.

An information report from August 2006 reads: 'Source wants to know if any other person has helped as much as she has and if anyone comes close she needs to be told so she can try harder.' Gobbo was told of her 'comfortable lead!!!'.

When White chatted with Gobbo in a recorded conversation in mid-2006, her nasal tone flared with feeling. She sounded weary, older than her thirty-three years, more Kalgoorlie than Kew, like a no-nonsense country girl after a long day drenching sheep.

What Gobbo said scuttles any claim that both she and Victoria Police were oblivious to the legalities of her informing. Gobbo knew what she was doing. 'I've chucked ethics out the window,' she said. 'I've chucked legal professional privilege out the window. I've chucked my career out the window. If any of this ever came out ... I would be so fucked it's not funny.'

* * *

There was one bright spot ahead. A big date was coming up: 16 September. It would be her twelve-month anniversary as an informer. In that time she had produced more than 1250 information reports at an average of almost 3.5 a day, including Christmas Day. Her productiveness as an informer was rising as the months wore on.

Gobbo wanted her handlers to make good on their promise: she wanted a celebratory lunch.

It's unclear if it actually took place, but it's fair to assume that her handlers flinched at her insistence on being appreciated. Two handlers and Gobbo did meet in the Mercure Hotel in Swanston Street at the end of October 2006. The get-together lasted more than four hours. Gobbo ordered a large strong skinny latte, and later some white wine.

The easy rapport between the informer and her keepers jumps out of the transcript. At one point, a handler mentions that Gobbo seems happy: 'What's going on? Had a bit of bang, bang, bang?'

The attendees knew the meeting was recorded but must have assumed the recording would never be aired. Milad Mokbel was an 'idiot'. He owed many people money — including $30,000 to Gobbo. The Mokbels had suffered for their arrogance; they'd assumed their might would eliminate threats from within. Greed and hubris had brought them down.

Gobbo felt 'old-fashioned Catholic guilt' for having once helped such bastards with their legal concerns. And affection for one of the Chemical Brothers, who 'would give you the last twenty cents in his pocket'.

At a certain point in the transcript, one of the dirty secrets of the Gobbo conspiracy is revealed in all its devilishness. Gobbo dons her glasses to peruse the Purana briefs of evidence against the arrested Mokbel crew members.

Here was the beginning of a pattern that would continue throughout her years as Informer 3838. She acted as a one-stop shop: she helped apprehend the crooks, then assessed the evidence against them for weaknesses.

Her instinct for self-preservation drove these improper exercises. Gobbo was ensuring that the evidence did not identify her as having betrayed her clients.

She met repeatedly with investigators to assess associates' draft statements, which she concluded were thorough. She helped one of them with forty statements that would help convict up to ten others. His statements conflicted with one another. He lied to exclude Gobbo from statements and hide her involvement from the Mokbels. Statements, mind you, that Gobbo helped prepare.

A sense of omnipotence oozes from the police information reports on this topic. The crims were pawns to be manipulated. The courts would be told only what Gobbo and the police wanted them to hear. She and her handlers tweaked the official narrative to suit their needs.

They breached legal professional privilege and they stacked the deck against fairness and transparency.

They thought it was OK, so long as no one found out.

* * *

As soon as they were arrested, all of the Chemical Brothers charged as a direct result of Gobbo's information, bar Horty Mokbel, rang her for legal advice.

Milad Mokbel was sentenced to eight years in prison for trafficking amphetamines.

Brother Horty was not charged until April 2007. Represented by Levi Diamond, he was accused of trafficking methamphetamine and precursor chemicals. His case was suppressed from public view, but he was cleared of the charges despite a snitching associate's evidence against him.

Mr Beautiful was charged in June 2006, and agreed to give evidence against Tony Mokbel and others. He received a suspended three-year sentence for trafficking MDMA. Gobbo was desperate that Mr Beautiful was spared jail time. She was infatuated with him and confided to a legal colleague that she wanted to marry him.

When he was picked up by Detective Senior Constable Paul Rowe in June 2006, he asked to speak to Gobbo on the phone.

'Do you want me to come down there?' she asked Mr Beautiful.

'Yeah, absolutely,' he replied.

Gobbo then asked him to put Rowe back on the phone.

'He wants me to come down there,' she told Rowe. 'Do you want to ring me back when you get back there and I'll see if I can avoid coming there?'

So much for unfettered legal advice.

The Apprentice was charged with one count of drug trafficking. One of his former mates was the star witness against him, in a trial featuring allegations against Gobbo. In 2015, the Apprentice would write a letter to Justice Murray Kellam, who was inquiring into Gobbo's behaviour for the Independent Broad-based Anti-corruption Commission (IBAC).

'I'm adamant Victoria Police acted improperly in their dealing with [an associate] and others,' he wrote. 'The lengths police went to to orchestrate convictions and ensure my demise, in what can only be described as shady, dishonest and corrupt undertakings, are mind-blowing.'

Five years later, the man still seethed in jail.

Six years later, he was freed on bail over concerns that Gobbo's conduct had tainted his conviction.

He knew the truth on his release: Gobbo had betrayed them.

Mr Average, on the other hand, had no idea. He was very close to Gobbo, his 'best friend', through the years before and after his incarceration, and he applied to the Parole Board to live with her on his release. The application was unsuccessful.

The pair exchanged 40,000 text messages. After his release, he and Gobbo would call one another 'precious' in some of these messages. She told him about a party dress she planned to wear without underwear.

'Let me thank you so much for a lovely dinner, Nic, and great company,' he wrote in one message. 'Despite all of your ailments you look incredibly beautiful, and to be totally honest I was a little lost for words and didn't say half the things I intended to say.'

Earlier, Gobbo had written to him: 'Am home tucked under a blanket on my couch reading and just thinking how nice it was to see you and have a laugh. You haven't aged at all and still have an incredible knack for telling stories in a very funny way. Years may have passed but it doesn't feel like it in lots of ways. Will be in touch … Drive safely, hun, and don't let anything overwhelm you because you are one in a million. Xxx.'

* * *

The Hodsons were a first stumble on Gobbo's journey, and the Mokbel operations the next. Another instalment of Gobbo's crazy adventure was her involvement with 'Shifty', a hitman who became the first 'supergrass' of modern Gangland. He and Gobbo set out to destroy the upstart responsible for starting the Gangland War: Carl Williams.

10

Deal or No Deal

Falling Out with Carl Williams
2003-2006

It was December 2003. Carl and Roberta Williams had welcomed their first, and only, child Dhakota into the world two years earlier, and they wanted to celebrate with everybody — now that Carl was not in jail. So they hosted a $150,000 christening bash at Crown Casino. Vanessa Amorosi belted out tracks, and the master of ceremonies was Carl Williams's dependable lawyer: Nicola Gobbo.

Dowsley later found a photo, now infamous, of Gobbo at this event, her arms around Carl Williams and Benji Veniamin, her breasts spilling out of her skimpy dress. Next to Veniamin, she looked like a female basketballer alongside a jockey. He'd evidently made up with Gobbo since she had represented Lewis Moran in July 2003 and Veniamin had called her a 'fucking dog'.

A swag of lawyers attended the event, though Gobbo later said she was the only one 'stupid enough' to make a speech. The police heard every word. 'I've been asked to make a special thank-you that Carl could be with us tonight,' she said. Gobbo offered a mock toast to 'the boys at Purana and, especially, Stuart Bateson'.

Gobbo didn't feel so silly at the time. She was the focus of jubilation. Her client Carl Williams was rapidly building a reputation for criminal grandeur. He was on stage beside her, deferring to her banter. Roberta Williams was miffed by the ease with which Gobbo stole the attention. She felt Gobbo overwhelmed her daughter's event.

Gobbo was by then a pseudo member of Williams's crew, a fixture at lunch and dinner meetings, some at the fast-food restaurants Williams preferred. On the morning of the christening, she had visited Paul Dale in prison, during which Dale said, according to her, that he would have attended the event if he could and he didn't care what the police thought. In a few months, he and Williams, according to the latter, would allegedly plan the murder of Terry Hodson, and Gobbo would act as a go-between for the two men.

Gobbo had known Williams since 2002. She met him and his father George after Mokbel pointed out Carl in Port Phillip Prison. She would go on to represent both father and son on various charges between 2003 and 2005. She met them for coffees, she later said, though she did not frequent nightclubs with Carl as other lawyers did. She accepted a burner phone from Williams's associate, whom Dowsley and Carlyon call 'the European'. The Williamses wanted to be able to speak to their lawyer without having police listen in.

Williams trusted Gobbo, even if his wife didn't. As Roberta Williams now describes it, Gobbo just materialised one day and ensconced herself. Gobbo acted like one of the boys, and the boys didn't betray Carl. Gobbo's role was to help him stay out of jail. Why would he suspect that she was actually trying to put him *in* jail?

Around the time of Dhakota's christening, Gobbo was on the point of snitching to Bateson, but had recently defended Williams in a hearing *related to* Bateson. Carl and Roberta really didn't like Bateson. 'Stuey' turned up on their doorstep so often that they reserved a chair for him in their living room, set apart from the other furniture.

In a tapped phone call to a mate in Barwon Prison, Williams had allegedly threatened to kill Bateson and 'chop up' his girlfriend. During Carl's arrest at Port Melbourne on 17 November 2003, *Age* newspaper photographer Angela Wylie famously captured Williams's scowl as he lay handcuffed on the ground, like hog-tied game.

Gobbo, as Williams's lawyer, sounded outraged in the courtroom when his case came to trial. She applied an odd logic reserved for defence barristers. She wanted to cross-examine Bateson's girlfriend, because the girlfriend's claim to being 'extremely scared' did not necessarily mean she feared for her life.

Williams was bailed just two days before his daughter's christening. He never suspected Bateson and his lawyer were growing allies, rather than adversaries.

* * *

Yet Gobbo's best work in putting Williams away for life would be done at Barwon Prison's maximum-security Acacia Unit, soon to be known as the Deal or No Deal Unit.

This was no Hotel California, à la the Eagles' ballad. You could 'check out' at any moment — as in be killed — but you could leave too. As Shifty the supergrass would show, you could walk into Acacia after confessing to a few murders and ask to be home in a decade.

Shifty, also known as 'the Driver', drove the getaway car at the Jason Moran and Pasquale Barbaro killing, and the murder four months later of Michael Marshall outside his home in South Yarra. The Assassin pulled the trigger both times.

Shifty was Supergrass Number One in the Gangland race of the rats. He was considered so critical that he merited a personal visit from Assistant Commissioner Simon Overland in maximum security prison. The Assassin was Supergrass Number Two. There's nothing new about police strategies that induce one criminal to snitch on his criminal mates in the hope of setting off a domino effect. But nowhere has the duplicity of a criminal lawyer been intrinsic to the scheme. Gobbo gave legal advice to both Shifty and the Assassin because they were fellow members of Williams's crew.

* * *

Shifty's early days read like a page from a handbook for creating a monster. His parents were Nazi sympathisers. One or both of them held his head under water to stop his habit of holding his breath.

He was a target of bullies at school. He began misbehaving as a child, triggering a pattern of aberrance that a psychiatrist would call a pursuit of validation. He became violent and abusive.

Yet Shifty defied hitman stereotypes. He blended in and went unnoticed in a chameleon-like guise of normality.

'What went wrong?' Bateson asked him following his arrest.

'Oh, when you don't get a chance at one sort of life,' he replied, 'people fall into other things.'

Shifty took up ice. He fell in with Carl Williams, who by then was obsessed with exterminating the Moran family.

Williams had recruited the Assassin when the pair were in prison together. The Assassin was in jail again when Williams rang him, mouthing off about Bateson and his girlfriend.

The Assassin and Shifty, who claimed he did not like guns, became one of the top three hit-teams of Gangland. 'If you came across [Shifty] in the street, you wouldn't pick him as a hitman,' one close observer would tell Dowsley and Carlyon. 'If you came across [the Assassin], you would run the other way.'

The killing of Michael Marshall, a hot-dog vendor, on 25 October 2003 was recorded by police as it happened. The hitmen were suspects in the earlier Moran killing and police had bugged Shifty's car. Investigators knew the pair were planning something — they had returned dozens of times to the same South Yarra block where Marshall lived. But police were unsure whether Shifty and the Assassin were contemplating a burglary, an armed robbery or a hit.

When the shots were fired, detectives heard muffled bangs via the car bug, but to this day say that the positional tracker on the vehicle was not working at the critical moment. That the tracker — but not the audio — dropped out for seven minutes was a quirk of fate that even Purana's bosses wondered at. Simon Overland, says one of the investigators, was 'paranoid that we were prepared to let' the murder take place. He came to the task force offices and demanded to hear the recording.

Investigators heard the Assassin and Shifty in the adrenaline-soaked minutes after the kill.

'Should I ring the Big Fella?' the Assassin asked. He later did, and told Williams, in what would become one of Gangland's most notorious quotes, that 'I think that horse got scratched'. The pair were arrested by heavily armed police at a pub the same day.

Shifty was giving up little, despite the evidence against him. He spoke to Purana detectives in November 2003. A few weeks in custody had been ample time for him to weigh up his options. The case against him was strong; he was going to jail for a long time. But he wanted to barter. He had information that implicated those further up the chain. He wanted to become a 'supergrass'.

It was the first crack in what Gobbo would describe in a 2015 letter to police brass as the underworld's 'dam wall of silence'.

Shifty sat in a white Commodore for the trip from Melbourne's custody centre to the St Kilda Road Police Complex. He hadn't eaten for three days when he spoke to Bateson and other detectives.

The record button was secretly switched on for the car ride. Police routinely chat to prisoners outside of the official interview and use the conversation as evidence against the suspect.

Bateson tried to establish a rapport, asking if Shifty had lost weight. He'd heard from Gobbo that her client was on a hunger strike. Did Shifty want food? Bateson asked. 'I'll get you whatever you want.'

Here began a masterclass in suspect negotiation, building to the turning point when a hitman became a snitch.

Bateson fed Shifty's hope that his car could be returned to his family. He didn't dismiss any of Shifty's banal requests. His was a slow-release technique over three hours, leading to the punchline: the police could help Shifty, but only if Shifty helped himself.

Shifty was evasive at first, yet he threw out hints. The Assassin had produced a gun on the way to Marshall's home. 'He pointed the thing at me and suggested, "Well, you're coming with me" sort of thing,'

Shifty said. 'Well, after he pointed this thing I thought, "This is going to be more serious than I fuckin' thought."'

He told them he thought he was on a debt collection job; he feared the Assassin would shoot the victim in the knees to encourage the repayment of a $200,000 debt.

Shifty was spouting nonsense. He was aware police had already identified him as the getaway driver for the Assassin's shooting of Jason Moran. Anyone who knew the Assassin knew he preferred head shots.

The detectives asked about Jason Moran's murder.

'I knew that, ah, that person [Williams] didn't like him very much and probably there was a number of people who wanted him dead, him included ...' Shifty said.

Asked how much a hit on Moran would cost, Shifty said it depended on who wanted it done.

He then blurted out, for no apparent reason, that Tony Mokbel had 'got half a mil on fuckin', ah, Mick Gatto'. This assertion was never proven.

Shifty was loosening up. Here was a kind of verbal shimmy, each party sounding out the other.

In the car after the Marshall shooting, Shifty had asked whether the Assassin shot the victim. 'I've whispered to him, "Did you?" and he said, "Yeah." And I said, "Where did you put them [the shots]?" And he said, and then he pointed, he put them all over the victim's head. And I've gone, "Fuck", and then you guys grabbed me.'

He spoke of discussions with Benji Veniamin over a plan to kill Lewis Moran as part of Williams's jihad against the family. He hinted that Veniamin had killed Nik Radev: 'He's a definite possibility you should be looking at.'

Shifty was asked about the Gangland kingpins. There was no top dog, Shifty said. Different players had different pursuits. Fights flared all the time. Tony Mokbel had the most money. Carl Williams was the smartest. Never talked in cars or homes because of bugs. Who was the scariest? Probably Mokbel, because 'he's got fuckin' a hundred people hanging off him'.

Mick Gatto could be the next target. Or Lewis Moran. Not that Shifty could explain who would fund such a hit. Not in the absence of incentives, anyway.

Shifty imagined he wielded leverage. In an earlier chat with another officer, he had indicated the initials 'C.W.' Just free me to be a snitch, he suggested to Bateson, and he would help pin drug charges to Williams.

Finally, having led Shifty to hope that he need not spend several decades in jail, Bateson steered him back to reality.

'[Shifty], you're on remand for murder ...' he reminded him.

Bateson said he didn't believe Shifty had been surprised when the Assassin gunned Marshall down. But he would consider reshaping his view if further information were forthcoming.

'As I said to you, [Shifty], we are always willing to listen ... Always ...'

* * *

Gobbo later said she played a 'pivotal role' in Shifty 'withstanding undue pressure from the Williamses' crew [and Tony Mokbel] to try to get him to stay silent'. The crime bosses suggested a psychiatrist could discredit Shifty if he 'rolled' on his bosses. Gobbo told them that Shifty was not rolling.

Bateson has since couched her influence as 'insignificant'. In 2019, he would argue in royal commission evidence that Shifty was always going to roll, regardless of his barrister's advice.

Yet Shifty's credibility would have been shredded in court if he'd stuck to his role of unwitting accomplice on the way to a debt collection. Bateson had flagged his disbelief to Gobbo after Shifty's first statement. After speaking to Gobbo, Shifty changed his story to make it sound more plausible. Yes, he belatedly declared, he knew he was driving a hitman to murder Michael Marshall.

His original claim was then replaced by this updated version of events. His first — and conflicting — statement ceased to exist. It was scrubbed from the record as if he had never made it.

* * *

It's likely that Carl Williams dispatched Gobbo to see the Assassin after his arrest for the Marshall killing in October 2003. She met the hitman in the Melbourne Custody Centre, an underground facility known as 'the Submarine' for its lack of natural light.

Killers have families too — even those who front for a DNA cheek swab, as the Assassin once did, with his own shit in his mouth. During his meeting with Gobbo, the Assassin rubbed his fingers together in the universal sign for cash. He later said he asked Gobbo to tell Williams that his hit fee should go to his mum, whom he'd saved from being stabbed to death by his father when he was a teenager.

Gobbo would dispute the Assassin's claim. Her notes at the time recorded the Assassin as speaking instead of money stashed at his property, not of hit fees he wanted paid. She later wrote a statement, partly as a defence: if the Assassin was telling the truth, Gobbo could have been charged as an accessory to murder after the fact.

The Assassin would provide fifteen statements to police, and Bateson would rate his intelligence as even more critical than Shifty's. The Assassin surprised many observers when he rolled on Williams and Mokbel in his first statement about the Marshall killing. The Assassin was hardcore and institutionalised; in rolling, he was disobeying the criminal code. He later said he did so because he was miffed that Williams had shortchanged his mother on the hit fee.

* * *

While he was being grilled by Bateson, Shifty named another Williams henchman as a suspect in the Moran and Barbaro killings — an accomplice who soon became the *third* Gangland supergrass. Gobbo represented him, too.

Like Shifty and the Assassin, this client's real identity cannot be published. The European didn't stand out in Gangland circles, though his house was firebombed once in an extreme case of vocational stress.

The European was close to his lawyer. They had even attended family events together.

A detective from the new Purana Task Force, Detective Senior Constable Peter Kennedy, thought Gobbo's relationship with the European was 'more than just professional', and had wanted her put under surveillance after Jason Moran's killing.

Another close observer wondered why Gobbo was talking to the European so often. 'I thought she's either sleeping with him or knows what's going on,' the source now says.

Phone records show that the European and Gobbo talked on 21 June 2003 at 9.33 am — about an hour before Jason Moran's death. The European's car e-TAG beeped under a CityLink gantry on the Bolte Bridge, about thirty minutes' drive from the oval where Moran's kids played footy, at about the same time as the Gobbo call. He and Carl Williams were getting blood tests together, citing a shared desire to lose weight, and establishing an alibi for the Jason Moran hit.

Gobbo received the European's call while waiting to fly to Bali, after being driven to the airport that morning by her biggest client Tony Mokbel. Gobbo and the European had also talked at about midnight the night before. They were in constant contact during these weeks. They spoke again after the Moran hit was carried out by the Assassin and Shifty.

The European would say in royal commission evidence in 2020 that Gobbo knew about the impending murder (which he would be convicted of plotting): a claim that seems impossible either to confirm or to disprove. What's undeniable is Gobbo's intimate proximity to the Jason Moran hit that tilted the Gangland War.

* * *

The European also played a part in the downfall of Williams, after Shifty's snitching forced him to do the same.

After Gobbo's stroke in July 2004, the European visited her in hospital. He was about to be charged by Bateson for the murder of Jason Moran. Bateson had spoken with him — they met at McDonald's — and the European was considering cooperating with police to reduce his sentence.

Her phone conversations with the European made her part of his alibi for Moran's death. Gobbo was never further than a phone call away from murder. Most lawyers are not called before, during and after the crime. Her purported conversation with the Assassin after Marshall's killing framed her as a witness in *that* murder too.

Meanwhile, she was receiving orders from Williams and Mokbel to silence the hitmen. She was acting as a player instead of a lawyer. Conflicted beyond measure, Gobbo shouldn't have represented *any* of these people.

* * *

On 9 June 2004, Williams was arrested and taken in for questioning about a conspiracy to murder Mario Condello, the Carlton Crew's money man. Williams had been due to go to court the same day to try to alter his bail conditions for drug-trafficking charges. It was his last-ever day of freedom: goodbye Mambo shirts, hello prison-issue red trakkies.

His arrest was hailed as an end to the Gangland excesses. Had Purana finally got their main man?

Shifty's decision to sell out his associates became public knowledge two months later. His real name was published in a newspaper. He was labelled the biggest supergrass since Gianfranco Tizzoni named the purported Mafia killers of anti-drugs campaigner Donald Mackay in the 1970s. Shifty would have to go into hiding and assume a new name.

His snitching had set a precedent and started a domino effect. After Shifty, Gobbo became the lawyer for other supergrasses of Gangland, as well as being the lawyer for the Gangland bosses they incriminated. She sneakily guided her snitches through conflicting statements, under the direction of Victoria Police. She charged these clients legal fees even though she was deceiving them.

But the complications deepened. The farce of her charade was illustrated when she represented the European as his barrister at a hearing in September 2004.

Bateson was in the witness box, to be potentially grilled about the changing statements of Shifty, who had by now rolled on the European.

The European's defence lawyer should have scythed the changing versions of the 'truth' in Shifty's statements against her client. But the European had a problem: his lawyer was Gobbo.

She asked Bateson nothing in court about Shifty's statements. How could she? To do so would expose her unholy collusion with Bateson in amending them. Gobbo had higher priorities than her client's best interests. She had to protect herself.

'Well, do you think that you gave [the European] value for money when you appeared for him on that day?' Gobbo would be asked at the royal commission in 2020. Gobbo replied that she had no recollection of the hearing, though she conceded, 'I could hardly ask Mr Bateson a question in which his answer would be to reveal myself.'

At a bail hearing for the European, Nicola Gobbo did not want her client to get bail. The police wanted the European to be thinking about how he could shed the privations of prison by giving up his mates and cutting his sentence. So Gobbo ensured that her client did not get released.

The conflicting demands of this moment were just another everyday conundrum for Gobbo. She needed to masquerade as a staunch defence barrister, but corrupt her courtroom arguments so artfully that neither her client nor the judge noticed.

Gobbo was the secret agent pursuing the police's agenda. To this end, she had to hide the growing paper trail that exposed her duplicities. She fixated, understandably, on her anxiety that documents would reveal her mixed loyalties. If they did, she could be killed.

Police diaries were the obvious problem. Police officers are bound to fill them with details of conversations and meetings. These are not personal notes, but official records.

Defence teams scrutinise these diaries. They also seek transcripts of secret hearings, such as those of the Australian Crime Commission and the Office of the Chief Examiner. These interrogations, under oath, can discredit prosecution witnesses if they reveal discrepancies in their stories.

Defence teams study the police briefs of evidence to decipher whether a snitch helped in a police investigation. Police informers are given numbers to denote who they are without revealing their identities.

Yet Gobbo's role in these cases never came up at all. The police made certain of it. She didn't appear in these documents.

But it wouldn't remain that way. Documents hinting of her double-dealing started to grow from about this time in 2004. More and more of them would hint at her unethical behaviour, no matter how carefully she and police tried to mask it. One oversight could bring down the greater conspiracy. These records would come to lurk under the surface like unexploded mines.

Bateson helped her out for the committal hearing against the European in 2005. He had expunged her from his diary notes, as if she had never existed, so that any subpoenaed material hid her involvement. Gobbo now says she cannot remember her exchanges with Bateson, but accepts she thanked him for hiding her from official scrutiny.

In September 2005, Gobbo again consulted Bateson about covering up their conduct in changing Shifty's statement. Lawyer Zarah Garde-Wilson had spoken of chasing unedited police notes for the upcoming murder trial against her client Carl Williams.

Bateson assured Gobbo that Garde-Wilson's subpoena push would be resisted. He also listened as Gobbo explained her official new role as a registered police informer.

* * *

Gobbo's duplicities in these processes bathed her in extraordinary powers. She held court far beyond the cobblestoned alleyways of Melbourne's CBD. As an agent of police and their star recruitment officer at the Deal or No Deal Unit, she could visit prisoners at Barwon Prison — located near Geelong, an hour's drive west of Melbourne — virtually whenever she liked. Her freedom there conjures images of a cloaked governess floating down candlelit corridors to the drip of a leaking tap. Of huddled conversations in which the sanctity of life, and the taking of it, were reduced to numbers games.

One of the wardens during the mid-2000s told Dowsley and Carlyon of the goings-on 'here that should never have occurred'. He claims that Gobbo was allowed to enter the prison at any time of the day or night. Purana police officers ran the prison, the warden says, and placed inmates where they were most susceptible to influence. Gobbo advised her handlers on how best to punish or reward her own clients to encourage them to roll on other prisoners.

These practices, which persisted when Gobbo became Informer 3838, had their roots in the years when she was unofficially informing to the Purana Task Force. Yet little record of this liaison survives because Bateson wrote Gobbo out of his documentation. Her history was *un-written*, for her own protection.

Bateson's erasure was in keeping with police attempts in the years ahead to swaddle Gobbo in an invisibility cloak. Had her cooperation on the Shifty statement been revealed, her intimate relations with Victoria Police would have been exposed years earlier. If she had been shown to be manipulating her clients, as well as the justice system, Gangland might have exploded with bloody payback, including the death of Gobbo.

* * *

In one of her first meetings with her official police handlers, Gobbo expressed her fears about reprisals for her assistance to Gangland snitches.

'In the period of acting for [Shifty] he turned on half the underworld,' Gobbo explained to her handlers in 2005. 'And that brought considerable stress and pressure to me, because I didn't want people to find out that ... through me he'd gone down that path. I went through the most significant period of paranoia in my life ... And I still live in fear of that coming out.'

Her double-dealing had remained undetected. By the start of 2006, though, she faced mounting scrutiny from Gangland players about her improper coaching of supergrasses.

At the time, Gobbo was guiding the European through the process of turning against Williams as she gave her handlers regular updates on his state of mind. He vacillated between helping police and telling them to 'fuck off'.

Gobbo was tempting fate. Tony Mokbel had warned her not to talk to the European. She believed Mokbel would kill her if he discovered she had, and Mokbel could find out from an increasingly suspicious Williams, also doing time in Barwon.

Gobbo decided she needed a jailhouse meeting with the European, Williams and Garde-Wilson. Gobbo's bold plan, it seems, was for the European to lie to Williams's face.

Williams wouldn't be the only threat to Gobbo at such a meeting. By now, she and Garde-Wilson were like repelling magnets tossed into a jar, frenemies who detested one another.

The get-together never happened. On 21 April 2006, the trial judge, Justice Betty King, called the two lawyers for a meeting. In 2020, Gobbo would recall her 'panic' before the 'dressing down' by King.

Had the judge figured out the depth of her deceptions? Not quite. Justice King, renowned for her shows of exasperation, told Gobbo not to represent the European because she had previously represented Shifty, who had rolled on the European. Gobbo was professionally conflicted.

How did Gobbo respond? The next day, she went to see the European, and continued to advise him to plead guilty and roll on Williams. During the same prison visit, Gobbo spoke with Williams, too, as a legal advisor. That day, one of Carl's associates was due to be arrested for drug manufacturing, not knowing Gobbo was the very person who had dobbed him in to police. She waited for the newly arrested crook's inevitable phone call as she connived to betray some of the other baddest criminals of Gangland.

Gobbo retained a note Williams wrote at the time, canvassing options for discrediting the Assassin's statement against him. Gobbo had purported to advise Shifty, the Assassin, the European and Williams himself. Professional conflicts aside, she acted against all of them as a police agent. And Williams had almost nutted it out.

Gobbo, the accumulator of information, visited Williams again in July. This time, her shtick in plausible deniability failed her. The once-trusted advisor was treated with suspicion. As summarised in her account to her handlers: 'He's got it in his head that 3838 must have known re [the European] and lied … He said that everyone is saying that 3838 is a dog and police informer.'

He had killed for trifling reasons, but Williams was not as one-dimensional as he seemed. Actor Gyton Grantley's caricatured portrayal of him in *Underbelly* was memorable, but not necessarily true to life. Williams played the buffoon and joked that he was a celebrity with courtroom reporters. He was open-mouthed and bug-eyed when he was convicted of the Marshall killing in November 2005. Yet that wasn't the full picture.

'People have this view of Carl that he's like the character in *Underbelly*,' says a lawyer close to the events at the time. 'That's nothing like him. He was a really smart guy. He's the guy who would make 200 phone calls a day. He wouldn't tell anyone anything, he'd never give anyone up. But he'd put all of those pieces, all those chats together, and he'd create a pretty real picture of what was happening.'

The bad news for Gobbo? Williams now wanted to destroy her. The good news? Williams put aside his guns for hire and picked up a pen.

He wrote letters. In one, to an associate, he described Gobbo as a 'double-dealing snake'. He said she'd advised Shifty and the European to make full statements to police, 'to try and put us in prison for a long time if not forever'.

'To put it bluntly, she is a DOG & I will show her up for what she is, I believe people have a right to know …' he wrote. 'I don't declare people unless I am 100% sure … in this case I am a million % sure.'

Williams wrote to his trial judge, Justice King. He wrote to the legal ombudsman to say that Gobbo 'had acted improper and unethical in regards to a matter that involves myself'.

'In regards to [Gobbo] I am 100% correct as much as I didn't want to think I was right, the writing was on the wall,' Williams wrote to a friend in August 2006. 'I had a lot of time for [Gobbo] and stuck up for her quite a lot of the time with different people. [Gobbo] admitted to Milad that she told or advised [the European] to go with police and make statements against me and others.'

Williams sent further letters to the Director of Public Prosecutions and the Law Institute. Roberta Williams also wrote letters demanding an official review of Gobbo's legal conduct. She acted unofficially too: she rang Gobbo and called her a 'cunt'.

Williams's letters triggered an inquiry into Gobbo's behaviour, but no disciplinary action resulted. Legal observers now express surprise that he was unable to expose Gobbo's conflicts. His claims certainly had merit.

Even stranger? Williams and Gobbo had kept speaking during his poison-letters campaign against her. Both had sought to milk the other for information in a relationship best described as keeping your enemies close.

* * *

Shifty pleaded guilty to the Marshall killing. When he was sentenced to a minimum of just ten years on 19 January 2005, Supreme Court Justice Bernie Teague said his cooperation had been 'of enormous value'.

His was a generous deal that, to this day, leaves observers wondering at notions of justice. The upside was undeniable. Without Shifty's statements, as edited by Gobbo, Williams might never have been charged with six murders.

Yet Shifty's statements didn't always sound true. His evidence in a trial for the murder of Mark Mallia was dismissed by a magistrate in July 2007 as 'greatly and almost totally unreliable'. The three defendants were accused of torturing Mallia with a soldering iron after Mallia was lured to a house in Lalor in Melbourne's north.

Similar scepticism greeted some of the statements of Mr Average, the Assassin and the European. Their evidence landed convictions. But their credibility in the witness box brings to mind the *Anchorman: The Legend of Ron Burgundy* movie line about a repugnant cologne called Sex Panther: 'Sixty per cent of the time, it works every time.'

The European eventually offered fourteen statements about Gangland goings-on. He claimed insights into the Hodson killings.

He spoke of a confession to Victor Peirce's murder in 2002, linked to Benji Veniamin and his associate Faruk Orman. He talked a lot about Mokbel, with whom he went a long way back, and Williams. Some of his claims were probably true.

Gangland killer Evangelos 'Ange' Goussis did not cooperate with police like the others. They got on the bus, as Justice Betty King once put it, while Goussis got *run over* by the bus.

Goussis was jailed for two Gangland murders on the evidence of another informer, 'Jack Price', a triple murderer known to lie. Goussis was convicted of the killings of Lewis Caine, the partner of Garde-Wilson, and Lewis Moran. Detective Inspector Gavan Ryan, then head of Purana, once said in court: '[Jack Price] would sell his own mother down the river.'

Goussis coined the 'Deal or No Deal' label for Barwon's Acacia Unit, where hitmen and drug traffickers lined up to barter for their freedom. In a thoughtful 2014 letter released to the press, he claimed their statements were induced and often unreliable.

'I'm not for one minute suggesting that the Gangland War was something that didn't need to be addressed,' Goussis wrote. 'Of course it had to be investigated and stopped; it put a lot of people in danger and it created a lot of tension in the general community. But it's what developed from this that has to be investigated, the process Police adopted in the way they gathered their evidence and the way they collaborated with witnesses and coached them to get their story right in order to secure a conviction.'

* * *

The Assassin was sentenced to jail until 2029.

It appears that Gobbo did not guide him through the rolling process, though investigations are ongoing. Fourteen years after his arrest for murder in 2003, the Assassin's evidence was still being used in Gangland trials. He would give evidence against Stephen Asling, another underworld hardnut, convicted in 2017 for the 2003 shooting of Graham Kinniburgh.

The reliability of the Assassin's evidence was challenged during Asling's trial. But he would have been framed as a liar had the police produced Gobbo's statement about their conflicting accounts concerning their conversation about money in his post-arrest meeting after the Michael Marshall killing.

They didn't.

* * *

Shifty may live among us. It's unclear whether he has been released back into the world he menaced, masquerading as another bloke you wouldn't notice if he walked past. He may go straight. Or resume a lifetime of choices that, as one lawyer put it, mark him as 'a psychopath'.

The European was sentenced to twenty-three years on 27 September 2006, but got out of prison after about ten. He may live next door to you. How would you know? For helping police, he was granted a new name to replace his old name, which cannot be published anyway.

Like Shifty, the Assassin — and Gobbo — the tricky parts of the European's history officially never happened.

11

The Stitch-Up

Chasing Mick Gatto
2006-2007

In late 2006, Gobbo was just getting started. She had survived the threats of Williams, Gangland's biggest killer, yet she wanted more.

Victoria Police were less certain. Assistant Commissioner Simon Overland declared that Gobbo needed to be 'eased out' of informing. The Gangland toll was slowing. From the end of 2004 until 2010, only three major Gangland figures were killed, compared with the carnage of 2003 and 2004, when sixteen underworld figures were gunned down. Melburnians could again celebrate their city's 'world's most liveable' status without stepping over blood pools in the gutters.

Gobbo had received a dozen or so threats in 2006, and Purana head Gavan Ryan said he was concerned, 'because I felt, you know, it's one wrong word, one wrong thing, someone says something, or someone puts two and two together and she's in a body bag'. He was describing Gobbo's death to colleagues as 'inevitable'.

She had by now virtually collapsed the Mokbel empire, even if Tony was currently on the run, in events explored in more detail in subsequent chapters. Soon, Carl Williams would be jailed for thirty-five years, largely because of her assistance. In little over twelve months, 3838 had disarmed the biggest Gangland generals and their most murderous soldiers. Victoria Police had restored peace and preserved the grotty secret of their success.

It was time to part ways. Wasn't it?

But Gobbo didn't want to stop. Nor did Victoria Police; they were 'greedy', as one of their own officers would later tell Dowsley and Carlyon. The force kept receiving Gobbo's intelligence, even though the relationship was bad for her and — if anyone found out — bad for the police too. Like a forbidden affair, built on danger and empty promises.

Gobbo remained manically active as Informer 3838. She wasn't even halfway through shaping the Gangland narrative. Her hardest hits — and highest hurdles — were still to come. They would involve Carl Williams, Tony Mokbel and 15 million ecstasy pills. But first, she had her sights set on another Gangland figure.

* * *

Mick Gatto was not an obvious target for manipulation. He cared about his reputation. This was a problem, because Victoria Police did not.

Gatto was not someone to mess with, and he still rails against links with Gangland. Gatto presented civility to the wider world. He still holds charity events for special causes, and has constantly referred to the scourge of drugs in the community. Yet Gatto shared something with his opponents of the time: like them, in cosying up to Gobbo, he might as well have spoken into a police microphone.

This is why Gatto matters to the Gobbo sagas. She tried to break him just as she broke Williams and the Mokbels. She tried to implicate Gatto in murder by selling out another of her clients, Faruk Orman. He was considered a weak link, and it was hoped that, under the nefarious guidance of his lawyer, he would cooperate in the same way as Mr Average, Shifty and the European. Yet Orman never gave her what she wanted; he has always said he was wrongly convicted.

Gatto was the target of a scheme that could have cost Gobbo more than her career. She came so close to being exposed that chasing Gatto ultimately bowed to the greater need to keep her secret.

She tried to stitch up Gatto, but failed. And in doing so, she played a major role in a significant miscarriage of justice.

* * *

Detectives had suspicions that Gatto was linked to the 2002 shooting of Victor Peirce. So Nicola Gobbo started to schmooze Gatto to try to prove it.

Gobbo's pursuit had begun by March 2006. At the time, Gobbo was midway through a major Tony Mokbel cocaine trial. She was organising a Chemical Brother's birthday party, and informing every day about them and many other associates.

She relished Gatto as fresh prey. She had been informing on Orman with a likely eye to the bigger prize of Gatto. She told police what cars Orman drove — a Ferrari, then a Mercedes — and who he was associating with. But he wasn't the main event. Befriending Gatto, she told her handlers, would be an 'amazing golden opportunity' for police. It would also get her more legal work.

One police theory was that Peirce had been shot by Benji Veniamin. But Veniamin wasn't thought to have worked alone on the Peirce hit.

Veniamin grew up in Sunshine West around the corner from a conservative Turkish family, the Ormans. Opportunities were limited for the uneducated around this part of Melbourne. Faruk Orman was just a teenager when he started doing odd jobs, such as driving, for members of the Carlton Crew

Today, in his late thirties, Orman is said to be well-spoken: a 'nice normal kid from a blue-collar background', says his current lawyer, Ruth Parker. At twenty, however, he was more of a 'young punk'. He was there when Gatto shot and killed Veniamin in a pizza restaurant. (Orman walked away as Carl and Roberta Williams joined the rubberneckers outside for a sticky beak.) Gatto was later acquitted of the murder of Veniamin on the basis of self-defence. And Orman would be charged with being Veniamin's getaway driver for two murders: Paul Kallipolitis and Victor Peirce.

Orman was thought to be there when Veniamin shot Kallipolitis dead in his West Sunshine bedroom in October 2002, but the case against Orman collapsed. Five months earlier, Veniamin had fired two shots through the driver-side window and killed Peirce before Orman allegedly shuttled him away.

The Peirce hit lay unsolved for years. Public murmurings greeted a police reward of $100,000 — was Peirce worth the effort? Off stage, a *lot* of effort was being expended.

The investigative breakthrough was Gobbo's old client, the European. He first triggered police interest in Orman by giving evidence under coercive questioning in 2004. In later statements, the European said that Orman and Veniamin had told him they killed Peirce.

After the European's claims, police trawled telecommunications data from 2002. Investigators concluded Orman had picked up Veniamin in a stolen car before both men turned off their mobile phones at the time of Peirce's murder.

Gobbo began representing Orman in October 2006, after he was accused of beating up a Gold Coast nightclub bouncer. She gushed with insights for police, then complained when they weren't put to use. She wanted to be in charge of the sting, and felt underutilised.

'3838 frustrated as SDU [Source Development Unit] and Purana investigators are not using 3838 to assist in the investigation of Orman,' an information report from mid-2007 said.

Orman told Gobbo in early 2007 that he was 'very concerned' that an informer was working against him. He trusted her entirely. How could he know that he was seeking advice about an informer *from* the informer?

* * *

In May 2007, just before Orman's arrest, the force took its secret mistress to dinner. The State's most important police investigators came along. The alternating heads of Purana, Jim O'Brien and Gavan Ryan. Gobbo's handlers.

Flanked by security, they clinked glasses at a swanky venue, nestled in the rolling vineyards of the Yarra Valley east of Melbourne, overlooking two exclusive golf courses.

O'Brien had arranged the event to reassure Gobbo that police cared about her. But it didn't go well. Gobbo was in agony with neuralgia, a nerve pain comparable to a frozen screwdriver being twisted into your face. She wasn't in the mood to talk. Nor was Ryan, who felt uneasy and left soon after Gobbo was presented with a pen.

She was toiling, under threat of death and/or seduction, to jail one of Gangland's remaining names. Gatto was sharpening in her sights.

But the thank-you dinner did not please her. She was still seething eight years later in a letter to police command. After years of risking everything to help Victoria Police, Gobbo would write, all she got was a stupid pen.

* * *

Orman was arrested for his alleged part in the murder of Victor Peirce on 22 June 2007.

Gobbo raged that she had not been notified beforehand. 'This frustrates her and makes her angry,' an information report stated. 'Basically told her this is how we work and she will not be told about operational timing of investigations unless it directly affects her. This is an old argument. It will never change. She has to get used to it.'

The resigned tone of her handlers deepened. They managed a complex character. Their reports show Gobbo had warmed to Orman. 'She says it is refreshing to speak to someone polite and nice on the phone who asks how she is. As opposed to the Mokbel pieces of shit,' one report read.

Like Mr Average, the European and Levi Diamond before him, Orman was Gobbo's friend even as she tried to destroy him.

Remanded after his arrest, Orman's first phone call was to Gobbo. He could have called any other lawyer in Australia and probably avoided the next dozen years in jail.

Gobbo fed police insights into Orman's nature, such as his obsessive tidiness. She suggested psychological cruelties to induce a confession. 'He also needs people around him — always,' an information report stated. 'Therefore if he is isolated and left in messy conditions, HS [human source Gobbo] is positive that he will not cope.'

While awaiting trial, Orman endured three years in solitary confinement, which allows prisoners one hour a day of contact with others. It appears German shepherds were run through his cell to upset his need for order. The tactics sound more Alcatraz than Australia.

Almost eighteen months after his arrest, Gobbo's handlers wrote that the 'Purana tactics re Orman' are working, 're not seeing Gatto, making life as difficult as possible. HS reckons he is now at his lowest in terms of coping with being inside. HS suggests no phone calls at all as a possibility. Likelihood of him ever rolling is N/K [not known].'

* * *

Gatto and Gobbo dined together many times in the months before and after Orman's arrest. Gatto was funding Orman's defence, and he wanted to know the details of the case against him.

Gobbo was intimidated by Gatto. She claimed that once when she hugged him, she noticed what felt like a gun tucked into his pants. Yet she was undeterred.

She advised him on the merits of a *60 Minutes* interview, which doesn't appear to have happened. They were photographed, side by side, attending a funeral. They became close — too close, according to Gobbo. 'She fears that he has an infatuation with her and it could get messy,' a handler wrote in 2007.

Here was another recurring theme: once it was Mr Average and now it was Gatto who, she told police, was besotted with her. In Gobbo's version, her handlers promoted the intimacy. They were as keen to nab Gatto as they had been Williams and Mokbel.

She represented Gatto at a secret coercive hearing at about this time, prompting her handlers yet again to make a point: might she refrain from representing the people she informed upon?

She had dinner with Gatto on the night of Orman's arrest.

Plainly, she would not refrain.

* * *

Police informing is a fraught business. Loyalties and credibility are fluid; it is difficult to know who is providing what, and why.

One of the Armed Robbery Squad's best informers in the late 1980s was known as 'the Sock'. Back then, police protocols were routinely ignored. Officers would put an informer's name in an envelope and place the envelope in a superior's safe, which was supposed to safeguard both police officers and the informer, who tended to be named 'Mickey Mouse' or 'Donald Duck'.

'The Sock' always claimed his titbits were unhelpful. Police, however, say that the informer, otherwise known as Mark 'Chopper' Read, was *very* useful.

Others were not so lucky. When a Victorian informer was shot in the head and stomach in 2002, the incident was recorded on a concealed tape recorder he wore. As described earlier, Terry Hodson, another informer, was killed along with wife Christine while he watched TV in his trakky daks.

Gobbo was by now the most influential secret informer in Victorian history. But in mid-2007, she came close to joining this list of victims when her conflicted past with the European was very nearly exposed.

The European was to be the star witness against Orman. Yet the police had stripped him of his assets. He was thinking about telling them to 'get fucked', prompting Gobbo's handlers to report in November 2007: 'She thinks he needs a Purana visit to put him straight.' Five days later, police duly visited the European in Barwon Prison. Perhaps Gobbo *was* running things, after all.

But investigators were slipshod in their attempts to hide her documented role in the European's snitching. Her name was redacted in places; elsewhere it was not. 'They might as well have highlighted her up she says,' a handler wrote.

As the police visited the European in prison, she was due to have dinner with Gatto at Society restaurant in Bourke Street. She was frantic that he had seen the documents and figured out her conflicted status.

She was still planning to act as Orman's junior defence barrister, under senior barrister Robert Richter QC. (Like all self-respecting Gangland figures, Orman wanted a silk as his senior counsel.) Richter, known as 'the Red Baron', had successfully defended Gatto on the Veniamin murder charge.

In a breach of legal professional privilege, Gobbo told police in October 2007 that Orman's defence would be simple: he was not at the shooting.

The European's evidence against Orman was crucial because he claimed the killers had confessed to him. She didn't tell Orman, her client, about the depth of her history with the European, including her role in turning him into a police snitch. As she put it to police, she knew about the '30 to 40 lies and contradictions' in the European's evidence. If Orman and his defence had found out about these lies, the European's testimony would have been shredded in the witness box. Instead, Gobbo conspired with police to try to hide them.

Gobbo fretted that Richter would find out the full extent of the European's lying and that her role would be exposed to the underworld. As a handler wrote: 'Richter will know that 3838 lied to him but this will be irrelevant because 3838 will be dead.'

The stingers were being stung, and the tensions prompted fresh police discussions about ending Gobbo's informing. They kept raising the option as the threats against her kept multiplying.

Handlers helped her invent lies to avoid appearing for Orman because of her flagrant legal conflicts. 'Too busy', she told them, wouldn't work anymore. Once again, she was perilously close to being exposed through court processes aimed at transparency.

Her anxiety peaked in mid-2008. She asked for police protection for a court hearing. She feared Gatto would hear the rumours that she was in Purana's 'back pocket', as well as scuttlebutt that she was sleeping with a detective.

Gatto generated headlines when he hosted a $1000-a-head charity dinner, attended by 400 business associates and friends, to raise money for Orman's legal bills. Auction items included a cricket bat signed by Sir Donald Bradman. Orman needed hundreds of thousands of dollars. A QC commanded at least $5500 a day.

Orman, in his ignorance, still hoped Gobbo could co-represent him. When she eventually told him she could not, in January 2008, Orman was as supportive of her as ever. 'Orman says 3838 looks unwell,' an information report states. 'Is not suspicious of 3838's way out of acting for him. He is happy with this. 3838 feels has comforted him sufficiently so that he won't drive 3838 mental.'

* * *

Orman was tried between August and November 2009, a suppressed process because, at the time, he was facing separate charges over the death of Paul Kallipolitis. At his sentencing on 25 November, Judge Mark Weinberg pointed out that the case 'depended heavily upon the evidence' of the European, which was uncorroborated.

The European had said that Orman and Veniamin had told him about the Peirce shooting as the trio walked near a particular apartment block at Southbank. Yet that apartment block did not exist at the time. His accounts kept changing, and close observers believe that Gobbo improperly coached him through the discrepancies in his claims.

Orman would still be rotting in prison in mid-2019, any chance of a reduced sentence ruined by his pleas of innocence. He was just as polite as Gobbo claimed he was a decade earlier. He drank chai tea. 'He was just a little pawn kid hanging out with the big boys,' lawyer Ruth Parker said.

But that was not the end of Orman's story.

As for Gatto? He survived Gobbo's attempt to implicate him. He was acquitted of the murder of Veniamin. He has since morphed into a commodity, signing autographs on the street. He rages against a police claim that he threatened Gobbo and against suggestions that he is a Gangland heavyweight, and he initiated defamation litigation against the ABC in April 2019 for repeating those suggestions.

In staying alive and out of jail while everyone else fell, he has written and amended his Gangland history. By his reckoning, Jason Moran was a 'red light' and Carl Williams lacked the dash of ex-wife Roberta.

Gatto has Orman's name tattooed on his chest. He has a catchphrase that serves him well.

'I'm not worried,' he says.

* * *

If Nicola Gobbo was pretend chums with Gatto, she was also pretend chums with his foe, Tony Mokbel. Few people boasted shared intimacy with two underworld enemies at the same time. No one, bar Gobbo, could claim to have betrayed them both in the space of twelve months.

12

My Big Fat Greek Odyssey

The Tony Mokbel Manhunt
2006-2008

At the start of 2006, the Mokbel drug fiefdom was still intact. Third son Tony was facing a court appearance over a relatively tiny importation of three kilograms of cocaine back in November 2000.

He was relaxed in the days before the case began. He promised Gobbo, his junior barrister, his Mercedes SL55 if he beat the charges.

His image as 'Teflon Tony' rested partly on Gobbo and her senior barrister, Con Heliotis QC, known as 'the Golden Greek'. Gobbo and Heliotis made a formidable team. She filleted documents with eagle-eyed zeal, while he graced courtrooms with a stage presence.

Two weeks into Mokbel's seven-week trial, she told police he might tamper with the jury. She felt that he had a slim chance of beating the cocaine charges through a 'clever no case submission', and that legal wrangling could stymie the case being presented against him.

Mokbel, by this time, knew the prosecution case was strong. The scandal now is that the police *knew* that he knew it. His legal professional privilege, the enshrined right of any accused person, was tossed aside in *The Queen v Antonios Sajih Mokbel*.

* * *

The cocaine case was nearly over when Mokbel became aware that charges of murder were set to be laid against him. The Assassin, the shooter in

156

the 2003 Marshall killing, had snitched on his purported bosses. He said that Mokbel had co-funded the hit. The Assassin and Shifty, the getaway driver, had first implicated Carl Williams in the murder back in 2003, but admissible evidence of Mokbel's involvement was fresh information.

Gobbo could tell Mokbel was worried: he was over-eating. He told her twice not to ring him on the third weekend in March 2006. This was 'very strange', Gobbo told a handler.

On the following Monday, 20 March 2006, Mokbel didn't turn up to court.

He'd gone.

* * *

Mokbel's escape itinerary is well documented. He initially went to a friend's property, in a town two hours northeast of Melbourne, where he received deliveries of his mother's cooking. He was visited by his girlfriend, Danielle McGuire, an acquaintance of Gobbo's.

McGuire and Gobbo met at a South Melbourne café, days after Mokbel's disappearance. McGuire was paranoid about bugs. She didn't allow Gobbo a mobile phone or even car keys at the meeting. But she mouthed the words: 'He is OK.'

Gobbo was fielding media requests for comment. Privately, she expressed joy at Mokbel's absence. He was the reason why Gobbo had opted for the unconscionable and become Informer 3838 in the first place. Now, she felt free. The 'Mokbel monkey' was either dead, as some thought, or at least elsewhere.

'3838 brought up irony of the situation, in that 3838 currently very happy to have TM out of her life, but is attempting to ascertain info that may locate him,' an information report read. 'Very apparent that 3838 demeanour changed dramatically, now laughs and jokes a lot, says people constantly asking 3838 why so happy?'

Gobbo pumped all her criminal associates for information, in phone calls, at dinners and over drinks. But she was circumspect. Curiosity was a dangerous trait in such circles, especially after the arrests of some of the Chemical Brothers in 2006 heightened doubts about her loyalty.

McGuire was more forthcoming over coffee two weeks after their first catch-up. Gobbo would tell police that McGuire implied Mokbel was 'involved in paying for murders'. Another source and Mokbel associate Karl Khoder told Gobbo that Mokbel was still in Australia.

Subterfuge prevailed. Soon after, McGuire headed overseas for an extended holiday, and police — assuming Mokbel had paid millions of dollars to be spirited swiftly out of the country — tracked her sojourn through France, Italy and Turkey. They hoped she would lead them to their quarry.

But Mokbel was holed up in a white house on a dirt road in Bonnie Doon, a stop on the Maroondah Highway marked by the roar of speedboats and jet skis at nearby Lake Eildon.

McGuire and Mokbel conceived a child there, some time before or after her European holiday. Mokbel spent the rest of his time watching TV and checking in with the private-school-educated druggies who had replaced the foot soldiers he'd lost in the 2006 drug-lab sting. He also plotted his overseas escape, to which he had not turned his mind before his sensational disappearing act.

* * *

In November, eight months after his disappearance, Mokbel crossed the Nullarbor in a car, which he rarely left during the journey. Should the car be pulled over, he was to pretend to be a mute called Wes.

Around this time, as McGuire, who had since returned from overseas, prepared to secretly join him, Dowsley dropped in at her hairdressing salon in South Yarra. The pair sat in a back room, on the floor.

McGuire was measured in response to Dowsley's questions. She told him that she would prefer Mokbel free rather than a prisoner 'in a cage'.

* * *

A 17.3-metre yacht, the *Edwena*, fitted with a custom-built toilet, soon took Mokbel from off the coast of Western Australia to Greece, where McGuire met up with him.

Mokbel was seasick for forty nights straight, though he later remembered the journey with some fondness. Perhaps he distracted himself, as others have reported, with the single CD on board, a Barry White greatest hits album. He still sends cards, from prison, featuring boat sketches.

* * *

Mokbel's disappearance had conjured whispers about priestly garbs and shootouts in downtown Lebanon. Rumours fed off rumours, and Mokbel's associates were overheard on their phones laughing about an inaccurate newspaper report. Soon, a $1 million reward was posted.

Throughout his absence, Mokbel ran his drug operations over the phone. These communications were his downfall. Police relied upon an informer from within Mokbel's circle, known as 3030, for phone bugs that pinpointed Mokbel's whereabouts in Greece. The informer, a musician with a history of drug use, was linked to Mokbel through Bart Rizzo, who handled some of Mokbel's finances.

Informer 3030 downloaded the syndicate's financial records concerning drug quantities and distribution — apparently while Rizzo was in another room. Mokbel's operation, 'the Company', produced forty-two kilograms of speed while its boss was on the run. Informer 3030 thrilled at his informing and took extreme risks — just as Gobbo did.

But finding Mokbel was difficult. His mention of Glyfada, a ritzy suburb of Athens, to one of his associates over the phone narrowed the search to a few square kilometres. Mokbel was pursuing an outwardly normal life of coffees and property discussions. When he said in a call that he was watching his five-month-old daughter Renate's swimming lesson, Greek police rushed to the public pool but arrived too late.

Police knew where he was — almost. But they didn't know what he looked like now. They had staked out a Starbucks and other places Mokbel visited, but the final critical clue was proving elusive — until Mokbel unwittingly told police where he would be and when.

* * *

Tony Mokbel was found in Athens on 5 June 2007, fifteen months after his disappearance, twenty days after police discovered his Athens location, and five days before his favourite role model, Tony Soprano, faded to black in the final episode of *The Sopranos*.

Mokbel had called a friend to arrange a meeting near the waterfront at the Delfinia Café at 11 am. When local police confronted a man in a baseball cap at a rear table, he produced a passport in the name of Stephen Papas. Wearing a moustache, and an unconvincing wig, Mokbel was held for ninety minutes before two Australian detectives identified him.

Mokbel congratulated them on their detective work. According to an intimate account in the book *Mokbelly*, by John Silvester and Andrew Rule, he shook their hands and said: 'I don't know how you did it but whatever you did it was bloody good ...' He then announced that he would not return to Australia unless police dropped the 'bullshit' murder charge against him for the killing of Lewis Moran. (He was yet to be charged for the Michael Marshall murder.)

Mokbel's capture prompted praise for police ingenuity. Here was a police fable of hunches and hard yakka. His arrest ended the *Where's Wally?* merriment that had enveloped his disappearance. Like that of Elvis, his absence seemed to have doubled as a career move.

His disguise opened new avenues of ridicule in the press. 'Big Wig Caught' read one Melbourne headline; 'All Wigged Up and Nowhere To Hide' read another. Mokbel's hair choice offered a punchline for the capture of a man who had dominated barbecue chatter since the previous year. Mark Knight, the *Herald Sun* cartoonist, depicted the wig raising its hands in surrender. Assistant Commissioner Overland later hung a photo of a bewigged Mokbel on his office wall.

* * *

Mokbel now says that Gobbo, the lawyer ratting him out to police, advised him to 'fuck off' overseas. So he did.

It's a curious notion that Gobbo would tell Mokbel to flee justice when he was about to be jailed for a long time. Given her hidden loyalties, it doesn't make sense.

In favour of Mokbel's version of events is an unlikely source: Roberta Williams. She told Dowsley and Carlyon in 2018 that Gobbo told her husband, Carl, to leave the country soon before he was imprisoned in 2004. Both Williams and Mokbel independently claimed, years apart, that Gobbo told them to disappear.

It's hard to know if their declarations are accurate. Getting Williams or Mokbel out of her life by advising them to escape would have offered Gobbo reprieves from her day-to-day turmoils. The idea would support notions of Gobbo's reckless sense of empowerment. Then again, the claims seem to suffer from an unlikely lack of strategy on her part.

Gobbo certainly knew about the pending murder charge against Mokbel, because Purana's Stuart Bateson told her about it when they met at the Martini Café in Melbourne's CBD on Saturday, 18 March.

At the time, though, others received most of the blame. Lawyer Zarah Garde-Wilson was soon accused of tipping off Mokbel about the murder charges. She had been Mokbel's solicitor and presented as an easy mark. But no, Garde-Wilson would tell Dowsley and Carlyon a decade later. She did not tip off Tony Mokbel.

* * *

Mokbel, sans wig, was escorted from the seafood restaurant and tossed straight into a Greek prison, where he intended to stay forever, if necessary. He knew he faced a murder charge for Michael Marshall, and he was peeved when police also charged him with the murder of Lewis Moran. He didn't want to come home.

He was on the phone to Gobbo straightaway, unaware that she had tried to track his whereabouts for Victoria Police. She reported the entire conversation to her handlers.

He told her he was sorry he hadn't said goodbye. He wanted her to get on a plane to Greece, and she considered doing so. His practised bravado radiated down the phone line. He asked her to 'ring up that Overland'; he would consider speaking to police if she managed the legalities.

She played a straight bat: 'Hang up, ring me next week and let me speak to Simon Overland for you.' She told her handlers later that the absurd suggestion was 'a bit of a headfuck'.

Mokbel told Gobbo that he was prepared to wear twenty years' jail time for drug trafficking. 'But I will not deal with murders,' he declared, arguing that he had committed none.

She was concerned about representing him, voicing belated panic over the immorality of her deceit. 'How can I represent him and charge him money for my services when I am talking to police and I am largely responsible for him being where he is?' she asked her handlers within days of Mokbel's capture.

Yet at the same time, she wanted a piece of the $1 million reward — most of which would be paid to Informer 3030. She claimed her mention of a man called Jeffrey Jamou, two months after Mokbel disappeared, led to Mokbel's capture. Follow him, she'd claimed, and you'd find Mokbel.

There is no mention of Jamou in official accounts of Mokbel's capture, and it is unknown whether Gobbo received any reward money. Questions remain about her influence on events leading to Mokbel's capture.

Her conversations with Mokbel continued. Generally he was polite, though at one point he asked if Gobbo still had a home in Port Melbourne, which she took to mean: 'I know where you live.' He tossed around legal strategies and likened his treatment by Australian authorities in Greece to the abuses of terror suspects at Guantanamo Bay.

Once again Gobbo was expressing regret over her deception, but she sounded relaxed. 'Well, one of the many ironies of all this is I have so many conflicts with the bloke but what does he know,' she told a handler soon after Mokbel's capture. 'He doesn't know about any of them. They'll all stay hidden.'

Gobbo's handlers now expressed concerns about Gobbo's reckless disregard for the boundaries of confidential client information. They were spelling out when they would and would not pass on her information to other police, because 'legal defence strategies for Tony Mokbel are not to be disseminated'.

There had been no such recognition of the protections of legal privilege during Mokbel's cocaine trial two years earlier, when Gobbo had fed strategies to her handlers. There had been no such recognition when police arrested Mr Average. Or Carl Williams. Or Faruk Orman.

Sandy White would later say his Source Development Unit never passed on confidential information to investigators. But the records suggest otherwise.

* * *

Mokbel was well connected, even in a grotty Greek prison cell. He heard the rumours that Gobbo was 'a dog'.

'In his heart of hearts he knows that 3838 would not dog on him,' Gobbo's handlers wrote.

Soon, though, Gobbo was inundated with vile threats.

In July 2007, she received a text message reading: 'Made any false statements you cunt.'

In August, she was told that a Mokbel associate was saying she 'deserves to die'.

In October, this popped up on her phone: 'YOU cock suckiering dod [sic] watch your back.'

That same month, she rang her handlers, shaking. She had received a letter addressed to 'Dog — XXXXXXXXX'. Inside was a sympathy card and two bullets — one for the heart, the other for the head. 'You won't see your birthday next month if you keep talking to the pigs,' the card read.

She feared that someone was trying to convince Mokbel of her betrayal. She implored her handlers to suggest ideas that 'assist with [showing] 3838 is not working for the police'. In a display of deft deflection, one handler replied that her strengthening links with Gatto might assist.

Mokbel was shifting moods in each conversation with Gobbo. Alternately charming and self-pitying, he persisted in asking questions about her clients who had rolled, such as some of his crew. She told Mokbel that she never helped clients assist police, and to suggest otherwise was 'bullshit'.

Mokbel mentioned that she had not been sighted with a boyfriend recently, which she took to mean: 'I'm watching you.'

She was rattled, and talked to her handlers about commencing a 'normal' life. If she 'did not start moving out of these criminal circles, the issues will never end'. She made an announcement: she would limit her calls to the SDU to one a week, as opposed to multiple calls a day. She would 'move on' once the Mokbel trials ended. Yet within weeks she was again asking her handlers for jobs to do. She kept coming back despite their admonitions. It's hard to grasp, given that the death threats against her were rising.

In November, an anonymous caller barked down the phone at her. Some level of police protection sounded like the prudent option.

In December, she received text threats from a source with a black sense of humour: the phone was falsely registered in the name of Purana detective Jason Kelly.

Five threats turned up by text message on the same day. Police were looking for someone who couldn't spell.

'You need to get raped first then pissed on then kicked in the fucken' dog head and then shot and splattered,' said one. And another: 'Its near for you dog shit the fuck up no pigs will help you just watch when you in good soon I mite in your bedroom waiting or maybe get you in the car park as you in home. Anyway its near for you pig lover dog.'

As Detective Inspector Gavan Ryan later pointed out: 'You don't know what it's like going home every day wondering if you are going to get bumped.'

The pressures rose still higher. In April 2008, following more warnings that she was to be shot in the head, Gobbo's BMW 330CI Tourer was torched on the street as she sat inside a South Melbourne pub. This was her new normal: a $100,000 car incinerated, bags of money in the boot. 'My God, I've never seen so much cash,' a witness said.

The scene raised an obvious question: why was a lawyer driving around with bags of cash? It's notable that, despite the esclating dramas and poor publicity, Gobbo still harboured hopes of becoming a magistrate at this time.

Mokbel called Gobbo from Greece a few days later and expressed sympathy about the car fire. 'He said it seemed obvious that she had obviously broken someone's heart deeply and asked who that could be,' a handler's report read. 'He told her to make sure she tells the police that she has broken someone's heart.'

Gobbo believed that this was Mokbel's way of claiming responsibility for the fire. It tallies with the recollections of a close observer at the time. Was the firebug a Mokbel fixer working on the orders of Horty and Milad Mokbel?

* * *

Mokbel's choice of hideout was unwise: Australia shared an extradition treaty with Greece.

During long stretches in solitary confinement at Korydallos Prison, Mokbel started thinking laterally. His fight to be extradited was reduced to a mantra: no fair trial, no coming home. He was becoming a second Christopher Skase, just with less hair.

From his first court appearances in Athens, Mokbel had spoken of five levels of Greek court appeals. Victoria Police Minister Bob Cameron later said that Mokbel threw 'every chair and hurdle in the way' of his extradition.

Mokbel floated crazy schemes with Gobbo over the phone. Repeatedly, he denied any involvement in the murders of Moran and Marshall. He now faced fifteen charges in all, including running drug labs while on the run.

He wanted to employ a media company to track prejudicial stories against him. He wanted statements from convicted Gangland killer Ange Goussis and others to show that the evidence of convicted criminals was being relied upon to convict him.

He spoke of alleged Purana Task Force harassment of his associates. He cited public statements from the Premier and the Chief Commissioner, which he argued would impede a fair trial.

He also wanted the Lebanese Government to extradite him before Australia could. It is speculated that that pursuit involved a bribe from Mokbel's associates, one of many totalling $200,000 that achieved nothing except deeper pockets for crooked officials on the other side of the world. Mokbel later said that allegations of bribery were 'remarkable'.

By May 2008, when his appeals in the Greek courts had dried up, Mokbel wanted another postponement to appeal to the European Court of Human Rights. His lawyers wanted to prove that his life would be endangered by a return home.

This, too, failed, and hype mounted.

The media called Gobbo constantly. When was her client Tony Mokbel arriving back in Australia? She was miffed that her handlers would not give her the exact date.

They discussed her planned professional split from Mokbel once he returned. She finally wanted to break up with him, after six dysfunctional years.

Her handlers advised her to be firm. To offer no help if Mokbel sought her advice on alternative representation. To tell him not to call again. She needed to 'go off at him'.

Mokbel touched down in Melbourne in a chartered Gulfstream jet on 17 May 2008. Gobbo wanted to see him face to face. But in the end, it was a phone call.

Fickle of manner, and loaded with contradictions, Mokbel is no easy study. Putting aside scruples, of which he has none, Mokbel can be generous and thoughtful, belligerent and menacing.

On this occasion, he flicked the switch to puppy dog. He claimed he didn't know why Gobbo was leaving him but he expressed guilt about his treatment of her. After a 'stunned silence', he asked her: 'Are you deserting me?'

Gobbo was relieved. Saying goodbye hadn't been as scary — or dangerous — as she'd feared. 'It was not left like he was fuming at her and thinking "fuck you",' a police handler wrote.

Gobbo could have walked away from Tony Mokbel years earlier. She could have stopped representing him long before his wig was mounted like a trophy of war at the Victoria Police Museum. She could have stopped accepting his money, instead of charging him $1800 in legal fees from the time of his Athens arrest. But she didn't.

Now, she wanted more than to walk away. She wanted to hurt him, to have him suffer because of her choices, perhaps because she felt so used by him.

She seemed to relish her betrayal, like a spurned lover who enjoys destroying the other person's happiness. Just as it is easy to imagine that Gobbo gloated when Mokbel found out about her deceptions years later, so too Mokbel must have grieved that he had been conned by a confidante.

It didn't matter that in stinging others she was hurting herself.

'So, you really are leaving me?' Mokbel asked.

Gobbo was firm. She'd got what she wanted.

Yet she wasn't free at all. An information report from the time read: '3838 says all she has got out of all of this is fear for the rest of her life.'

It would be years before Gobbo's informing was revealed. But Gobbo already knew the risk: that the criminals would gradually work it out, and the threats would never stop.

* * *

Tony Mokbel was chirpier than most convicted drug barons about to be sentenced to jail for the next few decades. He bounded into the Supreme Court on 3 July 2012, as though his charcoal jacket were lined with cheap watches and the witness box were his Bali beach.

Everyone was his mate. The journalist he clapped on the back. The lawyer who got a wave. He said hello to a police officer in Lebanese. The officer replied, just as amiably, in Greek.

Put aside the oily charisma and misplaced audacity, though, and he was just another dumpy bloke in a red tie. The fleshy jowls and hooded eyes lent him a rough resemblance to his idol Tony Soprano.

He had lost almost everything. His siblings were in jail. He had no contact with his youngest child, Renate, because her mother, Danielle McGuire, no longer spoke to him. The Mokbel cartel had collapsed, its fortunes — estimated at $60 million — taken away, as guided by Gobbo, under the extended police powers won by Nixon and Overland after the Hodson murders.

Yet Mokbel seemed fine. A suspected killer of two or more Gangland victims, he threw winks to members of the press and looked more at ease than the judge who was about to jail him for twenty-two years.

Justice Simon Whelan held his face in his hands and contemplated his sentencing 'minefield'. Mokbel's behaviour on bail, from fleeing justice to refusing to return to Australia, had been 'just unbelievable'.

Even as he listened to this dressing down, Mokbel wore the impish grin of someone who knew more than anyone else.

He didn't. He still wouldn't in 2018. He didn't know the extent of his old lawyer's betrayal more than a decade earlier because Victoria Police feared that the truth of Gobbo's informing would set him free.

* * *

Gobbo's perils and her power were never higher than at the time she broke up with Tony Mokbel. On the same day he was found in Athens in 2007, Gobbo presented her handlers with a piece of paper that led directly to the jailing of a mafia syndicate of drug traffickers for almost three centuries.

13

Can of Worms

The Tomato Tins Drug Haul
2007-2016

An Italian crime confederation, a bikie chief and the drug king Rob Karam came together in 2007 to carry out what was then the biggest ecstasy importation to have been attempted anywhere.

What they didn't know was that their lawyers Joe Acquaro and Nicola Gobbo would later be outed, separately, as police informers. (The extent and timing of Acquaro's relationship with police is unknown to this day.)

Nicola Gobbo was the reason why the Tomato Tins drug haul was doomed before it arrived. By the time 15 million ecstasy pills reached Australian shores, hidden in Italian tomato tins, Gobbo had already pinpointed exactly what police should look for and where. She betrayed the Calabrian 'Ndrangheta crime gang — a sure way to die young — as well as clients who considered her a friend — Rob Karam chief among them.

* * *

Gobbo met Karam through Tony Mokbel some time after 2001. She introduced Karam to another of her clients, Joe Mannella, who owned a freight-forwarding company that would be linked to Karam, John Higgs and major crimes.

John Higgs had been convicted of manslaughter in 1970. Within years of his release, he was regarded as one of Australia's biggest methamphetamine producers. He was smart, and careful. Higgs had dodged at least eight task force operations to remain free — and thriving.

These shadowy networks explain critical aspects of the operations of any serious drug baron. He needs a good drug cook at home. But he also needs a specialised freight-forwarder, a docks man, to negotiate the red tape — and the authorities — in order to bring illegal drugs into the country and off the docks. For Mokbel, this was Karam.

Mannella and Gobbo were friendly. They shared coffees and discussed underworld goings-on. When asked by Dowsley and Carlyon, the man himself would deny any knowledge of criminal matters. Amiable, without the hard charisma of Gangland's bigger names, Mannella laughed off suggestions of wrongdoing.

But Gobbo alleged in a 2007 audio recording that Mannella was the designated docks man for a record importation of ecstasy pills. They had been produced in Belgium before passing through Italy to be packed in tomato tins and sent to Melbourne.

At the time, Mannella had legal woes. Though he wound up winning his appeal, he thought he was going to jail for importing ninety-five kilograms of ecstasy in a shipment of barbecues a couple of years earlier. So, as Gobbo told her handlers, he handed the all-important shipping paperwork for the upcoming importation to his mate Rob Karam.

Karam was a big-time punter who imported even more illicit drugs than Mokbel. Indeed, the Mokbels were only some of his co-conspirators. His specialty was identifying local businesses that could be used, unwittingly, as dummy destinations for consignments. He chose businesses unlikely to attract the attention of Customs.

More audacious than Mokbel, but also more discreet, Karam lacked the caricatured stylings of Gangland notoriety, even though his nickname was 'Pizza'. In court, Karam wore the slumped features of a suburban accountant at tax time.

From 2005, he treated his lawyer Nicola Gobbo as his 'go-to' girl. Gobbo and Acquaro would also represent Pasquale 'Muscles' Barbaro, the head of what came to be known as the Tomato Tins drug syndicate.

The barrister and the solicitor were the glue sandwiching together the drug shipments and police investigations that followed.

Barbaro was a member of one of the most powerful 'Ndrangheta clans, the Barbaro 'Ndrina, which has a presence in the orchards of Griffith, New South Wales. Marijuana plantations have long nestled alongside the fruit trees of the region. Barbaro's father, Francesco 'Little Trees' Barbaro, was thought to know something about the death of anti-drugs campaigner Donald Mackay in 1977.

The 'Ndrangheta's power flows from villages in the Calabrian hills, where olive groves and ancient ruins are the backdrop for tax evasion and the art of bloody payback. On this occasion, Barbaro's Calabrian masters had arranged an expert delivery. Melbourne made sense as the destination: Calabrian mafia cells had run illegal shipments to Australia for generations, and affluent Australians paid some of the highest prices in the world (about $40 a pill). A Belgian syndicate could produce the pills more cheaply than Australians could, even allowing for the obvious risks of shipping such a massive haul. The tins were professionally packed in Naples, some of them loaded with gravel so that the total weight of the 3034 drug-filled tins matched that of 3034 tins of tomatoes.

Fruit and vegetable man Frank Madafferi also played a role in the Tomato Tins syndicate and he was arrested at 12.30 pm on 8 August 2008, the day the Australian Federal Police launched coordinated raids on properties across four states and arrested seventeen people.

In a 2019 statement, Madafferi would remember being visited by Acquaro and Gobbo in the cells beneath the Melbourne Magistrates' Court following his arrest.

'Don't worry,' they told him. You will be 'able to go home soon'.

He was bailed the same afternoon and went straight to Acquaro's office, to find that Gobbo was already there. Madafferi and his lawyers had a drink and talked through his legal bother.

Madafferi had first met Gobbo a few years earlier, when Acquaro introduced her at a lunch as his 'very good friend'. Madafferi thought she was just another blonde on his arm, but Acquaro explained that she was a 'barrister giusto'. She was 'on our side', he said, and it couldn't have hurt that she could speak the native language.

Gobbo had stood out because of the plaster cast on her leg (for reasons unknown) and her 'relentless' questions. She'd asked Madafferi about the presence of the Honoured Society — as the 'Ndrangheta was known in Australia — at the Melbourne Market and elsewhere. Madafferi was Melbourne mafia, a boss who guarded his rule against interlopers. Mafia bosses don't generally share how things work with outsiders — especially not 'Mad Frank', who had a notorious reputation for violence which had followed him from Italy.

Helping Madafferi and others had bestowed a special status on Acquaro within the Honoured Society. He straddled an unusual line between the respectable and the criminal, and his mix of vanity and pride may have led to his downfall a decade later, after Gobbo's deceptions began to trickle into public view.

The Honoured Society is built on loyalties and grudges. Its bosses don't forget. Madafferi would come to trust Gobbo entirely, he later said, because Acquaro vouched for her. 'They did a lot of things together, went everywhere together and spoke on the telephone all the time,' Madafferi said of Acquaro and Gobbo.

According to Madafferi, he saw his new barrister more than twenty times over the months following his Tomato Tins arrest, sometimes at weekend barbecues hosted by Acquaro. She would ask Madafferi questions unrelated to his case, such as his role at the Reggio Calabria Club in Parkville. The social club became a hotspot of official interest after a botched hit attempt on Pasquale 'Muscles' Barbaro's cousin there in July 2008.

But it was not Frank Madafferi who gave Gobbo the information that helped put the Tomato Tins syndicate away. It was Rob Karam.

* * *

Karam also trusted Gobbo completely. He was a bad man, blacklisted from Crown Casino and linked (unsuccessfully) to murder plots. But he had a playful side. He wanted to bed Gobbo, according to her, and tried various versions of charm.

Their intimacy was sometimes conventional. They went to the movies together, and to nightclubs where he was ushered past the queue at the door. He once tried to impress her by booking a restaurant table under the name of 'Robby Rockstar'.

But there were less normal elements too. Gobbo arranged dinner with his friends, who happened to be big-time drug lords, to thrash out failed deals and questions of retribution. (They particularly enjoyed dining at the Red Emperor restaurant in Southbank.) Like Mr Average, Gatto and Tony Mokbel, Karam might as well have spoken into a police microphone at these catch-ups.

Karam took a perfectionist's pride in his drug smuggling. He paid people on the docks. He planned ahead so that their shifts looked routine. He relied on a quantity equation; losing the odd shipment was the price of business. He conned lawful customs brokers into exchanging legitimate documents, including bills of lading, which list a ship's cargo.

He told his friend Nicola Gobbo all these things. He pointed out failings in Customs systems that he exploited. In early 2006, after informing her of an impending drug shipment, he said: 'I can't believe I just told you that.'

He told her about the time a container of illicit drugs landed in Sydney and had to be abandoned because the contents were 'off'. Horty Mokbel was to blame, he said, because he was late with the paperwork and set off official flags.

This paperwork, which included false names and phone numbers, was vital: drug shipments could be transported 12,000 kilometres, then sit on the docks for weeks or months until the required documents were produced.

Karam told Gobbo what was happening, who was fighting whom, and when the next shipment was due to arrive. Gobbo passed on everything he told her. She rang her handlers after she went to the footy with Karam and sat in a corporate box. And from the toilets of a Japanese restaurant minutes after she, Karam and another man had dinner.

Her handlers gave her tasks, such as providing registration numbers. When they wanted the number of Karam's latest burner phone, Gobbo and a handler discussed the dangers of sending herself a text message from the phone and deleting the sent message. One handler's report read: '3838 believes that Karam would think that 3838 simply couldn't tell anybody about what he tells 3838.'

Gobbo got results, there's no doubt. She bragged that containers she told police about never got from the docks into the community because of her spywork. In some of these cases, her intelligence was used to stop drug imports but charges were not laid. Gobbo was a committed one-woman war on drugs, and backhanded credit is due. Her informing almost certainly saved lives.

But Gobbo wanted convictions. And in the words of the master puppeteer, Shakespeare's Iago, Karam was being 'led by the nose, as asses are'.

* * *

The so-called 'Ceramic Tiles' haul was the biggest ecstasy seizure in history when it was intercepted in Melbourne in 2005. More than one tonne of pills — the weight of a Clydesdale horse, as a journalist pointed out — with a street value of $250 million, hidden within eight pallets of ceramic tiles, was seized after the haul arrived on board the cargo ship *Matilda*.

Authorities had received a tip-off, and replaced the pills with sugar tablets, when labourers were busted delivering the consignment to a northern Melbourne warehouse.

Karam was thought to be the Ceramic Tiles mastermind and was duly charged. But being on trial for importing five million ecstasy pills in June 2007 did not slow him down. He was a high roller who averaged a gambling splurge once every three or four days. He liked risks. In between court hearings over the Ceramic Tiles case, he was waiting on the delivery of a haul that would set a *new* world record: 15 million ecstasy pills in tomato tins.

His cockiness was born of experience. Karam knew that convictions for sophisticated criminal enterprises demand a flawless prosecution case. Good defence barristers are trained to pick holes in thousands of pages of documents, where a mis-signed statement or a minor error of fact can exclude evidence or establish reasonable doubt.

He also knew that the accepted police practice of arresting drug movers in the act got the lackeys but often failed to get the bigger players. Karam also pondered grimmer solutions. For the Ceramic Tiles case, Karam had concerns about one of his co-accused, Anton Claite, and Gobbo told her handlers that Karam had plotted to kill him.

Despite a textbook police approach, the four alleged ringleaders in the Ceramic Tiles case — including Karam — walked free, while the two sods who unpacked the pills faced life in prison. Karam was as Teflon-coated as his mate Tony Mokbel. He walked free from charges of importing 550 kilograms of ephedrine in 2001, as well as charges over the importation of three tonnes of hashish the same year. For every consignment that drew official attention, there were probably dozens that slipped through unnoticed. No wonder he felt bulletproof.

The irony was that while he was being cleared of the Ceramic Tiles pill importation, he was being implicated — largely from his own mouth — for the even bigger Tomato Tins importation he was planning.

He did not know the fuller story of his capture until he pieced together the revelations in Anthony Dowsley's story about a police informer in the *Herald Sun* in 2014. Even the Australian Federal Police (AFP), who made the arrests, appear to have been deprived of the whole truth.

* * *

On 5 June 2007, twenty-three days before the MV *Monica* delivered her illicit cargo from Naples, Karam gave Gobbo the ship's bill of lading for safekeeping. They were having a morning coffee before another day in court, and he did not want to be caught holding the incriminating document.

She asked Karam if the bill of lading related to ecstasy or cocaine importation, to which he replied: 'Bit of this, bit of that.' He told her it was the biggest importation those involved had carried out.

Gobbo held the bill of lading for no more than a few hours before she gave it back: ample time for a professional spy. She had copied the document and passed it on to her handlers, a single act that stopped 4.4 tonnes of ecstasy pills, many of them stamped with kangaroos, from flooding the Australian market.

The bill of lading referred to a shipping container known as MEDU1250218. Police now knew where to find the container, and they knew of its illegal cargo. Gobbo, ever helpful, even translated the document from Italian for them.

Despite the pressures of Tony Mokbel's capture in Greece and a rush of death threats around this time, Gobbo was an enthused secret agent. She exchanged mischievous text messages with Karam in court, both participants aware that police were monitoring the communications. She was in his Volkswagen Golf after he found a police-planted bug in it. There was a 'bit of cock teasing going on' with Karam, she told handlers, as there had been with Mr Average before him.

Police wanted more than the bill of lading. '3838 very confident [3838] could talk to Karam about it without bringing suspicion. TASKING: 3838 tasked to speak to Karam and find out who is involved, what phone numbers used and the name of the freight-forwarder.'

So Gobbo gave them more. And more.

* * *

The official story — which went unchallenged until 2019 — was that the AFP were tipped off about a large ecstasy consignment by overseas agencies. The case became a celebrated study in policing excellence, and a little luck. Customs officers supposedly conducted a wide search and discovered the drugs in a container of Italian tomato tins. The AFP removed the ecstasy and replaced the haul with fake pills, then waited for the importers to pick them up.

The fuller story is more tangled. The AFP version omitted critical details, perhaps out of ignorance. Victoria Police did not trust the AFP with their Gobbo secret, in just another case of interagency suspicion. But they did tell other federal crimefighting bodies, such as the Australian Crime Commission (ACC), about the incoming haul. Customs or the ACC told the AFP. A joint operation was in place before the MV *Monica* berthed in Melbourne.

After the haul arrived, the investigation shifted unexpectedly. A freight-forwarder chose not to call the number listed on the shipping paperwork — a false phone number offered by the drug syndicate, which hoped that the legitimate company would never know that it had officially ordered tonnes of tinned tomatoes. Instead, the freight-forwarder found the *real* number of the company on Google. She was told by the listed company that no tomatoes had been ordered. The drug importers, consequently, never received the expected call asking them to collect their tomato tins.

The container then sat in a Melbourne docks warehouse. Hearing nothing, the criminals couldn't try to retrieve it because they feared the cops were waiting to see who collected it. A game of cat-and-mouse began, an AFP investigation that would consume 10,000 hours in surveillance, 185,000 hours of tapped phone calls, and 287,000 work hours.

Victoria Police kept Gobbo's informer identity a secret throughout. They even took her phone after she gave them the bill of lading, because of fears the AFP would tap her number.

* * *

A month after Gobbo copied the Tomato Tins bill of lading for police, she had an explosive revelation for Karam. According to him, it happened when they were standing outside the Melbourne Magistrates' Court in a lunch break during the Ceramic Tiles case.

'I've just run into an AFP officer in the County Court who says there is something big at the docks, and you might not know about it now but you will soon,' Karam would allege that Gobbo told him.

Minutes later, according to Karam, he was sitting at Wheat restaurant with Gobbo and Higgs. '[Gobbo] then repeated the AFP comment to Higgs,' Karam would say. 'In the course of that conversation, Higgs told me he wanted to speak with me at the request of Pasquale Barbaro, whom I had never previously met.'

Higgs left, Karam said — to be recorded later the same day, talking to Barbaro and others. Barbaro was staying in Room 609 at the Pacific International Suites in Little Bourke Street. The room was bugged by the AFP, who already suspected Barbaro was involved.

Whether Gobbo was instructed to plant this seed of panic, or did so of her own volition, is unknown. One might speculate that this was a police play to provoke incriminating conversations to be picked up on bugs or tapped phones. If so, it worked: the syndicate members largely implicated themselves in coming months by blathering about the ecstasy haul stranded on the dock.

It's unclear why the syndicate did not write off the haul right then — except that hundreds of millions of dollars would have been lost. They hadn't received their call, and Gobbo had apparently warned them of AFP surveillance at the docks.

From July 2007, Australia's biggest-ever drug haul importers exhausted every diabolical and farcical scheme imaginable to first find, then remove, the 4.4-tonne consignment for the final leg of its journey — perhaps a few hundred metres from the Port Melbourne docks to the streets, where it was worth $440 million.

Syndicate members turned on one another in a dazzling display of buffoonery and bastardry, naïveté and arrogance. Police monitoring of their movements later exposed their desperation in humiliating detail.

The syndicate waited for news from Karam; he was the point man for the safe collection of the consignment. Tension built and errors multiplied.

Higgs thought Karam had got the container when he received a 'Delivery successful' text message. But he'd misunderstood his phone. The message was an automated response to his sending of a text. 'It's hard to fly like an eagle when you're surrounded by turkeys,' another syndicate member, prison escapee Jan Visser, was recorded as saying.

Barbaro faced a chilling prospect: going to Calabria to explain 15 million missing ecstasy pills. His Calabrian bosses suspected they had been ripped off by their Australian partners. There was nothing public at the time to indicate police intervention.

After landing in Italy on 22 July 2007, Barbaro was escorted to a car at gunpoint, taken to an unknown destination, and questioned for days. He had to tell his masters that the drugs were probably lost, then was told he must 'lick their wounds'. To borrow from John F. Kennedy, success has a thousand fathers but defeat is an orphan.

A deal was struck for reparations of $10 million and the promise of more drug importations. After Barbaro's return from Italy, the Calabrians sent an observer to Australia to monitor events. The syndicate was to be under *two* sets of surveillance: their 'Ndrangheta overseers and the Federal Police.

Barbaro attempted to get media coverage of the drugs being found by police. He used a burner phone and a fake identity to send a brazen text message to *The Age*'s Nick McKenzie, which implored the journalist to report on the seizure of the biggest ecstasy haul in history. 'Stan' wanted an article to show his Calabrian bosses. But McKenzie wasn't persuaded.

Troubled times produced a blaze of ideas. For out-of-pocket drug barons, greed was the mother of necessity. They had two mammoth tasks: to retrieve the drugs or at least show that they had been seized, *and* find a way of raising the $10 million they now owed. The solution? New drug importations to pay for the failed drug importations.

Barbaro was miffed that Karam, who tended to use other people's money for drugs purchases, still owed him $600,000. He had told Karam to pay with money 'or with your life'.

Police knew this, because they recorded a conversation in a park near Shepparton, north of Melbourne, in April 2008. Barbaro and others had gathered there in the belief that police could not eavesdrop. They spoke freely, and every incriminating word would be later used in evidence against them.

Barbaro didn't kill Karam over the $600,000 debt; instead, the pair arranged a July 2008 importation of 150 kilograms of cocaine from Panama. Yet this too failed, when an irregularity in the Colombian coffee bags in which the cocaine was shipped was detected by a Customs X-ray.

Some gang members, including Karam, were later ripped off by Indian criminals when they paid for 100 kilograms of fake chemicals.

Karam was extra-busy setting up other drug importations. He hatched a scheme to buy pseudoephedrine for making tonnes of ice. He headed to Asia for meetings with high-level Chinese gang members. He met one particular gang member called 'China Eddie' again and again. In March 2008, China Eddie suggested he and Karam travel to Hong Kong to meet 'Michael', a Triad member higher up the chain who would lend Karam money if a drug deal could be arranged.

Karam was unaware that China Eddie and Michael were both international undercover police agents.

One of Karam's associates, at his behest, sold $100,000 worth of ecstasy to Michael's supposed criminal associate in Melbourne, a woman called 'Rosie'. Karam was on a losing streak: 'Rosie' was an undercover AFP agent. He had been entrapped into seeking drug deals that would never happen.

He also plotted murders, or so said the police. Syndicate members believed that Fedele D'Amico had stolen from them, leading to a scheme to kill him at a kickboxing tournament in Melbourne's Docklands, then, when that fell through, a second plot to kill him at the wedding of Mick Gatto's son the following day. That didn't happen either.

Police detected a separate plan to kill a target related to Barbaro at the Reggio Calabria Club in Parkville in July 2008. (Hence Gobbo's later questions to Frank Madafferi about the club.) AFP officers monitored these events as they happened, and they observed the alleged hitman's car breaking down on the way. The hitman was Graham Gene Potter, who once murdered a woman and decapitated her. He fled in 2010 despite the close attention of the AFP. A master of disguise, Potter wears wigs and fat suits and has been on the run ever since.

* * *

Fourteen months after the drug consignment arrived from Naples, the Tomato Tins syndicate had still not attempted to recover it.

Authorities believed, correctly, that they now had enough evidence to convict the cartel.

They pounced in co-ordinated, nationwide, pre-dawn raids. In a Carlton apartment Barbaro shared with his mistress, Sharon Ropa, police found 2000 ecstasy pills and thirty mobile phones. The flat had doubled as a meeting place for drug business, and police bugs had already recorded many incriminating conversations in the months before.

Karam needed a lawyer when he was arrested at his home in Melbourne's inner east (coincidentally down the road from the Hodson home). He rang the very barrister he did not know had set him up for such a grand fall. So did other members of the doomed syndicate. Gobbo gave legal advice to and/or represented Karam, Madafferi, Barbaro, syndicate member Saverio Zirilli, and of course her old client John Higgs.

If you accept one member's claims, Gobbo was encouraging her clients to plead guilty from the time of their arrests. It's suggested that she urged them to roll on other members of the syndicate too. None did.

Karam was taken aback, while awaiting trial in June 2009, when he was arrested and interviewed about the alleged conspiracies to kill their associates. He was asked by police if he wanted a lawyer. Once again, he called Gobbo.

What was her advice?

'Tell them everything' was what she said, according to Karam's later testimony.

Karam squirmed at this; he would be implicating people who would kill him if they discovered his candour. But he says he accepted at the time that Gobbo knew best. He told the police everything.

Later, Gobbo spoke of turning the admissions into a draft witness statement, for Karam's 'best interests'. Karam was fretting about the interview, fearing that he would be charged with conspiracy to murder. When Gobbo produced a typed document for him to sign, he declined.

* * *

Karam was again flummoxed when he was compelled to give evidence to a secret hearing in 2011. This is an invitation that no one wants

181

to receive. The usual rights of silence are tossed aside. There are two options: tell the truth or go to jail.

Karam was uncertain about his approach to the interrogation. By then, Gobbo's career and reputation had flatlined, yet Karam overlooked her stench of double-dealing.

He wanted her to represent him but she said no. When he suggested another barrister by name, she replied: 'Why would you take that souvlaki with you?'

Karam was questioned over a day and a half. He thought he would be queried about the conspiracy-to-murder allegations, but grew uneasy about questions over the Tomato Tins drug importation.

It appeared that Gobbo had learned from previous mistakes. She had been at a hearing in 2004 where her client, the European, was questioned, and her conflicted loyalties had almost been revealed as a consequence of her presence.

Now she was too smart for that. In breaks from his interrogation, Karam trotted over to a nearby spaghetti bar, Maria's Trattoria, to receive legal advice from Gobbo, a police agent who would help put him in jail for thirty-seven years. Like an ass being led by the nose.

* * *

Thirty-two members of the Tomato Tins syndicate faced court between 2012 and 2014 for the failed importation. Justice Betty King gave Karam, Higgs and Barbaro the highest sentences. Barbaro was sentenced for life, Higgs for eighteen years and Karam for nineteen. They would still be in jail in 2020 because of Nicola Gobbo.

For two years before his 2012 trial, Karam now says, he spoke to Gobbo almost every day. She was his lawyer and his friend — or so he thought.

In 2016, after the Lawyer X story broke, Karam argued that Gobbo manipulated legal strategy to protect her role in the Tomato Tins investigation. He said her advice often contradicted that of his senior counsel, Chris Dane QC. Higgs's solicitor, Levi Diamond, also wondered about her advice, though he did not suspect her of informing until the *Herald Sun* outed 'Lawyer X' in 2014.

The trial for Karam's planned importation of twenty-six tonnes of chemicals from Hong Kong was discontinued, ostensibly because of the cost, but the Michael–Karam conversations led to a conviction for selling almost 11,000 ecstasy tablets to AFP officer Rosie.

He was tried for that charge, plus the failed Indian importation and the South American cocaine haul. Then on 23 June 2015, he was sentenced to a further eighteen years over the Tomato Tins seizure. With a total non-parole period of twenty-five years, he would be in jail until at least 2037, when he would be seventy.

In 2016, Karam accused Gobbo of entrapping him twice. As well as accusing her over the Tomato Tins case, he blamed her for setting him up with China Eddie to recoup money owed to her.

'I discussed all of what occurred with [Gobbo],' Karam said in his appeal. 'I sought her advice on my involvement …'

It's logical to assume that she passed on every detail to police.

'I sought advice from Lawyer X [Gobbo] about my conduct and, on the basis of that advice, continued in the way that I did,' Karam said. 'Everything that I heard or was told during this period, Lawyer X knew about.'

Peter Hanks QC, representing Victoria Police at Karam's 2016 appeal hearing, labelled Karam's claims as 'paranoid fantasies'. It's fair to argue that some parts of Karam's story are more convincing than others. Yet subsequent events have shown that some of Karam's claims were in fact extremely accurate.

* * *

Karam's proximity to multiple massive drug importations tends to preclude him from victim status. But he does not accept his drug-trafficking convictions — not when he knows that his lawyer and confidante was betraying him for years.

He is said to be the subject of 2200-odd information reports out of the 5500 produced during Gobbo's official informer period from 2005 to 2009. She told police everything about him, down to his tacky shows of chivalry. In jail, Karam has been fighting for years to access these police information reports to overturn his convictions.

'Pizza' refuses to do porridge until he's an old man. He still believes Gobbo's role in implicating him was hidden by the prosecution in the court cases against him.

He was the first of the Tomato Tins cartel to claim that his conviction was unlawful. Others still in jail in 2020, including Barbaro, are all seeking appeals. A winning play could spare Karam and his mates decades in jail.

* * *

Gobbo scored perhaps her biggest triumph in putting the Tomato Tins drug lords away. Yet by the time their cases went to trial, she was officially off the police informer books — thanks to a startling revelation by one of the biggest names of Gangland.

In seeking to wean themselves off the Gobbo drip, Victoria Police did the one thing guaranteed to heighten the risk to her life. They led her into a deadly dance with a serial killer: Carl Williams.

14

Secrets, Lies and Audio Tape

Informer 3838 Turns Witness
2007-2009

Carl Williams was just another bare bum in the jailhouse shower. But he was about to make life very difficult for the woman who was once his trusted lawyer.

On the outside, he and Tony Mokbel had boasted such infamy that they were known only by their first names. They also shared an honorific. Carl was 'Fatboy' and Tony was, naturally, 'Fat Tony'. They were the headline acts.

On the inside, Williams was serving one sentence for murdering Michael Marshall and was awaiting trials for five more charges for ordering the deaths of Lewis, Jason and Mark Moran, Mark Mallia and Pasquale 'Little Pat' Barbaro. He was also charged with a failed plot to kill Mario Condello.

Looking for ways to reduce a long sentence in prison, Fatboy put pen to paper — he was yet to get his prison computer — and told tales about an unfortunate trio from back in 2004: himself, ex-detective Paul Dale and Nicola Gobbo.

Williams was in the back of a prison van when the van turned around and headed back to court on Justice King's orders. Williams had told his lawyers that was willing to strike a deal — he was prepared to plead guilty to three murders and wanted a minimum sentence of no more than thirty years. This was a turnaround: he had told a court hearing in December 2006 that he would fight the charges.

His mother Barbara tried to talk him out of making a deal. But Williams wanted one — not just for himself, but also for his father George, who remained a suspect in the Lewis Moran killing, and for his ex-wife Roberta. (Their marriage had fizzled in early 2007, with the latter confiding to the *Herald Sun*: 'he just wanted me to move on'.)

Williams's statement of April 2007 was aimed at reducing his combined sentence for the murders of Jason and Lewis Moran and Mallia, and conspiracy to murder Condello. The charges for the murders for Mark Moran and Pasquale Barbaro were dropped as part of the deal.

In it, Williams described the so-called 'Hillside meeting', when Dale purportedly asked Williams if he was prepared to kill Terry Hodson for him, an allegation Dale has always denied. The statement also named Gobbo as the liaison between him and Dale in the weeks before the Hodsons were killed. (A second and third statement, both made in January 2009, would be more detailed.)

'What am I going to get?' he kept asking his lawyers.

One of those lawyers, Sharon Cure, received Williams's draft statement about Dale in a sealed envelope in the hours after it was made. She had an office in Crockett Chambers, a prestigious cradle of leading QCs — as did Nicola Gobbo.

Barristers had resisted when Con Heliotis QC, the Golden Greek, offered Gobbo an office in the chambers the year before. Gobbo's reputation had preceded her, in part because Carl Williams had fuelled gossip that she was 'a dog'.

Cure had Williams's statement in her office for an hour, perhaps two. She had not had time to read it before Detective Sergeant Stuart Bateson arrived. According to Cure, Bateson closed the door behind him and asked her to hand over the sealed envelope. She complied.

Was Bateson seeking to protect Gobbo's alleged role as a go-between for Williams and Dale from being revealed? Cure would not read the statement until the 2019 to 2020 royal commission.

* * *

Fatboy was sentenced on 7 May 2007. Justice Betty King, donning her signature red glasses, had received Williams's sealed statement ten days earlier.

The statement didn't help. Williams copped a minimum sentence of thirty-five years for the extra three murder and murder-conspiracy charges. He was thirty-six, and doomed to remain in prison until 2042. It shouldn't have surprised him. Already sentenced to twenty-one years for the Marshall killing, he got an extra fourteen years for ordering the two public executions of Lewis and Jason Moran, and for the deathly torture of Mallia. Charges for the deaths of Pasquale Barbaro and Mark Moran were dropped in the plea deal Williams negotiated with prosecutors.

Williams's pen-pal girlfriend, mum and dad were at the sentencing; so was Judy Moran, the matriarch of brothers Mark and Jason. Justice King labelled the defendant as 'arrogant, almost supercilious'. Williams had acted as 'judge, jury and executioner'.

As she pronounced her sentence, Williams was no longer winking at his family through the Perspex encasing the witness box. 'Ah, get fucked,' he said, announcing that he had 'expected nothing less' of King.

Barbara joined in, yelling at Justice King: 'You are a puppet for corruption, you are a puppet of Purana, you don't deserve your wig and your gown.'

Judy Moran was disappointed too — that Williams was 'still breathing'.

Williams's barristers David Ross and Cure withered under a tirade of Williams's abuse after his courtroom exit. Cure didn't represent Fatboy ever again.

* * *

Purana detectives rejoiced. Many of them gathered in their matching striped ties to hear a judge condemn the Gangland kingpin to be locked up until he was seventy-one. Purana detectives could bask in the satisfaction of having outmanoeuvred such a societal menace. Assistant Commissioner Overland summed up the public reaction: 'Carl Williams is not a B-grade actor. He is actually a serious criminal.'

Gloating Purana detectives downed pints at a pub near Melbourne's Supreme Court. They spotted Gobbo at a nearby bar and sent over a bottle of champagne.

Journalists noticed Gobbo's displeasure at receiving the bubbly. They thought the detectives were signalling 'up yours' to a Williams lawyer and acolyte. How could they know police were actually thanking Gobbo for her secret contribution to the conviction of Gangland's biggest name?

* * *

A bottle of bubbly wasn't going to give Gobbo's secret away — but Carl Williams just might. He launched an appeal against his sentence in the Supreme Court ten days after Justice King's condemnation. Williams's decision to plead guilty had freed Gobbo from possible exposure in a courtroom trial. But she was still meddling, terrified that legal documents subpoenaed by Williams's legal team would reveal her conflicted roles.

Gobbo needed to know. She still denies the following version of events, which labels her actions as criminal, but it is supported by police notes from the time.

On Saturday, 24 June 2007, when Crockett Chambers was deserted, Gobbo made her way up to the seventh floor where she and Cure both worked and entered Cure's office. She might have used a master key that sat in an electrical cupboard near the floor's kitchen; Cure says she might have left her office unlocked.

Cure no longer represented Williams but she had kept notes relating to his case. Gobbo rifled through them, finding phone records that showed the frequent calls between the European and Gobbo. Royal commission lawyers would call Gobbo's snooping 'burglary', the *Herald Sun* 'Gobbo-gate'.

Cure now believes that Gobbo was motivated by self-preservation: Cure had worked on the Williams case that Justice King had ruled

Gobbo could not be involved in. Cure thinks Gobbo wanted to find out what she knew.

'I couldn't stand her,' Cure says. 'I never trusted her.'

Gobbo was furious that police had allowed the release of the phone records and other documents to Cure. She was also incensed by Williams's statement against her and Paul Dale. She had obtained copies of these; it's unclear how and when.

Why wasn't she warned, she wanted to know, that Williams had 'made up shit' about her links to Dale? She was growing more and more contemptuous of her handlers. The relationship was turning sour. The hunter was now the haunted.

* * *

Soon Gobbo had better reasons to feel riled. She was about to be drawn into the Hodson murder investigation once more.

Under homicide detective Charlie Bezzina, the case had spluttered and stalled. It finally exploded afresh with the new allegations from Williams. As a response to Williams's statement, Assistant Commissioner Overland had launched the Petra Task Force in April to reinvestigate the deaths. He had always wanted a conviction, but he was also mindful of bad publicity about corrupt cops in the aftermath of the 2004 killings.

Bezzina and his homicide colleagues had been denied vital information possessed by Purana. The Petra Task Force grew to be just as secretive. Armed with Williams's statement, Petra's elite investigators became convinced that Paul Dale was guilty of murder. And Nicola Gobbo would be compelled to become a witness against him.

Petra investigators interviewed more than 200 people of interest, including Gobbo. Detective Sergeant Sol Solomon and Detective Senior Constable Cameron Davey wanted to know about her close connections to the Hodsons in 2003 and 2004. But this witness was to be treated unlike any other in Solomon's long career.

Gobbo was not to be contacted directly. Instead, Solomon and Davey had to submit written questions to be passed up the chain of police command. Such conditions were unheard of. Homicide detectives have always commanded unfettered access to any witness or person of interest.

Lump it, Solomon was told, without explanation. Follow the process or don't talk to Gobbo at all. He says he didn't know that Gobbo was a registered informer until it was revealed in the media.

Solomon and Davey interviewed Gobbo four times in 2008. They raised her use of burner phones in 2004 to speak to Paul Dale and Adam Ahmed, the man who ran the Oakleigh drug house burgled by Terry Hodson and David Miechel in 2003. Petra had teased out the phone connections, and Gobbo's use of burner phones appeared untoward.

Fear probably drove Gobbo's choice to cooperate. Usually she liked to show off her insider knowledge, but she was rightly uneasy about the Hodson case.

She must have known how unethical her past behaviour would appear in the glare. There was the other side, too, as constant as her need to protect herself: Gobbo liked assisting police, whether as an informer, meddler or de facto undercover operative.

Gobbo was a person of interest to Petra, but she was about to become an undercover spy for Petra too. In mid-2008, she agreed to a highly improper sting.

Her old client Andrew Hodson had long been a suspect in his parents' deaths. He failed a lie detector test in early 2008, and his acrimony towards his father was well known. Father and son fell out after Andrew was shown proof of Terry Hodson's informing — by Tony Mokbel — in 2002.

Investigators felt that Andrew would never hurt his mother, but some wondered whether he had provided information, including the layout of the house, to someone else who *did*. Petra decided that Hodson should be shaken up to shake out his knowledge.

Hodson told Dowsley and Carlyon he was picked up at an eastern suburbs shopping centre and taken to a nearby police station. Over several hours of questioning, Hodson, who was drunk at the time, denied any knowledge of his parents' murders. Officers told him he couldn't leave the room until he gave up information. 'I can't give you the answer,' he told them. 'I had nothing to do with it.'

Needing help, Andrew's wife Cindy rang his lawyer — Nicola Gobbo. Gobbo told her to bring Andrew down for a chat.

Gobbo was the sting. The police were provoking Andrew Hodson so he would go to Gobbo, who would wear a wire to record her confidential conversation with him. The hope was that Hodson would be looser with his lawyer if he thought his words were private.

The scheme lurched its participants into criminal realms, clearly breaching legal professional privilege. Gobbo and Petra sought to incriminate Hodson out of his own mouth — not in a police interview, but in a confidential lawyer–client discussion.

The sting failed: Hodson did *not* go to Gobbo for advice because he felt he did not need to unless police charged him.

Beforehand, Gobbo's SDU handlers had warned her not to participate, under threat of deregistration. But if you do record Andrew Hodson, they told her, give *us* the tape, not Petra.

Victoria Police, like every police force, has always been riddled with byzantine politics. But secretiveness had begun to flourish at the expense of crime-solving in a climate of mistrust.

So much for solving murders.

* * *

Soon Gobbo volunteered herself for *another* sting that had a very different outcome.

Solomon was at home when Gobbo rang him unexpectedly on Sunday, 30 November 2008. She was meeting Dale, she told the detective. Would he like her to record him?

Solomon was 'surprised' by her suggestion — not that he knew the bigger picture. She must have known the offer could trigger the fraying of the Gobbo illusion. She surely had the foresight to look ahead to calamitous scenarios. She understood the requirements of admissible evidence: she would be examined in a courtroom if her recording of Dale threw up anything incriminating.

This moment in the Gobbo story didn't make sense, at least to Solomon, and it still doesn't now. Perhaps Gobbo felt trapped, once again. By helping to snare Dale, was she hoping to shrug off the deepening scrutiny of Solomon and other Petra investigators over the past year?

Gobbo and Dale had stayed in touch since their relationship, born of fear, paranoia and booze, had first bloomed in 2003. The two of them met at table thirty-three at the Avenue Foodstore in Albert Park on a dim December day in 2008.

Gobbo ordered a large skinny flat white. The pair talked about the weather, his kids, and her struggle to give up the fags. They both hated shopping, they discovered, in the kind of light chatter that buoys café custom in bayside Melbourne. 'Oh, you've milked the cow, thanks,' Gobbo told a waitress after a forgotten coffee was finally delivered.

Dale had been the prime suspect in the Hodson killings from the moment the bodies were found. Almost five years later, nothing had changed, but he had never been charged and he has always denied any wrongdoing.

It made life tough, he told Gobbo. When he went to Perth to visit a police mate, the mate had sent him away. Dale had lost almost every friendship forged over seventeen years as a cop.

Gobbo, too, was frustrated. Health worries were still plaguing her. On the recording she sounds weak and fragile.

Her osteo-arthritis was sharpened by the Melbourne chill, she told Dale. She was still dosing herself on hillbilly heroin, but she had stopped taking morphine in the mornings. Her facial joint pain exhausted her by early evening, which meant she couldn't 'be bothered' to find a man. She took Botox to ease the pain; as she pointed out, she did not 'give a fuck' whether it smoothed her wrinkles.

Dale was fixated on his coercive examinations at the Australian Crime Commission about Williams's statement against him. The hearings came in waves, every few months. Dale, sounding outraged, believed he was being forced to appear at the ACC because of a vendetta headed by Overland. He likened the ACC inquisitions to a title boxing fight.

'Fucking hell,' Gobbo said, sounding sympathetic.

Dale told Gobbo how the ACC had played recordings of calls between himself, her and Williams from early 2004. He talked about Williams's statement to police, fingering Dale for murder. It was the kind of evidence that could get Dale charged, a prospective bridge between long-held theories and verifiable facts.

Gobbo flicked the switch from confidante to spy. As far as Petra were concerned, the hour-long chat could be reduced to this critical exchange.

'Accurate or not?' Gobbo asked Dale of the Williams statement.

Dale said it was 'very accurate': '... some things that came out that clearly only him and me know'.

Dale trusted almost no one anymore. His old confidants were scared to be linked with him. But he trusted his old friend Nicola Gobbo. She sounded like she was on his side.

She touched on truth when she said: 'I hope they don't think that *I* was involved in some murder.'

Dale's wife, Ditty, arrived with her son, and she and Gobbo exchanged stories about trying to lose weight. Ditty wondered about dressing her baby daughter in pink and Gobbo spoke of her baby goddaughters. They told exercise tales: 'I had a personal trainer for a while but he went to jail so I have to find a new one,' Gobbo explained.

The Dales had to go shopping. 'Anyway, have a wonderful Christmas,' Gobbo told them. 'I hope Santa comes to you.'

Gobbo rushed back to Cameron Davey and presented the detective with the hidden recorder she had worn. Her breezy chat with Paul Dale would lead directly to his being charged with murder.

It would also devastate Gobbo herself. When Overland, Sandy White and Superintendent Tony Biggin met to discuss Gobbo's status, they decided that Gobbo's value as a witness was more important than the 'perceived issues' regarding her safety.

This meeting took place the day *before* Gobbo had coffee with Dale. It was already decided that looking out for Gobbo's best interests rated second to the desire to jail Paul Dale.

* * *

In January 2009, a month after wearing the Dale wire, Gobbo was deregistered as an informer so she could appear as a witness at Dale's trial. She was no longer to contact her handlers but Petra investigators instead. Two Petra detectives were quickly trained up for the role.

It's unclear how this was supposed to work. To make this plan succeed, Victoria Police had to cheat the justice system.

As an informer, Gobbo's identity could be protected by police, but as a witness, her name could be aired in open court — potentially leading to the exposure of her informer history. All her betrayals, and her possibly criminal conspiracy with Victoria Police, could be revealed to the world.

Her informer number had been changed in early 2008: '3838' became '2958'. But a computer-generated designation would not shift human nature. Informer 3838 was a source not only of police intelligence, but also of police gossip.

By then, Gobbo's handlers had been considering exit strategies for a year or more. Their notes depict a genuine regard for her safety. For three years she had avoided serious scrutiny over the Hodsons. But Williams's 2007 statement had reframed her usefulness.

In approving Gobbo's transition from informer to witness, Overland had said he was 'aware of the consequences', but that 'corruption trumps everything'. Notes of senior command meetings depicted a bleak certainty: police protection would be the only way to keep her safe.

Yet Gobbo's controller, Sandy White, fought her transition to witness. White didn't think Overland understood that Gobbo's shift in police status jeopardised her life.

His fears had been shared by Detective Inspector Gavan Ryan when the question was first raised in 2007. Ryan, who left Victoria Police in early 2008, knew of her informer role, but his Purana investigators say they did not.

An intra-departmental war erupted, with Gobbo as the spoils. Gobbo's handlers feared that her innate eagerness to please could trigger events that revealed her informer past. 'Do not provide too many clues to Petra,' a handler advised her.

Her handlers' concerns seemed well placed. Now reporting to both SDU and Petra, Gobbo appeared to relish the competing attention. She basked in a fresh audience of curious investigators, and continued to inform to both departments for the next twelve months.

An SDU information contact report from February 2008 fed the theme that she treated her duplicities as a game: '[Gobbo] makes a point of stating [she] could never believe that [she] would be in this position when [she] began [informing] two and [a] half years ago ... [Gobbo] enjoys the experience and attention of this questioning and the fact that [she] has extensive knowledge.'

But Gobbo had no idea then how badly her shift to Petra would go.

White and Ryan were right. Overland was wrong.

Overland's decision to change Gobbo's status would blast the edifice of the Gobbo illusion. It was the first step towards Gobbo's exposure.

* * *

No rule book could have accommodated the seesawing periods of flattery and rejection, submissiveness and ruthlessness, that stamped Gobbo's behaviour as Informer 3838. She bent the rules of play to satisfy personal intentions that no one had foreseen.

Her information reports — all 5500 produced between 2005 and 2009 — offer an intimate insight into her unorthodox thinking, and the lengths to which her handlers went to indulge her.

Gobbo was wired to fret, as many successful people are. Her highly strung nature thrived on the strategies of her dangerous game. Yet she was trapped by her unusual dependency.

To this day, her handlers claim pride in their management of Gobbo. But when it came to Gobbo, the protocols got tossed out. Her interactions with her handlers lacked any bearings for comparison. She wasn't like any other police spy.

Her relationship with them was possibly the closest of her adult life — part professional, part counselling and part venom. She gushed, railed and even got beauty advice. Cucumber eye masks, a handler told her, could be purchased at The Body Shop.

Her handlers received mountains of legally privileged details, which they would later say they did not pass on to investigators. They labelled these gushes of confidential client details as 'venting'.

They indulged her demands to scrap speeding tickets and her tax complaints. She rang at all hours and expected to be heard. She raged when a handler was tending to a sick child and couldn't take her call. In her mind, her assistance trumped some kid in hospital. As one handler now says, sounding weary: 'We had a job to go milk the cow. When it got mastitis, we rubbed it.'

Now she was cast adrift. The woman who had wanted to be the best informer ever, the source who put away drug barons and murderers, had been excised like a cancer from Victoria Police's informer roster.

After risking so much?

* * *

Sol Solomon had worked with Paul Dale on the Lorimer Task Force, which had investigated the shooting of police officers Gary Silk and Rod Miller a decade earlier. They used to carpool to and from work. Now Solomon had enough evidence to charge his former colleague with murder.

He labelled Gobbo's recording of Dale a 'breakthrough': Dale appeared to have implicated himself in the Hodson deaths. Dale was charged on 13 February 2009, during the numbing grief following Black Saturday, the unprecedented Victorian bushfires that killed 173 people, and led to a royal commission that queried police leadership during the emergency.

Dale was placed in solitary confinement. In refusing him bail, Justice Marilyn Warren found that he posed 'an unacceptable risk of interfering with witnesses'. The witnesses included Gobbo.

Solomon would later say that when Gobbo was asked about testifying against Dale in January 2009, she appeared to be 'totally committed to the cause'.

He gave her a 'welfare check' the following month, and she raised no concerns. She was considering going into hiding, and Solomon observed little trepidation on her part. (She, of course, might offer an alternative view.)

Gobbo was listed as 'Witness F' for the murder trial — that is, her identity was not to be revealed. It's a reasonable assumption that Gobbo demanded anonymity in return for giving evidence. But suppressing her name meant a hearing in the Supreme Court.

On 4 March 2009, Dale's solicitor, Tony Hargreaves, was present when the court heard arguments about shielding Gobbo's identity. Hargreaves, who had known Gobbo for years, was rocked by the revelation that she had worn a wire. Returning to his office, he walked past Gobbo having a cigarette at Wheat. He wanted to say something, but wisely chose not to.

Dale was told the next day when his lawyers visited him in Barwon Prison. He was incensed. He claimed that Gobbo had broken the 'cardinal rule' of lawyer–client privilege; she always argued that privilege did not apply except on the very few occasions she officially gave him professional advice, such as the time in December 2004 when she had visited him in remand after he had been charged with burglary — never mind that she breached the privilege on these occasions anyway.

Dale's belief in the confidentiality of their café chat was not entirely misplaced. During their discussion, Dale had expressed fears that police might overhear his gripes about the secret ACC hearings. To which Gobbo had replied: 'At least you can use the excuse of my being a lawyer.'

* * *

News of Gobbo's wire-wearing was spreading fast. Although the name-suppression hearing had taken place in a closed court, the story was too juicy to be kept a secret. The wider legal fraternity was shocked when 'Witness F' was identified as Gobbo. Her penchant for playing outside the accepted codes of behaviour was finally being leaked.

Gobbo's professional reputation had long ago been dented by her choice of company. Her name could have been destroyed by any one of her hundreds of unethical choices over the years. Yet it was this single act, which she presented as a noble choice about helping the victims of a murder, that scuttled any hope of a bright legal future.

Dale's then barrister, Ian Hill QC, worked out of Crockett Chambers. Gobbo was evicted from the chambers within twenty-four hours of the suppression hearing. An emergency meeting that included two of Melbourne's most eminent barristers, Robert Richter and Phil Dunn QCs, raised issues concerning the safety of office staff, because of Gobbo's clientele.

Gobbo's office had been next to Con Heliotis QC's and across the hall from Richter's. Her tenancy was mired in suspicion and disdain. The Crockett barristers feared her tarnish. 'She was far too close to the clients,' one of the QCs at Crockett says. 'She was mixing in too much with them.'

Paranoia seeped from Gobbo. Many women instinctively flinched from her practised lines in melodrama and victimhood. Male colleagues, conversely, sometimes seemed slow to read the kind of wiles that women can identify in other women. At an office birthday party, Gobbo spoke of being set up with a man who said he was a carpenter but whom she suspected of being an undercover cop.

The decision to evict her had been urged by the wives of the leading barristers. These women were scandalised by Gobbo's tales of public promiscuity.

Many solicitors had stopped briefing her as a barrister. They could no longer trust her: a foreboding deepened by suspicions that she recorded conversations with other Crockett lawyers.

How this concern was first raised, or if there is any evidence for it, is unknown. Yet the implications are, as one of the affected QCs says, 'mind-blowing'.

Was Gobbo recording private conversations about legal strategies pertaining to high-profile cases? Was she passing this intelligence on to police? Had police asked her to record such conversations? If so, dozens of cases that did not even involve her stand to be queried.

Philip Dunn QC is one who believes the rumours, as does another Crockett QC. 'I reckon she did [compromise cases],' that QC recently said. 'It's bloody appalling, isn't it? ... It's a conspiracy to pervert [the course of justice] with the coppers who were handling her.'

The revelation, according to police notes, about Gobbo's possible snooping in Sharon Cure's office in mid-2007 would not emerge until a dozen years later.

How many lawyers moonlight as cat burglars on the weekend?

* * *

In the press conference room at the Victoria Police Centre in Flinders Street, Simon Overland was holding a meet-and-greet with journalists — including Dowsley — following his appointment on 2 March 2009 as Chief Commissioner of Victoria Police. That venue has hosted many shock announcements, but today's was unprecedented.

Overland told the media he was aware that many journalists had contacts within the force. Of course they did. Police officers helped journalists for a variety of motives, mainly to solve crimes or ease injustice.

Now, however, he was determined to stop leaks. From now on, any police officer found speaking to the media outside prescribed controls would be prosecuted for a crime.

The message jarred. Overland was supposed to represent freshness and transparency. How did this tally with prosecuting officers who unofficially chatted to journalists?

The meet-and-greet was a harbinger. Overland's command culture would be buried in internal suspicion.

* * *

Assistant Commissioner Noel Ashby was one of many senior police, including Deputy Commissioner Sir Ken Jones, to have his phone tapped over obscure media-leak allegations during Overland's time in the top job. Ashby remains livid that the Office of Police Integrity (OPI) also tapped the phone of his sixteen-year-old daughter.

He calls the OPI Overland's 'private investigation agency', and has labelled Overland, OPI head Graham Ashton and Assistant Commissioner Luke Cornelius 'the Three Amigos'. The trio knew each other from the Australian Federal Police and had imported the AFP's investigative techniques of surveillance, phone taps and listening devices.

Ashby has the righteous quality of the wronged. His police heritage is easy to spot as he hurries down Swan Street, Richmond, on a cold winter's day after coffee with Dowsley and Carlyon: the straight bearing, the briefcase, the long coat.

He tried without success to get hold of the affidavit that had led to the tap on his phone. At the time, he says, he boasted an unblemished 35-year record.

* * *

More than fifty of the phone tappings instigated by Overland related to the vexed Briars investigation into the 2003 death of the so-called 'vampire gigolo', Shane Chartres-Abbott.

The male prostitute, who claimed to drink blood, was accused of raping a woman and biting off her tongue. He was thought to have been killed by Jack Price as revenge for his attack on the woman, an exotic dancer. Price set off police interest when he wrote 'Vampire' on his hand during a jailhouse meeting with a police officer. Police came to believe the hit was carried out as a favour to the woman's boyfriend, Mark Perry.

Price, serving a lengthy sentence for three underworld murders, was the pin-up boy of the Deal or No Deal Unit. As already stated, he had cooperated with police on many Gangland crimes in exchange for reduced jail time, and his information was often unreliable.

In March 2007, Task Force Briars was set up to investigate Price's claims concerning Detective Sergeant Peter 'Stash' Lalor. Price told police that Lalor had given him the address of Chartres-Abbott. He claimed that a former detective sergeant, David Waters, a drinking pal, also had prior knowledge of the hit.

Waters and Lalor were the targets of a massive anti-corruption operation featuring multiple leaks and phone taps — including the one Ashby was subjected to. But Briars became a $30 million waste of time. The operation exploded into newspaper headlines and withered under widespread examination.

Briars shared many elements with Petra. Both were run with the assistance of the Office of Police Integrity. Both were triggered by the claims of known liars and murderers looking for a deal. Liars can sometimes tell the truth, certainly, but both Petra and Briars failed to snare their intended targets.

The intricacies of Briars defy easy explanation. In essence, the public was intrigued by a supposed nexus between dirty cops and underworld heavies, and police brass, including Overland and then chief commissioner Nixon, were sensitive to these impressions.

The secret-ops preoccupation that characterised Briars was the same acutely political, if not paranoid, approach that had allowed a source of intelligence like Gobbo to flourish.

A grand police hypocrisy shouldn't be overlooked. Under Overland's guidance, Briars deteriorated into a fever of petty hatreds that had little to do with solving a murder. But such onerous levels of scrutiny were never supposed to apply to Overland and his subordinates in their use of secret agent Gobbo.

* * *

As a witness in the Dale murder case, Gobbo was more vulnerable than ever. She had lost her professional reputation and her legal career seemed doomed. Dale knew she had cheated him, and most of the underworld was wondering if they, too, were victims of Gobbo's deceit. Perhaps most importantly, Gobbo had lost her handlers, who had offered her understanding.

By the start of 2009, she needed a holiday after a frenzy of death threats and double-dealing. A police detail tagged along with her everywhere she went: to Queensland, and Bali as well, on trips funded by the Victorian taxpayer, who also paid for her Victoria Racing Club membership and the Pink concert tickets she had to forego for safety reasons.

One officer, she later told Dowsley, got so drunk in Bali that she had to help carry him home. Another had a phobia about germs. She didn't feel very protected: her police entourage seemed incapable of looking after *itself*.

Petra paid $193,000 to protect her during this limbo of uncertainty. There were thirty-five flights in ten months.

The figures suggest that Gobbo flew business class. She was getting a $1000 weekly stipend. The police service came to a total price tag of $304,642, including the payment of a $113 parking fine.

Despite this taxpayer bill of $30,000-odd a month, Gobbo's lifestyle and prestige were gone. For two weeks, on and off, in June 2009, she was provided with 24-hour guard by a crack team of officers from the elite Special Operations Group, presumably after another threat was made against her. She was supposed to get permission before calling any clients or associates. She jumped on one plane after another under a false name to minimise the risks. Gobbo was right: this was no life.

Deputy Commissioner Kieran Walshe wrote to her about her 'necessary' inclusion in witness protection on 4 June 2009. He spoke of 'very serious threats against you', 'the major risks you now face', and how 'to date you have refused to enter the Program'.

In August 2009, Gobbo was admitted to hospital in Melbourne for seventeen days, for various conditions aggravated by stress. Detective Sergeant Sol Solomon was shocked by her appearance and mental state when he visited her soon after her admission. He encouraged her to eat some mashed potato. 'Physically she was thin, pale and had lesions over her body,' he would say. 'Mentally she was depressed and stressed. We tried to take her to dinner but she wouldn't eat.'

Gobbo regretted her involvement with the police, she told Solomon. Notions of betrayal festered as the implications of being a witness grew clearer. She had given so much, and now she felt burned in return. She had contemplated police protection in the past, but the neccessity of a new identity — and the loss of the old — had sharpened.

Gobbo was proud of her surname; she didn't want to surrender it. But she had no power to barter, not like this. Her rhetoric harks back to Melvin Udall, the malcontent in the 1997 movie *As Good As It Gets*, who spoke of being 'evicted' from his own life.

Promises had been broken. At times, Solomon would say, Gobbo was 'deranged with anger'. He tried to counsel her, but she said he didn't understand. 'If only you knew the truth,' she told him.

* * *

While Gobbo holidayed in Bali with a police entourage in May 2009, Detective Senior Sergeant Ron Iddles was given what sounded like a cushy assignment.

Iddles had hunted countless killers over a lauded career in homicide and was known for his Bradman-like conviction rate. Now, at short notice, he was to find his passport and go to Bali with his superior, Detective Inspector Steve Waddell.

Overland had issued an order. The two detectives were to hunker down in a luxury hotel and take a witness statement relating to the murder of Shane Chartres-Abbott.

On discovering that Gobbo was the witness, Iddles made sense of the secrecy and rush that had enveloped the trip. He already knew of her informing, and he was aware her life was in extreme peril. But he did not grasp the depth of her assistance to police.

Gobbo had represented David Waters, one of the two officers accused of links to the Chartres-Abbott murder, in 2004 and 2007, when Waters had been charged with and acquitted of drug offences.

She had since played her customary role of pretending to be a lawyer to disguise being a police agent. She'd fronted police stings that had sought to expose the detectives' alleged involvement in the murder. She'd furnished police with reports of Waters's goings-on.

On police orders, she'd tried to pin down Waters with questions about Chartres-Abbott. It wasn't her best undercover work. Waters now says he was struck by her odd questions, as if she were trying to extract incriminating information from him.

Taking her witness statement, Iddles found Gobbo 'hard work'. Informers often are, given that their information is normally negotiated or induced. She seemed happy enough to volunteer the material. Yet her statement took two and a half days in a room at the Hard Rock Hotel, due to the constant breaks for cigarettes by the pool.

In Iddles's view, Gobbo's unsigned statement contained little evidentiary value. But this was not his biggest concern; it was the other things she revealed that worried him. Over the course of those two and a half days, she helped him grasp the improbable: 'I crossed the line a long time ago. I've been acting in the interests of Victoria Police, not my clients.'

Iddles judged Gobbo to be very intelligent. And naïve: a description he also applied to the police commanders who had pressed for her statement.

Iddles and Waddell got the statement. Then, with an old-world wisdom that eluded some officers, Iddles refused to let her sign it. He told her she would be signing her 'death warrant'. Gobbo says that Iddles warned her senior command would 'burn' her.

Iddles also wondered at the fallout if she were to confront a thorough barrister under cross-examination. Two words kept flashing in his mind: royal commission.

Iddles relayed his concerns to Overland.

'You will get it signed,' he was told.

'But I didn't,' Iddles now says.

The full extent of Gobbo's work as a police agent was not known to Iddles until he sat down with her in Bali in 2009. When her unsigned statement was presented to the royal commission in 2019, it contained a sensational confession claim that Iddles says he had never heard.

Mark Perry, the key target of the Briars investigation, was said to have confessed to Gobbo, a lawyer he did not know, that he had ordered the killing of Chartres-Abbott. The conversation purportedly took place in the office of Perry's solicitor, James Valos, while Valos was taking a phone call.

Gobbo and Iddles had no recollection of the confession claim. Did it ever happen?

Waddell testified in 2019 that it did. Iddles and Gobbo said it did not.

It seems remarkable that an alleged confession by a suspected killer was never used in evidence against him. Then again, it was Nicola Gobbo who said she heard the confession, and to this day no one knows whether it was made or not.

There were further tangles in the Briars Task Force debacle. During Perry's 2014 trial for ordering the hit on Chartres-Abbott, Jack Price said that Gobbo had visited him in prison in 2006. He said that his conversation with Gobbo helped lead him to confess to killing Chartres-Abbott.

* * *

Paul Dale was granted bail in September 2009, after eight months in the Acacia Unit at Barwon Prison, mixing with the most feared murder and terrorism suspects in the State. He says that when he chatted with Tony Mokbel in an adjoining cell, Mokbel was stunned to hear that Gobbo had worn a wire to incriminate Dale.

Chief prosecutor Gavin Silbert SC had objected to Dale's bail: 'To put it crudely, organising an execution … has to be more difficult from prison than outside.'

The 'execution' Silbert was referring to was Gobbo's. She was still unwilling to receive police protection.

Deputy Commissioner Walshe switched focus. He wrote on 26 August 2009 to tell Gobbo that 'ad hoc security arrangements represent an unacceptable security risk to the health and safety of the police officers who have been protecting you'.

This was an interesting strategy. Gobbo had refused police protection, in part because she did not trust the police. In response, Walshe claimed that protecting Gobbo was *too dangerous* for the police.

By November 2009, there was fierce agreement on one point: Gobbo was struggling. Since 2004, she had had jaw, heart, neck, breast, ulcer and cyst surgeries, and suffered dramatic weight loss. Her figure was drastically thinner than it once was.

Svelte in a little black dress and heels at a 2008 funeral, she projected a glamour that had previously eluded her. She had shed the fleshiness that had once led Mandy Hodson to nickname her 'Sharon Twenty Stone'. The line of her jaw was slimmer, though photos also depict her features as tightened with tension.

She feared cancer, understandably, given the shedding of kilos and a possible genetic predisposition: the disease had already struck her father. She would be forced to confront that fear soon enough.

It's thought to be in Brisbane, during one of her 2009 trips to Queensland, that she called a police officer from the top of a building. She had had enough.

She brimmed with pique, scorn and self-defeating rage; the tone of her text messages at the time, reported later in this book, hint that anger was winning the battle against depression and ill health. Perhaps she was simply seeking attention.

'I'm going to jump!' she screamed to the officer on the other end of the phone.

15

The Butcher, the Baker and the Statement Maker

The Death of Fatboy Ends the War
2010

After almost six years inside, Carl Williams was 'broken', says one of his confidants. The bogan nonchalance of his TV portrayal in *Underbelly* was dimmed. (Not that the lead character himself thought much of the TV series, as he wrote to a friend: 'it would be lucky to be 5% of the truth'.)

'Some girls beg and some girls borrow, some girls lead and some girls follow, some bring joy and some bring sorrow, but the very best girls just suck & swallow!' read an SMS to another friend, written on 5 June 2004, just before his arrest.

Williams continued to tell dirty jokes in jail. After he got his computer, he wrote constantly from his Barwon Prison cell, dashing off hundreds of letters to family, friends and female admirers. Read in their entirety, Williams's words showed a wit and regard for others. He cared what people thought of him and offered favours freely.

If he sounded more human than public perceptions might suggest, he also sounded more vulnerable. The letters depicted an anguished soul who verged on depression. Williams was worried about time — too much of it. A 35-year-minimum stretch was 'one hell of a hill to climb'; he had missed his daughter's first day at school, and he would miss her twenty-first birthday.

'I am the first to admit that I wish that I could turn back time and what happened never did ... although I must confess I am certainly not ashamed of the lengths I was forced to take to protect myself and my loved ones,' he wrote to his mother Barbara.

'I killed or played a role in killing people who were planning to kill me and for that I have lost my freedom for the best part of my life. Everyday soldiers have to kill the enemy, otherwise the enemy will kill them.

'I am no saint ... but the people I killed were far worse people than I will ever be ... I never killed or harmed any innocent people.'

Where Pasquale 'Little Pat' Barbaro fits into Williams's thinking is muddled. Barbaro died because he happened to be sitting next to Jason Moran when the Assassin, a Williams-hired hitman, blasted Moran, then Barbaro. And what of Michael Marshall, who died in front of his son in a South Yarra street to protect a Williams lie?

But Williams nursed more immediate concerns too. He was heartbroken, perhaps for the first time in his life. He had become engaged to 22-year-old Stacey, an underworld groupie who visited him twice a week. He was so besotted, he admitted, that he had lowered his guard, which made the breakup all the more hurtful.

He was obsessed with small things too. Robbed of responsibility and power, drugs and menace, Williams's currency was gossip and perks.

For a time, he shared a jail unit with his father George. Then he shared Acacia Unit 1 with a good mate, 'the Watcher'. The Watcher was a 'great cook'.

Williams was healthier than ever, his baby face hardened by the giving up of everyday poisons. He pounded the treadmill daily because 'it keeps me sane', and he was now thirty kilos lighter than his arrest weight in 2004. The treadmill 'clears my mind', but also combated his daily battle with boredom. Heartbreak, Williams joked, was another way to lose weight.

Between 8 am and 3.30 pm each day, he and the Watcher shared the exercise room with Matty — Matthew Charles Johnson — another mate with whom Williams had asked to be housed.

Johnson was suspected of shooting a kid dead over a $50 debt. Two days later, on 24 May 2007, he broke into the wrong house and threatened an innocent couple in their bed. 'Where's Anton?' Johnson had asked, pointing a gun at the poor man's head.

Propelled by a combination of impulse and incarceration, Johnson projected a caged animal menace, coupled with an eerie death stare. He hated anyone who cooperated with police. Williams's selection of him as a cell mate was not Fatboy's shrewdest decision.

* * *

Williams had now made three statements — the last two in January 2009, to support Gobbo's wire recording — against Paul Dale. Each statement was more detailed than the last. His motivation for nailing Dale was simple enough: as he wrote to Horty Mokbel on 15 October 2009, 'Dale is a copper and like you said "fuck him".'

The police had agreed to colossal inducements — including the payment of his father's $576,000 tax bill — to get Williams talking. The biggest incentive of all was a ten-year reduction on Williams's sentence, in a deal negotiated with the Office of Public Prosecutions.

The deal hinged on Nicola Gobbo. Only her evidence against Dale, coupled with Williams's, could convict the former detective. But by March 2010, Gobbo no longer wanted to face the ordeal of cross-examination and possible informer exposure in the witness box. A few months earlier, she had tried to make a bargain: she would give evidence, she wrote to Victoria Police, for $20 million.

After police had resorted — unsuccessfully — to forcing Gobbo to appear in court, they conceded through their lawyers that they were 'not able to manage the risk to [Gobbo's] safety unless she agreed to enter the witness protection program on terms offered'. They argued that Gobbo refused to change her identity, or relocate to a safe area, and indeed 'refused to acknowledge and accept the existence of a serious risk to her security and welfare'.

She didn't try to find a compromise to the impasse by countering offers of protection with offers of her own. She too was nonplussed, and would complain that the police plan in case of a 'security incident' was 'run for your life'.

Tensions deepened. On a day in March 2010 when Gobbo claimed she was medically unfit to attend Dale's committal hearing, she was spotted 'enjoying the sunshine' at a Port Melbourne café, a crutch perched against her table. A month earlier, on the day when she had been subpoenaed to give evidence, she toted a walking stick or frame, as well as an oxygen bottle, in a scene that mimicked the latter years of Christopher Skase.

On another occasion, she tried to be excused from giving evidence by telling the court she was wheelchair-bound, but police put her under surveillance and photographed her walking unaided up the steps to her front door.

Dale's case had already been delayed. His defence team wanted truckloads of police documents, and the case went nowhere for months as the police gradually produced them. It has since emerged that Victoria Police did not in fact produce everything they were legally required to. If they had, Gobbo's informing would have been exposed almost four years before Dowsley sat down at his keyboard and wrote about Lawyer X.

* * *

From Barwon Prison, Williams avidly followed Gobbo's belated reluctance to testify against Dale.

On 22 March 2010, he wrote to Milad Mokbel: 'Yeah I see Nicola is ill, how ill though would be anyone's guess, if she told me the sky was blue, I'd have to go and check it … you know my thoughts on her — I don't think I'd be on her Christmas card list, nor do I wanna be. (ha ha)'.

He, like Gobbo, was reconsidering giving evidence — according to ex-wife Roberta.

On the morning of 19 April, his fellow prisoners howled like dogs. Williams was alarmed by the taunting. His assistance to police had been leaked. He had been identified as a snitch, and snitches got hurt.

'I don't want to do this, Bert,' he apparently told Roberta later that morning. 'There's too much at risk. I'm pulling out today.'

They spoke on the phone for about twenty minutes before Roberta had to go. She had a photo shoot with *New Idea*.

Williams had the *Herald Sun* delivered each day. He read that morning's front-page headline, which announced that his daughter's school fees were being paid by Victoria Police.

'Well, you've made the front page, hey?' a warder said to Williams.

'Yeah, I'm fine, I'm fine with it,' Williams replied. But he wasn't.

Williams was still reading the newspaper when Johnson crept up behind him, gripping the stem of an exercise bike. A metal bar that had added years to Williams's life would be reapplied as the bludgeon to end it.

Crack.

Williams fell at the first blow, which was probably fatal.

Johnson kept going, the Watcher looking on.

Crack.

Crack.

Crack.

Crack.

Crack.

Crack.

It was 12.48 pm. No one noticed for twenty-seven minutes, even though the room had 24-hour CCTV coverage. Johnson and the Watcher walked laps in the exercise yard until they tired of waiting for authorities to realise that the prison's most infamous inmate was dead.

'Miss, you need to press your buzzer,' Johnson told a female guard. 'Carl has been hit in the head.'

Photos of the pulp left by Johnson later circulated. Williams's skull was compared with a crushed egg.

Williams had been right, though not in the way he thought. Time *was* his enemy: he didn't have enough.

* * *

Roberta Williams heard the news straight after her photo shoot. She has radiated grief and outrage to this day.

Many others were less saddened — Paul Dale chief among them. With Williams's death, *The Queen v Paul Noel Dale* collapsed. The police dropped the case and proceedings were dismissed.

Nicola Gobbo benefited too. She had worn the wire to implicate Dale, but she no longer wanted to testify.

She was aware before the newspaper story that school fee payments were among Williams's inducements. She later had images of Williams's corpse — though exactly how she obtained these remains a mystery.

* * *

'I acted alone,' was Johnson's sole comment in his police interview after the killing. But did he? A fuller grasp is elusive.

Dale was an obvious suspect, yet the Driver Task Force, set up to investigate the murder, found no evidence of his involvement in Williams's death. Driver head Superintendent Doug Fryer called Dale an 'unwitting beneficiary'.

Johnson said at his murder trial in 2011 that Williams was 'spinning a yarn' in implicating Dale in the Hodson murders. He had seen Williams's statements before he killed him. '[Carl] said that they knew he had had dealings with Dale and he could just fill in the spots for the rest of it and they'd gobble it up.'

Such claims were never tested. Driver's disbanding after the Johnson conviction felt like unfinished business for some within Victoria Police.

The reasons Johnson turned on his friend are complicated. It is strongly suspected that money and pressure were involved. Disturbing theories, fostered in the vacuum of a police investigation that never amounted to much, are supported by some detectives who investigated Williams's death.

* * *

There is a macabre symmetry between the Williams murder and the Hodson killings. Williams, like Terry Hodson, was killed before he could give evidence against Dale. Both were let down by a police command that lacked the insight to appreciate the risk that the two men's knowledge posed.

Other facts bind Williams and Hodson too. Gobbo knew each of them was an informer at the time of his death. She knew both were offered massive sentence reductions to roll on Paul Dale.

And though their murders were almost certainly arranged beforehand, both men died immediately after prominent newspaper stories hinted of their police informing.

The day before he died in 2004, Hodson was alluded to as a 'police informer' in a *Herald Sun* story that spoke of a contract on Carl Williams's life. Hodson's informing history had leaked to the media as well as the underworld. The report said that Hodson, who was unnamed, had told a former Drug Squad detective (Dale) that he had been offered (and declined) a $50,000 contract to kill Williams.

Williams's inducements to betray Dale were splashed across the front page on the day he died. The identity of the source who gave the *Herald Sun* the tip-off that Dhakota Williams's school fees were being paid by the State cannot be revealed for ethical reasons.

Dale also had a known history with the Watcher, the third man in the exercise room where Williams was killed. The Watcher and powerful underworld figure Rocco Arico grew up in Brunswick together.

What few knew was that before Williams's death police were urging him to make a statement identifying Arico as the gunman in the unsolved Gangland killing of Richard Mladenich, a friend of Mark Moran, in a St Kilda hotel in 2000.

Arico heard of Williams's death before authorities even realised that someone was hurt: the Watcher spoke to Arico on a prison phone from the crime scene.

Arico had a motive for ordering Williams's death. Driver investigators scoured money trails to identify possible payments to Johnson's family for the killing. They probed whether large payments were placed into a betting account. But the painstaking analysis led to nothing.

Police got an unsigned statement from the Watcher about Dale and Williams after Williams's death. The Watcher said that Williams's first statement was true. The second and third statements were 'bullshit'.

He claimed Williams did not know that the Hodson murders were to occur on 15 May, but Dale was told and 'got busy with his alibi'. 'Dale's got a right to be pissed off. He's guilty but not the way Carl is saying,' the Watcher said.

The Watcher later disavowed his unsigned statement.

Williams, in his first police statement in 2007, spoke of Dale's purported plot to kill Hodson: 'He said it had to be done before his committal [a court hearing that precedes the trial itself]. I knew why because if the evidence goes in at committal it can still be used if the witness is dead at the trial.'

Williams and Hodson were both killed just before either could give committal evidence in cases against the same allegedly dirty cop.

It might be a coincidence. We can't say for certain, because Victoria Police — according to some of their own detectives — prematurely ended their investigations of the murders of both Terry Hodson and the Gangland king who said he organised Hodson's killing.

In shutting down Petra and Driver, police would no longer examine the role or otherwise of Gobbo in both killings.

* * *

The legal suppression of Gobbo's identity in the Dale murder case was lifted on 11 March 2010. The public, not just lawyers and underworld players, now knew that she had worn a wire. The same day, Gobbo went back to hospital. She was operated on to remove cancerous cells, in what she called 'radical vulva surgery'.

Gobbo was offered accommodation outside Melbourne with specialised protection, on the same day Williams was killed in specialised protection at Barwon Prison.

She rejected the police's offer the next day. She had a fair point: witnesses kept dying in specialised protection.

Nine days later, harnessing all her fear, loathing and distrust, she filed a lawsuit against Victoria Police. She claimed $20 million in compensation.

She spoke of empty promises. 'I was assured by Mr Overland that I would be compensated and that I would be left no worse off,' Gobbo told the ABC, during an exclusive interview on *Lateline*.

She projected the world-weary calm of a victim who knows the system. She nailed her talking points. 'Having had the courage and strength to become a witness for Victoria Police, I was required to give up my home, my security, my sense of life as I knew it,' she said.

Going to the media was a classic scorpion sting. It was also perilous, for she was telling only part of her story. Gobbo wanted the world to know that she did not feel safe. Yet it was what was implied, but not spelled out, that counted in her 41-page writ of claims: that she would use the secret of her informing against her own clients if Victoria Police did not give her what she wanted.

Six months earlier, she had tried to make $20 million a condition for giving evidence against Dale. Tallied up, she now said, that figure represented the cost of losing her career, her reputation and possibly her life.

A text Gobbo sent to a friend around this time warrants inclusion here. In it, her rage was stripped of any courtroom civility. She felt used up and spat out.

'I'm looking forward to cross-examining Simon [Overland] and his band of dishonest, perjuring clowns. They've picked the wrong person to fuck over, that much I promise.'

In August 2010, Gobbo was paid $2.88 million by Victoria Police in a confidential settlement signed off by the State's Police Minister, Bob Cameron. Petra detectives, against whom the writ was ostensibly launched, were perplexed by the speed and the size of the settlement. Detective Sergeant Sol Solomon would say the writ was 'unfounded and easily defendable'.

It stated that Gobbo could not be called as a witness against Paul Dale. The problem, however, was that Petra investigators had recently re-evaluated her involvement in events before the Hodson murders.

They suspected she had helped leak the Blue File, detailing Terry Hodson's informing, to the underworld in early 2004.

After the writ was settled, Overland issued a form for Petra investigators to sign, saying they were not to question Gobbo about the Hodson killings.

Solomon and Davey were among the detectives who refused to put their names to the form. They wanted Gobbo to be compelled to appear in a coercive hearing at the Australian Crime Commission.

Two days later, despite the significant breakthroughs it had made, Petra was shut down. The Hodson investigation was inherited by Task Force Driver, but Driver too would be dissolved before it uncovered any answers about the Hodson riddle. Instead, authorities would pursue other avenues for prosecuting its prime suspect, Paul Dale.

Solomon and Davey firmly believe their murder investigation was nobbled by their superiors because of the Gobbo secret. 'I have no doubt that the powers above did not like where we were proposing [to] take our investigation in relation to 3838 and our resistance to their instruction to cease all contact with her,' Solomon would write in 2019. He'd never felt more demoralised in his entire career.

Davey handed in his badge soon afterwards.

Solomon maintains he and Davey were never made aware of Gobbo's informing, even though her unusual status greatly impeded Petra's investigation. His professional zeal was rightly unfettered by the concerns of many of his Victoria Police superiors. His enthusiasm for solving the crime, rather than internal politics, probably explains why he was forcibly removed from the case.

As he put it, the 'interference' from police command was 'breathtaking'.

'It was not a fitting end to arguably one of the most significant murder investigations in the history of Victoria Police,' he later said.

* * *

Roberta Williams believes her family has been denied the truth about her ex-husband's death. In private, she is more measured than her public

216

excesses, which include street brawls and walking out of TV interviews. The screeching voice and woe-is-me styling are offset by her throaty laugh.

She has lost her home to the taxman and she embraces vulnerability in explaining her financial woes and her fears for the future. Her new partner shepherds her past her flashpoints and plays the role of comforter and diplomat.

Daughter Dhakota, a Gucci bag under her arm and her face fixed to her phone screen, has a gentler way than her mother. 'Mum doesn't have the patience,' she tells Dowsley and Carlyon over lunch in 2019 about her driving lessons.

Roberta Williams has been stamping her feet for a decade now. She wants an inquest. She wants to know: who *really* killed Carl?

* * *

The circus rituals die slowly.

The circling chopper, the bands of photographers, the arriving mourners, some sucking on a final ciggie before the service. These were the staples of Melbourne Gangland funerals.

As expected, Carl Williams's send-off radiated gangster chic, and starred sets of legs that rose to armpits, absurdly high heels, mini-skirts and designer handbags. If the turnout tapped wider trends, streaked hair was in.

The blokes, too, wore black. Those without hair plonked fat sunglasses on their domes. Goatees and rat's tails were dipped in peroxide. Where hair grew, hair product oozed.

There were the usual garish touches demanded of such events. A gold coffin masqueraded as a very big bullet, and the extended Williams family arrived at the Essendon church in a black Hummer with tinted windows and silver trimmings.

Naturally, there were security fears. A 'bouncer' stood guard over a news crew filming from a front garden across the road. Another private guard had apparently embedded a baton up his sleeve, just in case.

It felt colder inside St Therese's Church than it did outside. If you'd blocked out the whir of the chopper above, you'd have wondered whether you'd turned up at the right place. This was a 'private' service. Just friends, family and — in keeping with the rituals — members of the media who snuck in, including Carlyon and Dowsley and three other journalists from the *Herald Sun*.

But something was missing. Where was the requisite menace?

No children of the dead gave the finger to the media, as at Jason Moran's funeral in 2003. No henchmen clutched blondes who weren't their nieces, as at Alphonse Gangitano's send-off in 1998.

The man being commemorated wasn't like the media portrayal of him, said Father Bill Attard. He was a 'lost sheep'. Like all of us, Williams was part leper, part wolf, and he deserved to be prayed for.

Ex-wife Roberta spoke of 'Carlos' and his teasing quality, as did their daughter Dhakota. The nine-year-old recalled how her dad reworked song lyrics to stir her mum. Her older sister, Danielle, recounted how Williams, her stepfather, once gave her $500 for a lost tooth when he was drunk.

Hell, Williams didn't sound like such a bad bloke.

No underworld warlords dotted the pews to denote his grandness in criminal circles. For a moment, amid Roberta's breathlessness and Dhakota's lyricism, it could be forgotten that there was a simple explanation for this. The warlords were almost all gone — many because Williams killed them.

The slightest hint of Williams's notoriety could be observed in his service booklet, which depicted Melbourne's city skyline at night. This was *his* town. He once called himself 'the Premier' because he felt he ran the State.

A message from his father George was read out to the congregation.

It doubled as an unofficial postscript to the Gangland War. It really *was* over. Williams's shooting in a nothing park in 1999 started it; now his murder had ended it.

'No regrets,' the message went. 'What's done is done.'

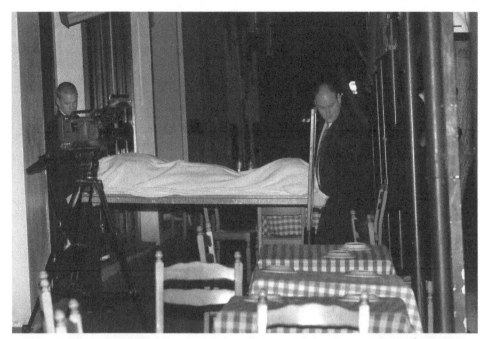

With bodies mounting in the streets, Victoria Police needed to stem the Gangland War. Here police remove the body of Carl Williams's hitman, Andrew Veniamin, who was gunned down at a pizza restaurant in Carlton in 2004. (Brett Hartwig/Newspix)

The grisly scene of Jason Moran's and Pasquale Barbaro's murders, with Barbaro still slumped in the passenger seat, at a junior football clinic in 2003. (Alex Coppel/Newspix)

Nicola Gobbo became known as 'the Bail Queen' for her talent of getting Gangland suspects freed before their cases were heard. Here she is with Tony Mokbel outside the Melbourne Magistrates' Court on 15 November 2004. (Jessica Lee/Newspix)

Gobbo and another of her Gangland clients, Calabrian mafioso Pasquale Barbaro, leave the Supreme Court of Victoria after a bail appeal hearing on 27 January 2009. (Michael Potter/Newspix)

Like Gobbo, lawyer Zarah Garde-Wilson boasted some of Gangland's most notorious names as clients. Garde-Wilson had long suspected Gobbo of wrongdoing. The pair were frenemies, like repelling magnets tossed into a jar. (Stuart McEvoy/Newspix)

The double murder of police informer Terry Hodson and his wife Christine in 2004 ought to have collapsed Gobbo's precarious house of cards.

Left: Terry and Christine's son, Andrew, clutches a photo of his parents. (Craig Borrow/Newspix)

Below: Their daughters, Mandy Hodson and Nicola Komiazyk, leave the Melbourne Coroners Court on 15 August 2014, after the final day of the inquiry into their parents' murders, which have never been solved. (AAP/David Crosling)

Former Victoria Police detective Paul Dale leaves the Melbourne Magistrates' Court on 4 June 2010, after the charge against him for the murder of Terry Hodson was officially withdrawn. Dale was never convicted of any crimes and maintains his innocence to this day. (AAP/Julian Smith)

Mokbel, sans wig, is escorted by Greek police officers after appearing at Greece's Supreme Court on 9 October 2007. He was captured in Athens after a fifteen-month manhunt. (AAP/Thanassis Stavrakis)

A Customs agent unpacks a tomato tin containing thousands of ecstasy pills in 2007. The 'Tomato Tins' drug haul, which was discovered because of Gobbo's secret assistance to police, was at the time the world's largest ecstasy bust. (Australian Customs Service via AAP)

CCTV footage shows prisoner Matthew Johnson (at rear) moments before striking and killing Carl Williams (sitting at the table reading the *Herald Sun*) with a metal pipe in Barwon Prison in April 2010. Ghastly images of the killing would be circulated after Williams's death. (Supreme Court of Victoria via AAP)

After months of investigation, journalist Anthony Dowsley reveals the first details about Nicola Gobbo, referred to as 'Lawyer X', on 31 March 2014. Years of legal battles with Victoria Police ensued, until the *Herald Sun* was finally able to tell the truth about 'one of the biggest scandals in Victoria's legal history' in December 2018. Gobbo herself told Dowsley he would 'win a Walkley' for the story. (News Ltd/Newspix)

Dowsley speaks to the media, while *Herald Sun* editor Damon Johnston looks on, at a press conference on 1 March 2019. The identity of Lawyer X was to be revealed later that day. (AAP/Erik Anderson)

Gobbo learned to use media coverage to her advantage early in her career. In 2010, days after Carl Williams was killed, she spoke to the ABC of living in fear as she launched a compensation claim against Victoria Police. She later gave an interview to the ABC's *7.30*, which aired on 9 December 2019, even though she claimed at the time that she was too unwell to testify at a royal commission. (ABC News via AAP)

Dowsley and Carlyon's revelations about Gobbo triggered the Royal Commission into the Management of Police Informants, which was established on 13 December 2018 to scrutinise Victoria Police's handling of police informers. Commissioner Margaret McMurdo presides over the hearings, while Chris Winneke QC acts as Counsel Assisting the Commission. (Royal Commission into the Management of Police Informants via AAP)

The royal commission hears evidence from (clockwise from top left) former Victoria Police chief commissioner Simon Overland (AAP/James Ross), Victoria Police Chief Commissioner Graham Ashton (AAP/James Ross), former Purana detective Stuart Bateson (AAP/David Crosling) and former Victoria Police deputy commissioner Sir Ken Jones (AAP/David Crosling).

One of *Herald Sun* cartoonist Mark Knight's takes on the Lawyer X scandal. (Mark Knight)

16

Tomorrow, When the War Began

Victoria Police Human Source 3838:
A Case Review
2010-2012

On Valentine's Day in 2011, Gobbo lost her mother to pancreatic cancer. Everyone liked Mary Gobbo. She was down-to-earth and friendly. No airs. Gobbo regularly had dinner with her mother on Saturday nights.

As teenagers, the Gobbo sisters had also lost their father to cancer after a long struggle. On anniversaries, even decades later, Gobbo told her police handlers that she was so despondent she couldn't speak.

Gobbo's lifeline through the currents of uncertainty was her sister Catherine, also a lawyer unafraid of saying what she thought. She had been by her sister's bedside when Nicola went to hospital, again, in the new year of 2010. Gobbo was so anxious that Detective Sergeant Sol Solomon feared for her future.

Catherine was again by her side the morning after their mother's death. There was a knock at Gobbo's door. Detective Senior Sergeant Boris Buick, unaware of the family's grief, had arrived to tell Gobbo that Paul Dale had been charged with lying to the Australian Crime Commission. Gobbo was to be called as a prosecution witness.

Buick, a former Purana detective who had arrested Faruk Orman for murder, had known since 2006 that Gobbo was a police informer. He later spoke of the 'awful timing' of this home visit. He might have returned at an easier moment. But time was pressing.

Gobbo had just cause to be stunned by the intrusion. Police were no longer supposed to contact her.

In conversations over the next twenty-four hours, Gobbo's sister pointed out to Buick that Gobbo could not be called as a courtroom witness under the terms of her confidential settlement with Victoria Police six months earlier. Buick told Gobbo that the Commonwealth Director of Prosecutions, who had charged Dale, did not feel bound by the agreement.

The day after her mother died, when she might have been receiving sympathetic calls and arranging a funeral, Gobbo was being squeezed again by Victoria Police. As Buick later recounted, he told her that the Dale matter 'hasn't gone away for her'. And it didn't matter that police had paid her almost $3 million to go away.

* * *

Some time later, Gobbo ran into her first legal boss, Levi Diamond, who was representing John Higgs, the co-accused of her client Rob Karam in the Tomato Tins importation case. Diamond offered her casual employment, obviously unaware that she had tried to jail him thirteen years earlier.

Diamond thought she seemed miserable, not at all like the young woman he had hired in 1997. He wondered about her advice to his clients that contradicted his own: he felt he was being undermined. She went behind Diamond's back; he wonders now, without evidence, if she was still acting as an agent of police at this time.

Gobbo's wider family had abandoned Nicola long ago, but the family unit, including half-sister Linda, tried to stay close. Catherine and Nicola fell out at some point; perhaps the stress got too much for the younger sister, whose own (commercial) law work presumably suffered due to the Gobbo stigma.

Nicola would say in courtroom evidence in 2017 that she told Catherine at a 'later stage' about aspects of her informing, probably before 2014. She would say in 2020: 'And I prefer if it is possible I don't say much about her because I've caused enough damage to her.'

As Diamond says of Catherine Gobbo, 'Nicola cursed us both. Catherine by birth and me as her boss.'

* * *

In mid-2011, a few months after her mother's death, Gobbo's secret history came perilously close to being exposed in open court. Steve Cvetanovski was facing a June 2011 trial for drug offences related to Gobbo's 2006 sting that uncovered a Mokbel drug lab.

Early in 2006, he had secured a meth lab site in Strathmore. Gobbo passed information about the lab to police, her first salvo against the Mokbel empire. Five years later, the star witness against Cvetanovski was in the witness box at his trial.

Cvetanovski and the witness were once mates. They'd shared an interest in strippers and in gambling. Cvetanovski once lost $400,000 in a betting splurge at Jupiter's Casino on the Gold Coast: the price of money laundering.

Cvetanovski's barrister, Michael Pena-Rees, was a thrusting personality with an ear for the absurd. He sought to sow doubt in the courtroom. Drawing on every available avenue, he trod the fraught line of impugning the reputation of a fellow barrister.

In attempting to discredit the star witness, Pena-Rees probed the man's perceived intimacy with Gobbo. He asked why Gobbo had been spotted with him on police surveillance tapes in the weeks before the drug-lab sting.

'Can I ask you now: when was it that you purchased a diamond ring for [Gobbo]?' he probed. 'Do you disagree that you've mentioned to many people, many of your friends that you purchased a $35,000 diamond engagement ring for [Gobbo]?'

The witness described the suggestion as 'rubbish'.

Pena-Rees declared that Gobbo's involvement in the case 'stinks'. Justice Jim Montgomery didn't go as far, though he did say that Gobbo appeared to be 'redefining conflict of interest'.

'Apart from the fact that she's a barrister and she seems to be, on the evidence of this trial, one of dubious ethical standards in relation to conflict of interest, she seems to be acting for everyone,' he said. 'Someone keeps telling me she's back in practice, I can't understand how.'

There was open-court discussion about putting Gobbo in the witness box. The case prosecutor was John Champion SC, soon to become Victorian Director of Public Prosecutions.

Champion told the court he would inquire about claims that Gobbo had 'conspired to concoct statements — false statements, with the concurrence of the members of the Purana Task Force'.

The suggestion didn't lead anywhere. If it had, Gobbo's secret might have emerged long before it did.

Champion, nevertheless, would be a key player in the Gobbo revelations over the years ahead.

In a 2015 letter, Cvetanovski claimed that the star witness had been improperly coached through contradictory claims in making statements against him. Cvetanovski felt he was the victim of an unethical conspiracy.

He was right.

* * *

Soon Gobbo would lose the most ardent keeper of her secret. On 16 June 2011, Simon Overland resigned after he was shown to have signed off on misleading crime statistics before the 2010 Victorian State election.

'I've always sought to act in the best interests of the organisation in an honourable way and I believe this is the appropriate thing to do,' he said.

Overland's announcement was not unexpected. Overland kept secrets, that much is obvious, though his biggest would remain hidden for a few more years.

Overland's deputy, Sir Ken Jones, had resigned the previous month. Overland exacerbated his long-festering feud with Sir Ken by ordering him to leave before he could serve out his notice.

Sir Ken had a formidable resumé built over years of policing in Britain and elsewhere. He was no yes-man. He had queried Overland's use of crime statistics, the directions applied to Petra investigators and the 2010 payout to Gobbo. Sir Ken was mistrustful of Overland's penchant for phone taps, and he wondered at their legality. In 2019 he said he made discreet inquiries about the use of Gobbo as an informer.

Sir Ken was popular; Overland was not. Overland's style of leadership had galvanised powerful enemies against him. He'd reached the top job because he'd supervised the jailing of Gangland figures, but he soon faced calls for a royal commission into his politics-over-policing style — from his former deputy, Sir Ken.

Instead, Overland would confront a royal commission into the bigger secret of Nicola Gobbo.

* * *

The case against Paul Dale for murdering Terry Hodson had been dismissed soon after Williams's death. But Victoria Police still wanted to nail Dale. This was why Buick had turned up at Gobbo's door. In charging Dale for lying under oath to the Australian Crime Commission, police relied on Dale's recorded café chat with Gobbo in 2008 as a key piece of evidence.

In response, Dale's lawyers once again sought documents relating to Gobbo. Once again, Victoria Police opted to impede the pursuit of justice by making the Gobbo secret the higher priority. They dragged Commonwealth prosecutors into the hidden conspiracy of Gobbo.

Behind the scenes, harried negotiations swirled between Victoria Police and prosecutors. In November 2011, Victoria Police sent their new Assistant Commissioner to plead the need for Gobbo's removal. Graham Ashton, of course, had been actively involved in the Gobbo conundrum for years, through his role at the Office of Police Integrity.

He was ostensibly concerned about the risks to Gobbo's safety if her informer past were teased out in the witness box.

Police boasted a transparent 'excuse' for Gobbo's removal from the trial: she was once again being threatened. A 'sympathy card' had been sent to her lawyer: 'Tell your client she is dead. Dogs die dead'. Police never traced the source of the menacing. It was of a kind that usually does not excuse a witness from giving evidence, yet it elevated Gobbo to the highest risk category.

At a meeting, the prosecutors rejected Ashton's argument for removing Gobbo. According to one source, Ashton then revealed Gobbo's informer status.

Victoria Police got their way. The ACC did not alert Dale's legal team to Gobbo's history of informing. Instead, they yielded and removed Gobbo from the case. At a preliminary hearing, a prosecutor told the court Gobbo would not be taking the stand.

It was odd that Victoria Police thought Gobbo could give evidence in the first place. It's unclear how she was meant to testify against Dale while avoiding questions of credibility. Was she supposed to lie under oath?

* * *

Off camera, the subpoena from Dale's lawyers had caused ructions within Victoria Police. If the request had been successful, documents exposing Gobbo's informing would have been introduced in open court.

Victoria Police hired barrister Gerard Maguire, who had appeared for the force in many cases over many years, to appraise the situation. In October 2011, he recommended a police review of all cases involving Nicola Gobbo. If some of Gangland's biggest thugs realised that Gobbo had snitched on them, he argued, they would start queueing up to claim that their convictions should be overturned.

His notion is hardly startling now, given the scandalised descriptions of Gobbo's informing that fill media waves. Nor should it have been that surprising within Victoria Police in 2011, given the brave voices within the force who had already questioned Gobbo's use.

Senior command, including Graham Ashton, met to discuss the issues. Victoria Police resolved to hire a former police chief commissioner, Neil Comrie, to produce a report. *Victoria Police Human Source 3838: A Case Review* was finalised in June 2012.

To this day, Comrie's findings are disputed by those who participated in the Gobbo subterfuge. Yet his analysis is a sensible starting point for understanding how the secret abuse of power flourishes when public officials set aside the rules.

* * *

Comrie is gifted with a plain style of writing foreign to most legal documents. His message was unambiguous, a portent of similar conclusions later reached by others. Comrie's message about police use of Gobbo was this: wrong, wrong and wrong.

Comrie quoted Superintendent Tony Biggin, who supervised the force's covert operations at the time, as saying that '3838 created an opportunity for Victoria Police that has never before been encountered, and in all probability will never be encountered again'.

Comrie described Gobbo as 'a complex, manipulative and conniving person', and spoke of her as 'somewhat bizarrely expressing desires to be the best human source to have ever assisted Victoria Police'.

He noted that she was initially motivated by her desire to eject the Mokbels from *her* life. Her unethical choices were driven not by community spirit but by displeasure at *her* personal circumstances. Upturning the justice system was, ultimately, about her.

The police, meanwhile, were ill prepared for an 'abundantly self-confident' source, 'possessing a very strong and forceful personality'.

Petra detectives, in particular, had had significant problems in managing her. 'This served to further empower 3838, who was now even more savvy and battle-hardened in making demands of Victoria Police.'

Comrie concluded that the Source Development Unit (SDU) records were incomplete and disjointed. Monthly assessments at management meetings were like cut-and-paste exercises in note-taking.

He compiled a step-by-step guide in due diligence. From day one, it should have been established that Gobbo must not provide privileged information to police investigators. Gobbo was 'somewhat misguided' in her grasp of the legal and ethical concerns, Comrie said. He queried whether Gobbo was informing to police to make money. If she was, it was 'inappropriate' for her to represent clients she had previously informed on.

Comrie noted that legal concerns were raised by SDU members in 2008 with Overland, then a deputy commissioner. Comrie discovered no records showing any further consideration of the legalities. He presented the SDU with a prospective get-out-of-jail card: given the lack of oversight and documentation, they were free to assume that senior management condoned their use of Gobbo.

Loss of public or judicial confidence in the use of informers would undermine the future effectiveness of the informer program, Comrie wrote. Conduct that sapped such confidence but was kept hidden from view could not be tolerated.

It was 'inappropriate for police to actively seek information from a human source when police are aware that this is being provided contrary to the human source's professional obligations'. The use of protected information, bar unusual circumstances, 'amounts to a conspiracy which undermines the justice system'.

'Entries contained in the 3838 [information reports], taken at face value, indicate that on many occasions 3838, in providing information to police handlers about 3838's clients, has disregarded legal professional privilege,' Comrie wrote. 'It is open to interpret that such conduct may have potentially interfered with the right of a fair trial for those concerned.'

There it was, in black and white, in June 2012: almost six and a half years before any of Gobbo's former clients would be notified of her deception.

* * *

What did Victoria Police do with the Comrie review?

Let's assume that senior command considered the convictions that might be tainted. And the individuals — perhaps dozens — doing lengthy jail terms as a result.

Let's assume that police brass considered the question of criminal conduct by some serving Victoria Police officers.

What did Victoria Police do?

They told the Director of Public Prosecutions, John Champion, about Gobbo, but they did not provide him with the relevant documentation.

Then they invoked the supreme protocol of all creaking bureaucracies. They ordered another review.

Operation Loricated had one job. It sounded simple, this secret police review prompted by a secret police review: compile all the police materials relating to Gobbo into a single file.

But it wasn't simple. The Victoria Police records were shambolic. It took eighteen months to decipher them.

Meanwhile, Tony Mokbel was sentenced for a string of drug-trafficking offences a month after Comrie's review was submitted, unaware that Victoria Police already knew his convictions might be tainted. Police had ample time to alert the courts to this potential miscarriage of justice. They did nothing.

Victoria Police knew that they had seriously erred, and that some of their officers might have committed crimes, years before Anthony Dowsley told the world about it.

And they've tried to hide it ever since.

17

The Case That Wouldn't Die

The Hodson Murders Revisited
2012-2015

Paul Dale's trial for allegedly lying to the Australian Crime Commission began in Melbourne's Supreme Court in March 2013. After Gobbo's withdrawal as a trial witness, many of the twenty-three charges against Dale were dropped.

Dale's barrister, Geoffrey Steward, branded Gobbo the 'baroness of treachery' during the trial. Steward had no idea that she was a registered police informer, yet he rightly described her as 'an excuse for a lawyer'.

The trial testimony was telling for other reasons. It revealed fresh insights into old Gangland goings-on.

The European — the supergrass helped by his once-lawyer Gobbo to roll on Carl Williams, Faruk Orman and others — gave evidence that Dale was 'working for us' before 2004. He said Dale's information to Williams was always 'on the money'.

In a 2009 statement tendered at the trial, George Williams described many meetings between his son and Dale. Usually, Gobbo received a call from Dale asking Carl to call him, George said. Williams senior found it 'a bit strange' that Gobbo 'seemed to be going out of her way' to assist Dale's desire to meet his son.

Despite these sensational allegations, a jury found Dale not guilty of all charges on 28 March. On hearing the verdict, Gobbo was said to 'scream down the place' with disappointment.

Dale was free, but puzzled. As he wrote in his 2013 autobiography: 'To this day, I don't understand why Nicola Gobbo crossed to the side of the prosecution rather than the defence. I can only wonder if the police had something on her to make her do it.'

Losing the trial galled police investigators. Like the aborted murder trial, internal feuding had blighted this prosecution of Dale. The quest to convict him was again sacrificed to the need to preserve the Gobbo secret.

But there were consequences beyond the bubbles of police intrigue. Legal observers had wondered about the decision to grant Gobbo leave from testifying after a threat. Among them was high-profile solicitor Rob Stary, a friend of Dowsley.

The irony is that the pursuit of Dale, through Gobbo's illicit recording, would condemn her and Victoria Police to a decade or more of examinations into their own possibly criminal conduct.

* * *

The Hodson children have never grieved properly. They are still locked in limbo. Nikki Komiazyk's handwritten pleas to various authorities for answers, dozens of them over the years, fill folders with lines of confusion and loss.

Nikki and her sister Mandy Hodson are easy to like. Both cry readily, but mask their brittleness with humour. Their mother 'went out with a bang', Mandy told a stranger over a cigarette in 2019. She cannot erase the memory of her mother's face, frozen in a permanent scowl as her body lay in the open casket.

This was why Mandy, and Nikki, agreed to meet Nicola Gobbo in a Southbank café in Melbourne's arts district in 2011 or 2012.

Komiazyk welcomed any interest in her parents. Everyone else had moved on, as if the mystery had dimmed. But Komiazyk still thought of her parents in the moments before she fell asleep each night, 'drinking glasses of champagne together'.

Komiazyk knew nothing about Gobbo's secret life. When they met, Komiazyk was struck by the obvious: tall, blonde, assertive.

Gobbo offered the sisters strategies in their quest for a coronial inquiry. Possibly she was motivated by guilt; maybe she thought there was a dollar in it. Or perhaps she couldn't shake her old habit of running towards the flames.

Komiazyk recalls a turn in the chat when Gobbo boasted about driving her black Mercedes. 'She ended up saying that the police aren't allowed to come anywhere near her,' Komiazyk says. 'She said she could run any red light in Victoria and they wouldn't pull her over.'

Gobbo was bragging about the perks of informing to those who had suffered because of her informing. If bystanders couldn't be privy to her powers, Gobbo could at least allude to her hidden influence.

Perhaps Gobbo already knew that police brass would not allow her to give evidence at the Hodsons' coronial inquest, should an inquest be agreed to. Victoria Police's reputation was inextricably wedded to the keeping of her secret.

* * *

The Hodsons' crusade for a coronial inquiry turned into an exercise in dashed hopes. The 2014 hearing only mashed an already tattered web.

A journalist informed the hearing that Roberta Williams had told him her ex-husband fabricated the story that Dale had ordered the hit. The court heard that Tony Mokbel had financed the murders — on behalf of Dale — in part because they shared corrupt information from the days when Dale was stationed at Brunswick Police Station. Dale denies having known Mokbel during the Gangland years.

Andrew Hodson was grilled on whether he had, wittingly or otherwise, explained to the killers how to get into his parents' home.

Here were more speculations, built on little evidence.

The suspected hitman, Rodney Collins, was excused from testifying. So was Nicola Gobbo.

The Victorian Government Solicitor's Office, on behalf of Police Chief Commissioner Ken Lay, wrote to Coroner Ian Gray on 9 April 2014, asking for Gobbo to be excused on safety grounds.

The letter represented the fourth time Gobbo would avoid answering questions about the Hodsons in the witness box. In seeking to protect her, and the force's image, Victoria Police once again stymied the pursuit of truth.

Gray had to follow the facts, and he didn't have enough of them. In his open finding, he neither accepted nor rejected the police argument that Williams, Dale and Collins were behind the hit.

The 'truth' of the Hodson killings had been apportioned, bargained over and solicited so many times that distorted theories had emerged in its place.

Gray *did* find that Williams and Dale met nine days before the Hodson killings: the so-called 'Hillside meeting'. But he could not conclude — given Williams, as the sole source, was 'unreliable' — that they had arranged a murder.

He also found that Terry Hodson should have taken greater precautions to protect himself, despite the Hodson children's submission that Victoria Police failed to protect their parents.

The confidential police submission to the inquiry set out Gobbo's 2004 use of burner phones, her liaising with Mokbel and Williams, and her conflicted status as everybody's lawyer. The revelations, a sliver of the bigger Gobbo saga, would appear in the *Herald Sun* in November 2014, after Dowsley got hold of a copy of the submission.

* * *

The coronial finding only compounded the Hodson children's despair. Some former and some serving police officers share the sentiment that too many aspects of the Hodson killings have been deliberately withheld from the light.

Outside the court, Nikki Komiazyk declared: 'It is my belief that Victorian police and the Victorian Government are avoiding a royal commission at all costs. And I feel sorry for anybody ever coming into witness protection or to become an informer. I'd advise you: don't do it, because your life's not safe.'

The Hodson children accept the prevailing view that Rodney Collins killed their parents. Mandy Hodson speculates that he wore a police uniform to gain entry, as he did to kill Ramon and Dorothy Abbey in 1987.

Sister Nikki encountered Collins, by chance, at a Lilydale supermarket not long after her parents' deaths. Collins knew her partner, Peter. Sporting white track pants and a reptilian leer, Collins applied the standard underworld greeting: 'Are they [the police] leaving you alone?'

Collins's casual evil deserves its own book. He was thought to have killed nine people and was jailed for life for murdering the Abbeys in May 2010. Inside, Collins, like everyone else, had tried to join the queue to swap criminal secrets for money. His price for information on the Hodson killings was $1 million.

Collins offered questions instead of insights. He sought to manipulate investigator Sol Solomon, and no deal was made.

Was he making mischief when he appeared to suggest that more than one person went to the Hodsons' home on 15 May 2004? 'But who was the person that was behind that known or trusted person, that followed him in?' he said.

Komiazyk blanches at the memory of meeting Collins. But her enmity towards Gobbo lies deeper.

The family wants Gobbo charged with crimes over their parents' deaths. Their open anger towards her is matched only by that of Roberta Williams.

'She's the master puppeteer,' Komiazyk says. 'She's dangerous. She's a very dangerous woman.

'She seems to have her finger in every little thing. And no accountability.'

Despite a royal commission, Gobbo has never been properly questioned about her improper proximity to the Hodson deaths. When Petra detectives wanted to treat her as a suspect, they were informed by police command that they could not; indeed, the unit was shut down shortly afterwards.

'I'll haunt them,' Chrissy Hodson said in defiance just before she was killed. And she did. Chrissy Hodson haunts everyone who cares for justice, including investigators and journalists.

She haunts Nicola Gobbo too. The Hodson murder mystery clings to her like a dag on a sheep.

* * *

Paul Dale declined to give evidence at the Hodsons' coronial inquest. He had previously hit problems in the witness box, though not always for criminal reasons. His family suffered from his admissions of infidelity in court, he says, and he cringes each time he reads about his sexual liaison with Gobbo in the press.

When Dale was charged with the Hodson murders in 2009, he spent eight months in solitary confinement in the Acacia Unit of Barwon Prison, alongside the hardened criminals he once tried to put in jail.

Dale says his time in solitary changed him. He developed a mental disorder. The 'atrocious behaviour of Victoria Police' is why he will be 'forever medicated'.

His bull-necked pugnacity did not appear to suffer, though. Since he acquired the 'accused former detective' honorific in the mid-2000s, he has strived to recast his reputation. He has quietly reached out to selected journalists to shape their coverage. More recently, in 2019, he has submitted to cross-examination by barristers seeking to trip him up.

They don't intimidate him. There is something compelling about Dale's insistence on being heard, and he has now published two books to tell his side of the story.

If he feels drained by the process, Dale still wears that country-boy pride of a family that has always thrown itself into town events. His mum, Jenny, was there for the indignities, the shackles and the red jumpsuits. She was her son's loudest cheerleader.

Dale is a tricky study: chatty, open to scrutiny to a point, and strident about the pain of his wife and children. His sense of having been robbed is genuine.

His vehemence invites a middle line, where he might have made poor choices but did not commit murder. Holes litter any prosecution of Dale, but holes also dot his defence.

Dale acts like another casualty of a jangled time when rules were broken and suspicions masqueraded as facts. He points to his main accusers, Terry Hodson and Carl Williams, and rightly raises questions about their credibility. Those questions will never be answered now, because both were murdered.

According to Dale's version, a conspiracy of police, criminals and Nicola Gobbo set out to frame a hapless victim.

Yet he isn't as hateful of Gobbo as you might expect. He feels sorry for her, because it's clear she was coerced by police. 'I wouldn't have gone near her with a fuckin' ten-foot pole,' he says, if he'd known she was a police informer. But he says it lightly, as if looking for a laugh.

He wonders at the why. Why did she help police, and why did she breach their friendship when she had so few left?

Journalists still come to his home, whose rounded driveway and manicured lawns used to raise questions because of its size and splendour. He sometimes talks to them. The message has never deviated: I am innocent.

He has not been convicted. But, as Dale lamented in his 2020 book *Cops, Drugs, Lawyer X and Me*, the legacy of his 'trial by media' has meant that 'most of the public think I'm guilty of something'.

* * *

Long before Paul Dale raged about the injustices perpetrated against him in his 2013 book *Disgraced?*, Nicola Gobbo had been trying to rebuild. Because she still refused police protection, Victoria Police could not keep her safe. She would not move elsewhere, because she trusted only her own doctors for her medical and emotional needs.

Police Deputy Commissioner Kieran Walshe was still urging her to go into hiding in January 2012. He judged her risk level to be 'extreme' and resorted to sending her an eight-page manual of 'personal security advice'.

New personal frontiers blended with old professional haunts. Gobbo's career was hurtling into reverse. She was back working with Levi Diamond where she began, alongside colleagues who remembered her as a twenty-something-year-old with a fag hanging out of her mouth.

Here's the weird thing: Gobbo was still trying to become Victoria Police's all-time greatest informer, even after they'd officially dropped her.

She generated hundreds of information reports after she was deregistered in 2009, many times more than some of the most prolific informers in Victorian history.

Police had tried to pension her off, and Overland had issued an instruction in August 2010 that Victoria Police stop receiving intelligence from her.

But Gobbo didn't go away. She kept presenting herself to offer new criminal insights. And Victoria Police kept listening to her.

We know Gobbo's tip-offs to police produced four, if not more, police information reports in early 2012, three years after she was deregistered, and two years after former chief commissioner Simon Overland ordered his officers to stop.

Who was addicted to whom?

* * *

At the same time, Gobbo was again appearing for Diamond's clients in courtrooms. Then, one day in September 2013, a judge was told that Gobbo couldn't be in court. She was delighted, radiant and a bit tired, the story went.

The County Court hears excuses every day. For once, here was a no-show that everyone could celebrate.

Nicola Gobbo was absent from court because she had just given birth to a baby girl.

Gobbo had always liked kids. She appeared to spoil her goddaughters; she learned a lot by babysitting the children of the Chemical Brothers.

In 2008, a close friend had gone through IVF treatment. Gobbo followed her friend's example. She had begun IVF treatment soon after being successfully treated for 'snatch cancer' (as she called it) in 2010.

Motherhood probably seemed like a natural step, even if her choice of partners often let her down.

The fairytale scripting was true enough — as far as it went. Gobbo had recovered and fallen pregnant; now she was bonding with her baby daughter and could not represent her client at a preliminary hearing for his upcoming trial on drugs charges. The client, Richard Barkho, went to prison for methamphetamine trafficking.

Here's where the fairytale took an odd turn. Normally, the lawyer–client relationship eases in the wake of courtroom machinations. Instead, Gobbo began visiting Barkho in jail.

Gobbo later had another child, a boy. She told people one or both of her children were fathered by a gay flight attendant. Others were informed she'd chosen her daughter's father through a sperm bank 'pick-a-face'.

Yet a lawyer who sighted Gobbo during visits to Barkho at a maximum-security prison heard her tell her daughter: 'Say goodbye to Daddy.'

The prosecution team in Barkho's case didn't know about Gobbo's relationship with him. Nor did the judge, Richard Maidment QC, who later stepped down from the bench and headed Tony Mokbel's legal fight against convictions that might have been tarnished by Gobbo.

'She told me it was a random selection process, picking faces to vet the donor,' says a man who declined to be the godfather of Gobbo's daughter. 'She was not telling me about Barkho.'

The flight-attendant and pick-a-face stories seemed to be motivated by a desire to protect Barkho from jailhouse reprisals for Gobbo's informing. They didn't work: in October 2015, Barkho was slashed across the face, requiring thirty-three stitches.

* * *

By then, the existence of 'Lawyer X' was a published fact. But her identity was still under wraps.

Gobbo had long feared the courts and the criminals would stumble onto her secrets. But soon her secrets would be out — and the entire world would hear them.

Part 2

From Rumours to a
Royal Commission

The Truth Comes Out
2013-2020

18

Truth or Dare

The 'Lawyer X' Story Breaks
2013-2014

Anthony Dowsley's search for the truth begins with a question of sex. Did a high-ranking police officer once have an affair with a barrister who represented some of the biggest criminals during Melbourne's Gangland War? Did they have a love child?

Dowsley much prefers investigating murders and mysteries. His usual job is to expose secrets, evil acts and the abuses of power — known in journalism as 'hard news'.

He once tracked down a notorious paedophile to a cottage near Melbourne's Flemington racecourse in 2005. It triggered the man's removal from the suburbs. Victoria's worst paedophiles released from prison were subsequently grouped, with provisional liberty, within the grounds of Ararat Prison.

Dowsley's 2006 anniversary story about a cold-case murder victim, Elisabeth Membrey, fed fresh police inquiries and murder charges after the case had stagnated since 1994.

Crime reporters like Dowsley trawl the sumps of depravity, which is why many veterans don't trust much in human nature. As one of them cynically put it once, their role is to 'harvest grief'.

Dowsley has been a crime reporter for a decade, but he isn't as jaded as some. He is obsessive, as the successful ones must be, and dogged about getting at the truth. But he is always glad to set aside the bandits and monsters to discuss Midnight Oil or the Western Bulldogs AFL club.

He is ambivalent about the Gobbo love-child claims. Salacious gossip gushes out of Victoria Police headquarters like the run-off from an abattoir. This Gobbo rumour, initially involving former assistant commissioner Jeff Pope, commands the usual sniggering from police when it's recounted to Dowsley in the pub.

Yet it is not the claim itself, but what it hints of, that makes it the unlikely starting point for Dowsley's uncovering of the biggest legal scandal in modern Australia.

* * *

Ironically, the rumour was unwittingly started two years earlier by Nicola Gobbo herself.

She has always blamed police leaks for the exposure of her informing. But who knows how it would have been revealed if Gobbo, in seeking to sting a man from her past, had not stung herself as well?

In October 2011, she gave a confidential police interview to Task Force Driver detectives investigating the death of Carl Williams, including Detective Senior Sergeant Boris Buick. It's unclear whether she was asked for or volunteered the information.

Call it boastfulness or revenge. Gobbo casually lobbed a grenade at a senior police officer who had rejected her as both an informer and (he says) a potential partner way back in 2000.

Assistant Commissioner Jeff Pope, in his second stint at Victoria Police, sat on the Task Force Driver steering committee responsible for the executive oversight of the investigation. He'd also been on the steering committee of Petra before that task force was disbanded in August 2010.

'I'll tell you something … just a skerrick of information that you'll laugh at,' Gobbo told the detectives. 'Do you know who the assistant commissioner was, who I only found out after the event, who was overseeing my handling when I was being looked after by Petra? Was Jeff Pope for a while, wasn't it?'

When Buick said yes, she went on: 'Would you think it was appropriate if I had a sexual relationship with you that you looked after that committee? How's that for [inaudible] for you? Have a look at Boris'[s] face. I wish I [could] take a photo of that.'

She explained that 'somebody told me that Jeff Pope was Assistant Commissioner in charge [of] the steering committee … and I thought, Jeff Pope, that sounds familiar, Jeff Pope, where do I know that name from? Then I saw him on TV and I went … I said to my sister … oh my god!'

'I just think it is hilarious,' she commented. 'Isn't that inappropriate? Can you imagine the complaint I could make about that? I bet you he hasn't declared it?'

The fallout was almost immediate. Pope stepped down from the Driver Task Force steering committee pending an investigation, never to return to the role. He vehemently denied any improper relationship with Gobbo and even signed an affidavit to make his point.

Yet he was hopelessly mired. There was no scope to prove or disprove Gobbo's claim.

He was condemned in 2013 in the court of rumours and nastiness on the say-so of a professional liar. The man who had wanted to be chief commissioner left abruptly in 2013 — rumour has it, ten minutes after a 'fireside chat' with Deputy Commissioner Graham Ashton.

Some people wanted to believe the gossip, whether it was true or not.

Pope had a neurological disorder that affected his stride, leaving him open to unkind comparisons with the Thunderbirds. He had just been diagnosed with bladder cancer, and now he was lugged with the Gobbo claims.

He had returned to Victoria Police a couple of years earlier, after a stretch with the Federal Police, to head up the Covert Services Division — and discovered that very senior jobs demand very tough decisions. In 2012, he had been asked to conduct a review of the division — including Gobbo's former handlers at the Source Development Unit (SDU). Drawing heavily on former chief commissioner Neil Comrie's report, Pope recommended the closure of the SDU in January 2013.

Pope's review found that Comrie had 'highlighted poor work practices of the SDU' that had 'significant ramifications'. Here was Pope's kicker: 'the structure of the SDU should not be sustained and whilst it continues to exist it will only be a matter of time before the unit unduly exposes a [human source] or [Victoria Police] to significant risk which cannot be mitigated'.

SDU members, to this day, are aghast at the decision to close the unit down, particularly given they were not consulted first. The SDU's head, Sandy White, blames personal animosities for the decision: his immediate boss was a 'bully', and a boss higher up the chain dismissed White as a 'Svengali'.

White believes his superiors were wrong to disband a first-rate human source unit. 'To be told that any document concerning source matters with my name on it is "toxic" is beyond comprehension,' he told a police colleague in 2014. 'This could only be the result of a campaign to destroy my reputation.'

* * *

When detectives feed Dowsley crumbs of gossip at the Palmerston Hotel that Christmas drinks night in 2013, Dowsley glimpses a story *behind* the story: about a defence barrister who is not as she appears.

In 2009, before Gobbo's role as a witness against Dale was made public, Dowsley overheard chatter in a St Kilda pizzeria about her secret cosiness with police. She's worth looking at, he thought at the time.

That night in 2013, he goes home at about 12.30 am and types some notes on his iPhone to remind himself of what he's just heard. Many journalists do this after drinks with contacts; some go into the toilets to leave themselves slurred voicemails, recording details that might otherwise be lost in an alcoholic haze. Dowsley is reciting scuttlebutt, not facts, based on chats with detectives who have had no direct involvement with Gobbo.

He writes:

- *Was she used as a human source to gain intelligence from her clients?*
- *Unit was shut down and its informers discharged.*
- *Pope suddenly moved from the job.*
- *Paid out $2 million to Gobbo.*
- *Major cover-up???*

This riot of rumours is what Dowsley begins exploring the next morning: the curious case of the police, a dodgy defence barrister, and a child of unclear paternity.

* * *

Gobbo is not the only chameleon in this story. Dowsley's knack is shifting gear without giving the appearance of any change at all. His faded T-shirts and unassuming manner provide cover for his astuteness.

He sets out to prove his suspicion that Gobbo is a human source, but he has to be cautious. Linking Gobbo to informing could trigger threats to her life, as well as Victoria Police efforts to kill his story before it is published.

Solicitor Rod Stary echoes Dowsley's suspicions. He contextualises some of the unseen machinations of the Hodson deaths. He tells Dowsley he took over Hodson's case from Gobbo after Hodson was charged in December 2003 — though by April 2004, Gobbo had taken back her client from Stary.

For Stary, her removal as a witness from the ACC trial against Paul Dale has provoked a recurring thought: what does Nicola Gobbo have over Victoria Police?

Dowsley delves into the paperwork of her 2010 civil suit, in which she claimed $20 million. Such an exorbitant price tag just for giving evidence didn't make much sense. Someone tells Dowsley of the tangled backstory behind the Gobbo settlement.

Someone else tells Dowsley the story of the stings that brought down the Mokbel empire from April 2006. It is an incomplete account about a controlled delivery of fake drugs to Milad Mokbel. Gobbo was improperly involved, Dowsley is told, but he learns scant details of her betrayals.

In the new year, Dowsley contacts one or two investigators who know Gobbo well. They are not chatty. If they're not across the breadth of her informer status, they are aware of her constant presence at police functions.

Others say it's odd to see a defence barrister, as opposed to a defence solicitor, in police stations. And Gobbo always seemed to materialise at police stations.

* * *

Dowsley is loaded with speculations, but he needs hard facts. He doesn't know what to believe. The notion of a double-dealing lawyer holds significant risks, primarily to her welfare. When Dowsley hints of it to trusted contacts, he is met with open-mouthed disbelief.

The fullest account of Dowsley's investigation cannot be recounted without breaching ethical imperatives to protect sources. By 2014, hundreds of people know about Gobbo's informing, within both policing and legal circles. Most know no more than snippets of the grander script.

Some of the sources who share secrets with Dowsley are motivated by their disgust at Victoria Police's disregard for the justice system. Gobbo's use conflicts with the notions of fairness upon which they built their careers.

Dowsley keeps collecting the hints, like a sparrow pecking at crumbs, trying to form a fuller picture. Suspicions are an occupational hazard of investigative journalism. It's an obsessive's trade, built on tips and conspiracy theories, often furnished by malcontents who mangle facts for their own ends.

In March 2014, Dowsley meets with one particular source who knows a few things from a long time ago, *when Gobbo first started informing to police.*

Pardon? Has Dowsley heard right? He's hunched in a city coffee shop, his faded black canvas bag at his feet, taking no notes lest the subject take fright and clam up. Is this the confirmation he's been seeking? The damning evidence that has shimmered just out of reach?

This source seems keen to talk. Dowsley asks another question. How did it start?

It was the late 1990s. Gobbo met a certain Drug Squad officer over coffee, the subject replied. (Later evidence will suggest this officer was Senior Sergeant Wayne Strawhorn.) Gobbo's motivation was neither betrayal nor greed, he says. She came eager to help. She said she couldn't look in the mirror when she defended such 'scumbags'.

The source knows of the controversy over Gobbo's role within police command during her period as an informer. Some senior officers feared her safety was being unreasonably jeopardised, particularly after she was deregistered as an informer to be a witness against Paul Dale.

Dowsley farewells the source then frantically scribbles down everything he can recall of the chat. He feels overwhelmed by the possibilities. Dating her informing to the late 1990s suggests that she was an informer for a very long time.

The notion still seems absurd to Dowsley. He has trawled newspaper clippings, seen Gobbo pictured with Mokbel and Rob Karam. Did she betray them?

Dowsley now knows that Gobbo was suspected of being an accessory in the Hodson murders — but then senior brass stepped in and abruptly shut down the Petra Task Force. Dowsley can't work out why, in 2014, she is yet to be held to account for her inexplicable choices in the lead-up to the double homicide. Factoring in his growing belief that Gobbo was a police informer, he wonders if the Hodson investigation was hobbled for all the wrong reasons.

He has a moment-of-truth exchange in February 2014 when he puts his Gobbo speculations to someone who is well placed to know. That person says nothing, but gives him a thumbs-up.

It is enough to tweak Dowsley's antenna. He is closing in on the full picture.

He rings Gobbo out of the blue in mid-March 2014. Now isn't the time to put allegations to her about informing; that's for the last minute, for when he is certain of the facts and has gathered enough material to publish a story. Instead, he asks about Pope and the apparent relationship many years earlier. Gobbo says it happened. Pope has denied sleeping with Gobbo.

Dowsley takes stock. He collates his notes to see what he knows, and what he does not. Some of his conclusions stem from what people will *not* talk about. Omissions, such as 'I can't say' or 'No comment', almost count for as much as admissions.

He has cross-referenced the dates; Gobbo was informing to police when Tony Mokbel and Rob Karam were her clients. It seems logical that she improperly helped police convict them.

Dowsley's email to himself on 17 March has some fresh points:

- *The endangerment to her life.*
- *The IVF baby.*
- *Remained a human source with one contact point, which she does not like.*
- *Still practising? Her addiction to underworld and men.*

He keeps sniffing.

* * *

In the final weeks of March 2014, Dowsley gets his cold, hard proof. From an unlikely place, he gets Gobbo's informer number, 3838, and the number of internal information reports she has generated. Dowsley is told there are more than 5000.

Someone tells him that Gobbo gave police the bill of lading that fingered the Tomato Tins ecstasy syndicate. He is across the police suspicions that Gobbo passed on Terry Hodson's informer history (contained in the Blue File) to the underworld. If Gobbo's informing is the centrepiece of his investigation, it also pales as only one aspect in Gobbo's bigger career of double-dealing.

Two months after his boozy night at the pub, Dowsley feels he finally has enough for an article. The latest revelations serve as a trigger;

he feels he cannot sit on the story lest another inquiring journalist should stumble across the same information.

Dowsley has fashioned a narrative, loaded with secrets, deceptions and speculations. This story has massive implications — some that not even Dowsley can foresee at this point. But he is canny enough to recognise that the justice system has been undermined and prisoners could be freed.

His hope of uncovering an informer scandal has exploded into something far bigger, involving secrets about the Hodsons and other Gangland murders as well as drug syndicates and the Calabrian mafia. He believes the secrets probably warrant a royal commission.

It's Sunday morning. Dowsley rings his editor, Damon Johnston, who is at the park with his daughter.

Johnston goes quiet at the mention of Gobbo's name. The *Sunday Herald Sun* had settled a defamation action brought by her in 2011 after the paper published details of her 1993 drug arrest and conviction. Hers was a bold play, given she was unlikely to have taken the stand if the newspaper had contested the claim.

Johnston was the editor of the *Sunday Herald Sun* at the time. He was 'arse-kicked' for the payout to her.

But Dowsley starts talking and Johnston is mesmerised. Dowsley's information not only rewrites the entire history of the Gangland War, but could also trigger the release of dozens of serious criminals. He is describing a wholesale corruption of the Victorian justice system.

'Are you 100 per cent on what you've told me?' Johnston asks.

'Yeah, yeah, I am.'

Johnston wants to publish the story tomorrow. Like Dowsley, he fears being scooped by a rival newspaper. Dowsley inwardly groans: he'll have to miss this afternoon's Western Bulldogs game to file the story.

Then Johnston asks the critical question: 'Should we name her?'

The answer will have huge ramifications over the next five years.

The newspaper *could* name Gobbo, which would strengthen the story considerably. But Johnston is mindful of the possible consequences for Gobbo's safety. He does not want a story about the secret abuse of power hijacked by a debate about editorial recklessness. Gobbo's identity as an informer, once out, cannot be retrieved.

He goes with prudence: no name.

He considers aliases for Gobbo. The 'Lawyer X' label, which will become so ubiquitous, is coined on the spot while his daughter Phoebe directs Johnston to 'keep pushing' her swing.

* * *

Gobbo herself does not know how many details Dowsley has uncovered — until he takes a deep breath and rings her later that same afternoon.

It's never easy to tell someone that you are about to upend their life.

Fears for Gobbo's safety have haunted Dowsley. What news organisation takes steps that could inspire the murder of a mother? How compelling is the public interest if its pursuit ends in a killing?

But when Dowsley tells her she's about to become front-page news, Gobbo isn't belligerent. She does not plead. Instead, she feigns ignorance.

She is neither talkative nor rude. She avoids denials. The professional liar, whose career has been preserved by mistruths and cover-ups, is once again protecting herself from a bullet.

She responds to the informer claim as if she's hearing foreign news. She knows things about police tactics, she counters, but deflects direct questions about police informing.

She gets off the phone with Dowsley and immediately calls the police.

Over the coming hours, Victoria Police will try to kill Dowsley's story. The police are mandated to hide Gobbo's identity as an informer. And a newspaper journalist is poised to tell the world.

* * *

At this stage there is little of the hype that Gobbo's story will generate later. Only a few people within the *Herald Sun* know the Lawyer X story is coming.

Unlike most exclusives, it's not treated as the biggest story of the day. Dowsley's story is page one, but only a strip, not the splash, or main story.

Published on Monday, 31 March 2014, 'Lawyer a Secret Police Informer' is a restrained collection of confirmed facts.

A prominent underworld lawyer was recruited by Victoria Police to inform on criminal figures running Melbourne's drug trade for more than a decade.

The controversial move to list the lawyer, whom the Herald Sun *has chosen to name only as Lawyer X, as a registered informer gave the force unprecedented access to information on some of Australia's biggest drug barons and hitmen, including alleged corrupt police and others involved in Melbourne's gangland war.*

The force's biggest secret in turning a high-profile criminal lawyer into an informer brings into question police ethics in cultivating 'human sources', which went spectacularly wrong after the informer became a witness in one of Australia's biggest criminal investigations ...

The article goes on to mention (in veiled terms) Gobbo's implication in the Hodson case before Task Force Petra was suddenly shut down, and the police-command email that excused her from giving evidence at Paul Dale's lying trial in 2011.

If such sources of information ever existed in the fight against the New York Mafia or the Chicago mob, they were never exposed. This is a Melbourne exclusive, and a world first.

These 504 words will shape years of courtroom wrangling, give prisoners hope of early release, and drive a police force to extreme lengths to hide its secret abuse of power.

Yet for Dowsley, the showtime moment after months of work is tinged with disappointment. His accumulated dossier of explosive truths has been stripped back to abstractions. The revelations raise more questions than answers.

To this day, he brings up the fact that his Lawyer X story was trumped by a page-one report about tenants trashing public housing.

* * *

The first edition of the *Herald Sun* goes to print at 8 pm. Dowsley is at the pub with Chris Tinkler, the paper's deputy editor, when a call comes through a few minutes before eight. Herein lies Dowsley's next disappointment.

The call is from police assistant media director Charlie Morton. Dowsley rang Morton while going to work on the tram earlier that day. Concerned about Gobbo's safety, Dowsley felt he should advise Morton that the story was about to be published.

Now Morton asks to see the story, by this time moments from being published. Tinkler and Dowsley don't *have* to show him, but acquiesce as a courtesy. They soon regret their choice, and to this day each blames the other for making it.

The next call, within the hour, is from Johnston, ringing from his kitchen. He tells Dowsley and Tinkler that a posse of police and lawyers has raced to the Supreme Court to prevent the story from being published.

The first edition, a small print run that goes to regional Victoria, has already been printed. In events lifted from a black-and-white newsroom movie, the police are trying to stop the presses before the Lawyer X story is published in the second and third editions, which comprise the overwhelming majority of newspapers printed.

Tinkler wonders at Dowsley's nervous smirk before the pair race from the pub back to the office.

He and his editors are captive to legal machinations. Lives are at risk, lawyers for the police argue.

In the end, the arguments are not put to a judge, as they will be in coming days, weeks and years. Instead, on this first night, police lawyers and the *Herald Sun*'s lawyer, John-Paul Cashen, reach an agreement outside the courtroom. About half a dozen facts — deemed to tend to identify Gobbo — are removed from the story published in later editions.

* * *

The following morning, Tuesday 1 April, is telling. Victoria Police, like any large organisation, usually rush media outlets to denounce a story when it's wrong.

But the force isn't saying anything in public about Lawyer X. Dowsley thinks he knows why. A well-placed source tells him that some police officers have broken the law by lying in court to protect Gobbo's identity. Victoria Police have a lot to hide.

Dowsley's tale is out — just. Yet the *Herald Sun* can't tell you who Nicola Gobbo is, why she became an informer or how the justice system was corrupted by her use. The newspaper can't even state her gender.

Legal circles are full of chatter over the story. The facts seem so unlikely, and so repugnant to any decent lawyer.

Johnston wants to apply pressure and keep running the Lawyer X story day after day. He uses the facts extracted under the temporary agreement between police lawyers and Cashen from the day one story and applies them to the day two story about the abrupt end of the Petra Task Force investigation into the Hodson killings.

> *A police taskforce into multiple murders was shut down to protect a high-profile lawyer used as an informer.*
>
> *Lawyer X, who the* Herald Sun *revealed yesterday was recruited to inform on senior crime figures for years, also pocketed a multi-million-dollar payout to keep silent, and as compensation, as the relationship unravelled …*

Johnston also publishes a *Herald Sun* editorial that goes straight to the point:

> *Extraordinary events over the past 48 hours have raised such deeply concerning questions over the integrity of Victoria Police that the* Herald Sun *believes Premier Denis Napthine has no alternative but to order a royal commission …*

* * *

Johnston will admit later that he should have acted differently on day three.

Dowsley's cracking story has grown from a front-page strip to a front-page splash. But before publishing this third story, Johnston wants questions put to Victoria Police. The questions are pointed, name Gobbo, and are sent with a message that the *Herald Sun* intends to publish them in the next day's paper.

Police receive the emailed request for answers from the *Herald Sun* late on the afternoon of 1 April — then dash to the Supreme Court again. They use the questions to argue in court that the story must be suppressed because Gobbo is endangered by the *Herald Sun*'s intimate understanding of life-and-death information.

The judge agrees.

The police action stops the *Herald Sun* presses. At about 8.20 pm, Johnston has to find a new story for the front page.

Inspiration under deadline pressure is a daily journalist's lot. That's how Johnston's replacement 'Fight for Truth' front page is forged. Legal threats may cost him sleep, but they will not dissuade him from the cause.

Designers craft a striking image featuring white print on a black background. Johnston is sending a message.

The Herald Sun *was last night silenced from publishing details on Lawyer X which it believes is of extreme public interest.*

Victoria Police took the extraordinary action of seeking a Supreme Court injunction at 7.30 pm preventing the newspaper from publishing any information about Lawyer X, whom the Herald Sun *had no intention of naming or identifying.*

As the hearing commenced, the Herald Sun *was ordered by the judge to stop its presses. Editor Damon Johnston said that Victorians deserved to know the full truth ...*

Legal battlelines are drawn, and it's clear now that Victoria Police have botched their choice of playing field. By trying to bury the story, they've plonked a cover-up on top of a scandal.

They think they've done enough. Deputy Commissioner Graham Ashton exchanges emails with Morton, who believes that Cardinal George Pell's imminent appearance at the Royal Commission into Institutional Responses to Child Sexual Abuse will smother the Lawyer X coverage.

'Dowsley has used all his best ammo already (I think),' Morton writes.

'None of the other journos have got anything different or are prepared to use it.

'The Pell stuff is coming tomorrow and will knock this way off the front page.

'Unless there are some serious appeals from convicted crims which might get up as a result of this, then I can't see this continuing with the same level of profile.

'There will be more, but I suspect we can weather it.'

The Gobbo sagas would be long gone by now if Victoria Police had offered a *mea culpa* response in 2014, instead of seeking to dictate what truths the *Herald Sun* could and couldn't publish. A police plea for understanding, lathered with contrition, would have limited the story's longevity.

Instead, Ashton avoids his regular commitment to appear on the radio show of 3AW's Neil Mitchell, who has backed Dowsley's report with thundering criticism of the police.

The Victorian Government Solicitor's Office issues a threat against all media: do not publish information that tends to identify Lawyer X, or the Chief Commissioner of Police might legally prohibit your organisation from doing so.

Herald Sun lawyer John-Paul Cashen issues legal instructions on 4 April for reporting on Lawyer X. It's Friday, and the newspaper is legally restricted from publishing most of the details it reported only on Monday. Lawyer X can no longer be called a police informer. Her associates cannot be named, as Tony Mokbel and Carl Williams were in Dowsley's 1 April story.

Asked by the press about the Lawyer X story on 7 April, Chief Commissioner Ken Lay says: 'I'm not in a position to make any comment about that at all and I don't propose to make any comment about the alleged payment or any matters around Lawyer X. Let me just say at this stage I am not prepared to say anything at all about this matter.'

* * *

Victoria Police also try to withhold information from the Office of Public Prosecutions (OPP). Senior police, and the head of Victoria Police's legal services, Fin McRae, meet with the Director of Public Prosecutions, John Champion, the day after Dowsley's first story.

Meeting notes taken by the OPP's Bruce Gardner recorded the discussion. McRae says it is unclear whether Gobbo provided information about her own clients, then alludes to eighteen 'instances/ information reports in which NG [Gobbo] may have given information to Victoria Police, re her client[s]'.

Meetings between the OPP and police command about Gobbo's relationship with police in fact began almost two years ago. As early as September 2012, according to Gardner's notes, McRae told the DPP, that 'there may be a suggestion that NG was providing information to Vicpol [Victoria Police] about persons she then professionally represented, including T Mokbel'.

By then, former police commissioner Neil Comrie had completed his scathing report about Gobbo's use by police. But the force did not hand over the Comrie review to the DPP. Not then in 2012, even as Mokbel's legal fights meandered through the courts, and not now in 2014. The obvious conclusion is that Victoria Police are covering up the cover-up.

Someone close to the April 2014 meeting offers Dowsley and Carlyon a sceptical tone about police priorities. If a teenager summed up the high-level meeting via text, it would read:

OPP: *wtf*
Victoria Police: *lol*

Meanwhile, the mystery of Lawyer X's identity fuels speculations. Observers from afar think Lawyer X is the better-known female Gangland lawyer, Zarah Garde-Wilson. As Victoria Police have failed to grasp, cover-ups are often just as intriguing as the misdeeds they seek to hide.

* * *

On the day Dowsley's second article is published, he speaks to Gobbo again on the phone. Again, she expresses no hostility. They find common ground: both of them are seeking information from the other.

Gobbo doesn't address Dowsley's specific questions — he hopes but does not expect that she might admit to broader aspects of her informing — but she doesn't dismiss them either. 'It's not about me, it's about VicPol,' she says. She thinks some senior Victorian police will be 'very worried'.

Dowsley asks her why she thinks the Petra Task Force was closed down several days after police command issued an edict to investigators not to interview her. If they'd tried to interview her, she says, 'I might retaliate.'

Dowsley asks how she is faring. Gobbo spouts wisdom: 'You cannot control things you cannot control.'

Yet Gobbo suffers as much as she ever has in the days after Dowsley's exclusive story. The death threats have started again. If Gobbo is the centre of attention, as she has often wanted to be, she is almost powerless to steer events. Her secret is leeching into public view, and she is reliant on a police force she does not trust to stop the leaks.

She has progressed well since her 2010 civil case against police, even if she has spent 'a fortune' rebuilding. Her health is much better, and she has a six-month-old daughter.

Dowsley's story has destroyed all that. Now, she is angry again.

After years of allowing her to run her own life, police once again swarm to protect her. They offer her protection within forty-eight hours of the first Lawyer X story, under the same terms she previously rejected: she and her child will need to be swiftly moved to another location, and she will cease contact with all family and friends — permanently.

Gobbo says no. She will not give up the treatment of *her* doctors. Anyway, she says, police protection is neither safe nor appropriate. She does not trust Victoria Police to keep the confidentiality of *any* agreement.

Victoria Police will spend untold resources to suppress her name, yet almost everyone affected by her informing already knows the identity of Lawyer X. That's what Gobbo herself thinks, anyway.

In 2016, she will testify that 'the whole world' knew what she had done after the story was published: 'When I say "the whole world", I probably should clarify that to anyone who would have a reason to harm me, because the people — a lot of people in prison, the *Herald Sun* is their Bible.'

She loses every remaining friend from the legal fraternity. She isn't even able to attend her own home auction, in bayside Melbourne, for security reasons.

* * *

On the twelfth floor of the *Herald Sun*'s Southbank office, Johnston and Dowsley have bunkered down for a long fight.

They have an early win. Within three days of Dowsley's first story, the awkwardly named Independent Broad-based Anti-corruption Commission (IBAC) — the successor to Nixon and Overland's Office of Police Integrity (OPI) — announces that it will investigate the Lawyer X claims. An inquiry into police management of an informer 'recently identified in the *Herald Sun* as "Lawyer X"' will be headed by a retired Victorian Supreme Court judge, Murray Kellam QC.

So much for the police source in an *Age* newspaper story who mocked the *Herald Sun*'s 'Watergate' story as more like 'Fountain Gate' (a suburban shopping centre).

* * *

Victoria Police set up their own review into Gobbo's use ten days after the *Herald Sun*'s first story. Operation Bendigo is tasked with assessing the potential legal conflicts arising from Gobbo's intelligence. Bendigo is directly triggered by Dowsley's stories. Its establishment goes to the power of the press: police have sat on Comrie's review for almost two years and done little to explore the implications of its findings.

Within Victoria Police, Operation Bendigo is described as a response to 'extremely serious' threats made to Gobbo as a result of increased media reporting. It will identify five possible legal conflicts relating to a sting involving a Mobkel henchman and his associates. The *Herald Sun*, along with all media outlets, will be kept ignorant of Operation Bendigo until court-released documents reveal its existence in December 2018.

* * *

A month or so after the initial story breaks, Dowsley meets Gobbo at a South Melbourne wine bar. She's in mother mode, fumbling with her toddler. She has put off previous scheduled catch-ups, citing clashes with her daughter's doses of *Peppa Pig*.

Gobbo is quietly dressed. No drawing of attention to herself. The short skirts and low-cut tops belong to an earlier life. The master spy is now a dedicated mum.

As Gobbo's little girl plays with the beads around her mother's neck, Dowsley sips a white wine. Gobbo is pleasant, easy to talk to, even if she appears more eager to receive information than provide it.

Afterwards, though, he will be struck by a pattern to the chat. Gobbo switches to the default setting she's used with killers who've asked similar questions over the years: she deflects them. She always responds to a line of inquiry by offering details on an unrelated subject.

She is complimentary of Dowsley's first story. 'You'll win a Walkley for it,' she says.

'Not if it's not true,' Dowsley replies.

He tries to ask questions about her informing. She listens to his insights, as if mentally building a dossier of what he knows and what he doesn't, but she neither confirms nor denies them. Instead, she asks questions of her own, probably because she is planning another civil claim against Victoria Police.

She knows lots of police, obviously, but denies knowing the officers whom Dowsley names as her handlers. Instead she focuses on her contempt for others in the force, such as the drunk detective she assisted as he stumbled home in Bali — when he was meant to be protecting *her*.

Dowsley asks her about Rob Karam and the Tomato Tins case. He knows she handed the crucial bill of lading to police. 'Rob is my friend,' Gobbo counters. 'I spoke to him only yesterday.'

Dowsley again asks her if she was a police informer. She again avoids answering.

He asks her about her threat to jump from a roof in 2009. She denies it.

Over two hours, Gobbo conceals the chaos set off by Dowsley's newspaper story. Off stage, police bemoan Gobbo's recalcitrance, while she shrieks about their breaching of her trust. Victoria Police and Nicola Gobbo seethe with mutual resentment, like a broken couple, post-divorce.

* * *

Dowsley, meanwhile, is being courted by stakeholders masquerading as his new best friends forever.

Mick Gatto is the first to call him on the morning of his exclusive story. He wants to talk about Faruk Orman. Gatto later feeds Dowsley pasta at his Carlton restaurant.

Detective Sergeant Steve Mansell, who has now left the force, has a coffee with Dowsley. He and Detective Senior Constable Paul Rowe were the two Purana detectives who first invited Gobbo to become an informer in September 2005, leading to her registration as 3838. He tells Dowsley that Gobbo wanted to inform after 'we put it on her', that is, compelled her to be registered as an informer.

Lawyers, too, are avid readers of Dowsley's stories. Robert Richter QC is intrigued; his client Faruk Orman was convicted in strange circumstances in 2009. He, like many in the legal circles, knows that Lawyer X is Gobbo. She acted strangely, Richter recalls, after their client Orman was arrested for murder in 2007.

Dowsley visits Zarah Garde-Wilson, who begins chatting about her old colleague and foe. She tells Dowsley about a kid arrested in a Mokbel drug house in 2006.

Criminal solicitors, like doctors, receive calls at all times of the day and night. This tale began with a panicked phone call to Garde-Wilson in the small hours. 'Come now. Right now. It's an emergency.'

Garde-Wilson's caller was an eighteen-year-old man, though he sounded even younger. He hadn't done much, except be in the wrong place at the wrong time. His best legal response to police questioning, according to Garde-Wilson? Say nothing.

She turned up at the St Kilda Road Police Complex as quickly as she could. And waited. This was how it worked. It might be an hour, perhaps three, before detectives allowed her to see her client.

This time, however, the ritual was interrupted. Gobbo materialised, all huff and bustle, to be ushered through by a familiar detective. His name would later turn up in confidential police documents. Detective Senior Constable Jason Kelly, of Task Force Purana, knew Gobbo well.

A text message from Gobbo beeped on Garde-Wilson's phone. She was being dismissed: 'All sorted. You can go home.'

Yet Garde-Wilson did not go home. She was finally allowed to speak to the young man. He was shaking. He was friends with the daughter of one of the traffickers. He had never been in trouble before.

The young man told Garde-Wilson that Gobbo had advised him to say he was there to cut up drugs. He should tell police everything to improve his chances of bail.

It was very poor legal advice, Garde-Wilson tells Dowsley. He would be implicating himself in crimes for which there was no other evidence. A 'confession' would also expose him to reprisals from Mokbel associates. He was entitled to bail whether he spoke to police or not, Garde-Wilson says, given 'they had nothing on him'.

Yet the young man made a statement to say he was helping to package drugs, pleaded guilty, and received a community corrections order.

His talking must have helped the police. Gobbo, his barrister, was not working for him at all, but for the officers who wanted to charge him.

Garde-Wilson thinks she was glimpsing the bigger Gobbo picture by then. She saw herself as 'a thorn in the side of police' at the time, because she expressed her concerns about Gobbo's strange behaviour.

This happened eight years before Dowsley went to the Palmerston for drinks, then published the truth in the *Herald Sun*.

* * *

Joe Acquaro, the Honoured Society lawyer who represented most of the Tomato Tins drug cartel, wants to discuss with Dowsley how dangerous people have spread misinformation about him. Among these nasty rumours are suggestions that *he* was Lawyer X.

Dowsley had rung Acquaro in August 2015 to talk about other things: the mafia's supposed tentacles in politics as well as a purported contract on Acquaro's life.

Dowsley doesn't know at this stage that Acquaro has deep links with Gobbo, or that Acquaro himself will later be accused of being a police informer. Details of such accusations remain clouded to this day.

Three years earlier, bullets were sent in the mail to Acquaro's parents. Perhaps it was then that he began talking to police. He was close to Gobbo during the peak period of her informing. Those convicted of the Tomato Tins importation have questioned both Gobbo's and Acquaro's roles as lawyers and informers.

Acquaro, to Dowsley's surprise, is candid when they meet. He is beset by myriad problems.

When he was seventeen, Acquaro was anointed as a rising star by the head of Melbourne's Honoured Society, Liborio Benvenuto. He has always liked to be known as the society's *consigliere*, the advisor and networker. He puts people together — as he did a decade ago, when he brought Gobbo to a lunch and Frank Madafferi thought she was just another of Acquaro's blondes. He gained mafia respect when he helped overturn a deportation order against Frank Madafferi, a decision that would politically haunt then immigration minister Amanda Vanstone.

But now Acquaro has been jettisoned from the cocoon. He has been accused of breaking the 'Ndrangheta's golden rule of *omertà* — the code of silence. He has not only lost his place within the Honoured Society, but he has also lost his sense of identity.

Acquaro has fought battles over legal fees, his ice-cream restaurant Gelobar, his three sons and a partner. Long-time friends the Madafferis have fallen out with him over his alleged 'Ndrangheta betrayal. Frank Madafferi turned up at Gelobar in 2013; a punch-up erupted and Madafferi was left bleeding. Acquaro borrowed from *The Sopranos* to smear Madafferi's blood on his face and declare: 'Now we will die together.'

Acquaro has forgotten about *omertà*. He swells with pride and reeks of loneliness. He has had to move his office, down the hallway and up a small flight of stairs — away from his old firm, which still advises the mafia identities he now fears. The room is dim and strewn with papers. Like an afterthought, or a place to hide.

Acquaro speaks softly over scotches, clinking Dowsley's tumbler with a '*Salute!*' He wants to write his memoirs. Violence clings to him; he speaks of a gun he once stashed in his roof. Threatening to share his mafia links is a fast track to the kind of beating inflicted upon him in 2002 (after Acquaro's mate fumbled for a pen-gun) in the basement of a Carlton pizza restaurant.

Acquaro will meet Dowsley again and again in person. He's in touch with a police officer at Purana, and with his psychic, Sarah Kulkens.

One night in early March 2016, Acquaro calls the detective repeatedly, perhaps about an upcoming case. The following week, he calls Kulkens four times over four hours on her 1800 line. Black magic has deep roots within the mafia. Major Gangland figures are known to seek spiritual assistance.

As Acquaro speaks to Kulkens, his killer lurks outside Gelobar on Lygon Street.

No one can be certain of the reasons for Acquaro's end. He has just closed his restaurant when he is shot repeatedly in the chest. His body is found in the street in the early hours of 15 March 2016 by a garbage man.

Seventy-year-old labourer Vincenzo Crupi will stand trial in 2020, suspected of killing Acquaro over a small debt for tiling work at Gelobar. Crupi and Acquaro fought at the restaurant in the weeks before Acquaro's death, and Crupi is suspected of having started a fire at the premises in January 2016.

Acquaro dies the way of so many victims who fall out with the underworld: paranoid and alone.

Gobbo has risked a similar fate for more than a decade.

19

Live and Let Die

Informer 3838: A Second Damning Report
2015-2016

Perhaps Acting Chief Commissioner Tim Cartwright reads the wrong report before he fronts the media. When the Kellam report's broader findings — but not its contents — are released in February 2015, transparency does not appear to be Cartwright's main consideration.

'There is no evidence at this stage of any threat to any conviction or any evidence of mistrial,' Cartwright claims of a still-secret report that in fact says Gobbo's use is 'primarily responsible for [a] grave risk ... to the administration of justice'.

Only three copies of the highly confidential Kellam report are handed out at this early stage. But Victoria Police will not be able to hide Kellam's findings much longer. Kellam's recommendations will be the next crucial step in the chain of events leading inevitably to a royal commission. In cooperating with one of those recommendations, police trigger the next phase in exposing their secret.

* * *

Justice Murray Kellam has gone further than former chief commissioner Neil Comrie. He has spoken to witnesses such as Gobbo's SDU handlers. He has studied more information reports than Comrie and taken a broader line of inquiry. He is also across the longer history: in 2002, as a Supreme Court judge, Kellam bailed Tony Mokbel because

263

of the delays caused by corruption charges against some Victoria Police Drug Squad officers.

Kellam's report is a dense document intended for legally minded readers, and lacking in the subtext of shock that lifts Comrie's findings off the page. Kellam is considered and careful. Like so many elements of the Gobbo tale, the most telling of his findings are buried in the detail.

As a starting point, he cites the Victorian Bar Incorporated Practice Rules: 'A barrister must seek to advance and protect the client's interests to the best of the barrister's skill and diligence, uninfluenced by the barrister's personal view of the client or the client's activities.'

If these rules were breached, his report notes, it amounts to professional misconduct and perhaps more: the criminal offence of attempting to pervert the course of justice.

Kellam has read the confidential information reports relating to Gobbo's convicted clients. It's clear to him that Gobbo *was not* advancing or protecting the interests of these clients, but *was* influenced by her personal view of them and their activities.

Kellam points out that most of the information a barrister receives from his or her client is categorised either as falling under legal professional privilege, or as confidential. There is also a third category of information that *can* theoretically be passed on to authorities: information that is 'subject to criminal activity falling outside the fiduciary relationship'.

Kellam finds that any recognition by the SDU of such categories was '(almost without exception) absent'. Furthermore, problems arose because Gobbo was allowed to 'self-interpret' the categories of her information.

Kellam cites an information report relating to Tony Mokbel to prove his point: '3838 advised to speak freely, and reassured 3838 re ability to speak to handlers regarding all matters, including those matters involving alleged corruption'.

Kellam finds it difficult to accept Victoria Police's claim that they avoided seeking legal advice to ensure Gobbo's informer status was not leaked. Barristers, he argues, keep professional secrets all the time.

Gobbo's assistance to police required the assessment of a QC familiar with the subtleties of legal professional privilege.

He raises the suggestion that Victoria Police did not seek legal advice because they recognised they would encounter untenable tangles. Had the police sought advice from the Victorian Government Solicitor's Office in 2005, Kellam says, the use of Gobbo would have been condemned.

Her handlers' attempts in 2008 to prevent Gobbo from becoming a witness for the Petra Task Force showed that they knew the legal lines had been smudged. They spoke of a royal commission.

'[The] basic reason for not being a witness is because of being an informer for the past 3½ years and not wanting to be in the witness box as the role as a Source may come out,' handlers' notes reveal. 'Numerous issues include the Source's personal safety but also include unsound or unsafe convictions because of the Source's involvement with witnesses and persons charged.'

The logical conclusion? Victoria Police knew the legal perils well before they belatedly sought legal advice from barrister Gerard Maguire in 2011. They didn't need lawyers to tell them they were party to a dubious scheme.

Kellam reserves an extra-large helping of scorn for Gobbo's practice of reviewing the police evidence against her clients, so she could check that her involvement had been erased from view. She relished reading the cases against her own clients and pointing out their deficiencies.

Kellam finds that police relied on Gobbo to provide tactical information against her clients, and to manipulate those clients so they would give evidence. He lists fifteen examples from her handlers' reports relating to the Mokbels and others, including this: '3838 believes the fact that 3838 assisted [a Mokbel crew member to] roll over will never come out.'

It appears that Gobbo's part in police investigations *was* officially erased. Yet police are legally obliged to disclose the details of every investigation to the courts. This includes their use of sources, even if they claim public interest immunity (PII) to cloak these sources' identities.

If police fail to provide these details, both the court and the defendant are denied the transparency demanded of a fair trial. Criminal sanctions, from contempt of court to more onerous charges, can apply. It seems that Victoria Police, in erasing their use of Gobbo, may have been guilty of illegal conduct.

Regrettably, scrutiny of such disclosure provisions appears to be beyond Kellam's remit. But he has other damning observations to make. He refers to Victoria Police's 'wilful blindness' and a 'serious systemic failure'.

Graham Ashton, now Chief Commissioner, has told Kellam that police were under 'considerable pressure'. When Gobbo 'comes on board that could potentially solve a bunch of ... murders or prevent others'. In an oft-repeated observation, Ashton spoke of Gobbo as a 'glittering prize' that 'sometimes diverts you from the necessary sense of steps'. A forbidden fruit too tempting to ignore.

Yet legal professional privilege (LPP) is sacrosanct, a tenet any TV viewer picks up from *Law & Order*. Breaching LPP can hardly be seen as an overlooked step; it is an affront to basic legal ethics. Legally privileged information obtained by a police informer is 'extremely unlikely ever to be admissible as evidence in criminal proceedings', Kellam writes, citing the United Kingdom's Covert Human Intelligence Sources Code of Practice. Published by the Home Office in 2002, the code dedicated a chapter to issues of receiving information from lawyers:

> *Where there is any doubt as to the handling and dissemination of information which may be subject to legal professional privilege, advice should be sought from a legal advisor before any further dissemination of the material takes place.*

He calls Victoria Police's failure to adhere to this principle 'a significant, and avoidable, oversight'. He says the 'apparent receipt and utilisation by police of prima facie legally privileged, or otherwise confidential information provided by the Source ... had the potential to contaminate the criminal justice system'.

Citing a High Court judgment, Kellam suggests that if a court is denied the 'true circumstances' of a case, it amounts to 'an attempt to pervert the course of justice'.

Kellam states that he did not find that any unlawful behaviour occurred. But he does identify 'negligence of a high order'. Officers' behaviour was 'improper', though this was mitigated by their lack of supervision.

Kellam indicts Victoria Police for Gobbo's perilous position:

The serious systemic failure of VicPol in relation to the management of the Source is primarily responsible for the grave risk which has now been created for the personal safety of the Source, for the good reputation and public confidence in VicPol and to the administration of justice in the State of Victoria.

* * *

Kellam's conclusion? He has identified nine of Gobbo's clients whose convictions are possibly tainted.

Gobbo's handling of an early client was a 'clear and obvious conflict' that Gobbo herself identified in mid-2006, in a recorded conversation with her controller Sandy White. This particular client was the source of her most conflicted feelings. She saw him as a kindred spirit and felt bad about betraying him, though it didn't stop her.

According to that client, she incriminated him, told him to plead guilty, compelled him to roll on his associates, then coached him through dozens of statements to be used against those associates. He might never have become a police witness if he had received independent advice.

Discount his evidence, and the cases against four of the other eight people on Kellam's list — Milad Mokbel, Frank Ahec, Karl Khoder and Mr Beautiful — are weakened.

Tony Mokbel was absent during much of the sting in 2006, busy fleeing to Greece, but Gobbo was sharing defence secrets with police before he was convicted *in absentia* for cocaine importation. Mokbel thought Gobbo was acting in his interests when he spoke to her from a Greek jail, and she was passing on his thoughts to police.

* * *

But for all the damning findings in Kellam's report, it is one simple recommendation that will prove to be Victoria Police's undoing.

It directs the Chief Commissioner of Police to provide a copy of the report to the Director of Public Prosecutions, John Champion. Champion is about to write another verse in the lengthening chorus of shame being played to Victoria Police.

* * *

By March 2015, the Lawyer X story has been subjected to multiple suppression orders and driven from the news cycle, despite *Herald Sun* editor Damon Johnston's efforts to circumvent the legal barriers.

Each time the *Herald Sun* publishes a Lawyer X story, police rush to court to further restrict what the paper is allowed to publish. Now Victoria Police successfully suppresses the use of the term 'Lawyer X' itself, despite the fact it was Johnston's own invention. The force is relentless in pursuing the paper, and never mind the countless taxpayer dollars.

Johnston digs in, but his scope is contracting. As the court orders, 'the Lawyer X case' becomes 'the police informer scandal', which will become 'the police corruption scandal', which will become 'the justice system scandal'.

Other media pick up the story, but the scarcity of available information hampers efforts to explain its intricacies. For years, Dowsley will wonder at the long silences that punctuate the Lawyer X scandal. It feels as though it's too impenetrable to be pursued.

In what Johnston now calls a 'long, lonely legal fight', police will engage in court battles with the *Herald Sun* over fifteen separate issues. They play the legal version of the kid's game Whack-A-Mole.

When Dowsley writes a July 2016 story about drug baron Rob Karam's appeal ambitions, he assumes (rightly) that Victoria Police will immediately seek to legally suppress the information. Lawyer X has been reduced to barristers at twenty paces, armed with affidavits and billable hours, buzzing about like flies on dung.

As Johnston says: 'It would still be a secret today if it wasn't for Anthony Dowsley, and the company's determination to back him in at great expense and legal risk.'

He identifies another salient point: police claims about the dangers to Gobbo lack specificity. They argue 'environmental' dangers. 'But they put her in there, and she put herself in there, it wasn't us,' he says. 'That was what I had to fall back on: "Well, we're just doing our jobs here."'

He begins writing a newspaper editorial about the course of the fight, not knowing when, or if, it will be published. For years he will tinker with the words in quiet moments in his office. Its walls boast framed front-page milestones, which now include the Lawyer X 'Fight for Truth' promise.

'In an era of immediacy and social media and instant gratification, I don't remember anything else in my career that spans old-school traditional typewriter journalism and instantaneous social-media journalism,' he says now. 'You think about everything that went on [between 2014 and 2019 when Johnston left the *Herald Sun*]. It wasn't the only thing we were working on but, Christ, it felt like it sometimes.'

Johnston maintains a 'civil' back-channel relationship with Victoria Police. He uses occasional face-to-face meetings to reiterate his determination to fight the legal threats. He also calls Lawyer X staff planning meetings from time to time, as much to remind staff about his commitment to the long game as to set strategies.

Yet there is an unexpected upside to the police crusade to shut down the fight. In fighting Dowsley's 2016 story about Rob Karam's appeal pursuit, Victoria Police's lawyers take a drastic mis-step.

Their affidavit refers to an examination of Karam's conviction in the Kellam report, whose findings are still suppressed. It cites Kellam's finding that 'the use of information provided by a police informer or informers may have compromised the fair trial of criminals including Rob Karam'.

Johnston has always been convinced the *Herald Sun*'s stories are correct; Dowsley knows too much, and the police's 'brutal and swift' response has lacked transparency.

Now he has written confirmation of the facts, from the police themselves — albeit in the course of their attempts to stop him publishing those facts.

He scribbles 'Holy Shit!' on a pink Post-it note and sticks it next to the Karam reference. He will revisit his 'Holy Shit!' dossier when police seek charges against the *Herald Sun* for an alleged breach of court orders in 2017. The dossier is so overloaded by then that the documents threaten to spill from the pile in his office.

He believed then what he says today: that Victoria Police command are 'protecting their arses, and willing to blow millions of dollars of taxpayer funds to do that'. That if major criminals are released from jail, it will be entirely the fault of police.

'I think in Victoria, there's a collective thought that our police are better than Queensland and we're better than New South Wales,' Johnston says. 'This wasn't corruption with cash in brown paper bags as it was in Queensland. Potentially ... this was corruption at a far grander scale, at a systemic scale, and a far more damaging scale.'

It contracts to a catchphrase that will drive countless confidential *Herald Sun* strategy meetings over the months and years before the Lawyer X scandal breaks afresh in December 2018.

Did they break the law to end the war?

* * *

Dowsley suspected Gobbo was planning something when they met in the wine bar in the weeks after his first Lawyer X story broke. In October 2014, she wrote a letter to Chief Commissioner Ken Lay. After receiving a response that was 'nothing but disingenuous and offensive', she writes another letter to Assistant Commissioner Steve Fontana in June the following year.

Taken together, the two letters are a manifesto of jilted pride. Small errors of spelling and syntax suggest they were both typed in a huff, as if the writer were keen to leave her rage on the page.

They were not penned as therapy, however. The letters are compelling for what they do not say as much as for what they do. They are intended as weapons.

Together, the two letters run to more than 4200 words, but can be distilled into a single demand: 'Give me hush money.' Gobbo received almost $3 million in 2010, after demanding $20 million. She wants more — lots more — for her pain and suffering. Privately, she says Victoria Police have offered her nothing but 'broken promises, threats and bullshit'.

In her second letter she writes:

Since the 'Lawyer X' publicity started, it would be fair to say that my mental, emotional and physical health are in decline and I feel the impact of this nightmare almost every single day.

In addition to my anxiety, fear, severe depression, PTSD [post-traumatic stress disorder] and paranoia, my reputation is gone and I will never be able to work as a lawyer again ...

I would like you to try to put yourself in my shoes for a moment to try to comprehend my almost complete disillusionment with the very organisation which assured me as an informer, that what I did for Police and the detailed information I provided, would remain a highly protected secret and would never see the light of day.

Now, but for my children and a handful of loyal supportive friends and family, each day is a nightmare as to what might come out next or indeed, the consequences for my safety and wellbeing.

She feels trapped. She blames police for putting her life at risk. Her informing was motivated by a hatred of injustice. She did the right thing for the right reasons. She feels no guilt; she's a victim who is now being punished.

In her 2014 letter, she claimed the death threats against her — from Tony Mokbel, among others — were multiplying. But there's another school of thought on this point. A jailed underworld figure close to Gobbo has been mouthing off. He says he sent her a death threat — on *her* urging.

In both her letters, Gobbo seeks credit for shaping the solution to the Gangland War. She sets out the cause and effect, with the clarity of a student solving a maths equation. As an informer, she writes in 2015, 'There was no topic, criminal, organised crime group or underworld crime that was "off limits" during the many debriefing sessions that occurred.' Her thousands of information reports will help account for her 'actual value, reliability and work'.

She has kept count. At least 386 people have been arrested and charged because of her information. In her letter to Fontana, she even provides a top-ten list of her greatest stings. Her help has led to asset and property seizures worth more than $60 million, she tells him, based on figures in a newspaper report. Quantifying the veracity of the claim — Gangland seizure estimates vary from $40 million to double that — is impossible. There is no way to measure Gobbo's influence in monetary terms.

She now wants her rightful due, she tells Fontana. Until now, all she has received is a Victoria Police pen, she says, conveniently overlooking her $2.88 million payout in 2010. She is proud of her work, but she also seems aware that it may bring disgrace upon herself and Victoria Police. She says that if the police do not compensate her, she will launch legal proceedings.

The unsubtle threat lies not in the proceedings themselves, but rather in their public nature. She wrote to Lay in 2014:

I am prepared to meet with you to try to reach a mutually acceptable agreement. I would encourage you to consider this option seriously because it is in no one's best interests for my role and involvement as an informer/human source to be detailed in a Writ or explored in civil proceedings.

Yet this virtually ignores the concerns that explain why documents about the Lawyer X scandal fill rooms. In her 2015 letter she explains away the ethical knots of her informing in a single sentence: 'I maintain …

that anything told to me or said in my presence about crimes being planned or committed cannot ever fall under the protection of legal professional privilege by a client.'

She overlooks the reasons why some legal experts think that murderous bastards will walk from jails, and some police officers ought to be charged with serious crimes. She ignores the fact that she betrayed clients yet accepted their fees.

It's unclear if Fontana or a representative ever replies to this letter. If they do, Gobbo surely finds the response most dissatisfying.

* * *

Victoria Police do as Kellam has instructed, and deliver his report (by hand) to the Director of Public Prosecutions (DPP), John Champion, within a week of its release. Over the next twelve months, Champion reviews nine cases in which miscarriages of justice have potentially occurred.

Champion's confidential report, completed in February 2016, offers a neat encapsulation of the Gobbo conundrum:

> It appears to me highly likely that on a number of occasions [Gobbo] acted improperly in informing against her own clients. It appears highly likely that there were breaches of legal professional privilege, and of confidences between the lawyer and the client on multiple occasions, over a lengthy period of time.
>
> There were, almost certainly, serious conflicts of interest occurring in her actions ... The overall circumstances of the role and activity of this person, and the associated legal implications, may be extremely difficult to unravel.

His letter to Chief Commissioner Graham Ashton, on 10 March 2016, is another smoke bomb for Victoria Police.

Champion proposes more than just another damning report. He has examined the cases of the nine convicted Gobbo clients identified by Kellam, and he wants to tell seven of them that their trials may have been tainted. His letter says they should be informed 'expeditiously', in notifications known as 'letters of disclosure'.

Champion is mindful of the risk to Gobbo. He is not seeking to provide the full Kellam report to the convicted men, but 'it will be necessary to provide sufficient information in order for those people affected to embark on a rational and informed decision-making process as to what steps they may wish to take from this point onwards'.

How do Victoria Police respond? That's right. They say no.

Deputy Commissioner Shane Patton writes to Champion to say that the risk of death to Gobbo if her role is disclosed will rise from 'possible' to 'almost certain'. He advises Champion that disclosure is the wrong way to go. Victoria Police will invoke public interest immunity protections.

If Champion wants to challenge this view, he can go to the Supreme Court.

Victoria Police have repeatedly battled with the *Herald Sun* over publishing the Lawyer X story. Now they're seeking to shut down any other forms of revelation, on the grounds of protecting police informers.

The next battle is looming.

20

Timothy's Choice

Victoria Police v The Truth: A Secret Trial
2016-2017

It's 22 November 2016. Dowsley is slouched outside a courtroom in an upstairs corridor of Melbourne's Supreme Court. QCs file past, each one shutting the courtroom door behind them with a click.

No one is supposed to know that this case is taking place, bar the participants, who are sworn to secrecy. Their notes will be kept in a safe and later destroyed.

This court trial is not publicly listed; even court staff are unaware of it. Secrecy is so tight that the judge, Timothy Ginnane, will even entertain arguments about the security clearance of courtroom cleaners.

A few months back, Dowsley trailed Justice Ginnane through the courts in an attempt to confirm the existence of this case. Dowsley's investigation has propelled the hearing. Yet he isn't allowed in. There are no bouncers on the door, but there may as well be.

The civil case will come to be known as *AB & EF v CD*. This jumble of initials means nothing to anyone without knowledge of the case's cast.

It's highly unusual. Victoria Police (AB) usually work *with* the DPP (CD) to prosecute crimes. But the police are taking the DPP to court. Victoria Police and Gobbo (EF) have skirmished for years. Now they're actually on the same team.

The DPP, John Champion, is seeking to fulfil his mandated duty to inform seven criminals that their convictions may have been tainted.

275

Victoria Police and Gobbo, both armed with millions of taxpayer dollars, are seeking to stop him. Whatever happens, this case will likely cost Victorians more than a massive Tattslotto win. But if Victoria Police win, Victorians won't ever find out.

Solicitor Justin Quill, a regular advocate for the *Herald Sun* in court, is inside the courtroom, on the behalf of Dowsley and the *Herald Sun*, seeking to gain entry for the journalist. He counts five QCs inside and many more lawyers milling.

Quill is a media lawyer who applies a dapper touch and quick wits. He fights suppression orders that prevent public insight into suspects, sentences and courtroom dramas. He scraps and charms, beholden to judges, who generally abhor unexpected delays.

Speeches about the freedom of the press, and the public's right to know, tend to glaze eyes. Here, in an archaic enclave of wigs and cracked leather benches, one of those moments beckons. Yet it's anything but dull.

Quill tells Justice Ginnane that Dowsley is sitting outside, eager to come in. Quill invites Ginnane to 'look in the whites of the eyes of the journalist and make clear the importance of the undertaking' to keep proceedings secret. To read Dowsley — at this moment idly scrolling his phone for stories about the Western Bulldogs — 'the riot act' if need be.

Quill strikes at the police resistance to scrutiny over Gobbo, which now dates back more than a decade. He figures that the public, as the lawyers' paymasters, 'at some point ought to know what's occurring in this courtroom'.

Victoria Police's barrister, Peter Hanks QC, counters with reasons why Dowsley should be kept out. Hanks knows the *Herald Sun* has risked judicial censure by publishing carefully worded stories that skirt the growing pile of court-imposed suppression orders.

'There is such an avid pursuit of this story — and that's the business of newspapers, of course — that any undertakings that are given would have to be so watertight ... that they might run to reams of paper,' Hanks says. The pursuit of journalism 'regrettably ha[s] to be constrained'.

'This is an extreme case,' Hanks emphasises. 'The life of a person is at stake.'

Quill is irked by the odd procedures. He was ejected from the courtroom while Hanks was speaking. He could not dispute Hanks's arguments because he could not hear them. Secrecy, it seems, trumps fairness.

The *Herald Sun* loses this particular legal battle. Dowsley and Quill leave the Supreme Court like footballers dragged unwillingly from the field.

Transparency has been the first casualty of the Gobbo legal war. It will be another two years before the public gets an inkling of this case. Editor Damon Johnston is compelled in the meantime to publish 'nonsensical' stories about AB, CD and EF in which the *Herald Sun* cannot say who or what AB, CD and EF are. Johnston tries to tell readers what they need to know, even though the readers aren't *allowed* to know what the newspaper is trying to tell them.

The truth will be teased out in ponderous detail throughout 2016 and 2017, in the kind of courtroom marathon that lands lawyers beach houses. The trial will delve into the why and the diabolical depths of the how. But the public is not allowed to know anything about this battle over 'the public interest'.

* * *

Whispers say that more than 600 letters of disclosure ought to be sent to Gobbo's former clients as a result of her activities. When Champion asked Victoria Police for the names of the people charged with offences after Gobbo informed on them, he received a reply from the Victorian Government Solicitor's Office. He was told the information he wanted was not relevant to resolving the issues before the court.

It seemed *very* relevant to Champion.

The police want the court to bury the whole issue. They argue — and Ginnane accepts — that disclosures of Gobbo's informing will have a 'chilling effect' on all Victorian police informers, paralysing the force's ability to solve serious crime. It will also lead to her 'almost certain' death.

The competing public interest is the contamination of the justice system, and the fact of seven — and perhaps hundreds more — potentially unsafe convictions.

It all has to be laid out. Gobbo's recorded conversations with her handlers, her incriminating of her clients, and her critiques of police briefs against them.

The price for Gobbo was high: anxiety, hypervigilance, depression. She got stressed when she spoke to the crooks and she got stressed when she dealt with Victoria Police.

The crux of the issue is her unwillingness to receive police protection. It's fundamental to the police's argument. If she accepts police protection, the police will have to rely on other arguments to mount their case. But because Gobbo will *not* accept protection, police argue, she will probably be killed if her informer status is revealed. Days of evidence delve into her resistance.

Gobbo has hinted she may finally go into hiding after all. She appears to be yielding to the realities of her jeopardy, and police contact her physician about signing forms.

In hindsight, Gobbo was probably teasing. She was never close to entering police protection. Such a choice, according to evidence given by her treating psychologist, would almost be as dangerous as exposure.

* * *

Gobbo has had a long and chequered history of seeking psychological help. Her handlers first urged her to visit a psychiatrist just months after she turned informer. By late 2006, Sandy White was so concerned about her 'dependency issues and welfare', he suggested she see a psychologist. Though she'd declined the previous invitation, this time she reluctantly agreed.

It didn't go well. Gobbo queried the woman's credibility and understanding. An information report stated that Gobbo 'attempted to bully' her.

By 2010, though, Gobbo was seeing a psychologist she trusted. The professional sessions with this woman would continue for some time past 2017.

Casual observers have plonked various diagnoses on Gobbo over a long period, including borderline, histrionic and narcissistic personality disorders. Her more extreme choices show symptoms of all.

Her long-term psychologist says most in her profession would not take Gobbo on as a client. Yet she has not diagnosed any personality disorders.

Gobbo's treatment includes cognitive behavioural therapy, which involves being goal-directed and purposeful. She takes an anti-depressant, Lexapro, and anti-seizure medication. She has been encouraged to meditate and use other relaxation methods. Yet no techniques can alleviate the strain of always looking over her shoulder.

Gobbo wants 'unique' conditions that disqualify her from the protections offered by police, such as a personal bodyguard detail. Her grandiose demands conjure visions of a luxury villa nestled behind high walls, with a terrace where she accepts pina coladas from the butler as the kids splash in the pool.

She refuses to give up her name. She doubts she can blend in. As her psychologist says: 'I think that she feels that you can't alter her physical presence. I think she feels that it's unlikely that she could just disappear in that sense.'

The psychologist testifies that Gobbo will become suicidal if taken from the support of friends and family. It's unclear who these people are, but the possibilities are limited given Gobbo has told so few loved ones about her informing.

'I very much feel that if she was to be taken out of this environment she's in now and put into some kind of isolatory ... protection program without support of myself and [name redacted] she would eventually think there was nothing really worth living for,' the psychologist says. Going into hiding would trigger a 'catastrophic mental health breakdown'.

'Well, I suspect she'd end up in a psychiatric hospital and potentially with major depressive disorder if it becomes treatment resistant ...

which just means that she's not responsive to the anti-depressants that she's on. If she's not able to function, then you start looking at much more serious kinds of treatments, so electroconvulsive therapy ...' Gobbo is taking so much medication that any new doctor introduced to her dosage would be shocked. (Or so says her own doctor.)

Access to Gobbo's medical records is argued over at length, ironically for reasons of privilege and privacy. But when the DPP's legal team are finally granted quick access to examine them, they discover evidence that could potentially turn the case.

They find the letter Gobbo wrote to Assistant Commissioner Stephen Fontana in 2015 that included her 'top-ten stings', in essence spelling out her informer history — what she did, and how.

It's a dog-ate-my-homework moment. Victoria Police have not produced the letter for the trial, a bad habit that has frustrated every inquiry into the force's use of Gobbo.

But there are bigger moments to come. By September 2016, before the trial begins, Ginnane has determined that Gobbo herself can enter the witness box.

* * *

Gobbo is holed up at the Novotel in St Kilda. Dowsley has just written a highly incriminating article about Rob Karam and Pasquale 'Muscles' Barbaro, both of whom she has informed against. Gobbo now thinks she's being followed.

She is summoned to a meeting at the hotel by senior police officer Cindy Millen. When Millen contacts her, Gobbo braces for bad news.

'Do I need to bring a lawyer?' she asks. 'Am I being arrested?'

It's urgent, Gobbo is told in response. 'I can't tell you anything. You need to come to this meeting.'

Gobbo arrives to be confronted by police and lawyers. She is handed a three-page document, an 'originating motion' describing the court hearing at which she will give evidence. She is surprised by the list of the seven criminal clients who might have been affected by her informing. She'd thought there would be more names.

Gobbo now has a choice: admit wrongdoing or fight. She decides to fight.

She will tell her story to a public audience of none. Not even those she betrayed can know of the events in this courtroom.

The force has earlier argued that Gobbo should not be made aware of the case at all. Now they argue on legal grounds that she shouldn't testify, again prompting questions about their motivations. 'It wasn't about her,' a well-placed source says now. 'It was about them. They were worried about their own exposure.'

But now Gobbo *wants* to give evidence. She wants to rationalise choices that have debased the cornerstones of her calling.

Her testimony looms as a security challenge. Since the first *Herald Sun* article, she has masqueraded, sans police entourage, as just another suburban mum. Yet Hanks now argues that she should give evidence remotely. The court's protective officers will not be enough. Hanks wants a 'special arrangement'.

He wins concessions. Over five days from late February 2017, Gobbo gives her evidence in the County Court instead of the Supreme Court because it offers better security.

* * *

The trial transcript runs to thousands of pages, yet Gobbo's emotions on the stand can only be guessed at. She takes medication during breaks in giving evidence. Her kids are being babysat but they are on her mind.

She presents none of the coquettish vulnerability she has applied to other audiences. Her behaviour is equal parts brassiness and naïveté. Perhaps she's not as worldly as she thinks she is.

There's something else, too. Gobbo bristles at being grilled on her behaviours. Narcissist or not, her mental defences tighten under attack.

She has few regrets, she tells the court. Her informing was 'altruistic', prompted by seeing how hardened crooks such as Carl Williams and Tony Mokbel manipulated justice. She did not breach legal professional privilege or confidentiality, she claims, despite the vast quantity of documents and recordings that suggests otherwise.

Reading between the lines of the transcript, one imagines Gobbo mentally squirming as she offers the same lame responses to questions about ethics. Plausible deniability does not fly in this forum. Gobbo is telling others what she wants to hear.

She does not relinquish her mental bullet points, even when they look flimsy under scrutiny. She appears to be following an internal script, and she's sticking to it, no matter how it conflicts with rules of law or established facts.

Dr Sue McNicol QC, representing the DPP, guides her gently through the quagmire, as though by the hand.

McNicol exposes contradictions and forces corrections and qualifications. She questions Gobbo on her choices as an informer and then on the unfortunate consequences of those choices.

Gobbo tends to confuse these two elements. She doesn't accept that her choice to become an informer is why her life is now so troubled. She shirks the responsibility and blames the police. In her own mind, she did good things, only to become a victim of forces beyond her control.

'It was an unbelievable kind of time in my life because there were people that I saw one day who were literally murdered by the next day,' she says.

The unanswered question is this: why didn't Gobbo walk away? The simple answer is that she didn't want to — nor did Victoria Police want her to. Yet the caped-crusader routine will not fly in court, mostly because a close examination of her informing reveals the absence of both a cape and a crusade.

Recordings are played of her chats to her handlers, and in them Gobbo sounds as though she is relishing their attention. But she is shocked to hear a recording of her first meeting with the SDU in 2005. She was told at the time that it was not to be recorded. 'It puts a new light on things when you know you've been lied to from the very beginning,' she tells the court.

McNicol probes Gobbo's ironclad belief that her identity as an informer could be protected. This projected belief, it should be added, does not tally with her behaviour and paranoia at the time of her informing. She read police briefs for oversights that identified her, and probably broke into a colleague's office in search of incriminating evidence against herself, which she denies. She didn't trust the police to protect her at all.

In the witness box, Gobbo explains that there are two types of informers. She was not a criminal and did not need a 'get-out-of-jail card'. Her premise wobbles when one recalls that she offered herself to police as an informer in 2005 because she feared she was perverting justice and committing crimes.

'There was never going to be an occasion where your secrecy and your identity was blown?' McNicol asks. Gobbo seems to think that conventions, of both gossip and criminal law disclosure, do not apply to her. Perhaps it reflects her living-outside-the-rules thinking. She 'sadly, regrettably, trusted and believed what I was being told' by police.

Yet she also admits, under repeated questioning, that she was aware informer secrecy could *not* be guaranteed. Gobbo knew that an informer codenamed E292, who infiltrated a major drug operation headed by John Higgs, was put at risk after his files were stolen from the Drug Squad offices in January 1996.

She herself, in 2002, correctly identified a hidden informer as Terry Hodson. She had successfully argued in court that the identity of an informer could be revealed, on behalf of Tony Mokbel in 2005, even as she began snitching on him.

Gobbo reiterates her belief that criminals would need an official 'piece of paper' to act against her betrayals. Again, her fears at the time do not align with this statement. She tells the court about 'conversations over a number of years where this topic arose and I was repeatedly assured that if a subpoena was issued, for example, or some kind of proceeding in which material was called for that may identify me, that the police would fight it on my behalf and claim public interest immunity'.

Yet her contempt has since grown. She says Victoria Police gave her assurances about 'unprecedented circumstances' should she need to be placed in protection. She took these to mean special privileges not usually reserved for those in hiding. These were to be put in writing but they never eventuated.

There were threats to remove her children from her for their safety in 2015, which Gobbo interpreted as a nasty incentive for her to accept police protection.

She instead took personal precautions, at her own expense, which she does not detail to the court. She has told few people about her informing, besides several health professionals and the barrister representing her in her successful 2010 claim against police.

Her informer role was confidential 'until Anthony Dowsley put it on the front page of the paper'. Should her name be released through the court, it would put 'a bullet in my head'.

McNicol offers a kind of dénouement. In closing, she calls Gobbo's use 'simply abhorrent'. Hearing the simplest facts of this case 'causes one's jaw to simply drop'. This case is more than 'a stain'. 'The criminal justice system has been contaminated.'

McNicol queries the arguments Victoria Police and Gobbo have used for so many years. 'EF [Gobbo] should not be able to dictate the outcome ... by refusing to go into wit sec [witness security]. She has asserted that Victoria Police cannot be trusted ... but the point is that her personal choices are not relevant.'

Brind Zichy-Woinarski is the *amicus curiae* — counsel known as a friend of the court — whose role is to advance courtroom arguments for those affected by Gobbo's informing, while not officially representing them. He points out that the court has heard a lot of evidence about Gobbo's safety. This consideration needs to be balanced by the administration of justice, and the question of whether Gobbo and police have interfered with that.

He raises scenarios that have gone unmentioned by Victoria Police's and Gobbo's barristers. He argues that if the possible misconduct of the police and Gobbo is not revealed to those who may have been denied justice, it will restrict the courts' ability to investigate the legality of using a barrister as an informer, and the question of whether criminal charges need to be laid.

'The weighing process will require Your Honour to determine whether — and we'll say you'll find there has been — just how serious a corruption of the criminal process system there has been not only by [Gobbo] … but knowingly by Victoria Police.'

* * *

Victoria Police accept that they have erred — within the cocoon of a closed courtroom. They concede that some of their officers have obtained information in 'an improper manner'.

Hanks acknowledges perceptions that Gobbo's informing is a 'fundamental breach of the criminal trial process'. 'Perhaps it's said that the police have learned its lesson,' he admits.

Victoria Police ask Justice Ginnane to put their misdeeds aside, and never mind the hapless goons betrayed by the grand deception. Yes, internal police reviews have listed possible miscarriages of justice. As a result, nothing at all should be done, the police argue, in arguments straight out of TV's *Yes, Minister*.

For years, Victoria Police ran the risks of Gobbo and repeatedly chose to avoid the consequences. The organisation seems to be saying, 'Yes, we created the inequity, but trying to repair it would only cause more damage. And no, we have not disciplined any officers for their behaviour. But our supervisory systems are better now, and check out all our new acronyms.'

The absurd line belies the gravity of the ruling Ginnane will need to make. He faces a choice that would haunt any person of conscience. He is known for his serious-minded approach to the law (as well as his involvement in preventing Dowsley's beloved Western Bulldogs from folding in 1989).

This case is in a different league. The law seems to have cast off its bearings of right and wrong. Murderers and drug traffickers have become the victims. Their guilt or otherwise does not matter here; what matters is that they may not have received a fair trial, as all are entitled to.

If Ginnane is not thrust into the role of God, he at least carries the burden of Abraham. His conundrum is complicated by many months of evidence from doctors and police officers. He has to decide which of two competing public interests outweighs the other.

Does the sanctity of life come before the administration of justice? This can be reduced to an even more basic question: will Ginnane protect Gobbo's life or not?

* * *

Justice Timothy Ginnane doesn't call it the pub test, but he may as well. He poses the questions that ordinary, 'reasonable' observers have asked since the Lawyer X scandal erupted.

Weren't the criminals that Gobbo informed on guilty anyway? And why offer them a chance at being freed 'when the consequence may be the murder of EF [Gobbo] and harm to her children'?

Ginnane concludes that the police evidence about the lethal danger to Gobbo is compelling. Gobbo acted to get the 'Mokbel monkey off my back'. So why should Ginnane put it back on?

'A reasonable person with knowledge of these facts might well wonder what end of justice is achieved or advanced by making the proposed disclosures,' Ginnane writes in his judgment, delivered on 19 June 2017.

He then answers himself: everyone is entitled to independent legal advice. Everyone. As they are to a fair trial: an enshrined requirement that should not be confused, in some of these cases, with the notion that an innocent man was convicted.

Ginnane's judgment sets out the extraordinary lies that Gobbo perpetrated. It lurches into questions of criminal behaviour by Gobbo and police.

Ginnane walks through the cases of each of the men, now known as the 'Secret Seven'. One of them, Tony Mokbel, is serving a long sentence in jail. Three others — Milad Mokbel, Frank Ahec and Karl Khoder — are now free men. Steve Cvetanovski was granted bail in 2020. Two others who cannot be named received shortened sentences for rolling on their drug-dealing colleagues.

Tony Mokbel would certainly benefit from learning of Gobbo's informing role. The knowledge would provide him with 'substantial assistance in challenging his convictions, at least those in 2006, on the basis that he did not receive a fair trial because he did not have independent counsel'.

Gobbo's betrayal of one particular client forms the essence of the Ginnane judgment. He was the springboard for the subsequent convictions of Milad Mokbel and four other members of the Secret Seven.

All five men were entitled to know how this man's evidence against them was elicited, directly or otherwise, through Gobbo's actions. Had they known this during their trials, those trials almost certainly would have been aborted.

Ginnane finds that the man's case demonstrates the complexity of the issue. He assumed that Gobbo was representing his best interests. He, too, could argue that Gobbo's dual role led to a miscarriage of justice, despite his pleading guilty.

Victoria Police and Gobbo have argued that the information in the proposed DPP letters to the seven criminals will not tell those men 'anything of value'. It's a bold gambit, given the findings of internal police reviews, and the subsequent talk of court appeals and enormous compensation payouts.

Ginnane finds it 'highly likely' that legal professional privilege was breached. His desire to satisfy the paradoxical demands of the law is detailed in the fourth-last point of his sixty-page finding.

'I do not pretend that this conclusion answers the question that I have suggested a reasonable person might ask,' he writes, 'but I consider the public interests in our nation's rule of law and system of criminal justice requires this outcome.'

Telling the world about Gobbo, even at the cost of her life, is the only choice.

Victoria Police have lost. Again.

What do they do? They say no. Again.

The force appeals Ginnane's decision to the Victorian Court of Appeal. On 21 November 2017, the three judges unanimously uphold Ginnane's decision.

So Victoria Police seek leave to appeal to the High Court.

21

Game, Set and Catch

The High Court Decides
2017-2018

In early 2017, as the Supreme Court case drags on, Dowsley and Carlyon come together again to work on an unrelated story. Their last big joint venture was an investigation of the serial rapist Adrian Bayley, who killed journalist Jill Meagher in 2012. Their new case will prove to be equally eye-opening.

James Gargasoulas is a crazed man who took ice then stabbed his brother in the early hours of 20 January, just days after getting bail for previous offences. Gargasoulas was finally shot by police around 4.30 pm after he careered through crowds of pedestrians in Melbourne's Bourke Street, driving a stolen car. He injured twenty-seven people and killed six, including a baby boy thrown sixty metres from his pram, and no one knew why.

Carlyon speaks to victims and witnesses, as well as the medicos who treated Gargasoulas in the same hospital as many of his victims. As previously, Carlyon is struck by Dowsley's knack of speaking with police officers in a way that earns their trust. He may write stories that displease them, but he never exposes them for their unofficial assistance.

Nothing is on the record. No notes are taken until the officer leaves, when both journalists scribble madly on random bits of paper and each hopes that the other has recalled what he forgot.

Dowsley spends his work days on the phone, often not settling at his computer to write until half an hour before deadline. Carlyon covets time to impart a sense of being there, to make what a former colleague once sarcastically referred to as 'powerful observations'.

They blend their strengths in a partnership long forged by their mutual need for coffee — and a shared desire to prove their old newspaper editor, Shirley, wrong in her assessments of them.

Dowsley starts explaining the Lawyer X scandal during these breaks from work.

At first, Carlyon doesn't understand what Dowsley is talking about. Dowsley speaks of Gobbo's baby daughter and rumours of illicit encounters. But the details of the Comrie review, Kellam report and the Supreme Court goings-on remain hidden at this point, even from Dowsley.

Dowsley explains — with diagrams — several times before Carlyon understands the case's import. Carlyon grasps legal tenets, partly from a brief fantasy he once had of studying law.

Dowsley takes Carlyon to meet Nikki Komiazyk, Terry and Christine Hodson's daughter. Dowsley is necessarily careful. His knowledge is legally forbidden, under suppression orders, and he can't tell Komiazyk much.

From Carlyon's point of view, Komiazyk bathes the Gobbo tales in humanity. She cries, a lot, and her distress clarifies the jumble of extraordinary facts. The Gobbo scandal is not just about the disregarded legal rights of drug traffickers and murderers. The bigger story is the suffering of real people through a barrister's abuse of power.

Readers can relate to that. But how to explain the mess to anyone without a law degree?

Dowsley buries Carlyon in confidential documents, then patiently interprets each for him. The coffee breaks turn into after-work drinks, when Dowsley switches from coffee to bourbon and Coke.

Most striking to Carlyon is the way police politics have interfered with the pursuit of truth. If police always set priorities as they did for the Hodson investigations, many more cases would go unsolved.

Carlyon wants in. He goes to see editor Damon Johnston at the start of 2018, right after his Christmas break.

Johnston doesn't yell, like most newspaper editors, yet Carlyon fears a negative response. Newsrooms are shrinking rapidly; journalists must keep busy across many things. Carlyon wants to indulge in the luxury of longer-form journalism at the expense of writing daily news. He's challenging a modern media paradigm in which a story's merits are measured by the number of online hits they generate. Like sports analysis, journalism has become hijacked by nerds and numbers.

Johnston opens up his Lawyer X 'Holy Shit!' dossier, and flicks through clumps of paper as he describes the legal battles between the police and the newspaper. It's a story he likes to tell, and he can't tell it to many people.

Carlyon bluffs his way through the ins and outs: a common theme in his first months on Lawyer X. But he understands Johnston's 'cat and mouse' analogy. He warms to Johnston's pride in the innovative ways the newspaper has avoided legal censure.

Fighting for the truth has cost six-figure sums, in a time of declining readership and revenue across the industry. It could also land Johnston in jail. Both he and the police know the fight will end if a sympathetic judge bows to the police argument about Gobbo's safety.

But there's no room for compromise. The Lawyer X story will be properly told — or it will not be told at all.

Johnston agrees to Carlyon's suggestion that he work exclusively on the story with Dowsley for the next few months. Carlyon and Dowsley are dispatched to another floor, amid the curious murmurs of their colleagues. Sarcasm greets their attempts at secrecy. Their 'little project' casts them as precious.

The alternative floor has been stripped: redundant space in a shrinking organisation. Tape is strung up around areas of unsafe flooring, like cordoned-off crime scenes. Tradies drill and hammer, and wonder why these two blokes are in their worksite.

Dowsley and Carlyon hunker down in their disused-boardroom office, spill dozens of documents onto the table, and wonder what to do next. Here, over countless hours, they 'solve' the Hodson murders again and again.

At some point, perhaps day three, they confront the vastness of their task, as colleagues start finding excuses to sniff around. They poke fun at the pair's whiteboard, which is turned to face the wall before the office is locked each night.

On the board Dowsley is building a cast of characters and a list of topics. A 'Who Knew' section includes three Victoria Police chief commissioners. Soon, the whiteboard is dotted with squiggles, as if a toddler with a Texta has come to consult. The story and its incestuous connections defy neat answers.

Dowsley and Carlyon go to see lawyers and police officers and criminals. Carlyon sometimes wonders which are which. He notes Dowsley's ability to juggle their conflicting interests without once misleading an interviewee.

Dowsley and Carlyon write about 30,000 words: a lot of copy for a tabloid newspaper, especially with no guarantee it will ever be published. The pair rework the ghosts of Gangland. Williams and Mokbel, as well as Karam and the Honoured Society, are recast with a blonde woman as their puppeteer. For Carlyon, the who, what and how aspects of the Gobbo story fall into a loose chronology, but the why remains elusive.

'The Scorpion's Sting', the first instalment of what will be an eight-part exposé, is written working blind. The pair do not possess a single Gobbo police information report.

* * *

On Wednesday, 9 May, Johnston calls Dowsley and Carlyon to his office. They're being shut down, perhaps permanently. Victoria Police have won the right to appeal to the High Court. The saga could drag out another year or more, and Johnston cannot spare that time for two journalists to work on something that may never appear in print.

The force's blind determination to kill the story reminds Carlyon of the cyborg cop in *Terminator 2*. The reputations of those chief commissioners listed on Dowsley's whiteboard seem to matter just as much as the courtroom claims about Gobbo's safety.

On that last day, Dowsley gets an exclusive tip-off that hitman Rodney Collins has died of natural causes in a prison hospital. Dowsley, Carlyon and colleague Mark Buttler write the story up for the next day's paper, emphasising that Collins was the prime suspect as the hitman who killed the Hodsons.

Collins has taken his secret to the grave. His death is another obstacle to uncovering the truth. Did he murder the Hodsons on the say-so of a dirty cop?

Over three months, Dowsley and Carlyon have published only one story related to the Lawyer X scandal. At this rate, they've produced an average of just seventeen published words a day. Their 'little project' stinks of misplaced faith in truth and justice.

The pair tape up boxes of Lawyer X documents, sweep up the empty Diet Coke bottles, and go to the pub.

* * *

Gobbo is still eschewing overtures to accept police protection. She continues to treat the offer as an unpleasant lifestyle choice rather than a lifeline. She doesn't hide — unless the shortening of her Christian name is aimed at confusing hitmen. 'Nicola' has become 'Nicki'. She has a new identity: Supermum.

Her patch is Brighton, a preserve of bayside Melbourne known for blonde women in expensive cars. Here, if anywhere, surely she can blend in, though not all her choices are conventional. Another lawyer spots Gobbo at Baby Bunting in neighbouring Bentleigh as she's getting a child out of the car, a smoke dangling from her mouth.

The mother of two helps out at the Brighton Playroom, her kids' childcare centre. Website photos show her at an event at the centre with local politicians, who wear the fixed smiles of ho-hum electoral duties.

Gobbo has always had a softer side; not that it had much chance to be expressed throughout her informing history. She reminisces about her own childhood under the tutelage of two giving parents. That she might seek to give to others as a parent is not as jarring as it first seems. Volunteer work lacks the thrills and dangers of informing, but Gobbo embraces it as a natural calling.

The Gangland weapon shows 'skilled and selfless leadership' at the centre. She is 'practical and passionate'. She engineers 'transformational changes — from strengthening child safety policies to finding ways to help disadvantaged families'. Gobbo helps create a 'true community hub' at Brighton Playroom.

How do we know all this? It comes from a Victorian Premier's Award citation in September 2018.

Gobbo picks up her volunteer's award from Victoria's Early Childhood Minister Jenny Mikakos at Government House, the one-time residence of her uncle, Sir James Gobbo. Hailed as the Brighton Playroom's saviour, she beams for the media's cameras. She looks younger and fresher than she did a decade ago. Her sculpted features prompt murmurs that she has 'had work'.

Now she's just another Gobbo doing good things, and never mind the death threats.

Johnston does not let the opportunity pass. He dispatches a *Herald Sun* photographer to the event to snap Gobbo in case the legal suppression of her identity is ever lifted.

In early November 2018, as president of her daughter's Brighton kinder, Wilson Street Kindergarten, Gobbo attends an end-of-year celebration at a local park. The mums sip wines from plastic glasses, while the dads watch over the kids as they ride bikes and climb on the play equipment.

Gobbo has maintained an illusion of normality for several years. The other mothers don't know anything about the police threats to forcibly remove her children if she doesn't change her name and move away. Nicki is just another mum, a kindly person who accommodates parents seeking to change session times, even if her trademark bluntness has survived her shift of roles. 'If you don't behave, I'll put you in the boot,' she is overheard telling her son tongue-in-cheek.

The normality is about to end, and Gobbo knows it. The same week as the kinder park catch-up, she is spotted at Flight Centre in Bentleigh.

She needs a ticket overseas, she tells staff. 'You'll know all about it next week.'

* * *

Dowsley gets a call around the same time — a few days after the running of the Melbourne Cup on 6 November.

The reliable source speaks in code. 'That thing. I'd start writing.'

The murk clears in ensuing calls, equally secretive, with other sources. The High Court has made its decision.

Dowsley and Carlyon are told that Victoria Police won't like it.

* * *

On 25 November, over six months after Carlyon and Dowsley downed tools, events can finally be mapped.

The High Court decision remains a closely guarded secret. Off stage, Victoria Police are still scrambling to conceal Gobbo's identity on safety grounds. Indications — and they are only hints — suggest the High Court has denied Victoria Police's appeal.

It will announce its decision publicly at 9 am on Monday 3 December: 1708 days after Dowsley's first Lawyer X story.

The police can no longer hide the truth.

* * *

Strange as it may seem, the almost certain knowledge that Gobbo's story can finally be told is *not* met with high-fives at the *Herald Sun*. Dowsley jiggles, Johnston calls the company lawyers. Carlyon swears absently. He had come to assume that, like his chances of placing a winning Melbourne Cup bet, this moment would never come to pass.

Then Carlyon and Dowsley scramble again. Deputy editor Chris Tinkler doesn't carry a whip, but perhaps he should. He, Dowsley and Carlyon second an office — on the same floor as the *Herald Sun* newsroom this time — which they promptly fill with fast-food wrappers.

The secret is unofficially out. Colleagues no longer snigger about the crazy story that seems bigger and longer than any other.

Suppression bans prevent disclosure of the High Court decision before 3 December. But stories alluding to a big announcement — without naming the announcement itself — are an occupational necessity. Another news outlet could scoop the *Herald Sun* on a story that the newspaper single-handedly brought to public attention.

Dowsley and Carlyon write a front-page story on 30 November. It is a 'teaser' that flags 'one of the biggest scandals in Victoria's legal history'. The next day, a story about Tony Mokbel's bid for release is headlined 'A Wig and a Prayer'.

Disbelief tinges these days. Carlyon wonders whether Victoria Police will stymie the High Court judgment, but doesn't doubt that they will try. Dowsley picks up snippets: that letters of disclosure will be sent to a handful or more of convicted criminals, but that perhaps 600 cases will be affected.

The moniker of 'Lawyer X' is coming back, but will Gobbo's name and age still be hidden from view? Will she be able to 'tend to be identified', through details such as her gender and background?

Different versions of newspaper stories, with differing levels of detail, are prepared. Scrupulous checks and balances are applied: depending on legal restrictions, all references in draft stories to 'Nicola Gobbo' may have to change to 'Lawyer X'. The *Herald Sun* assumes the police will fight to prevent every scrap of truth from being published.

* * *

Carlyon wakes on the morning of Monday 3 December and sneaks in a comfort cigarette to prepare for the intense day ahead. Dowsley has slept poorly.

In their frenzied skimming after the High Court judgment is released at 9 am, they find a strident denunciation that vindicates Dowsley's years-long pursuit.

The High Court ruling is unequivocal. It encapsulates the astonishment of other judgments and reviews over the past six years.

The seven judges express naked wrath at Victoria Police and Gobbo. They find that the Gobbo subterfuge was 'deliberate' and 'most likely a criminal offence'.

The High Court appeal bid was held under the easiest of conditions for Gobbo and Victoria Police. The individuals affected by Gobbo's informing, the prisoners languishing in jail, could not be heard. They could not contradict the evidence of the police or Gobbo.

When Gobbo gave evidence in the Ginnane trial, she invoked legal professional privilege to refuse to answer questions about clients. Now she can no longer dictate the outcomes. Both she and Victoria Police have failed to appreciate the impact of their behaviour.

The court cites a 1908 judgment that states 'the end does not justify the means'.

Victoria Police are guilty of reprehensible conduct in knowingly encouraging EF [Gobbo] to do as she did and were involved in sanctioning atrocious breaches of the sworn duty of every police officer to discharge all duties imposed on them faithfully and according to law without favour or affection, malice or ill-will. As a result, the prosecution of each Convicted Person was corrupted in a manner which debased fundamental premises of the criminal justice system.

Gobbo's vetting of police briefs — against her own clients — and Victoria Police's concerted efforts to conceal it are described with particular eloquence by the High Court: 'They poisoned the fountain of justice.'

The court will suppress Gobbo's name for three months for safety reasons. Yet if Gobbo and her children are endangered by the court's decision, the responsibility does not lie with the judiciary: 'If EF [Gobbo] chooses to expose herself to consequent risk by declining to enter into the witness protection program, she will be bound by the consequences. If she chooses to expose her children to similar risks, the State is empowered to take action to protect them from harm.'

* * *

Later that morning, Dowsley and Carlyon happen to be standing together in the *Herald Sun* newsroom when they hear a radio news report. Premier Daniel Andrews has made an announcement following the High Court's decision.

Carlyon turns to Dowsley. 'Ha,' he says. 'You got your royal commission.'

* * *

The days after the revelations of 3 December 2018 are odd for many of the main players in the Gobbo saga.

Lawyer Ruth Parker is outraged when the Gobbo conspiracy against her client Faruk Orman is revealed. He is featured in Gobbo's list of top-ten stings in her 2015 letter to Steve Fontana. He was convicted of murder in circumstances in which the court, and his defence team, were denied critical knowledge about Gobbo's deceit.

Parker gets on ABC radio and demands police documents relating to her client's case. She calls the Gobbo revelations a 'disgrace'. It works, too: she receives the confidential police information reports about her client long before other lawyers who deploy the more conventional path of paper wars with Victoria Police.

But Parker's win comes at a price. It concerns the strange story of the $250,000 S450 Mercedes parked outside her home in Melbourne's southern suburbs. Parker is preoccupied with preparing for a trip to Bali and doesn't notice the car herself, but neighbours do when it sits unattended for days.

She leaves for her holiday in December, having mentioned her departure to friends and colleagues in phone and email correspondence. At the last minute, a relative decides to housesit.

The day after Parker's departure, the keys of the strange Mercedes turn up on her kitchen island — *inside her locked home.*

How did they get there? And why, if there was a break-in, was nothing stolen?

Parker has theories. She thinks the car keys were left behind by an intruder, who got a fright after he entered the house. He did not want to take anything, she suggests, but rather add an unwelcome extra: an electronic bug.

The scenario sounds removed from reality, but her suspicions are heightened after she calls police about the car keys in her home. Police later tell her they have no record of her report.

Some of her fellow lawyers worry that their offices have been illegally entered, and that their phones have been bugged.

Other reactions vary.

Roberta Williams seethes. 'Give me five minutes with that woman ...' she begins, before launching into violent fantasies.

A Gangland judge is overheard in a Richmond shop: 'I could kill her. It was always me, me, me with her.'

Garde-Wilson feels vindicated; she almost worked out the Gobbo secret years ago.

Dowsley, too, wonders if police have ever listened to his phone calls. An unexpected police attempt to suppress the name of the European occurs a day or so after Dowsley muses on the phone with Parker about the European's life outside of jail.

Carlyon wonders about men in trucks listening to his blather about bad bets and school drop-offs, and he pities them. Intermittent drop-outs during phone calls may be a giveaway of surveillance — or a sign of Bluetooth unreliability.

The media cavalcade mob the obvious targets. Simon Overland, now a local council chief executive at Whittlesea in Melbourne's north, faces questions about being the architect of Gobbo's use. And more questions about the misgivings of his old deputy, Sir Ken Jones, who wondered if some police officers perjured themselves.

Journalists also mob Detective Senior Sergeant Ron Iddles, who speaks of a wide group of police officers, reaching high within the organisation, who knew about the secret.

The public wants the truth. Overland says nothing, except to berate a *Herald Sun* photographer camped outside his inner Melbourne home.

Former chief commissioner Christine Nixon is silent too. So is Assistant Commissioner Luke Cornelius, and the force's head lawyer, Fin McRae.

Dozens of officers enveloped by the Gobbo conspiracy, serving or retired, are called to a crisis meeting. Some of them are miffed; they had no idea that closed-court battles have been raging for years.

The only one who *does* speak is Chief Commissioner Graham Ashton.

Ashton projects confidence for the TV cameras. He uses desperate-times-desperate-measures rhetoric to defend the use of Gobbo in the struggle to stop the Gangland War. The Gangland murders slowed after Williams was jailed in June 2004, fifteen months *before* Gobbo was registered as 3838, but the timing does not figure in his analysis.

He labels the damning language used by successive judges to describe police as 'colourful'. He doesn't elaborate on his own role in Gobbo's use, or reveal that his knowledge of her informing traces to 2007 or earlier.

Put side by side, the earlier police admissions in court and the Chief Commissioner's comments for the cameras do not gel. Corporate image appears to drive the public strategy.

His 'high-risk decisions in high-risk times' comments get some traction. Legal professional privilege and the 'golden rule' of disclosure may be pillars of justice, but they pale into abstractions for those seduced by the Gangland folklore.

Victorians ask the same 'reasonable' questions posed by Justice Ginnane in the Supreme Court: does the depriving of legal niceties owed to Carl Williams and Tony Mokbel matter when both men sold drugs by the kilogram? These bastards belong in jail, don't they? A *Herald Sun* letter writer wants Gobbo crowned as Australian of the Year.

In Barwon Prison, prisoners jostle for instant release. Russell Street Police Headquarters bomber and jailhouse lawyer Craig Minogue drafts documents for fellow prisoners. Mokbel reduces his freedom timeline from years to months. Every jailbird suddenly seems to be connected with Lawyer X. 'I'm fucking outta here, darling,' says a well-known prisoner.

* * *

Carlyon and Dowsley slog through days of twelve hours or more in the weeks after the High Court announcement. Even so, their succession of front-page stories can't match the longest run of splashes in *Herald Sun* history: the fallout of an affair between AFL footballer Wayne Carey and a team-mate's wife in 2002.

Dowsley and Carlyon feel, once again, like little players in a larger scrum. Other journalists, very good ones, have revealed isolated truths about Gobbo's informing since Dowsley's exposé. Now he has to share the secret he uncovered almost five years ago with the rest of the media pack.

Yet, thanks to Melbourne's historical reserve — elsewhere labelled snobbery — the story doesn't reverberate nationally as it would have had Lawyer X happened in Sydney.

* * *

Parker, meanwhile, sets a precedent. After using the media to get her hands on the internal documents other lawyers have sought for years, she petitions Victoria's Attorney-General, Jill Hennessy, who will send Faruk Orman's case back to the Court of Appeal on 25 June 2019. Orman's appeal options ran out back in 2011.

Yet Victoria Police are still reluctant to disclose any information to Tony Mokbel or Rob Karam. Both criminals have fought long appeals with their eyes closed. Documents to support their claims have repeatedly been refused, despite the now-established premise that Gobbo incriminated them while she was also representing them.

Gobbo is yet to be named, but she is disarmed of her survival mechanism of plausible deniability. She is cleansed from the internet as thoroughly as Victoria Police can manage. Her Premier's Awards citation disappears from the web. She will cease to exist by all the measures she holds dear.

She has remained close to her half-sister Linda, and may have spent Christmas with her just weeks after the High Court's bombshell.

The new Elvis sightings are of a peroxide blonde who stands out in a crowd. Gobbo is 'sighted' in Rome, Capri, London, Asia, Victoria's Mornington Peninsula and yes, Brighton too.

The whispers of exotic destinations hide an uglier prospect. Like many of those she once incriminated, Gobbo is serving a life sentence, trapped by her past.

Gobbo's predicament brings to mind Isaiah's verse about turning to the left or right, before hearing the voice from behind. She can no longer walk her own path. The courts have shepherded her in directions not of her choosing. She has everywhere to hide and nowhere to go.

And as 2019 begins, the pressure will mount.

22

The Reckoning

A Royal Commission, and the Naming
of Nicola Gobbo
2018-2019

The launch of a royal commission by Victoria's Premier Daniel Andrews was a political no-brainer. Not that the police accepted this. They had received the High Court ruling before it was published and pleaded with Jill Hennessy, who had just been sworn in as the State's 77th Attorney-General. Their message was simple: please don't call a royal commission.

Hennessy wasn't swayed. As she told the press during the High Court announcement on the morning of 3 December: 'Only a royal commission will get the answers needed so that something like this can never happen again.'

But until 6 February 2019, no one bar Victoria Police knew the startling detail that changed everything.

After the High Court decision in December, it was officially revealed — as Dowsley had long believed — that Gobbo was previously registered as an informer in 1999.

But in June 2018, confidential papers from the pre-computer era of police record-keeping were uncovered in an archive centre. They showed that Gobbo was first registered not in 1999, but in 1995. Senior police did not confirm Gobbo's 1999 registration during the Comrie, Kellam or Ginnane inquiries into her informing. It appears they didn't know about her earlier registration.

302

She was an official informer, on and off, for fifteen years, not the three and a half years that numerous hearings were told about. Gobbo was Informer G395 before she was Informer MFG13, before she was Informer 3838, before she was Informer 2958.

Police only get around to telling the royal commission about it the following Australia Day, eight weeks after the commission is launched. The informer registration — two pages of handwritten notes in answer to *pro forma* questions — has been overlooked by Victoria Police over eight years of reviewing themselves in relation to Gobbo's use. The oversight doesn't say much for the force's powers of detection, organisation, or commitment to the task of transparency.

The revelations are symptomatic. The Gobbo devils lie buried in the detail, like gem specks that only flicker in bright light. And the details keep changing: as a consequence of the 1995 registration discovery, the commission's terms of reference have to be formally amended.

The new terms also give the commission scope to examine the possibility that Gobbo informed unofficially as well. The best chances of making sense of her tale are scattered among the scribblings of decades-old log books, police diaries and information reports.

* * *

The opening statement of Commissioner Margaret McMurdo, on 15 February 2019, sets out the royal commission's lines of inquiry. It will determine how many cases have been affected by Gobbo's duplicity throughout the entire period of her informing, and to what extent. It will scrutinise police handling of informers in the light of their professional obligations of confidentiality.

Royal commissions are the outliers of the justice system, change agents that apply a legal blowtorch to perceived improperness. Criminal acts identified by a royal commission can only be prosecuted by other agencies. The 2019 Royal Commission into the Management of Police Informants looms as a paradox, a potential launching pad for the criminal prosecution of the criminal prosecutors.

McMurdo is perched above a crowded gallery in a sixth-floor room of the Fair Work Commission in Exhibition Street, Melbourne. No Gobbo-style mini-skirts or exposed cleavages in *this* hearing room.

Dowsley is here, dressed as though he's slept in, as is Carlyon, who wears a Hugo Boss suit he cannot really afford. Unlike the lawyers he temporarily resembles, he does not earn up to $10,000 a day.

The gallery whispers about Tony Mokbel's life prospects. He was stabbed and badly beaten in Barwon Prison a few days ago, in an incident unrelated to Nicola Gobbo, though it occurred not long after he composed 500 legal questions about his former lawyer. He was carried out of jail and into intensive care.

Twenty-two lawyers huddle at the bar table, including seven QCs. Waiting journalists fish for a collective noun and settle on 'a murder of crows'. 'There's never been such a shitstorm,' one of the QCs later declares.

McMurdo reads from the High Court's judgment, which essentially found that the administration of justice trumped Gobbo's life: 'EF's [Gobbo's] actions in purporting to act as counsel for the Convicted Persons while covertly informing against them were fundamental and appalling breaches of EF's obligations as counsel to her clients and of EF's duties to the court.'

McMurdo is a former president of the Queensland Court of Appeal. Her in-court persona — pearls and a queenly bearing — is replaced out of session by leather jackets and a breeziness described as 'boho'. She likes stage shows and retreats from work by heading to the beach. McMurdo will foster commission staff loyalty by bringing fruit to share each day.

She is across the wider commentary on the Lawyer X issue. She knows that ordinary people wonder why the Lawyer X commotion may offer freedom to the guilty. 'Some members of the public may query the outrage expressed by the courts, professional associations and legal academics at the conduct of EF [Gobbo] and the police, arguing that it had a positive effect, namely, the conviction of serious offenders,' she says.

'But, as the courts have explained, these are matters of high principle, fundamental to our democracy. The Rule of Law requires that everyone (the rich, the disempowered, the poor, the mighty, individuals, governments and their agencies, police officers and corporations), everyone is answerable to the same laws before independent courts.'

McMurdo adjourns the hearing soon afterwards. She stands, bows to the gallery in keeping with courtroom etiquette, and tries to leave through a door behind the bench.

But the door will not open. The unexpected delay is the first of many unexpected delays ahead.

Even leaving aside the debacle of Victoria Police's belated Gobbo disclosure, this royal commission is hamstrung from its inception. It has subpoena powers and the right to raid properties. It has authority to compel killers and disgraced cops to give evidence, as well as countless serving officers who either can't remember or don't want to. What the royal commission does not have is time.

Its deadlines have been forged in hell: seven months for interim findings, and just over a year to finish. Thousands of documents have to be produced, dozens of people examined. Many of them will receive aliases, checking the media's ability to add context to complicated issues.

There are other challenges. In its first weeks, the inquiry is legally suppressed from naming the lawyer responsible for its launch. Gobbo is protected as an official ghost for three months after the High Court ruling. Who said justice was blind?

Elsewhere, legal machinations rumble anew. Police have not given up. Outed for 'atrocious' and 'reprehensible' behaviour, the force once again seeks a permanent block on publishing Gobbo's identity.

Victoria Police have returned to the High Court since the unfavourable judgment to argue that the court's decision to name Gobbo endangers her life. The legal logic of the strategy, after a succession of failed claims, is unclear, though the vigour of the force's fight cannot be questioned. Here is a boxer, knocked down again and again, who just keeps getting up. The police want the genie back in the bottle — or, to use the journalists' vernacular, the shit pushed back in the donkey.

Victoria Police have failed the demands of justice and, yes, failed the needs of Gobbo too. But they're still arse-covering, despite being dacked over and over.

Gobbo is considered to be in less danger than previously, however. She is a commodity worth more alive to the crooks she has betrayed than dead. She could give evidence that will help free them.

Victoria Police's High Court submission is opposed by the *Herald Sun*, the royal commission and the Directors of Public Prosecution, both State and Commonwealth. The police will lose this legal battle, as they have every other significant legal contest since Dowsley's 2014 story. Gobbo will be named and her picture will be published.

* * *

Friday, 1 March 2019 at 4 pm looms as a ta-da moment, when pictures of Lawyer X can finally be published alongside her name. For the first time, Dowsley is confronted with *being* the news instead of reporting it. He stands at a press conference that morning, wearing a suit for once, in front of the microphones and not behind them.

He has been interviewed dozens of times over recent months, but has never faced a press pack. He has trained himself not to let Gobbo's name slip, a legal breach that could see him jailed. He thinks how it would be just like him to stuff it up and name Gobbo only hours before he's officially allowed to.

It's almost five years since Damon Johnston elected not to name Gobbo in Dowsley's original story. Mind you, throughout this time, the more curious could easily have identified Gobbo through a 'Lawyer X' Google search. Finding her name, even with some of the poorest search speeds in the developed world, took about four seconds.

Carlyon wonders whether naming Gobbo is necessarily the breakthrough it appears to be. Her mystique will dissolve.

Naming Gobbo frightens Dowsley; five years on, he's still concerned about her safety.

As 4 pm approaches, and the *Herald Sun* readies its online story, 'Nicola Gobbo Is Lawyer X', nerves and excitement coalesce among the huddles in the newsroom.

Johnston has slain a legal bully. But the release of Gobbo's name is tinged with unease, not triumph.

'What happens now?' Dowsley thinks, as he and Carlyon sip office beers, a rare festivity in a modern newsroom. He avoids the misplaced sense of jubilation that tends to infect journalists on the taking of a scalp. Here is a serious moment, with potentially serious consequences.

Then he realises he's drinking Victoria Bitter. Of all beers, he hates VB the most.

* * *

Victoria Police have never welcomed royal commissions. One of the last Victorian police probes was the Beach Inquiry in 1975 and 1976. It recommended charges against fifty-five Victorian officers after examining old-school practices of false confessions and evidence-planting. Of the thirty-three officers eventually prosecuted, none were convicted, and two later rose to be deputy commissioners.

Public pressure for an inquiry into links between corrupt cops and murder exploded after the Hodson killings in 2004. Premier Steve Bracks toyed with the idea of launching a royal commission. Chief Commissioner Christine Nixon privately threatened to resign in the face of continuing calls for a royal commission into police corruption. Instead, Victoria got the Office of Police Integrity and the Office of the Chief Examiner, controversial bodies with coercive powers.

Nixon was jolted by her experience at the Victorian Bushfires Royal Commission in 2010. She was embarrassed by revelations that she left the emergency control centre at about 6 pm on 7 February 2009, the night of the Black Saturday fires. 'I had to eat,' she later said on radio, unwisely, given it emerged she had received reports that many Victorians would die in the inferno.

The onslaught she was subjected to in 2010 reinforced her long-held doubts. She felt royal commissions tended to be hijacked, derailed or ambushed. 'A royal commission process can become the worst kind of kangaroo court if it is not managed properly, and it is all about playing to the audience,' she wrote in her book *Fair Cop*. 'It becomes a public flogging. It doesn't say much about us as an evolved community if that sort of method is still considered appropriate.'

Victoria Police disdain the current royal commission as much as they have every inquiry into their conduct over the past century. This is obvious from the very first day of hearings on 27 March 2019.

Predictably, the inquiry does not begin hearing evidence that day at the prescribed time of 10 am. There are to be hours of legal wrangling first. Yet again, Victoria Police apply all the arguments that have failed over five years of lengthy, taxpayer-funded court proceedings.

The pattern of the months ahead is set in those first minutes. Victoria Police cannot locate the relevant documents within the prescribed timeframes. They need to make redactions before documents can be released. They fear for the safety of this or that person. No issue seems too small for their consideration.

'Life isn't easy,' McMurdo remarks in the early weeks.

'It's not in here,' replies junior counsel assisting her, Andrew Woods.

Soon enough, legal suppression orders fill the door of the media room, which adjoins the hearing room. They spread to the next wall, like concert posters pasted at a railway station. One or two solicitors from the legal firm representing the police sit in the gallery each day, like props borrowed from *The X-Files*.

The Victoria Police approach is effective, at least insofar as it ensures the royal commission is soon weeks behind what is described by Counsel Assisting the Commission, Chris Winneke QC, as an 'ambitious' timetable. Observers will be ejected from the room almost daily for *in camera* arguments. The constant objections of Victoria Police's barrister Saul Holt QC, an urbane and witty fixture outside the courtroom, will feel like death by a thousand 'buts'.

Police have dedicated 100 people, over four floors, at an estimated cost of $1.5 million a month, to the royal commission demands of disclosure. Their purported inability to find, redact and readily produce internal documents seems self-serving.

Much like the German war machine of World War II, Victoria Police have written almost everything down. This royal commission is like a never-ending onion: layer upon layer of events first depicted in the *Herald Sun*, peeled back by the participants, some of whom reach for the Nuremberg defence of 'following orders'.

Gobbo herself referred to the volume of police material during the Ginnane Supreme Court trial in 2017: 'What I was told on a number of occasions was that — and it was over time in an increasingly joking kind of way — there was literally a warehouse-sized vault full of documents, diary entries and recordings,' she testified.

Yet these documents are not being handed over in a hurry, with police asserting they are struggling to keep up with the sheer volume of requests. Have police misplaced the warehouse? Observers wonder why police were not compelled to hand over every document up front, then invited to seek to suppress or redact each document on a case-by-case basis.

'Can I suggest to you and those instructing you, remind your clients [Victoria Police] that this notice to produce, and their obligations under it, which are ongoing, that it is an offence not to comply with it and an agency of the Crown, under the *Inquiries Act*, can be charged,' Ms McMurdo says in June 2019.

Her wry asides have come to stamp the process. In May, she reaches for analogies. She joins in 'having a whinge about Victoria Police'. The initial statement of Detective Sergeant Sol Solomon, so damning of senior brass's handling of the Hodson murders, appears to have been held back deliberately.

McMurdo doesn't say explicitly what everyone else is thinking: that the police's inefficiency is a tactic. The Court of Appeal has voiced similar concerns in appeal applications by Tony Mokbel, Rob Karam and Steve Cvetanovski. By withholding documents, the police have dictated the flow and speed of the telling of Gobbo's tale. It seems wrong, given it's the police who want to *impede* the telling of the tale.

'Historical suppression and non-publication orders and constant public interest immunity claims sometimes make my task in moving this commission forward in public akin to a boxer in a fighting match with one hand tied behind his back and the other bruised and bleeding,' McMurdo says after less than three months of hearings. 'But I am still upright and focused on a positive conclusion.'

McMurdo receives some good news soon afterwards, on 25 May. Her commission budget is almost quadrupled, to $27.5 million (later lifted to $39.5 million), and she now has until July 2020 (later extended again to November 2020) to finish her report.

But there's bad news too. In August, time-stamping shows that Victoria Police have failed to provide documents that they reviewed months earlier. This confirms what was already suspected. Starving examiners of time to assess what's before them by last-minute delivery of voluminous documentation is a craven strategy usually employed by corporations and politicians with things to hide.

Echoing the thoughts of Christine Nixon, Victoria Police appear to be treating this royal commission like a kangaroo court. They didn't seem to mind, during the Gangland War, when a newspaper published the real name of Shifty, the getaway driver in the Michael Marshall, Jason Moran and Pasquale Barbaro killings. Shifty was the first in Gangland to roll; that was a *good* news story.

Now, in response to *bad* news stories, the force tries to keep changing the names of informers. Police demand new pseudonyms to replace the old aliases.

The force presents an obsequious front in presenting arguments about informer safety. Yet cynics identify other motivations, such as fear and loathing.

Senior brass are potentially facing criminal charges, as are those further down the chain of command.

* * *

The commission takes a chronological approach, starting with Gobbo's earliest encounters with police. Dozens of police officers give evidence in these first months, answering the questions of a team headed by Winneke.

Like Carlyon, Winneke loses his father in 2019 — in his case, eight days after the royal commission hearings began. No one would have guessed.

Winneke is patient, conducting a verbal tap dance with witnesses. He is methodical, devoid of TV-lawyer theatrics. He does not inflate at the sound of his own voice as some barristers do.

Certain officers appear to admit to perjury in protecting Gobbo, yet Winneke does not seek to brand them as criminals. His understated approach brings to mind Paul Keating's 1992 riposte 'I want to do you slowly.'

Winneke questions officers on their understanding of client confidentiality, which they all learned about in training. He wonders why they ignored this training in their dealings with Nicola Gobbo. Some officers say they felt uneasy about Gobbo's use, especially her omnipotence before, during and after the Mokbel drug empire was brought down. But most take their cue from a force steeped in intransigence against scrutiny.

On 1 and 2 April, Jeff Pope tells the royal commission that before taking on his role at the Covert Services Division, he informed superiors, including Sir Ken Jones and Simon Overland, about his professional history with Gobbo. He figured then that his work might involve her.

It's tempting to sympathise with Pope in the witness box. He's represented by a barrister who earns a reputed $1100 an hour, but the price cannot protect Pope's name. His forehead is sheened in sweat, his wedding ring shiny even in the dim lighting.

Yet he projects complete certainty on the sex question. He utterly denies a liaison with Gobbo two decades earlier. Had he slept with Gobbo, he says convincingly, he would never have returned to Victoria Police for a second stint.

Dowsley and Carlyon feel sympathy for Pope for another reason. In the witness box, Pope is accused of revealing Gobbo's informer status to Dowsley. Dowsley did not discover the secret from Pope.

David Miechel, the former Drug Squad detective and Dublin Street drug-house burglar, is quietly spoken in the witness box on 22 May, after almost thirteen years in jail. His exit is choreographed to ensure he does not encounter his one-time co-accused, Paul Dale, outside the hearing room.

Dale gives evidence on various dates between 22 May and 25 June. On the stand, he is so belligerent that Winneke reminds him that he was not 'a baby' at the time of the Hodson killings, but a 'grown-up' detective.

Like Gobbo, Dale prefers to dwell on the consequences of events than on their causes. He is obsessed with his treatment by police, but he isn't as interested in explaining how they arrived at their suspicions.

He becomes flushed, in a rage that remains unvarnished fifteen years after he was accused first of burglary, then of murder. His hands are hidden from view; at times, they are surely balled.

Victoria Police's legal team have the opportunity to cross-examine Dale, a suspect in a notorious unsolved murder. And pass. It's a recurring frustration for journalists: that unprecedented insights into murders and serious crimes go unexplored because they do not slot into the commission's terms of reference.

Dale tells Dowsley and Carlyon he was pleased when a truck turned up at his northern Victoria home in early 2019 and took away thirty-three boxes of documents for the royal commission's use. 'I was just alleged corrupt cop Paul Dale and no one will listen,' he said. 'But it's all starting to come out now … slowly.'

He leaped into the royal commission witness box in 2019 with 'great excitement', he says. He described police who 'perjured themselves', in a day's evidence marked by his ability to turn his answer to any question into a tirade about police corruption.

* * *

'[T]he people we're investigating are murderers and drug dealers,' Purana detective Paul Rowe tells the commission during his second day of evidence on 1 July. 'We can't just go, "It's all too hard, we don't do it." There's risk that comes along with it. We do our very best to manage the risk and keep people safe.'

Rowe was the officer who took the phone call from Gobbo that led to her becoming Informer 3838. He defies the cookie-cutter caution of most police in the witness box. He is much more forthright than his colleagues. He says Gobbo was no 'delicate flower'. Police were 'not running a day-care centre for barristers who have lost their way'. 'All we cared about is criminal activity that was ongoing that was right there in front of our face,' he says.

'I think a heap of Victoria Police members would be more relieved if she had … just disappeared into the sunset,' he continues. 'That would have been a win for certainly the Purana Task Force and probably the majority of Victoria Police. No end of grief was caused, no end of grief.'

On 1 and 2 July, Stuart Bateson sounds assured, but he admits that Gobbo helped him change her client Shifty's statement. Later, he offers his perspective on the sorry scandal.

Bateson argues that it is possible to be both a barrister and informer. He also queries whether a criminal was entitled to 'independent counsel'.

'I think you can do two things,' he tells Winneke. 'Would this ever happen again? Clearly not. But my view is you can be a human source and a barrister at the same time.'

Yet Bateson concedes that if he knew then what he knows now, he 'probably' would've acted differently. He is cool in the witness box, as if channelling his *Underbelly* TV character Steve Owen. In between sittings, he exchanges pleasantries with Dowsley.

Between 30 July and 5 September, Gobbo's controller at the Source Development Unit, Sandy White, speaks down the phone to give evidence — for seventeen days in all. 'Mr White' blends with the pseudonyms of his subordinates, including 'Mr Green' and 'Mr Black', which also nod to Tarantino-esque stylings. The joke goes around that no one wants to be Mr Pink.

Gobbo's old handlers have opted for separate legal representation from Victoria Police, fearing they could be scapegoated by senior brass.

As they give evidence, one after the other, the absence of a female voice reasserts Gobbo's solitary place as a woman in a man's world.

White is proud that his team solved numerous serious crimes, and defiant in the face of suggestions that they cheated the legal system. But his clear-cut judgments are smudged by the emerging evidence.

Why didn't police seek legal advice about its use of Gobbo at the start? White 'did not think it was necessary' to consult with the police legal department. Nor does he think Gobbo committed any crimes in her dealings with his unit.

White's superior, Overland, a trained lawyer, didn't see fit to check the legals either. The available evidence suggests that he and White didn't want to. Inspector Andrew Allen, the first head of Purana, says he would have sought legal advice. He didn't know about Gobbo's informing; to him, she was 'just a crooked lawyer', a female 'Walter Mitty'.

Victoria Police knew the arrangement was questionable. It hid Gobbo's informing from scrutiny from day one and it's still trying to hide it at the commission, fourteen years later.

* * *

The first ex-con in the royal commission witness box is also one of the first whom Gobbo double-crossed. Pistol Pete — who gives evidence as 'Person 12' on 21 and 22 May — was set to be a Crown witness against four cops from St Kilda Police Station in 1999 but pulled out. What he didn't realise was that his lawyer was sleeping with one of them.

He is 'shocked' about his lawyer's romance with a police officer whose legal case conflicted with his own. If he'd known, he says, drawing gasps, he would have asked her 'when it was my turn'.

Pistol Pete is a convicted killer. He speaks the shorthand of the underworld. He offers a refreshing counterpoint to the police defence of Gobbo's use. He seems to grasp the wrongness of Gobbo's intimate associations better than any royal commission witness wearing a police badge. His views are later shared by a Mokbel drug dealer, and the European.

Soon enough, Pistol Pete will decide to sue Victoria Police for an obscenely large amount. His lawyer will be Levi Diamond, the one-time employer of Gobbo whom she helped police try to jail.

None of the criminals who give evidence sound like they need a royal commission to know that what Gobbo did to them was wrong.

* * *

In secret hearings, the royal commission has deeply probed the question of whether prosecuting lawyers knew that they were working on cases built from Gobbo's informing. Were they in on the secret when they prosecuted the likes of Carl Williams, Tony Mokbel and their henchmen? These secret hearings could be the great untold element of the Gobbo story. Did the conspiracy seep further than Victoria Police?

The evidence suggests not. But the controversy still raises concerns about what prosecutors knew, and when. Dowsley and Carlyon are told that some Commonwealth prosecutors *did* know at Paul Dale's trial for allegedly lying to the ACC in 2011, in speculations later borne out in royal commission testimony. Although it's not clear whether they knew the full extent of her double-dealing.

If any prosecutors *did* knowingly bring unfairly presented cases to the court, they, like Gobbo, probably broke the law.

* * *

Royal commission lawyers turn up at Melbourne's Court of Appeal on 26 July 2019. They want to see this. So do the BBC and other international media, as well as a lone Purana detective who tries to become invisible. Observers, so crammed that they can't shed their winter coats, sweat for the first time since the annual grey enveloped Melbourne.

Faruk Orman, the convicted murderer of Victor Peirce, has waited twelve years for this moment. He is about to become the first criminal to be freed from prison because he was cheated by Nicola Gobbo. He walks into the first-floor hearing as a baby-faced assassin and walks out as a victim of injustice.

This is no ordinary mention hearing. Orman's guards do not try to settle his exuberance. He wears no shackles. No scowls. A suit balloons on his thin frame, as if he has borrowed clothes from a big brother, feeding the notion that time stopped when he went away.

The court hears about the 'fundamental breach' that goes 'to the very foundations of the system of a criminal trial'. Orman listens to accounts of his unwitting error on 22 June 2007, when he was arrested and his first call was to Gobbo.

She was determined to get him. She was also the lawyer for the European, the main witness in the murder case against him. She advised police about convincing the European to give evidence against Orman ('put him straight') after he hesitated about testifying. She lined a criminal up against a suspect, and she didn't care about the conflicts until there was a risk that her devilishness would be revealed.

Descriptors for Gobbo's behaviour flow around the courtroom, from 'improper' to 'outrageous'.

Yet the police's use of her in informing against Orman does not feature. Her client conflicts alone are enough to quash Orman's conviction. Victoria Police get a leave pass. Their underhanded and multi-pronged approach to getting at Orman through Gobbo is not examined in this forum.

Orman does not wallow in bitterness after he is freed by the court. He expresses gratitude to the Attorney-General, Jill Hennessy, for accepting his petition for mercy after all his avenues of appeal were gone. Talk of multi-million-dollar compensation claims is for another time.

Orman's history has been unwritten. His release is not a validation of innocence necessarily, but a recognition of justice undermined. In his case, Victoria Police rigged the odds in their own favour, like a football team that fields too many players.

Robert Richter, the lead barrister at Orman's original trial, was unaware of Gobbo's subterfuge until later. He didn't know about it when she pulled out of acting as his junior, and he still didn't know about it when he helped expel Gobbo from Crockett Chambers years later. He laments the Orman case as one of three — including his defence of Cardinal George Pell — that did not go the way he expected.

Will Tony Mokbel, Rob Karam and others imprisoned by Gobbo's informing be released too? In 2020, their appeal lawyers will still be waiting for the necessary documentation from Victoria Police. The force isn't to be rushed — either in the royal commission, or in addressing the wrongs identified by Neil Comrie back in 2012.

Gobbo's deception of Mokbel and Karam, as well as mafia boss Pasquale 'Muscles' Barbaro and his Tomato Tins syndicate members, explains why they all itch to be freed from prison, and why many fine legal minds believe that this is now an inevitable consequence of the Gobbo conspiracy. It doesn't matter that Mokbel is Australia's El Chapo, and Karam Australia's Pablo Escobar. Everyone is equal before the law. When Victoria Police hoodwinked Karam and Mokbel, among others, they hoodwinked the justice system. Them one day, you the next?

* * *

As December dawns, police top brass past and present — Overland, Nixon, Ashton and the like — are finally about to take the stand, as is former deputy chief commissioner Sir Ken Jones, a rare dissenting voice. They were flagged to give evidence months ago, but the commission schedule keeps being pushed back.

By now, the possibility of criminal charges against senior police is being freely voiced. Victoria's former chief Crown prosecutor, Gavin Silbert QC, speaks of 'extraordinarily unethical behaviour'.

Talk about their testimony even rivals curiosity over the appearance of Gobbo herself.

Among the first orders McMurdo made in February 2019 was for Gobbo to appear at the royal commission. Yet by year's end she still has not provided a written statement. Originally she was to give evidence in June 2019; her appearance was then pushed back to September. She privately expressed hope of appearing, but by October she officially did not want to give evidence anymore. The spy did not wish to come in from the cold.

As 2019 nears its end, her lawyers say she is unfit to give evidence, citing 'mental anguish'. Five or more reports by psychologists and psychiatrists are tendered. They are current reports; Gobbo has found time, in hiding, to visit a number of professionals in recent months. One psychologist says she has 'no support' and 'no self-esteem'. Drugs cannot address her psychiatric conditions or severe depression, prompting an ominous phrase: 'therapeutic nihilism'.

Two of the experts say Gobbo cannot testify, while another says it would be helpful for her. It's difficult to form judgments given these differing points of view.

By now, Gobbo's potential crimes include burglary, attempts to pervert justice, perjury and obtaining financial gain by deception. In 2010, Gobbo was suspected of being a conduit in the lead-up to the Hodson murders. Police have also queried her knowledge of the Jason Moran hit a year earlier.

Police are leery of hearing Gobbo air her views in public. Her evidence promises insights that have so far eluded the most thorough exploration of the scandal of Nicola Gobbo.

Victoria Police are just like everyone else. Waiting for Gobbo.

23

See No Evil, Hear No Evil

The Top Brass Take the Stand
2019-2020

It is almost eight months into the royal commission hearings when those who matter most to the Lawyer X story are called to give evidence. Their testimony is largely overlooked at the time due to the nation's preoccupation with a bushfire crisis. But their evidence shouldn't be ignored.

* * *

The witness box of a royal commission is historically unkind to Victoria's police chief commissioners. Yet Graham Ashton seems unflustered.

For almost a year, he has maintained he did 'nothing wrong' in relation to the Gobbo scandal. He was the first police officer to publicly do so. He openly confronted the High Court's finding of 'reprehensible' behaviour.

In the witness box, he sits calmly, bar the odd leg jiggle. He avoids the combat pose of some royal commission witnesses. He never gets animated in public, whether in open court or on talkback radio. He appears unfazed, on this day in December 2019, when his memory conflicts with the documented evidence. If Ashton doesn't play poker, he should start.

Ashton was the Assistant Director at the Office of Police Integrity during the Informer 3838 years. He was mandated to investigate corruption within the force.

Gobbo's use as an informer was plainly wrong. But Ashton identified nothing at the time to warrant scrutiny. 'There wasn't anything at play suggesting there was any integrity or misconduct concerns,' Ashton says.

'So you're not prepared to concede to this royal commission that it would have been advisable for you to do a little bit of probing just to find out what was going on?' Chris Winneke asks.

'With the information that I think was available to me at that time, I don't think I did the wrong thing.'

Ashton explains that he was late to the Gobbo informing secret, if twelve years ahead of the Victorian public. But he knew about her odd behaviour as a lawyer long before he learned of the bigger deceit.

Ashton asked questions about the defence barrister soon after the killings of Terry and Christine Hodson in 2004. He heard Gobbo was probably sleeping with the chief suspect, Detective Paul Dale.

He also suspected that Gobbo had passed on intelligence reports about Terry Hodson's police informing to the underworld, leading to the Hodson murders. He wanted her to face coercive questioning under oath in 2006 and 2007. But, like so many other police investigators, he appears to have been stymied in his pursuit of the truth — by the very force he now commands. All the evidence points to his withdrawing Gobbo from the 2006 compulsory hearing because Assistant Commissioner Simon Overland asked him to.

This would mean that the fierce independence of the OPI got lost in Victoria Police politics. The protections supposedly offered by an independent overseer dissolved when a senior police officer begged a favour.

Yet Ashton cannot recall why the OPI hearings were called off. He plays down his relationship with Overland. It was a good working relationship, he says, that did not veer towards a social friendship.

He says he didn't know about Gobbo's informing until a year later, in 2007, when Gobbo was eventually examined and the OPI hearing was abandoned for unknown reasons after she was warned she was being untruthful.

That's how he remembers it, Ashton says, and so what if a mountain of documents suggests otherwise?

He seems unmoved by questions about his not keeping a diary when he was at the OPI. It is standard practice for police officers to keep a diary across the Western world. Notes protect police officers from nefarious speculations fostered in the absence of written documentation.

Ashton was asked why he had not mentioned Gobbo's 1999 period of informing during the secret Ginnane trial in 2016 and 2017. It hadn't occurred to him, he said.

But he does have concessions to make. He has jettisoned his 'high-risk decisions in high-risk times' language in response to Gobbo's exposure in December 2018. He sought then only to explain his officers' thinking, not excuse their behaviour, he now says.

When he accepted the top job in 2015, he named the Hodson killings as a case he was determined to crack. Yet in the witness box, Ashton speaks about the internal police machinations that help explain why it remains unsolved to this day.

* * *

Call him the Outsider.

Sir Ken Jones wanted to move to Australia because the idea appealed to his family. The British police officer's work had already taken him to Hong Kong and Zimbabwe. He applied to be Victoria Police's chief commissioner after Christine Nixon announced her retirement in 2008.

The Outsider was a big chance. He was interviewed as one of the final two applicants by Premier John Brumby. A few weeks after Deputy Commissioner Simon Overland was chosen as top cop, he then accepted an offer to join Victoria Police as Overland's deputy.

He's never got over it.

Jones admired many aspects of Victoria Police culture on his arrival, but he questioned others. His foreign perspective was unwelcome. He grated on the ingrained culture. Within six months, according to him, Overland was trying to sideline him by relocating his office.

By then, Jones was already arranging an exit strategy from Victoria Police. He resigned in 2011, then was told to leave before he had seen out his notice. Overland reported him to the OPI because Overland believed Jones was leaking to the media and undermining him. Jones felt 'completely and utterly' humiliated.

His phone was bugged, his reputation tarnished. His wife's mental health collapsed after a red laser rifle-sighter was trained on the couple while they walked their dog along the Tan Track in South Yarra.

These experiences explain why the Outsider sits in the royal commission witness box, as opposed to giving video evidence from his home in the United Kingdom. He wants to confront the demons in person and set the record straight.

Jones has a clipped beard and wears a striped tie. He presents as neat and precise. The Outsider offers unsettling perspectives about the inside of Victoria Police. He wants the world to know that Victoria Police was 'toxic', 'dysfunctional' and 'wrong'. He seeks to right the wrongs that cost him so much.

He says the police bureaucracy was driven by 'absolute loyalty' to the boss. Some junior officers made choices that conflicted with their professional ethics. Tracking waste and accountability was like 'knitting fog'.

Jones wondered at joint investigations by Victoria Police and the Office of Police Integrity. How could the regulator work alongside the regulated? They 'sank or swam' together, it seemed.

Jones didn't become aware of Gobbo's informing until 2010, after the death of Carl Williams. He joined a small list of private naysayers. To him, her informing was nothing less than the 'industrial abuse of the criminal justice process'.

'It quickly descended into chaos,' he says in the witness box. 'By the time the train had run away from them, they didn't know how to stop it.'

At the time, after Williams's death in 2010, Jones consulted a retired judge, then the Ombudsman's Office, which he felt did not grasp the wrongness of Gobbo's use as an informer. Jones believed some police officers had perjured themselves. He queried the swift payout of the 2010 civil suit launched by Gobbo.

Yet he did not speak to his boss, Simon Overland, about his concerns. He says he sought independent scrutiny that would not tip off those suspected of improper behaviour.

Jones says the Hodson murder investigation was hamstrung by internal police secrets that amounted to an 'unforgiveable betrayal'.

As for the Carl Williams murder? Jones speculates that it was pre-planned. He oversaw Task Force Driver, which investigated the prison killing, and concludes the murder involved 'corrupt actors inside and outside the prison'. Jones said he held concerns that investigators had found nine dormant bugs, illegally installed, in Williams's Acacia Unit 1.

His statement is unequivocal: 'On the face of it the Williams murder was unimaginable in that the most important State witness in the history of Victoria could be murdered within the most secure unit, which itself was located within our most secure prison.'

Speaking of the phone tap he was subjected to after his removal, Jones describes a police culture of secrecy and paranoia, 'hopelessly clouded by petty personal sensitivities and concerns'. It does sound extraordinary that a former deputy commissioner's phone was bugged over such flimsy preoccupations as media leaks.

As for keeping a police diary? It's accepted practice across the world. Not to keep one could expose you to claims of corruption, he says.

Of course Jones kept a diary.

* * *

Nicola Gobbo has spoken.

Not at the royal commission, where she would be confronted with criminal allegations, but to a news crew instead.

The ABC announces the TV interview early on the morning of 10 December 2019. It becomes *the* talking point of the royal commission hearing room. Why is Gobbo talking to the media but refusing to talk to the powers that matter?

Close observers suggest that McMurdo has rejected Gobbo's claims of ill health. Gobbo, it's said, is retaliating.

So Gobbo speaks — on her terms. There is a last-minute flick of the hair, and an uncertain darting of her eyes as an ABC producer theatrically snaps a clapboard and announces that the camera is rolling.

'It's complicated ...' Gobbo begins.

She presents a measured candour in choosing her words. Her reflections seem hard-earned. As if it is time to dispel the almost daily allegations from the royal commission. Yet her choice of forum invites more questions than answers.

Carlyon and Dowsley knew they would never get to interview Gobbo. She holds Dowsley personally responsible for her plight. But they have often spitballed the questions they would ask her. They could be reduced to three. 'Why?' 'Any regrets?' And 'What the hell were you doing in the months before the Hodsons were killed?'

By giving a TV interview, Gobbo avoids the exacting details that Dowsley and Carlyon seek to understand. Gobbo instead perpetuates her victimhood line, unfettered by the inconvenient facts that contradict her chosen narrative.

Gobbo says she was extorted by the criminals, then extorted by the police. 'It's not the first time that they [Victoria Police] threatened me in relation to toeing the line and doing things their way or they would take my children ...' Gobbo tells the ABC.

She has claimed such concerns since 2015.

'It remains their [her children's] belief that they were chased out of their home by police that are trying to take their mummy away, and that, to any parent, is beyond devastating.'

Gobbo's life is hellish. Physical pain is compounded by threats to her safety. She is 'stranded' and 'stateless', she says, fed 'to the wolves' by Victoria Police.

In words later stridently condemned by the Police Association, Gobbo says: 'There's always going to be a [safety] risk, but my greatest fear is the police themselves.'

After his second day of evidence to the royal commission, Chief

Commissioner Graham Ashton is compelled to address Gobbo's claims. She need not fear police, he says. They are doing 'everything they can' to keep Gobbo safe.

So how much of Gobbo's take on historical events is accurate? Her ABC TV interview is a terrific journalistic scoop, hard earned and well executed, but lacking the controls for an unvarnished rendering of her state of mind.

Dowsley and Carlyon are frustrated that they cannot put forward supplementary questions in response to her answers. For example, Gobbo speaks of people being murdered, and police threats compelling her to continue to inform. Yet she also says her assistance 'morphed into a dependence upon Victoria Police'. And we know that Gobbo kept offering up information, even after she was officially jettisoned by Victoria Police in 2009 and again in 2010.

The two positions — threats and dependence — do not bind readily. Her reasoning from 1995 to 2012 needs to be tackled over many hours to make sense of her choices.

'It began as a moral and ethical dilemma for me,' she tells the ABC interviewer, harking back to the same issues that prompted her to contact the AFP in 1998 about becoming an informer. Gobbo didn't like her criminal surrounds within a month of becoming a barrister. This is easy to understand. What is not is that Gobbo did not absent herself from those surrounds over the next thirteen years.

Gobbo's wellbeing once relied upon deceiving drug barons and speed freaks. Her gift for lying — or what she has called 'plausible deniability' — is why she is still alive today.

Gobbo speaks to the ABC of suing Victoria Police for personal injury against herself and her two children. Her greatest source of guilt, she says, is the impact on her children. Finding sympathy for her daily privations of pain and dislocation is not difficult.

Less easy to embrace is Gobbo's blaming of others. She portrays herself as misused and manipulated, whereas the police have cast her as an informer and a suspect, most notably for her proximity to two Gangland hits — the Hodsons and Jason Moran — and four deaths.

Gobbo deflects questions that contradict her projection of herself as a victim. She denies that she burgled the office of a colleague in 2007. Yet she is not confronted with the documents suggesting that she bragged about the break-in to her police handlers.

We can compare Gobbo's statements on the ABC to chats she had with Dowsley in 2014. She denied to him that she was an informer. She also denied sleeping with Paul Dale (though she now tells the ABC they were romantically intimate, once, a claim Dale supports).

Gobbo bats away the questions she doesn't want to answer — ironically by claiming that the answers are only for the ears of the royal commission that she does not want to appear at. She has neither the time nor concentration to prepare for such a grilling, she says.

As the royal commission points out, however, Gobbo has had *lots* of time. The commission has waited for her statement since March this year, and off stage seethes about her TV interview.

'Ms Gobbo has been represented at community expense and continues to be represented throughout the life of this commission at virtually all its hearings by solicitors and by both junior and senior counsel,' a commission spokeswoman says. 'Whilst Ms Gobbo's lawyers commenced preparing a statement on her behalf, it was not completed.'

Gobbo has spoken, choosing to make a very different kind of statement. But the bigger questions still shimmer in a haze of doubt.

Why did she inform to police for three separate periods between 1995 and 2009, starting with a sting on her then housemate?

How does she defend the mounting raft of criminal claims, from fraud to worse, of which she now stands accused?

These questions can be addressed only when Gobbo talks — on terms not of her making.

* * *

Gobbo *has* spoken to the royal commission in 2019, but no one knew about it at the time. Three phone conversations have taken place: in March, April and June respectively.

She did not swear to tell the truth, as she would have in the witness box. Time was short: the three calls lasted about six hours in total. She popped a painkiller every two hours to dull her chronic facial pain. Her memory, understandably, was patchy on details.

Despite the context, she would describe the first chat as the 'most stimulating conversation I have had in months and months'.

'G'day, Nicola,' Winneke opened, with a casualness that defied the old-world customs of courtrooms. To her, he would be 'Chris'.

Gobbo had a lot to say about her 'voluntary second job', much of it in conflict with the prevailing Victoria Police line. Like them, she was not about to take responsibility for the appalling breaches of legal process. But she *was* prepared to blame police for threatening her. She is the weapon they couldn't stop wielding.

Take Mick Gatto. Gobbo said one of her handlers had suggested she sleep with him to build his trust — '[T]ake one for the team,' she says he urged, in just another allegation that highlighted her status as a lone female in a swamp of men.

She'd wondered at the start how and when her informing would end. 'Well, that, that was the problem,' she told Winneke. 'As time went on, they kept coming up with new people and targets that they, that they were specifically interested in.'

She recalled the depth of the subterfuge. Like the time officers 'raided' her office for documents. It was a sham raid that had ended with detectives 'sitting around drinking coffee'. Gobbo would have provided the documents, but police needed it to appear as if they had grabbed them by force.

By the end of the third conversation, Gobbo's evidence was still incomplete. There was never going to be enough time. But she did express a regret. Her stroke in 2004 was a wake-up call. She should have taken a step back, but 'I didn't'.

* * *

It's painful sitting in the royal commission gallery. The hard chairs yield little comfort over the long hours. The middle back starts to protest, first with a niggle that cannot be stretched away, then a chronic ache, in a kind of symptom of the inexorable volume of material to be scrutinised by the inquiry.

Yet the gallery seats are nothing like the trials in the witness box. You are captive. There is nowhere to go. The level of detail asked for requires memory and patience, and both are bound to elude you at times. It is a perch that no one wants to try. Certainly not former chief commissioner Simon Overland.

* * *

Noel Ashby stares at the man only a few feet from him in the witness box. Ashby has spent many years wondering about Overland, who investigated Ashby, then assistant commissioner, in 2007 — even instigated an Office of Police Integrity investigation to tap his phones — and laid (unsuccessful) criminal charges against him.

But Overland isn't interested in Ashby. He is a solitary figure in a room buzzing with twenty-two lawyers, like a giraffe gazing down at the zebras.

Overland is the most significant figure in this forum, bar Nicola Gobbo herself. They never met, but Overland supervised her unholy relationship with Victoria Police, built on a shared desire to jail Gangland figures.

Overland has had a tough year, including accusations of historical mis-steps concerning the use of Gobbo and his sacking as a local council chief executive just a week ago. He has never relished close scrutiny.

But he defies expectations on his first day of evidence. He appears relaxed in the witness box, even risking a few lighter moments. He seems to know what he wants to say. His evidence is imparted so uneventfully that a man in the gallery falls asleep.

In 2005, he had never before heard of a barrister who was also an informer, but Gobbo's circumstances were extreme. She faced a 'death sentence' one way or another, because of her intimate relationships with criminals.

Overland argues that Gobbo's informer registration was the 'least-worst decision based on the information'. He didn't intervene because

328

he did not want to be in a witness box answering questions about her death.

He says he cannot recall whether he knew Gobbo was representing Tony Mokbel in a high-profile 2006 drug case — while his officers used her in a sting aimed at collapsing the Mokbel empire.

Winneke suggests Overland put his 'head in the sand', which Overland denies. He did not know she was breaching legal professional privilege, he says, challenging all common sense.

Winneke allows himself a brief moment of incredulity, then shows Overland a 2006 newspaper article that quotes him alongside a photo of Gangland lawyer Gobbo, helpfully captioned as one of 'Tony Mokbel's barristers'.

Yet Overland maintains that public references to Gobbo as Mokbel's lawyer escaped his notice. He was too busy.

Winneke reaches for the obvious conclusion. Overland's claim of ignorance 'beggars belief'.

* * *

Cross-examining Overland, Chris Winneke QC is almost knockabout in his style, using lots of 'yeahs' and 'all rights'. He doesn't do condescending. He rarely raises his voice. He charts a course and won't be distracted.

'They need a prick up there,' says one vested observer during a break of Winneke's counsel-assisting role. He wants Overland savaged. 'But they don't have a prick up there.'

Instead, Winneke is the barrister's equivalent of Glenn McGrath, the former fast bowler. He puts the questions on a line and length with a relentless constancy that can induce impatience at their sameness.

Overland discovers this on his second day on the stand, when he admits that Gobbo's use may have been a perversion of justice.

He doesn't need to say what comes next, but speaks as if he ought to concede something. 'I certainly agree that the ethics were fucked,' he says, drawing on Gobbo's own language to her police handlers in 2006.

But, like Ashton, Nixon and every other police officer in the witness box, Overland is not about to accept responsibility for Victoria Police's behaviour.

* * *

By the end of his second day of evidence, Overland's position is becoming clearer. He says he was not kept abreast of intricate operational details that go to the ethics and legality of Gobbo's use.

In the *Herald Sun*, Dowsley and Carlyon reduce Overland's evidence to a few simple sentences.

- *I solved the Gangland War but I wasn't across the details.*
- *My investigators made choices without my knowledge, and they possibly broke the law, but I did not fail in my leadership.*
- *I was 'concerned and surprised' by the registration of Gobbo as Informer 3838 in 2005, but yes, the documents show I was across her registration within days, if not earlier.*

If Overland's recollections sound unlikely, his evidence is about to be torpedoed on another front. His insistence that he did not keep written records is smashed about half an hour before he finishes his evidence, just before the Christmas break.

It is forty-four degrees outside, the sky tinged red by the lifted dust of bushfires. The assembled journalists are salivating over imagined beers.

Then the story of the day happens.

No, I didn't keep a diary, Overland has said repeatedly.

But his former chief-of-staff Shane Patton has remembered differently, telling Victoria Police his boss *did* keep a diary. A renewed hunt leads once again to the Laverton storage facility, west of Melbourne, where Gobbo's 1995 informer registration lay unnoticed for almost a generation.

Laverton has echoes of Area 51, the United States Air Force base in Nevada thought to contain extraordinary secrets. In an overlooked box labelled 'Miscellaneous' lie blue hardback books embossed with the Victoria Police insignia. They are Overland's diaries, from 2003, 2004 and 2007.

Overland did keep diaries, after all. And their contents will conflict with much of what Overland has said in the witness box.

His recall of events until now has seemed disingenuous. He has a month to reconsider his evidence.

* * *

Sergeant Schultz from TV comedy *Hogan's Heroes* does not appear by name in the royal commission's transcripts, but former chief commissioner Christine Nixon channels his ghost when she gives evidence. She offers the most credible of excuses when asked about the use of a defence barrister as a police informer.

She knew nothing.

Why didn't she know? Nixon doesn't know. She brings to mind the Socratic paradox: 'I know that I know nothing.'

Nixon did not know about Gobbo's pivotal use in the discovery of the world's then biggest ecstasy bust in 2007, and the prosecution of Gobbo's own clients in the case.

Nixon is poised and considered, as always, yet the content of her evidence conflicts with her presentation. She seems to know less about Lawyer X than the average radio talkback listener.

The obvious reason? Her once-subordinate Simon Overland never told her.

Nixon is at ease describing organisational charts of Victoria Police hierarchies from various eras. She speaks of management reforms aimed at overcoming 'cultural isolation'. This is her language, the preserve of company boardrooms, and it is foreign to the splatter and stench of a murder scene.

She is evidently proud of her efforts to stem Drug Squad corruption after taking over in 2001. Yet the public face of the force, presented on TV to deflect bad news, says she didn't know about the biggest corruption of all.

Nixon had seen Gobbo on TV, walking into court with clients. She knew Gobbo was to be a witness against Dale in 2009. 'I thought that was a significant matter,' Nixon said of the fact that a defence barrister was being used by the prosecution.

But Nixon says she was never briefed on the extensive history that precipitated that choice.

'I don't recall being told she was a source, ever,' she says.

Indeed, Nixon says she did not know anything about the Lawyer X scandal until the *Herald Sun* broke the story in 2014. At the end of 2018, when the High Court decision against Victoria Police was handed down, she thought Lawyer X was another lawyer, perhaps Zarah Garde-Wilson.

Here was the biggest corruption of process in legal history, under the watch of a crusading corruption-buster. Yet Nixon says that she did not know what 140 police under her leadership *did* know.

Indeed, Ms Nixon doesn't seem to know much about some of the biggest crimes that took place during her time as Victoria Police Chief Commissioner between 2001 and 2009. She receives the words 'Dublin Street', the shorthand for the Hodson–Miechel burglary in 2003, with a blank stare.

Her subordinates should have sought legal advice about Gobbo's use, she says. She should have been told about Gobbo, she agrees. If she had been, she would have been 'extraordinarily surprised'.

Instead, Nixon knew only about the results. She attended a presentation, alongside Premier Steve Bracks, about the operation against Mokbel's crew, known as Operation Posse, apparently a high watermark in policing.

Yet Nixon was ignorant of the fundamental truths behind that sting — of ethical breaches so profound that the decades-long convictions stemming from the operation stand to be overturned.

She doesn't know why she was not told. Perhaps the officers managing the risks felt that the risks were being managed. The same risks, mind you, that explain the need for the Lawyer X royal commission.

Nixon notes that 'hindsight is a wonderful thing'.

The top job sounds like the most 'culturally isolated' position within Victoria Police. The glib conclusion from Nixon's evidence was that the boss needed to know nothing.

Nixon stands to be condemned by an oft-repeated line from the New South Wales Wood Royal Commission in the mid-1990s. She used the line in 2001 when she addressed Drug Squad members and disbanded the unit.

Some detectives complained that they were unaware of corrupt colleagues in their midst.

Her parting shot to them?

'If you didn't know, you should have.'

* * *

Christmas must have been strained in the Overland household. After a month to consider his options, Simon Overland has to get back in the witness box, and he has to change his evidence.

He has read the belatedly discovered diaries he kept a decade or more ago. In light of what they reveal, Nixon's apparently marginal place in the story will also have to be reconsidered. Was she so irrelevant?

On 21 January 2020, Overland tells the commission that it seems from his diary that he briefed Nixon about Gobbo within days of Gobbo's registration as 3838. But he has no memory of ever telling Nixon about their most critical Gangland weapon.

Overland sounds cornered.

'Having now reviewed my diary, I note that I was involved in fourteen meetings with Ms Nixon regarding Purana Task Force matters and I believe that I did, in fact, inform her of Ms Gobbo's recruitment on 29 September 2005,' he says.

'I have no independent recollection of this meeting, but note the contents of my diary entry that indicates I did tell her about the registration of Ms Gobbo as a human source.'

Overland apologises for his stated belief that he kept no diaries. He says six separate requests from Victoria Police for materials did not yield them, triggering his mistaken recollection.

He gets emotional when recalling the Gangland carnage. Police confronted 'death and destruction', he says. He remembers the pressures Victoria Police felt at the time.

But there's still an elephant in the room: who knew what and when? Overland has offered no clarity. From the start, his stated evidence has conflicted with the written documentation of events at the time.

Winneke sums it up neatly. Overland's arguments are 'incongruous'.

* * *

Fin McRae, the director of Victoria Police's legal services, is next in the witness box. His role in the story is muddled; he represents the 'legal advice' that police investigators avoided for so long. His evidence goes to the layered understanding of Gobbo's use at the time and immediately afterwards.

McRae came into the circle of knowledge when Gobbo sued police in 2010. He says he discovered she was informing to police at that time, but not that she was informing *on her own clients* until 2012.

At one point, asked about his handling of the marathon issues surrounding Gobbo, McRae begs time to compose himself. He recalls how Gobbo supposedly stabbed herself in the leg with a pen. He gives evidence that echoes the line whispered by anonymous police sources that the Gobbo secret seeped beyond Victoria Police.

McRae spoke to John Cain, who headed the Victorian Government Solicitor's Office, about handling Gobbo's 2010 lawsuit claim in a 'safe way'. He provided written advice to Cain that outlined Gobbo's informing history. The two then negotiated a $2.88 million payout aimed at making the informer scandal go away. McRae says Gobbo's informer role was openly discussed at a meeting that included Cain and the Office of Police Integrity.

Yet Cain has told the royal commission, in a statement, that he was 'completely astounded' when he discovered Gobbo's informing past *five years later*, on reading the 2015 Kellam report. Channelling Overland, he says he was too busy — with the Black Saturday bushfires royal commission — to be across the details of the written material at the time.

What did Cain know, and when? No one can say. The royal commission cannot call him to the witness box. As Victorian State Coroner, he cannot be compelled to give evidence to the royal commission.

A Gangland barrister as a Gangland snitch? It is 'unthinkable', McRae protests, even though he has managed much of the fallout for a decade.

As Commissioner McMurdo earlier commented, her inquiry is becoming more and more 'Kafkaesque'.

24

'A Spectacularly Good Liar'

Nicola Gobbo Finally Faces the Commission
2020

It's 9.30 am on Tuesday, 4 February, and Nicola Gobbo is supposed to begin her testimony to the royal commission. But there is an unexplained snag. Of course there is.

At 9.50 am, Commissioner Margaret McMurdo speaks of 'some delays' but promises a 10 am start. Journalists in the gallery speak of placing bets on whether Gobbo will give evidence or not, then pass the time ruminating on McMurdo's passing resemblance to a younger version of former governor-general Quentin Bryce.

Gobbo is facing what she has long avoided: telling the truth in a public courtroom. But she has gained concessions. With a nod to the absurd, the hearing room will follow Winneke's lead and stare at an empty chair in the witness box while Gobbo tells her story over the phone. There will be no vision of her testimony, just a disembodied voice, prompting speculations about a new look, perhaps plastic surgery.

McMurdo has sensibly adopted a pragmatic line. Something is better than nothing. Imposing the usual rules on a witness who is emotionally unstable — or so says a succession of medical reports — might compel her to refuse to pick up the phone.

Gobbo's version of the truth is certain to diverge from the police line presented to the inquiry over many months. The Lawyer X scandal is *her* story. There is the why — the first question everyone wants to ask — and there is the how.

Can Gobbo steer the commission away from suggestions of her own criminal behaviour? Will she rekindle her past powers of hidden influence to cast the blame elsewhere?

The most pressing question is answered at 10.02 am. Finally, Gobbo is on the other end of the line.

'Nicola Maree Gobbo,' she answers from an unknown location, before being sworn in.

Gobbo is throaty, and her voice will turn more nasal over coming days. As usual, she sounds measured and calm, in defiance of her drastic behaviours. If she doesn't quite speak roughly, she sounds as though she has addressed many rough people on their own terms.

She makes concessions about her breaches of privilege and unethical behaviour — in the face of the damning evidence, how can she not?

'In retrospect,' she says repeatedly, drawing distance between the person she was and the person she now claims to be. She admits that she acted improperly and made choices that 'potentially' broke the law. But she describes this behaviour as if she is speaking of someone else.

Her matter-of-factness exacerbates the jolt of her more extraordinary admissions, as if the systematic deception of the justice system equates with the reckless impulses of a speeding driver.

What Gobbo says doesn't change everything. But her thoughts lift some cryptic choices into the glare. Winneke guides her through a chronology that seeks to make sense of the unknowable, and the audience is rewarded with Gobbo's singular logic in describing the illogical.

We already know that she accumulated knowledge at the expense of her ethics, that she thrilled to the power of knowing more than anyone else. Yet Gobbo's humiliating tell-all over five days is coupled with disclaimers. She will say that she is a victim of police forces bigger than she is.

She sounds pitiful and scathing, forgetful and sharp, helpful and recalcitrant, proud and shameful. The clues lie in her unfiltered contradictions. Observers finally get to glimpse the clouded links in her thinking. Gobbo is the keeper of all the secrets, but how many will she share?

The commission hears how Gobbo's legal career started with a lie, and how she was breaching her professional ethics as soon as she became a barrister. Australia's greatest ever legal scandal was triggered by a law graduate with 'self-esteem' issues.

Winneke ponders the affidavit Gobbo submitted to the Legal Admissions Board in 1997. In it, she omitted crucial facts. Her career could have ended before it began, if she hadn't fashioned a story in conflict with the facts of her 1993 guilty plea to drug use and possession.

She didn't mention in her affidavit that her ex-housemate and drug trafficker Brian Wilson co-owned her Carlton property. Or that he returned to live with Gobbo two years after their house was raided. Or that she had used amphetamines herself.

She tries to blame her lawyer at the time for her untruthful affidavit. Winneke is sceptical, and Gobbo finally agrees that *she* misled the board of examiners, and that she might have been rejected — or faced other repercussions — had she set out her true circumstances back then.

Point one is that Gobbo's law career was built on wilful distortions. Point two is that she was an informer before she was a lawyer.

She wasn't a good university student, she says, just one who applied herself under pressure. Study, as later with the Law, was cover for other pursuits. Her informing against Wilson in 1995 is critical to the Gobbo narrative. It began, she says, because her ex-housemate wouldn't leave the house.

From 1998, she was feeding police information that her employer, Levi Diamond, was laundering money.

The police came to *her*, she says. There was nowhere to turn: a chronic Gobbo problem. She is 'embarrassed' by her poor judgment back then, she says: another recurring theme. She was threatened with being charged for crimes concerning money-laundering and attempting to pervert the course of justice if she did not assist officers, and she was too green to recognise the emptiness of the threats.

A pattern was set. She met her first unofficial handler after qualifying as a lawyer, Senior-Sergeant Wayne Strawhorn, in a South Melbourne coffee shop. She says she was 'petrified' by his perceived power. She says he seemed 'predatory' and 'manipulative'.

'My then level of maturity and naïveté was very different to what it is now,' she says.

'I don't want to labour the point but the simple point I make is this: you say you were providing, you believe, albeit in a naïve way, information to a police officer about matters that you knew of as a result of you being a lawyer and acting for people,' Winneke says. 'How could that possibly be acceptable?'

Gobbo replies: 'Well, you say matters that I became aware of in the context of acting for someone as a lawyer, yes, that's correct, but not all those matters that I'm aware of because I'm acting as a lawyer are necessarily privileged.'

It's a weak defence. As Victoria Police barrister Saul Holt QC later says to Gobbo, of all the defence lawyers in Australia and abroad, none bar Gobbo has abandoned their ethics because a police officer invited them to.

Strawhorn passed on his chatty coffee companion to Senior Constable Jeff Pope, from the Asset Recovery Squad, who to this day denies that he slept with his secret source.

Winneke wonders why a newly minted barrister would agree to be handed over to another police handler. Gobbo's reply touches on a critical point in her story. She 'found saying "no" very difficult'.

Gobbo later informed to Inspector Peter De Santo, who investigated Strawhorn for drug trafficking. (Strawhorn was eventually charged and sentenced to seven years' jail.) De Santo was a master manipulator like Strawhorn, Gobbo says, but more polished of manner.

These tales are intended to explain the formative exchanges of a master informer, and they're not terribly satisfying. By Gobbo's account, her career in subterfuge began because she did not know how to stop it.

Gobbo also tried to inform to the Australian Federal Police in these early days. And to the National Crime Authority (NCA).

She approached these agencies herself. She *wanted* a double life. She slept with an NCA officer, it emerges, though her memory is patchy. 'Is he balding with blond hair?' Gobbo asks, prompting involuntary smirks in the hearing room.

The genesis of the greatest legal scandal in modern Australia lies in these connections. Gobbo was informing to three different arms of police at the same time as she was being hailed in the *Herald Sun* as one of Victoria's youngest-ever female barristers, at twenty-six.

She was a full-time barrister from 1998 until 2009. And she was informing, unofficially or not, right throughout those years. After she was deregistered in 2009, she tried to start informing again.

Gobbo offers another fresh clue. After completing a Masters in Law, she hoped in 1998 to do a doctorate paper about the 'illegality' of police–informer relationships. 'I know it will sound laughable in a sense when I say this now,' she comments.

Let's put it another way. Gobbo was fascinated by informers when she began informing. She was a spy in search of a master. At the same time, she was forging social as well as professional relationships with organised crime figures who were the clients of her boss, Levi Diamond.

'It's not funny, in a funny way, but it's very ironic that I'm telling you this in a royal commission,' she says.

Gobbo's parting sentiment on this first day of evidence might be shared by the detectives who exploited a lost soul: she has had a blinding headache for four days or more.

'If Mr Winneke is going to keep going,' Gobbo says, 'can I take more painkillers please?'

* * *

Nicola Gobbo wants to set the record straight. It's day two, and she is more forthright than yesterday. She never stayed at Tony Mokbel's house, she tells the royal commission. He never stayed at hers. Nor does she use illicit drugs.

As for her reported 'promiscuity'? 'My privacy has been invaded comprehensively, but the picture that has been painted of me is far from the truth in many respects,' she has written in a slim seven-page statement to the commission.

Yet a tawdry hook-up epitomises the Gobbo enigma. It will dominate today's evidence because it is an episode with no good answers.

Gobbo puts aside her occasional spurts of belligerence in talking about the events of 2003 and 2004. She boasts a sharp memory (despite health issues), and negotiates the pseudonyms of protected identities without hesitation. Yet Gobbo sounds uncertain about her choices leading up to the murders of Terry and Christine Hodson.

She agrees with Winneke. That she did not act like a lawyer at the time. That she tried to impress the people around her. It seems she gloried in the power of forbidden knowledge.

Gobbo was involved with every stakeholder bar Miechel in the 2003 Dublin Street burglary. This was her perfect storm. She toyed with everyone in her twisted pursuit of power. She played the crooks and the cops and the officers who investigated both.

Gobbo presents a sorry study in naïveté, as if she were far younger than her thirty-something years at that time. Her emotional maturity seemed pathetic. Of course she would do it differently if she had her time again, her mantra goes, in an if-I-only-knew-then-what-I-know-now lament.

When Gobbo describes herself as 'out of my depth' amid 'out-of-control events', Winneke plucks alternative adjectives out of the air. He calls her behaviour 'untenable' and 'improper', and Gobbo is too canny to try to argue.

Gobbo's entanglement traces to the night of the 2003 AFL grand final, when the Dublin Street drug house in Oakleigh was burgled. She represented the burglars and the burgled. She met her clients in the guise of a lawyer but she was acting as a police agent. She sent Hodson to Inspector Peter De Santo and his Ethical Standards Department to snitch on dirty cops. Then, she cooked up extra dollops of crazy. Within two weeks she caught up with one of the suspect cops, Paul Dale, for drinks.

The pair fell into bed that night. Gobbo made herself the prize in a tug-of-war between De Santo and Dale.

Winneke: 'Do you believe you acted inappropriately?'

Gobbo: 'Looking back there were a lot of things that were, that were, um, at best confused, um, and at worst, yes, totally inappropriate ...'

Winneke: 'Well, why did you continue to do it?'

Gobbo: 'Well, I mean I, I, I don't want to come across as making excuses but where my mind was then was obviously quite different to ... how I can look at it from this point in my life.'

Winneke: 'Where was your mind then? I mean, you'd studied law, you'd studied ethics, you knew very well what was ethically right and what was ethically wrong ... What's the explanation, was it the desire to help police?'

Gobbo: 'Well, it was a combination, I think. It was a desire to ... help Mr De Santo and to, you know, I know it sounds pathetic but to live up to what his expectations were of me ... I was also being pushed in the background by Tony Mokbel, who wanted to find out what, as much as he could about what police did and didn't know ... Dale wanted to know if Tony wanted to kill him because he'd burgled a place that belonged to Tony. Um, so, yeah, it was all — there was — I felt pressure from all around and you're right, I should have walked away from all of them.'

Winneke: 'Look, the reality is you weren't operating as a legal practitioner, you weren't operating as a barrister, you were operating as an accumulator of information either for yourself or for other people, isn't that the situation?'

Gobbo: 'Yeah, I can't disagree with that.'

Gobbo denies a police theory that she passed the Blue File, detailing Terry Hodson's prodigious history of informing, from Dale to Tony Mokbel. She said her burner phone contact with Dale — which ended just before Hodson's death — probably ceased because the phone credit ran out.

'I want to make it clear that I'm not offering this as ... a cop-out excuse,' Gobbo says, in what sounds like a cop-out excuse.

Gobbo seems like she is describing a needy child. She wanted to be the keeper of the secrets but she could not keep them from spilling out.

She later fretted, quite rightly, about being implicated of criminality in the lead-up to the Hodson murders.

Winneke is spared the need to prove that Gobbo was a willing participant. Instead he asks whether she knew her behaviour was wrong at the time.

She sounds weary. Or is she ashamed?

'Of course I did,' she replies.

* * *

It seems Gobbo's inexplicable choices in 2003 and 2004 triggered her inexplicable role as a secret agent in the years ahead.

Over the next two days of evidence, she gets a chance to explain. Her testimony relating to the Hodson killings has been underwhelming; Dowsley and Carlyon both think she knows more than she's said.

The depths of her fixations remain untapped; perhaps they will never be understood. But Gobbo does throw up titbits that have never previously been revealed. They are signposts to her troubled motives and personality.

Take her hobby during these two years. In her spare time, Gobbo compiled chronologies of drug cases — not for clients, but for personal aggrandisement. She cross-referenced the chronologies, figured out informer identities, and tracked who was top and who was bottom of Melbourne's criminal netherworld.

Yet she had already wearied of her lifestyle. She harboured hopes of escaping criminal law, mainly because she felt so used by Tony Mokbel. The paradox, as she herself acknowledges, is that her remarkable choices over these two years laid the foundation for her official registration as an informer in 2005.

In too deep, Gobbo dived deeper.

By January 2004, Gobbo was telling De Santo everything he asked of her. Soon, she was doing the same with another 'smooth operator', Detective Sergeant Stuart Bateson of Purana.

After her stroke on 24 July 2004, she was 'scared and stuck', she told Bateson in a teary chat. She believed her position was 'intractable'.

Winneke calls her out on the claims. Her hospital recovery was a 'perfect opportunity' to walk away from her deceitful attempts at lawyering.

It wasn't that simple, she explains. She had massive property loans. She had no one to turn to for advice.

Soon, Bateson was asking Gobbo about her fellow Gangland lawyers. Victoria Police had instituted a push against lawyers they suspected of 'enabling' Gangland crimes by passing messages between criminals and accepting the proceeds of crime as fees.

Bateson and Gobbo met for coffees, sometimes at South Melbourne's Emerald Hotel. Gobbo volunteered supposedly damning details against another lawyer, known as 'Solicitor 2' under royal commission suppressions. The irony is that Gobbo herself was guilty of the same 'enabling'.

When Solicitor 2 was charged with providing false evidence to the Australian Crime Commission, that solicitor asked Gobbo to defend the charges in court. Gobbo accepted, even though she was informing on her client to Bateson, who had a 'specific level of hatred' for Solicitor 2.

'Do you accept that the concept of a barrister appearing for a person in relation to whom they are providing information about to the police is repugnant?' Winneke asks.

'Yes,' Gobbo replies, again citing 'weak and pathetic' self-esteem issues.

For the record, Solicitor 2 tells Dowsley and Carlyon that Gobbo's representation was poor. In court, Gobbo meekly agreed with the prosecutors' position against her client.

These choices reek of the righteous zeal of a dibber-dobber. Gobbo does claim a moral code; in her evidence she speaks of being 'disgusted' by specific examples of both police and criminal behaviour. But morals alone do not explain her snitching on other lawyers.

* * *

Gobbo speaks about her thinking in the lead-up to being registered as an informer in September 2005. She was being asked to betray her client, Mokbel henchman Mr Beautiful, and she felt she could not go on. Gobbo needed an out. So she decided to become a police agent.

She talks of this era as if it were a lifetime ago. She appreciates now that her handlers, and her controller Sandy White, played to her ego after they frightened her into submission. She calls the pitch of White and subordinate handler Peter Smith a 'bad cop, worse bad cop' routine.

White and Smith said they would know if she lied to them, before inviting her to tell them 'everything' about her client Tony Mokbel. They later told Gobbo she was 'on top of the ladder' of all-time greatest Victorian informers.

'In hindsight it was to obviously boost my self-esteem and to make me feel more important about what I was doing and, you, you know, my type-A personality was making me do more,' she says.

A little later, she adds: 'It was insane and idiotic and wrong on so many levels and what then transpired was just more craziness.'

Winneke pulls her up. Her graduation to official informing was a natural progression, he suggests. She had escape routes and chose not to take them.

Gobbo concedes the point with a contradiction. She was famed for excoriating witnesses in a courtroom, but chose to become an informer out of a desire not to disappoint anyone.

'My emotional functioning, my maturity, my stupidity, my mistakes ... I can't back away from any of that ... and my wanting to please everyone, inability to say no, I couldn't see the wood for the trees,' she says. 'I mean, for me to have thought that was a sensible thing to do shows that what you've just suggested, the kind of rational, logical, easy solution was not apparent.'

The police encouraged her to get closer to her first target, a drug dealer, who they hoped would implicate the Mokbels.

Winneke asks a question that may hold serious ramifications for Gobbo as well as the senior detectives involved. When the target was arrested, she was warned to ignore her handlers on seeing them at the police station.

'And you were aware that by turning up and providing advice to [the drug dealer] you were in effect doing things which would have a tendency to pervert the course of justice?'

'Potentially,' Gobbo replies.

She shared with investigators her mental dossiers of her clients' quirks and weak points. De facto psychological profiles were a signature extra during her years of informing. Gobbo represented the suspects she helped apprehend, then advised police on breaking them down.

Her relationship with her handlers came to resemble a toxic affair. First, the deep satisfaction, and the thrill of forbidden pursuits. Then, the side-effects: the ill health and anxiety. As Gobbo puts it, detectives compromised their ethics to protect the secret. They were good men, tethered to a dreadful choice.

Yes, Gobbo agrees fourteen years later, 'the ethics of it were all wrong'.

* * *

Winneke mentions details untold until now. He has the financial records that show the fees Gobbo charged her clients.

She helped police to charge Faruk Orman with murder, and he spent twelve years in jail before his conviction was overturned in 2019 because of Gobbo's conflicted role.

Gobbo charged Orman $32,000.

She charged Rob Karam about $60,000 while she was informing against him as 3838. She charged Tony Mokbel $1800 for legal assistance after his 2007 capture in Athens, at the same time as she was briefing police about his attempts to avoid extradition.

Tony's sister-in-law, Zaharoula Mokbel, was billed about $4000. Gobbo told investigators about the deficiencies in the fraud case against her.

Gobbo charged Carl Williams at least $1650, and his father George $14,000. Gobbo told Bateson in late June 2005 that George Williams had taken out a dodgy property loan to pay legal fees, perhaps those he owed Gobbo.

Put simply, her clients paid Gobbo money to help put them in jail. Was this a criminal conspiracy to defraud criminals?

In her view, though, her informer role meant she *had to* charge them money. If she did not, they would wonder why.

That word 'repugnant' again comes to mind. Gobbo cannot remember many of the details Winneke is recounting, but she is candid enough: 'Yes, I think I've already said, the entire ethics of all this were wrong.'

Winneke describes the deceit in harsher terms. He suggests the fees are evidence that she committed the crime of financial advantage by deception.

Gobbo counters that her handlers knew. 'Obviously wrongly, but I was led to believe that they were the police and anything that I was doing that was wrong, they would stop, they would stop me,' she says.

The issue festered. By July 2007, according to her tally, she had incriminated twenty people while acting as their lawyer.

Winneke returns to the question of crimes.

'Do you accept that that was wrong, that the people who you had represented should have known and they should have known that you were not providing them with independent legal advice ...?' he asks. 'And every time it did occur there was the potential for that case, for those proceedings to be perverted?'

'Or to be overturned, yes,' Gobbo replies.

* * *

Gobbo's house was searched by the royal commission some time after December 2018. There, in scattered envelopes marked 'Fees', lay bundles of cash.

In a box marked 'Evidence' was $5000 in an envelope labelled 'Car wash July rent'. Gobbo's co-ownership of an Avondale Heights carwash, where Gangland criminals chatted under the spray of water, appears to have been lucrative.

'I wish I had piles of $100 notes sitting in a box in *my* garage,' whispers a journalist in the gallery.

There was $2000 held by rubber bands inside a birthday card signed 'From Carl and Purana'. Gobbo says she knows nothing about it, nor the other wads of cash.

Did she make so much money out of the people she betrayed, and later the police she said betrayed her, that she could overlook $13,000 lying about her house?

* * *

Nicola Gobbo the police agent did not *have to* incriminate Rob Karam in 2007. She welcomed men like him into her orbit because she wanted to continue to inform after she'd destroyed the Mokbel enterprise from within.

The move to wind down Gobbo's informer use was first touted in May 2006, after Milad Mokbel was arrested. The following year, police talked of no longer tasking their secret informer with intelligence-gathering. Then they tasked her with intelligence-gathering.

Gobbo went to extraordinary lengths, with the encouragement of police, to try to jail Karam.

'... [W]hat we thought was going to be confined to the Mokbels, for example, just snowballed in a massive way and then all of a sudden there were people telling me about murders, bashing and abduction, labs, pill presses and drug importations,' she says. 'It was just what I thought was going to finish in a certain period of time just went on and on and on.'

Her handlers doubled as counsellors, assisting with her poor mental health and anxieties. Records from the time show they invited her to stop informing whenever she liked. She admits that she did not want to disappoint Sandy White, and she claims he wanted to get Karam.

So the relationship continued. She told her handlers about the thrill of her informer calling. In her evidence, she seeks to write off her child-like remarks at the time as good-natured banter, but there is a recurring sameness to them. Gobbo hungered for new targets and fresh intrigues, even though informing was bad for her health. She didn't — or couldn't — stop.

In 2011, two years after she was deregistered as 3838, and a year after she received a promise that police would leave her alone, Gobbo offered police fresh information about new crimes. At the end, as at the beginning, she wanted to be a spy.

A succession of police liaison officers was rotated to attend to Gobbo's needs. But in 2011 the police didn't want to hear from their 'best-ever' source anymore. As she put it, Gobbo was treated as a 'kind of problem'.

As police QC Saul Holt asks: 'Ms Gobbo, far from wanting to get on with your life, every time you have an opportunity you're trying to contact police officers and trying to give them the very information you were for years at the SDU?'

The affair had long since soured, and threatened to spill over into public view. Gobbo had kept her life, if not her health, and she had millions of dollars to start again. But the evidence suggests she had an inveterate need to keep going, like a boxer too punch-drunk to know that he should hang up the gloves.

'Would it be fair to say, Ms Gobbo, that you were an extremely enthusiastic informer?' asks Geoff Chettle QC, representing the police handlers at the royal commission.

'I think that yes, I think that's my personality,' she replies. 'I either do something 150 per cent or don't do it at all.'

Jeff Gleeson QC represents former chief commissioner Simon Overland. He asks about keeping the truth from her loved ones and lying on her application to become a lawyer.

Gleeson poses the headline question that encapsulates her secret career in informing.

'See, what I want to put to you, Ms Gobbo, is that you are a spectacularly good liar, do you accept that?

'Ah, yes.'

'And do you accept that you've lied so well and so often that you've lost the capacity to know when you're telling a lie?'

'No, I don't.'

'When did you give up your practice of being a spectacularly good liar, Ms Gobbo?'

Perhaps 2010 or 2011, she says.

The label sticks. It is put to her that she is lying about her lying. Gobbo appeared to mislead the court in her evidence at the secret Supreme Court trial, in front of Justice Timothy Ginnane, in 2017. She told that court that she did not know the contents of Shifty the supergrass's 2004 statements against his fellow criminals at the time she was representing him.

She is likewise unconvincing in her royal commission denials that she burgled the office of legal colleague Sharon Cure in 2007. Gobbo says it is 'rubbish' that she examined Cure's confidential papers. Yet she told her handlers at the time she had been 'looking around' Cure's chambers.

Holt points out apparent discrepancies regarding Gobbo's place in the Briars investigation into the 2003 killing of Shane Chartres-Abbott. She gave a statement to detectives Steve Waddell and Ron Iddles in 2009. Later, the unsigned document said the chief murder suspect, Mark Perry, had confessed the killing to her. Gobbo denies to the royal commission that she had told investigators about a confession by Perry.

Then Holt produces a text message written by Gobbo to a police officer after a newspaper report into the Briars investigation was published in late October 2009:

Good to see that VicPol have finally broken the story on Mark Perry, the murderer I told Briars all about. Read today's paper so you're up to speed … How fucking funny it is to be so instrumental yet treated with, at least, indifference. Circus.

Holt asks Gobbo if she told investigators about the supposed confession.

'It looks like it,' Gobbo says.

She has changed her mind. No one knows where the truth lies. It begs the question: does Gobbo simply say whatever she thinks the listener wants to hear?

She is quizzed over her claim that she never lied to her handlers. She told them the truth, perhaps, but not the whole truth. For example, she didn't mention her use of burner phones to contact Paul Dale in the months before the Hodson killings in 2004.

Gobbo does not impress when she is presented with letters written in 2011 by her then lawyer, Levi Diamond, to the Director of Public Prosecutions. He was sounding out a reward on her behalf for her giving evidence about the Hodson killings.

What sort of person wants a prize for playing games that end in murder?

* * *

After fighting so long to avoid giving evidence, Gobbo appears to be enjoying her questioning. As embarrassing as the process is, she seems buoyed by the attention.

If she cannot remember, she sounds genuinely apologetic.

But, in her own words, she is a liar. A professional liar.

The recurring charge gores her in questions about the aftermath of Dowsley's 2014 story in the *Herald Sun*. In a meeting with senior police, she asserted that she did not think she had acted improperly.

Yet, as she concedes in her evidence, Gobbo and her handlers knew that they were breaking the rules from the moment her informing began. They hid it as well as they could, lest the behaviour be 'judged in a particular way'.

When Winneke re-examines Gobbo, he almost snarls. The good-bloke persona has shifted to attack dog. He feels that Gobbo has twisted her testimony, as if seeking to agree with each of her questioners as they cross-examine her.

'Ms Gobbo, you said in your evidence, and I think you said it on a number of occasions, that you don't want to give anyone the wrong impression, do you recall saying that?'

'Yes.'

'Can I suggest to you on a number of occasions, during the course of your evidence, that is in fact what you have done, do you accept that?'

'Um, not, not necessarily intentionally, but if I have, I have.'

In her final minutes after five days of evidence, in transcripts that run to 222,000 words, Gobbo concedes that she cannot recall an actual sexual encounter with Pope. She provides no where or when, just an insistence that she knows it to be true.

'I can't think of a reason why I would make it up,' she says.

You have to wonder. Is Gobbo still the 'spectacularly good liar' she once was?

* * *

There is no goodbye at the end of Gobbo's evidence, not even a thank you. Commission staff seek to squeeze other witnesses into the forty-five minutes left in the day. Gobbo is off the line and back in the wind.

Her version of events has reshaped dozens of details.

The police were 'driving the bus'. They never said stop. She has scoffed at senior Purana detectives who have claimed in evidence that they knew little about her informing.

Stuart Bateson, Gavan Ryan and Jim O'Brien are fingered by name for their knowledge and application of unseemly practices. Winneke gets Gobbo to agree that only a judge could determine the legality of the Gobbo conspiracy, and no judge was ever consulted.

Under unbearable pressures, Gobbo did what she was good at — acquiring information, as power, to be dispensed at her discretion. She was used by the crooks and she was used by Victoria Police, and she in turn burned the crooks and Victoria Police alike.

The police line diverges from the Gobbo line, but they share a disingenuous theme. Each party blames the other. If there is something to see here, it isn't their fault.

'Noble cause' is a prevailing posture in the royal commission witness box. The right intent and the wrong execution. But many police officers have not raised their hands and accepted responsibility. The bosses blame the rank-and-file. The rank-and-file blame the bosses.

Victoria Police needed to solve crimes and they threw every available weapon at the cause. This is the accepted line. If perjury and other crimes were an unfortunate consequence, they should be treated like regrettable side-effects.

Many police officers have been less than forthcoming. They have hunkered in the shadows, as if hoping the light will not penetrate to the damning details.

There is a collective cravenness in this approach. Wilful myopia and a resistance to transparency still seem to thrive at Victoria Police.

Simon Overland was only one officer of many recalled to the witness box because fresh evidence — often delayed by the tardy processes of Victoria Police document production — required renewed examination.

The overarching conclusion is that Gobbo couldn't say no, and neither could Victoria Police. 'One thing led to a lot of other things,' she says.

The royal commission is now furnished with much of the how, when, where and who. It has identified ninety-six current prisoners who may have historical claims against Gobbo's behaviour among the 1296 people who may have suffered for receiving her legal advice. In 137 years of the Victorian Bar, no other lawyer has treated the courts with such contempt. Yet the Gobbo enigma has survived the process largely intact.

Who is she? Why did she do it?

We may never really know.

Epilogue

Girl on Fire

2020

Henry Hill, the mobster turned FBI informer, helped convict fifty New York Mafia figures back in the 1980s. Director Martin Scorsese told the tale in the film *Goodfellas*.

In the movie's final scene, Hill steps out his front door to fetch the morning paper from the porch. A two-toned station wagon sits in the driveway.

Henry Hill has survived, but only because he is no longer Henry Hill.

'Today, everything is different,' he says. 'There's no action. I have to wait around like everyone else ...

'I'm an average nobody. I get to live the rest of my life as a schnook.'

* * *

Since November 2018, there have been unconfirmed sightings of Gobbo in the Melbourne CBD and in beachside Brighton. But by 2020, she has disappeared. Has she gone her own way, or is she enjoying the tailor-made police protection she always demanded? Where is she now? No one knows.

Her destination seems certain, no matter where she heads. It's a sad place, where no one knows your name, and demons chatter when you walk down the street. Police protection or not, Gobbo will follow Henry Hill to Nowheresville. She is sentenced to be a schnook.

Boasting more convictions from her informing than Henry Hill wasn't the prime-ministerial role Gobbo yearned for as a student. But it suited her better. If she liked to draw attention to herself, it was always on her terms. As Informer 3838, she was a somebody, a confidante to both villains and cops, and so what if she was a walking catastrophe?

Gobbo put people in jail for decades and they never had a clue. She hoodwinked both the criminals and the judges by betraying those who trusted her most. Gobbo was a person everyone knew of and no one knew. She stung the good, the bad and the dastardly. She played life as though it were a game and she were the grandmaster.

Gobbo was, as one of her handlers admits, always two steps ahead. Her powers of persuasion topped those of any politician, even when she was playing to an audience of hotheads, speed freaks and goons.

She deceived Carl Williams, the bogan prince who killed over petty grudges. He sent his hitman to scare her in 2003. He wanted her blood, or at least her reputation, by 2006.

Yet she kept going. Despite the bullets in the mail and the firebombing of her car. Despite her alleged choking by Horty Mokbel and her eviction by her legal peers. When her handlers warned her to slow down, Gobbo responded with more gifts of information, like a needy lover who fears rejection.

Gobbo was a woman in a boys' world, where the female pioneers tended to favour muted tones and an air of entitlement — like the men. But she wasn't like any of the men or women of the Bar.

Gobbo incriminated her clients so that they were criminally charged. She accepted their money, but secretly worked for the police prosecution on the opposite side of the courtroom. Her clients were worse than alone in the face of the law.

No defence lawyer anywhere has had so little care for the rule of law. No lawyer except a Catholic girl with every advantage from Melbourne's exclusive inner east.

She maintained the control by masquerading as one person while conniving as another, and only she can explain why. Her choices were foreign to anyone who values sincerity, trust and a good night's sleep.

It was a solitary existence, layered with terrors. Gobbo always felt like she was alone. She staved off her fears of abandonment by creating chaos. She was a fugitive from the truth, and she couldn't stop running.

She cast herself as a victim in a righteous cause. This self-anointed vulnerability became a pattern: to rush at the flames of notoriety, then wonder why no one saved her from the heat.

* * *

Into her vortex flowed men. Bad men, some in the uniforms of the local police force. 'She rooted enough of us,' one of her handlers once told Dowsley.

Her men spun her moral compass. She wielded unlikely power by making herself available to these men as both lawyer and secretary. Nothing was too much trouble. Yet she was not as she appeared.

Gobbo made herself available in other ways too. Perceptions can be terribly unfair, but attitudes to Gobbo have been drawn over decades.

The ethical blur of her double life spread to her fraternising. Gobbo's numerous sexual encounters were hopelessly intertwined with her informing. She didn't seem to mind that people thought her behaviour loose. She slept with cops and criminals and everyone in her circles talked about it, often because her choices sounded more calculated than romantic. Call it, as a once-close colleague has, 'Sex, Lies and Recording Devices' (to misquote a well-known arthouse movie).

Sex matters to Gobbo's story, much as it counts in understanding Mata Hari, the alleged German spy who seduced men on both sides of the World War I battlelines. The Dutch dancer and the Melbourne barrister share several traits: both acted as solitary women among swarms of men; both knew how to please those men, and to get what they wanted in return.

Gobbo always liked to be talked about. For her, infamy was equated with relevance. The problem, as her psychologist said in 2016, was that infamy was bad for her mental health.

Rumours of sexual intimacy in public places can be traced back to her school days and her encounters at Tunnel nightclub. She herself fanned these tales, fellow students say.

Her university housemate, Brian Wilson, set an unfortunate benchmark. He was the first bad man among the dozens she fell prey to — and only some of them were on the wrong side of the law.

Sergeant Trevor Ashton first registered Gobbo in 1995. His subordinate Tim Argall — like Argall's old mate Paul Dale — has admitted under oath to having sex with her.

Argall, in answering an awkward question about an 'episode of physical intimacy', sounded ashamed in the witness box. Both he and Dale emphasised that they slept with Gobbo only once, as if the fact of the encounter were a blot on their judgment.

Such couplings were symptoms of the throwback culture of a police force yet to fully evolve in the early 2000s. Under the stewardship of Christine Nixon, Victoria Police came to emblazon inclusive ideals, such as gay rights, as well as conciliatory resolutions to violence. But chauvinist notions persisted. Nixon herself was derisively dubbed 'Big Kev', after an overweight cleaning entrepreneur.

Police work on the front lines leads to marriage breakdowns and drinking problems. It always will, even if emotional dysfunction is better understood now than it once was. Gobbo was later diagnosed with PTSD and major depressive disorders, the kinds of ailments that hardened police officers can suffer in their work.

She thrived in their blokey cohort of denial, where physical acts could be recounted later to your mates, and feelings were otherwise suppressed. She was one of the boys — until she went home *with* one of the boys.

People talked. Gobbo graduated from 'footy groupie' to 'badge bunny' to 'gangster's moll'.

Even as she informed on her criminal clients, she used sex as a weapon to gain their trust. Drug baron Rob Karam supposedly serenaded her with movie dates and dinners. She indulged Karam's overtures because she wanted to help jail him.

She might have slept with the European. She might have slept with Tony Mokbel, even if she vocally disputes such claims. The truth in either case is almost beside the point. Gobbo was spotted at intimate dinners where the body language invited labels of canoodling with criminals. Her lifestyle lent itself to the possibility that she slept with crooks.

If there was a pattern to Gobbo's romantic life, it was flings and one-nighters. The constant was the absence of a regular man on her arm. Gobbo *wanted* normal romances — at least she said she did. But the bad-man spectre never faded.

Years after her informing ended, while she embraced the ordinariness of kindergarten mums in the suburbs, Gobbo still visited drug trafficker Richard Barkho in prison because he was apparently the father of one, if not two, of her children.

In the language of Mata Hari's accusers, Gobbo was bathed in 'immorality' as one of the 'man-eaters'. She was the high-flying defence barrister said to be caught in a stairway encounter with a police officer at the now-closed Celtic Club. 'They didn't break stride,' a stairway witness says. Again, the important thing is not whether it did or didn't happen. It's that people accepted it *could* have happened. This tale circulated at Crockett Chambers and may have had a bearing on her eviction from the chambers.

When flowers were delivered to Gobbo's office at Crockett Chambers on her birthday, colleagues greeted the gift with squealing and lots of questions. Here's the sad part: some fellow barristers assumed Gobbo sent the flowers to herself.

Former crime commander Terry Purton never met Gobbo, but he was involved in many discussions about her role as a human source. He described general perceptions to the royal commission.

'It was sort of common knowledge that she had sexual relationships with people in the legal fraternity and there could have been some scuttlebutt that she sort of tried to drag members [of the force] into bed ... That was my gut feeling at the time, the same as the gut feeling with Tony Mokbel giving her a $25,000 Rolex watch. There was always something. Nicola was always the topic of discussion.'

Yet Gobbo was both a predator and a victim. A police officer is said to have once dropped her off at hospital after rough sex, only to fret over coming days that Gobbo would lodge a criminal complaint about her injury.

Like a cheater who comes to wonder if others are cheating *them* too, Gobbo never really trusted people. She seemed to cheat herself as well as her clients. She was smart and feisty, but her accumulated wisdom did not extend to protecting her reputation. She instead embraced a label that no lady wants.

Her cheating separates her from her closest counterpart. 'A harlot, yes, a traitoress never,' Mata Hari said in her own defence.

* * *

The Hodson tragedy obsesses Dowsley and Carlyon. In New York in late 2019 for a long overdue rest, Dowsley attended a Billy Joel concert in Madison Square Garden. His personal take on *She's Always a Woman* differed from that of every other fan that night, as Joel sang about secrets, lies and killer smiles.

When Dowsley met with Gobbo after his first Lawyer X stories were published in 2014, she sounded genuine when discussing the Hodson killings, stating that she wore the wire for the Hodson children. 'Wouldn't you want me to do it if it was your parents?'

If it's hard to believe her claim that her informing was motivated from the beginning by altruism or guilt, the notion of belated contrition might soften the easy view of Gobbo as a ruthless manipulator.

There is one other major mitigating factor.

Gobbo's choices were bathed in Shakespearean tragedy — in the timeless themes of ambition and greed. But she was abetted. She was a one-stop shop but no one-woman show.

Gobbo was manipulated by Victoria Police. Informer inducement is a niche of policing tethered to protocols, but in this case they ought to have known better — and many close observers think they *did*.

As if they were tossing the car keys to a child, Victoria Police wanted the world to look the other way while she swerved down the highway with an armed escort. They deliberately evaded the checks and balances of a system that serves to protect all from chicanery. The police and Gobbo appointed themselves as judge and jury despite protections aimed at ensuring that no person or entity should ever wield absolute power.

There were few officers who voiced concerns about the legal and ethical maelstrom of Nicola Gobbo. They are the only heroes in this tale of villainy, and the likes of detectives Chris Lim, Charlie Bezzina and Ron Iddles, as well as Sir Ken Jones, merit praise for daring to tell the truth.

Of course, *Gobbo* manipulated *the police* too. She decided what should be shared and who should be punished. When the police eventually jettisoned their weapon, the weapon took aim at *them*.

This Iago did not submit, as did the *Othello* character, to torture and execution for her crimes. 'I know *our* secret,' Gobbo implied, 'and if I have to, I will use my knowledge to destroy careers and reputations.'

Understandable, perhaps, given how she had suffered. Aspects of police behaviour are less so.

Within Gobbo's first fifteen months as Informer 3838, Victoria Police officers in the secretive loop of knowledge collectively came to believe she 'suffered psychiatric or psychological and personality dysfunction'. She told her handlers in one discussion: 'I'm a fucked-up person, but you know that.'

Simon Overland told the Kellam inquiry in 2014 that Gobbo had 'personality and attachment issues'. She was 'pathologically incapable of acting in [her] own best interests'.

Yet Victoria Police kept her on as an informer for three and a half years, when opening the letterbox or checking a text message might mean she was confronted by yet another death threat.

The release was her deregisteration so she could become a witness against Paul Dale in his Hodson murder trial. Yet her new circumstances, coupled with the burden of her old informer exploits, only condemned her to further risk. Her future was enveloped in her past.

Her controller at the Source Development Unit, Sandy White, spoke of all high-risk sources in 2019 as 'not quite normal'. This prompted a recommendation years after Gobbo was deregistered that any source exhibiting mental issues must be sent to a psychiatrist. White thought Gobbo was 'psychologically unstable'.

He described the informer program as a swamp of liars and nutjobs. 'I have found that the very best human sources are those who have big egos because they try hard to get a successful result,' he said. 'There is no doubt in my mind that Ms Gobbo fell into that category.'

When White sent her to get professional help in 2006, the female psychologist did not think Gobbo was at risk of suicide or self-harm. She also said that Gobbo's 'personality problems' were 'long-standing and not created by her role as a human source'.

Yet Gobbo was 'needy', as White called her years later. Her handlers had come to replace criminals as her social outlet.

Testifying to the secret Ginnane trial in 2016, Gobbo's long-term psychologist offered clues about the 'void' in Gobbo's life.

'So her father died when she was doing Year 12, so she would have been eighteen,' the psychologist said. 'Her mother had had two bouts of cancer prior to that and her father was quite a bit older than her mother. And ... there were two other children by the father's former marriage, so she has two half siblings. And her father died and that was relatively catastrophic for her, it was a very difficult event, and then her mother died in 2011 from pancreatic cancer, which is a very nasty condition.'

In the absence of a father figure, she sought to be validated by her handlers, and White in particular, who she later felt took 'advantage' of her need to change 'the situation'.

'So one of the things we've worked on, and this is a common treatment with trauma, is to help her deconstruct, if you like, and speak about the matters that occurred some years ago in relation to her relationship with Victoria Police,' the psychologist said in 2016. 'And so we've spoken a lot about why she got involved with that and her sense of there being a void in her life and that some of the people she got involved with at Victoria Police really fulfilled a father-figure

type of role. I think in that respect, she certainly would be a person …
vulnerable to that kind of experience.'

Gobbo told her psychologist she had spent thousands of hours
with White and was 'very involved in doing activities in relation to her
relationship with him'.

'I think she felt that he treated her as somebody special and valued
her contributions to the work they were doing together,' the psychologist
said.

Gobbo claimed she wanted to impress him. Yet the relationship also
made her feel 'trapped'. 'That was a, yes, repetitive theme …' Gobbo
said in closed court in 2017. '[White] gave me the impression that you
could never earn their trust 100 per cent, but I'd come close to that, yes.'

Gobbo had healthy relationships with her mother and at least one
sibling, but limited family connections beyond that. Her gregariousness
seemed to mask something even sadder. She didn't seem to want
anyone too close. Even her beauty therapist, who gave Gobbo night
appointments, felt her customer needed a friend.

As her psychologist testified, Gobbo relied on her and an unnamed
loved one for the kind of trust that others ordinarily share with partners
and *multiple* loved ones.

Yet Gobbo kept things from her counsellor, despite their many
hours together, such as her odd desire to be the best informer in history.
Her being is built on secrets and the keeping of them, and even those
she trusted most were deprived of the fuller view.

* * *

But Gobbo needed more than a shrink. The risks of her informing were
not monitored as the police informer textbook demanded.

The police would task her to get a phone number, say, or to chat with
a crook about his criminal enterprises. Get licence numbers, they said.
Find links. They learned the pressure points of the criminals without
leaving the office.

A cynic might identify a pattern that went: 'Please do the policing
on behalf of Victoria Police. And if it's unclear to us what you're doing,

and how you're gathering the information, we accept that. You might be a "bloody nightmare" [as a very highly ranked officer has called her], but we bow to you as an untameable force of intelligence.'

Victoria Police also cocked their leg to history. They ignored the 1881 Longmore Royal Commission, set up following the outbreak of the Kelly Gang, and the Kelley inquiries (1932–1933) into Victorian police brutality. The founding tenets of British policing, the 1829 Peelian Principles, didn't matter, including Principle 8, 'Police should ... never appear to usurp the powers of the judiciary.'

Rather, they seem to have borrowed from the J. Edgar Hoover rulebook, which said that 'Justice is merely incidental to law and order.'

The police kept one promise of the many they made to Gobbo. They vowed to hide her double life. When they couldn't, they built obstacles to the truth.

But it seems Gobbo was not persuaded to inform by promises. She could see no other way. Whether driven by naïveté or arrogance, she sought first of all to save herself. In choosing to inform, however, she sentenced herself to be never more than one misplaced whisper from death.

Simon Overland admitted to the Kellam inquiry 'that it was sometimes difficult to discern the exact circumstances in which [Gobbo] had come into possession of information ... because of [Gobbo's] own blurred lines of professional conduct with respect to ... clients'.

She broke protocols aimed at preserving her wellbeing, yet no one tempered her excesses. Her licence to thrill, bill and spill was revoked only when Victoria Police found another use for her as a witness.

Victoria Police can cite review after review of human source management. The organisation is a creaking bureaucracy, laden with protocols and procedures critical to policing in an unpredictable and changing world.

Yet Victoria Police appear to have tossed out the rules of risk assessment with Gobbo from the start. Gobbo never received anything in writing about the terms of her informing. There was no legal advice, not in 1995, or 1999, or 2005 onwards.

As former chief commissioner Neil Comrie wrote in his 2011 review, her informing career read like 'a case crying out for informed legal advice at the outset'.

Police did set out the risks — the risks to themselves. Gobbo needed to be corralled for the force's sake. Her second and final handler review in 2006 noted: 'Because of the Source's occupation and particular position, if compromised, the handling of this Source would come under extreme scrutiny. This could cause embarrassment of the force.'

There is another way to put this. Victoria Police were seeking to cover their own behinds from the time they signed on Nicola Gobbo as their Gangland secret weapon, despite their claims that they were protecting her. They knew the legal risks. Sandy White flew to England to research informer management before Gobbo was registered as 3838. But it appears that Victoria Police chose to ignore the international benchmarks.

In November 2005, Gobbo told her handlers that her informing posed 'no ethical or legal issues'. Such grandiose claims, from someone who was, according to Comrie, 'clearly manic', went unquestioned.

Her lifestyle was 'clearly unsustainable', Comrie wrote. Yet Gobbo's welfare seemed to be considered secondary to the welfare of the handlers who dealt with her.

Instead of being concerned for her wellbeing, Victoria Police were drunk on the possibilities. Here was a spy who could put away the meanest of criminals. Here was a way to end the Gangland War.

One-time Purana head Detective Inspector Jim O'Brien claimed at the royal commission that he 'never turned his mind' to Gobbo's possible breaching of legal professional privilege. The assumption appeared to be that such unconscionable breaches did not matter — again, so long as no one found out.

Thousands of words of Victoria Police internal documents were couched in management jargon and shrouded in high secrecy. Their sheer volume gave the impression of thoroughness. But read in their entirety, they invite other conclusions.

Victoria Police didn't care to assess the toxic overflow of Gobbo. The organisation was like a cheating husband who rationalises his deceit as a necessary part of his machismo. Victoria Police were as hooked on Gobbo as Gobbo was hooked on them.

This underhanded approach has been defended in the context of bullets and safety. But the 'extraordinary times, extraordinary measures' mantra doesn't seem to hold up. Gobbo's official registration in 2005 was a whole year after the spate of Gangland killings. Carl Williams was locked up and Tony Mokbel was about to be. Almost every other major player was dead or in prison.

The criminal justice system is imperfect, as everyone who works within it has to accept. Grey areas leech into the black and white. But a lawyer who informs on her clients, with the active encouragement of police, is no grey area.

That's why there are no known precedents for the systemised police use of a defence lawyer as an informer. Why didn't the FBI use a duplicitous lawyer to stem the Mafia death toll? Or British intelligence agencies mandated to stop the IRA bombings? Why haven't books before now described lawyers dedicated to deceiving their criminal clients?

Because, as the Comrie review found, the notion is 'ethically repugnant'. Convicted criminals are now lining up for get-out-of-jail cards and compensation payouts in the tens of millions of dollars. All because of a woman Victoria Police thought was crazy from the start.

Victoria Police face more of the same critical judgments that they secretly concluded about themselves a long time ago. They have fought against the shame and possible criminality, and are likely to continue doing so.

By permitting Gobbo's informing, they blighted trust and decency, citing community safety, as well as community pressure. But they also hobbled the pursuit of truth.

The mantra of police homicide squads goes that everybody matters or no one matters. In their use of Gobbo, and in covering it up afterwards, Victoria Police placed themselves on the wrong side of the equation.

* * *

We do know that Gobbo's informing always had to end. She dodged the bullets and the bastards, but could not shake off the curiosity of a newspaper journalist.

Observers, with the clarity of retrospect, can judge the outcomes as logical. Anthony Dowsley, or someone like him, was bound to come along, as was the royal commission that police fought so hard to avoid.

Dowsley tapped Gobbo's secret when murderers and judges could not. The risk — as Dowsley often told himself in the unwanted wakefulness before dawn — was that Gobbo would lose everything. But the stain was not Dowsley's to apply.

Gobbo's affront to ethics and honesty would come to define her, and there isn't much call for such skillsets outside the informing shadows. Once the Gangland spy who changed the war, Gobbo is now condemned to the life of an 'average nobody'.

Like Henry Hill, anonymity has been foisted upon her.

Gobbo dosed up on so much adrenaline that she is now severely depressed and largely unresponsive to treatments, like a wind-up toy wound too many times.

She has attempted to adjust to her loss of power and reputation. She has tried a personal trainer to dim the depression. She has had to find new meaning in the absence of her secret life. But it has been hard.

She spoke to Mick Gatto after Dowsley's 2014 Lawyer X exposé, and oddly Rob Karam, the drug baron fighting thirty-seven years in jail because of her deception. She spoke to others too, some very dangerous, knowing they were people who will kill you if they find out who you really are.

Was she trying to dim the fear of always looking over her shoulder? Or was she clinging to the only identity she knew?

Gobbo still wants to work. The law is gone, along with her professional reputation. Speaking to a police handler, she once voiced whims of being an air traffic controller or FBI profiler. She even proposed becoming a 'talent scout' for Victoria Police informers. All these roles would have played to her strengths.

Yet Gobbo spoke of another prospect. She didn't seem like someone who would bathe private parts or swap bedpans, but she expressed an interest to her psychologist in becoming a nurse.

The psychologist, a mother figure, did not point out that the ethical demands of nursing are just as life-and-death as those of her lawyer past. She believed that nursing could offer Gobbo an identity 'that wasn't around infamy'.

On the stand in 2016, the psychologist spoke of Gobbo's need to 'find other things she can do with herself that actually give her some purpose'. This is a challenge for someone who has always felt empty. Gobbo has never tried 'normal' before. As the psychologist said, Gobbo didn't know if she 'could relinquish her identity and still be who [she is]'.

Hill moved again and again, with his wife and children, in a twilight existence where being himself would have been fatal. Gobbo faces a similar erasure of her history. Perhaps she will chase the sun, as she always has.

The price of her chaos seems destined to be her greatest fear: abandonment. Everyone she has known has burned her or been burned by her. She is, as a former colleague has said, radioactive.

In exposure, she is like Hill, or Donnie Brasco, the FBI undercover agent credited with 100 Mafia convictions. She is alone and vulnerable, a nocturnal animal doomed to eternal sunshine.

Disarmed of righteousness and her unofficial police cloak, the scorpion has lost her sting and skitters for release. She has ample legal, health and welfare excuses for seeking refuge in dark places.

She thrilled to her informing with the same zeal as Terry Hodson. He felt like a dead man walking in his final months in 2004, and now Gobbo cowers under the same cloud of doom.

The drama of her double life always offered far more than the ordinariness of a mum who blends into the crowd. This is what Gobbo can now look forward to if she can avoid grimmer fates. Charges await, potentially, along with the ongoing humiliation that comes with the public judgment of your deceptions and mental struggles.

Nicola Gobbo stands as a case study in the abuse of power. Her exposure may lead to criminal convictions for the lawkeepers and freedom for the lawbreakers.

Yet her legacy will be something more. Nicola Gobbo broke the system, and she almost got away with it.

How will she pay? With a lifetime sentence of hiding in plain sight.

Postscript

Conclusions of Law, for Now

2020

Commissioner McMurdo releases her final report on the Royal Commission into the Management of Police Informants on 30 November 2020. Her findings are as pointed as every other judicial review of the Gobbo saga.

The criminal justice system was 'corrupted'. A number of Victoria Police officers 'fell short of their legal, ethical and professional duties and obligations'. Gobbo's conduct was 'inexcusable'.

She does not find that Gobbo or any former or current Victoria Police officers had committed any crimes; instead, she defers this task to a special investigator, who will assess the evidence for proof of perjury, perverting the course of justice, misconduct in public office and other crimes.

Where Gobbo is hiding, and whether she can be extradited from an overseas location to face any charges should they be laid against her, goes unsaid. But Gobbo faces years more of uncomfortable scrutiny.

For McMurdo's finding prompts an inescapable conclusion: that a saga that has played for six years on the public stage could continue for another six years.

McMurdo dismisses police claims that their desire for secrecy was driven entirely by concerns for Gobbo's safety.

She was disbelieving of police excuses, from Overland down, for why they did not seek legal advice for Gobbo's use from the start. 'It suggested an unacceptable willingness throughout the organisation to tolerate bending the rules to help solve serious crime,' she said.

'The Purana Taskforce and SDU officers involved in efforts to avoid adequate disclosure, claimed this was done solely out of concern to protect Ms Gobbo's safety. Another powerful motivator was likely to be the avoidance of reputational damage, public exposure and judicial criticism of their use of a prominent criminal defence lawyer as a human source, given that this may have put past and future convictions at risk. It also allowed them to continue to receive and use her valuable intelligence and tactical advice.'

She ordered the immediate release of police documents to those people whose convictions might be affected by Gobbo's misuse. It seems remarkable that police were privately aware of legal concerns over Mokbel's conviction in 2012, and yet, more than eight years later, still withhold materials they are legally obliged to produce for his appeal.

McMurdo leads us to an answer: that police officers acted outside the rules in part because the rules precluded Gobbo's use as a source.

Her findings become the official chronicle of a cover-up, her recommendations unknotting the tangle of police recalcitrance, conflicting agendas and a universal refusal to take responsibility. All of her 111 recommendations, which focus on continuing external review of police protocols for human sources, are immediately accepted by the Andrews Government.

A 'profound failure' is how Police Chief Commissioner Shane Patton describes Gobbo's use in his response to the royal commission's final report. Shows of handwringing are adopted as the prevailing political and police reaction to McMurdo's recommendations.

Patton's extended statement of contrition is an ungainly, if welcome, detour from the claims of his predecessor, Graham Ashton, who said that Gobbo's use passed the so-called pub test.

It didn't. By implying that officers involved knew this at the time, McMurdo sweeps away the self-serving veil that has marked the long-held police line.

Patton's language of a trust broken is recognition that the truth is finally out there. It does not mean, however, that Victoria Police will not resist it for many more years to come.

After all, as of the end of 2020, not a single police officer has been stood down over the Lawyer X scandal.

General Note on Sources

Had we written endnotes for this book, the endnotes might have been longer than the manuscript itself.

Instead, we have set out some of the thousands of general sources we used when researching this book.

The 2019 Royal Commission into the Management of Police Informants laid out the longer saga, piece by piece, in thousands of statements and primary-source documents that otherwise would have remained secret. The royal commission is an important source for the earlier days of Gobbo's informing from 1995.

Understanding her choices, which seem so contradictory, came late to the writing. They are detailed in extensive commission witness statements from police officers who worked with her at the time, some from Victoria Police, others from the Australian Federal Police.

The royal commission also revealed many of the 5500 police information reports about Gobbo's informing from 2005 to 2009. They are unedited and candid. We gave them pre-eminence, given that they generally recorded events as they took place, and were not skewed by the fear that they would be later scrutinised. We have relied upon them as a close link to what was happening, and what Gobbo was thinking, during those crazy times.

A plethora of books, from journalists John Silvester and Andrew Rule (*Mokbelly*, *The Gangland War*), as well as Adam Shand (*Carl Williams*, *Big Shots*), and serving and former police officers (Paul Dale's *Disgraced?*, Christine Nixon's *Fair Cop*), were drawn on to describe the Gangland machinations that erupted after 1999. Some of the players themselves have also written books, such as Roberta Williams (*Roberta Williams: My Life*) and Mick Gatto (*I, Mick Gatto*). These were very helpful in shedding new light on major historical events.

The newspaper articles written by courtroom reporters of the time were critical to understanding long-ago events. The likes of *Herald Sun* journalists Elissa Hunt and Katie Bice ought to be thanked, along with so many other reporters who kept their heads amid the bubbling chaos of Gangland's conniptions.

Comprehending Nicola Gobbo's place in the well-documented Gangland story was the trickiest part of the research. Her early associations with the likes of Tony Mokbel and his brothers and associates were elusive. Again, Victoria Police testimony in the royal commission witness box told much of the story of this era.

The so-called Comrie report, whose findings would be disputed by Gobbo's handlers, was the first formalised review of Gobbo's informing. Written in 2012, it was not publicly revealed until 2019.

That report precipitated the Kellam report, which provided more of the police information reports documenting Gobbo's behaviour and thinking. The Kellam report was directly triggered by Dowsley's revelations, published in the *Herald Sun* from March 2014.

The Kellam report preceded the civil trial of 2016 and 2017, in which Nicola Gobbo sided with Victoria Police in challenging the Director of Public Prosecutions in his wish to notify some of Gobbo's former clients that their convictions might be unsafe.

Dowsley waded through the months of transcripts of what was called *AB & EF v CD*, including those covering Gobbo's appearance in the witness box, to identify and highlight previously unknown facts.

The Hodson killings of 2004 were expansively covered by Dowsley in the *Herald Sun* over many years. The saga has also been comprehensively reported on by *The Age*'s Nick McKenzie.

Dowsley built a friendship with the Hodson children, and broke revelations about the police investigation into the killings in 2015.

But again, questions of motivation — and the sheer depth of deceit that Gobbo employed during that time — remained hidden until the royal commission. Her description in the witness box of feeling trapped in the triangular vortex of thrusting detective Peter De Santo, Tony Mokbel and Paul Dale (then under suspicion of burglary and murder) offered an explanation of sorts that had been lacking for more than a decade.

In specific instances, a particular reporter had written much of the historical narrative of a case. The *Herald Sun*'s Keith Moor, for example, almost single-handedly told the Tomato Tins saga in his book *Busted* (and also in his *Herald Sun* article 'World's Biggest Ecstasy Bust: How a Google Search Foiled Aussie Tomato Tin Mafia's Drug Plots', published 25 July 2016). In such instances, that previous work laid a blueprint for an understanding — with Nicola Gobbo's role overlaid — that otherwise would not exist.

Public archives, such as the State Library Victoria, as well as written judgments from various courts, were invaluable in the research.

Obviously, we cannot thank our many confidential sources by name. But there would be no book without them. These people risked their livelihoods, if not more, in providing information, and many were generous even in cases in which their proximity to the unethical conduct of Gobbo stood to reflect badly on themselves. They are owed a great debt.

They cover an impossibly wide sweep of professions, from lawyers to housewives to hospitality workers. They offered information on Nicola Gobbo's life from her schooldays to the present day. We have tried to honour their help by endeavouring to tell the truth as fairly as we can.

The telling of this story was complicated by legal restrictions against identifying particular people who are critical to the Gobbo story. Victoria Police have sought to suppress these people's names to protect their safety, and they have succeeded in a number of cases. As a result, we have at times been frustrated by an inability to narrate events in a logical way, or even provide the scantest sketch of this or that character.

Further Reading

Books

Paul Dale, *Disgraced? The Cop at the Centre of Melbourne's Gangland Wars*, Five Mile Press (2013)

Mick Gatto and Tom Noble, *I, Mick Gatto*, Victory Books (2009)

Keith Moor, *Busted: The Inside Story of the World's Biggest Ecstasy Haul and How the Australian Calabrian Mafia Nearly Got Away With It*, Penguin (2016)

Christine Nixon and Jo Chandler, *Fair Cop: Christine Nixon*, Melbourne University Press (2012)

Adam Shand, *Carl Williams: The Short Life and Violent Times of Melbourne's Gangland Drug Lord*, Penguin (2014)

John Silvester and Andrew Rule, *Underbelly: The Gangland War* Floradale Press (2008)

——*Underbelly: Mokbelly*, Floradale Productions and Sly Ink (2013)

Roberta Williams, *Roberta Williams: My Life*, HarperCollins Publishers (2010)

Websites

AB & EF v CD (www.supremecourt.vic.gov.au/case-summaries/ ab-ef-v-cd-proceedings)

Herald Sun: True Crime Australia (www.heraldsun.com.au/ truecrimeaustralia)

Royal Commission into the Management of Police Informants: Exhibits by Witness (www.rcmpi.vic.gov.au/exhibits-witness)

Acknowledgments

Big stories are never neat. They suck up your waking hours and invade your thoughts. Everyday responsibilities get overlooked. That's when friends and loved ones compensate for your absence of mind and body.

This book arrives six years after the story behind it was first uncovered. It follows a flurry of new material, mostly from the royal commission, that furnished assumptions and suppositions with hard facts.

It has been written out of the chronic chaos of a very tough year. It wouldn't have happened without the support of so many.

Andrew Rule has long provided wisdom to the authors. His knowledge of Gangland is surpassed only by his understanding of human nature.

He, along with *The Age*'s John Silvester, trailblazed Gangland media coverage in the 2000s. Any work about Gangland ought to bow to their example. They made sense of the confusing array of criminals and detectives. They made them real.

Damon Johnston, our then editor at the *Herald Sun*, gave us the time, resources and commitment to write this story. He was critical to the story's birth, and he backed it through the empty years when it mostly seemed that no proper story could ever be told. He cleared paths for information in a way that no amount of knocking on doors could.

Chris Tinkler, the *Herald Sun*'s deputy editor, steered us through the impenetrable permutations of ever-changing information. He was patient, even when he had cause not to be. He was the sounding board — and arbiter — for the hundreds of fresh leads that shifted the story this way or that.

It's fair to say that we grew to be myopic. What seemed simple enough to us — once we had mastered the tenets of confidentiality, independent counsel, unsafe convictions and a dozen more legal principles — threatened at times to read like turgid nonsense to the average reader.

Emma Dowden, our book editor, had the tricky task of editing a raw manuscript that was not only necessarily unfinished, but very bloody complicated. Her suggestions for simplifying the story and its themes were almost always right, even when we didn't want to hear them. She, too, showed wisdom and patience that contributed so much to the final result.

To the bigger team at HarperCollins, thank you. The then managing director James Kellow enveloped us in an enthusiasm that eased the sheer steepness of the task ahead.

Publisher Helen Littleton shepherded us through the long months when it was unclear which way was up. We are very grateful to editor Rachel Dennis, HarperCollins counsel Sophia Conomos and now managing director Jim Demetriou.

John-Paul Cashen legalled this book and most of the *Herald Sun* stories that appeared about Lawyer X. His even temperament was a cherished gift in those early years when the police fought the newspaper's right to tell the story through the courts.

He and colleague Justin Quill embarked on the legal equivalent of nailing jelly to a wall. They clamoured, finessed, and sometimes begged so that aspects of the story could be revealed years before anyone else glimpsed the bigger picture.

Tracey Matters at the Royal Commission into the Management of Police Informants was invaluable, and not only for the little treats she regaled the working journalists with. To this day, she receives every silly question with a smile.

Carlyon wants to thank his son, Charlie, for his care and concern. He thanks his daughter, Chloe, for reminding him that this book 'is taking a very long time'.

To Jack, thank you for watching so much TV with subtitles and the volume on mute. To Maddie, the mugs are great, but it's about time you made the coffee to put in them. To Tom, thank you for so many kicks of the footy with 'old mate'.

They all, along with Carlyon's partner, Susie, say that Carlyon has been trying during the writing of this book, and they are right. Carlyon thanks them for their kindness and patience, especially Susie after she tackled an early manuscript with a very red pen. Her brave appraisal was vindicated when Carlyon's mother, Denise, did the same.

Carol and Steph, thank you so much for helping out.

Carlyon's father, Les, liked to say that he taught his son everything his son knows, and Carlyon likes to say what Anthony Cummings, son of horse trainer Bart, once said: 'If only Dad had taught me everything *he* knew.'

Les Carlyon passed away four days after Nicola Gobbo was publicly named in March 2019. He can take credit for anything that works in this book.

There are many others to whom we are grateful. Peter Blunden, then managing director of the *Herald and Weekly Times*, backed the endeavour from the start.

Jill Baker corralled Carlyon for many years in newspapers and magazines. No other newspaper editor can compare with her for reader instincts. Her biggest gift? She always had faith.

So did Neil Mitchell and Garry Linnell, whose big-heartedness and overabundance of journalistic talent have always set impossible benchmarks to strive for.

As for Dowsley, he has learned from journalists Mark Buttler and Padraic Murphy for years. They are among the many colleagues integral to the telling of the Lawyer X story who remained largely behind the scenes.

Like Carlyon, Dowsley has ink in his veins passed down through his father, Jim, a lifelong newspaper man.

While Dowsley's drive, along with his dancing ability, comes from his mother, Lorna, his instinct for the law was inspired by watching his older brother, James, become a criminal lawyer. His sister, Susan, a teacher, taught him how to spell.

To Siobhan, who met Dowsley just months before this madness unravelled, journo life isn't always this hectic.

Dowsley cannot thank them all enough.

Lawyer Zarah Garde-Wilson was generous with her insights. To others in the law, we are indebted to you.

We would especially like to acknowledge Rob Stary, a great defender whose rapier wit and even sharper legal mind have been influential throughout this investigation.

To many others who have helped piece together the jigsaw puzzle of Lawyer X, we cannot mention your names. But you have shone a light on an unprecedented scandal that is still unfolding.

Lastly, to Nicola Gobbo. You are one of a kind.